The
# Hikers Guide
## to the
## Hawaiian Islands

# The
# Hikers Guide
# to the
# Hawaiian Islands

## UPDATED AND EXPANDED

### STUART M. BALL, JR.

**UNIVERSITY OF HAWAI'I PRESS**
Honolulu

23 22                    6 5 4 3 2


**Library of Congress Cataloging-in-Publication Data**
Names: Ball, Stuart M., Jr.
Title: The hikers guide to the Hawaiian Islands / Stuart M. Ball, Jr.
Description: Updated and expanded. | Honolulu : University of Hawai'i Press,
    [2018] | Includes bibliographical references and index.
Identifiers: LCCN 2018009752 | ISBN 9780824876371 (pbk. : acid-free paper)
Subjects: LCSH: Hiking—Hawaii--Guidebooks. | Trails—Hawaii—Guidebooks. |
    Hawaii—Guidebooks.
Classification: LCC GV199.42.H3 B35 2018 | DDC 796.5109969—dc23
LC record available at https://lccn.loc.gov/2018009752


University of Hawai'i Press books are printed on acid-free
paper and meet the guidelines for permanence and
durability of the Council on Library Resources.

*Cover photo*: Leaving Kalalau Valley. Kalalau backpack, Kaua'i. Photo by Kelvin Lu.

# ❈ CONTENTS ❈

Acknowledgments – ix
Introduction – xi
Changes in the Updated and Expanded Edition – xiii
Hiking Tips – xv
Hike Categories – xxiii
Hike Summary Table – xxx

## Hawai'i (the Big Island)

### HAWAI'I VOLCANOES NATIONAL PARK

1. Kīlauea Iki – 3
2. Kīlauea Crater Rim – 9
3. Makaopuhi Crater – 18
4. Halapē Backpack – 25
5. Pu'u Koa'e – 36
6. Ka'aha – 42
7. Palm Corrals – 48

### HĀMĀKUA

8. Kalōpā Gulch – 53
9. Waipi'o Valley – 59

### SADDLE ROAD

10. Pu'u 'Ō'ō Trail – 65
11. Mauna Loa (via the Observatory Trail) – 72
12. Mauna Kea – 80

### KONA

13. Kealakekua Bay – 89

# Kaua'i

KAPA'A

14. Nounou Mountain–East (Sleeping Giant) – 97
15. Kuilau Ridge – 102
16. Powerline Trail – 107

PO'IPŪ

17. Māhā'ulepū – 117

KŌKE'E

18. Kukui – 121
19. Waimea Canyon Vista – 127
20. Nu'alolo Cliff – 136
21. Awa'awapuhi – 144
22. Alaka'i Swamp – 150
23. Kawaikōī Stream – 157

HANALEI

24. 'Ōkolehao – 165
25. Hanakāpī'ai Falls – 170
26. Kalalau Backpack – 177

# Maui

HALEAKALĀ NATIONAL PARK

27. Sliding Sands–Halemau'u – 193
28. Hōlua – 204
29. Haleakalā Backpack – 210

KULA

30. Waihou Spring – 227
31. Waiakoa Loop – 231
32. Polipoli Loop – 236
33. Skyline Trail – 242

HĀNA

34. Ke Ala Loa O Maui/Pi'ilani Trail – 250
35. 'Ohe'o Gulch – 257

KĪHEI
    36. Hoapili Trail – 263

WEST MAUI
    37. Waiheʻe Ridge – 269
    38. Lahaina Pali – 275
    39. ʻŌhai Loop – 282

## Oʻahu

HONOLULU
    40. Kuliʻouʻou Ridge – 289
    41. Lanipō – 295
    42. ʻAihualama (via Mānoa Falls) – 302

CENTRAL OʻAHU
    43. Kamananui (Moanalua) Valley – 308
    44. Mānana – 316

WINDWARD SIDE
    45. Makapuʻu Point – 324
    46. Olomana – 330
    47. Maunawili – 337
    48. Kahana Valley – 343
    49. Hauʻula-Papali – 352

LEEWARD/NORTH SHORE
    50. Keālia – 359
    51. Waiʻanae-Kaʻala – 366
    52. Kaʻena Point – 374

Appendix: Trail and Camping Information Sources – 381
For Further Reference – 385
Index – 389

*Color photos follow page 190.*

# ACKNOWLEDGMENTS

Lynne Masuyama, my wife, joined me on most of the hikes in this book. She is an ideal hiking partner, providing support, guidance, and good company.

Mahalo to Joe Bussen, John Hoover, Grant and Joyce Oka, and Marcia Stone for their advice and assistance. Thanks also to John Hoover, Kelvin Lu, Lynne Masuyama, Joyce Oka, Deborah Uchida, and Nathan Yuen for their great photographs. Finally, mahalo to Allen Hoof for the detailed hike and section maps.

# ❈ INTRODUCTION ❈

Hawai'i is still truly a paradise for hikers. Despite the recent surge in trail use, most of the routes in this book remain relatively uncrowded. They will take you to active volcanoes, lush valleys, cascading waterfalls, secluded beaches, and windswept ridges and sea cliffs.

This guidebook includes fifty-two of the best day hikes and backpacking hikes on the islands of Hawai'i (the Big Island), Kaua'i, Maui, and O'ahu. Each island is equally represented with thirteen hikes. All of the hikes are open to the public; none require a permit or liability waiver.

Each hike has a section on highlights, directions to the trail-head, and a detailed description of the route. A narrative section covers points of interest and major hazards along the trail. As applicable, there are short notes about the plants, birds, geology, history, and legends of the area. Each hike also has its own topo-graphic map keyed to the route description.

As you will see, this guidebook is very detailed. The infor-mation in it, however, is neither perfect nor up to date because of changing conditions. New housing construction alters the approach to a trailhead. Recent lava forces a trail to be rerouted. A winter storm causes a landslide that blocks the route. Do not rely entirely on this book; use your own judgment and common sense, as well.

Good luck and good hiking!

# CHANGES IN THE UPDATED AND EXPANDED EDITION

Those of you who have used the first edition of my guide will notice some major changes in the updated and expanded edition. I have added fourteen new hikes: Halapē Backpack, Pu'u Koa'e, and Palm Corrals on the Big Island; Māhaulepū and Kalalau Backpack on Kaua'i; Haleakalā Backpack, Waihou Spring, and 'Ōhai Loop on Maui; Kamananui (Moanalua) Valley, Makapu'u Point, Olomana, Maunawili, Wai'anae-Ka'ala, and Ka'ena Point on O'ahu. I have also made major route changes in the Kīlauea Crater Rim and Kawaikōī Stream hikes. Lastly, Hāna-Wai'ānapanapa Coastal Trail changed its name to Ke Ala Loa O Maui/Pi'ilani Trail.

Unfortunately, I had to delete six good hikes. Hawai'i Volcanoes National Park closed the Halema'uma'u hike because of volcanic activity. Ma'akua Gulch remains closed because of the 1999 lethal rockfall at nearby Kaliuwa'a (Sacred) Falls. I also removed Kalu'uoka'ō'ō, 'Aiea Loop, Waimano Ridge, and Maunawili Falls to make way for some new hikes, especially on O'ahu.

For GPS users, I have added UTM and latitude/longitude coordinates to the route description for the trailhead, and midpoint or endpoint of each hike. The notes section includes expanded historical information from my book *Native Paths to Volunteer Trails: Hiking and Trail Building on O'ahu*.

Visit my website at http://stuartball.aditl.com for updated route and access information.

# ⊠  HIKING TIPS  ⊠

## CLIMATE

Hawai'i has two seasons, summer (May to October) and winter (November to April). Summer is the warmer and drier season. Daytime temperatures at sea level are in the 80s and nighttime temperatures are in the 70s. Trade winds from the northeast blow steadily to cool the Islands. The trades, however, do produce cloud buildup over the mountains and some rain there.

Winter is the cooler and wetter season. Daytime temperatures at sea level are in the 70s and low 80s and nighttime temperatures are in the 60s and low 70s. The winds are more variable in strength and direction, sometimes coming from the south or west. Southerly Kona winds produce mainland-type weather—clear skies or heavy cloud cover and rain.

## CLOTHING

For short, easy hikes, wear:

- hiking boots, running or walking shoes (with tread)
- socks
- tabis (Japanese reef walkers) or other water footwear for stream or shoreline hikes
- lightweight pants or shorts, nylon, cotton, or cotton blend (no jeans)
- lightweight shirt, short or long sleeve, polyester, cotton, or cotton blend
- rain jacket, breathable fabric
- hat, broad brimmed

For long, difficult hikes, add:

- additional upper layer, polyester or wool

## EQUIPMENT

For short, easy hikes, bring:

- daypack
- 1 liter water
- food
- sunscreen
- cell phone (fully charged)

For long, difficult hikes, add:

- extra water
- extra food
- first-aid kit
- space blanket
- flashlight and extra bulb and batteries
- whistle
- compass
- topographic map, hard copy or in-phone/GPS unit

For backpacking trips, add:

- tent
- ground cover
- mattress pad
- sleeping bag or liner for shoreline trips
- water purifier or filter
- knife
- toilet paper
- stove and fuel
- cooking gear
- other personal gear

Most of the hikes in this book are trash-free. Let's keep them that way. Pack out all your trash, including cigarette butts, gum wrappers, orange peels, and apple cores.

*Heiau* are early Hawaiian places of worship with stone or earth platforms. Do not disturb *heiau,* other ancient sites, or artifacts you may come upon while hiking. In addition, do not build new *ahu* (rock cairns), as they confuse other hikers and local archaeologists.

Unfortunately, the Islands have a number of invasive plants, including *Clidemia hirta, Melastoma candidum,* and banana *poka.* All three overrun native forests and overgrow hiking trails. The pests are spread by birds and, yes, hikers. Carefully clean the soles and sides of your boots after every outing.

All three pest plants are easy to recognize. *Clidemia* is an aggressive shrub with heavily creased, elliptical leaves. Mature plants have hairy blue berries containing lots of tiny seeds. *Clidemia* is widespread on Oʻahu and also occurs on the Big Island, Kauaʻi, Maui, and Molokaʻi.

*Melastoma* is a shrub or small tree found on Kauaʻi and the Big Island. It has velvety, elliptical leaves with a slightly curved tip and large pink flowers.

Banana *poka* is a woody, climbing vine and a member of the passion flower family. It has distinctive three-lobed leaves and a yellow fruit resembling a small banana. The vine is a serious pest on Kauaʻi and the Big Island, where it climbs native trees and shades them out, eventually killing them.

*Hiking Tips*

Don't have any! Seriously, come prepared with the right clothing and equipment. Bring along this book and follow the hike description closely. Start early, memorize key junctions, and constantly be aware of the route you are traveling. You can never be lost if you know where you came from. Above all, use your common sense and good judgment.

The mountains are a dangerous place for exhausted, disoriented, and/or injured hikers. If you do get into serious trouble, call the emergency number (911) on your cell phone, ask for Fire Rescue, and then settle down and wait. If the call is late in the day, you may have to spend the night out. You did bring your extra layer and space blanket, right?

Never rely entirely on a cell phone for emergencies or a GPS unit for route finding. Both can run out of power or become damaged. Phone reception may be poor or nonexistent in gulches and valleys. GPS results depend on the user and the quality of the unit and its maps.

It is still good practice to tell a relative or friend where you are hiking and when you will be out, especially if you are hiking alone. Make sure they know to call the emergency number and ask for Fire Rescue if you don't call or show up on time.

## HAZARDS

There are hazards in hiking, as in any sport. Described below are the main hazards you should be aware of while hiking in Hawai'i. With the right clothing and equipment and good judgment on your part, you should be able to avoid or minimize these hazards and have an enjoyable outing.

### Too Hot

Hiking in Hawai'i is usually a hot, sweaty experience. Drink plenty of water throughout the hike, as it is very easy to become dehydrated. Prolonged lack of water can lead to heat exhaustion and heat stroke.

The need for water on a hike varies from person to person. As a general rule, take 1 liter of water on the short, easy hikes. Take 2 or more liters on the long, difficult hikes. If you have to ration or borrow water, you didn't bring enough.

The sun in Hawai'i is very strong, even in winter. During midday, wear a broad-brimmed hat and use lots of sunscreen. Be particularly careful of the sun on the shoreline and at high altitudes.

### Too Cold

Hiking in Hawai'i can sometimes be a wet, cold experience. A winter Kona storm with high winds and heavy rainfall can make you very cold very quickly. Insufficient or inappropriate clothing leads to chilling, which leads to hypothermia.

Always bring a rain jacket to protect you from wind and rain. Most of the time you won't even take it out of your pack, but bring it anyway! On the high-altitude and long ridge hikes, take an extra upper layer of polyester or light wool that will keep you warm even when wet.

### Altitude Sickness

Altitude sickness occurs when you climb to high elevation too quickly for your body to adjust to the thin air. Symptoms can show up as low as 8,000 feet, depending on the individual. Symptoms include shortness of breath, headache, dizziness, loss of appetite, nausea, and general fatigue. The cure is to stop climbing, rest, drink plenty of liquids, and eat sparingly. If the symptoms persist or get worse, descend to lower elevation immediately.

### Leptospirosis

Leptospirosis is a bacterial disease found in freshwater ponds and streams contaminated with the urine of rats, mice, or mongooses. The bacteria can enter the body through the nose, mouth, eyes, or open cuts.

Symptoms resemble those of the flu—fever, chills, sweating, head and muscle aches, weakness, diarrhea, and vomiting. They may persist for a few days to several weeks. In rare cases, the symptoms may become more severe and even lead to death.

What to do? First, never drink any stream water unless you have adequately boiled, filtered, or chemically treated it. Second, wear long pants to avoid getting cut and don't go swimming in freshwater. That's harder to do. After all, people come to Hawai'i to wear shorts and go swimming. Only you can decide how much risk you are willing to take.

### HIGH STREAMS

Island streams can rise suddenly during heavy rainstorms. Do not cross a fast-flowing stream if the water is much above your knees. Wait for the stream to go down. It is far better to be stranded for half a day than swept away.

### NARROW TRAIL

Hawai'i is known for its knife-edge ridges and sheer cliffs. Trails in those areas tend to be very narrow with steep drop-offs on one or both sides. Oftentimes, the footing is over loose, rotten rock or slick mud.

If narrow sections make you feel overly uneasy, don't try them. There is no shame in turning back if you don't like what you see.

### ROCKFALLS

In the mountains, rockfalls occur sporadically. Most are small or take place away from the trail or when no one is around. Because of the steep slopes above, the narrow sections of the valley hikes are particularly susceptible to rockfalls. As they occur with little or no warning, there is not much you can do about them. If caught in a rockfall, protect your head with your arms and pack and hope for the best.

Lava is tough on your boots and feet. Wear sturdy hiking boots with plenty of ankle support and cushioning. Don't take new boots on lava unless you want to age them prematurely!

As you will soon find out, there are two types of lava: *'a'ā* and *pāhoehoe*. *'A'ā* flows are jumbled up heaps of rough, clinkery lava. They are virtually impassable without a trail. Even a well-worn path through *'a'ā* is difficult to walk on because of all the loose, uneven rock.

*Pāhoehoe* is lava with a smooth or, sometimes, ropy surface. The terrain of a *pāhoehoe* flow ranges from relatively flat to very humpy. A well-used trail on older *pāhoehoe* makes for easy hiking. Be careful, though, on new flows without an established treadway. Their crust may be thin and brittle in spots and can collapse when walked on.

### GOAT/PIG/BIRD HUNTERS

On the trips in the state forest reserves you may meet goat, pig, or bird hunters. They are friendly people, and their dogs generally are, too. They use hiking routes to access hunting areas; however, the hunt usually takes place off trail. Stay away from areas where you hear shots being fired or dogs barking.

### MARIJUANA (*PAKA LŌLŌ*) GROWERS

The danger from marijuana growers and their booby traps is much exaggerated. The growers do not plant their plots near recognized trails. All of the hikes in this book travel on established routes. Stay on the trail, and you should have no *paka lōlō* problems.

### THE OCEAN

All of the shoreline hikes visit beaches with no lifeguards. If you decide to swim, you're on your own. Ocean swimming is usually less hazardous in summer and along leeward coasts. The waters off windward coasts are often treacherous because of large swells and strong currents.

*Hiking Tips*

While exploring along the shore, remember the saying—never turn your back on the ocean.

### TSUNAMIS

Tsunamis are huge onshore waves that can rapidly inundate coastal areas. The waves are generated by earthquakes, either locally or along the Pacific Rim. If you feel an earthquake or the ocean recedes suddenly, move to high ground immediately.

### HURRICANES

Hurricane season in Hawai'i is usually from June to December. Before starting a hike during that period, check the weather report to make sure no hurricanes are approaching the Islands.

### A FINAL CAUTION

The hazards just described are the main ones you may encounter, but the list is by no means all inclusive. Like life in general, hiking in Hawai'i carries certain risks, and no hike is ever completely safe. *YOU HAVE TO DECIDE HOW MUCH RISK YOU ARE WILLING TO TAKE.*

# ❋ HIKE CATEGORIES ❋

Length is the distance covered on the entire hike. If the hike is point-to-point, the length is one way. If the hike is out and back, the length is round-trip. If the hike is a loop, the length is the complete loop.

Distance is given to the nearest tenth of a mile. The mileage is taken from park signs or trail maps, when available. Otherwise, distance is measured on the U.S. Geological Survey topographical maps. The plotted value is then increased by 10 to 20 percent to account for trail meandering too small to be shown on the map.

To convert the length to kilometers, multiply the miles by 1.609.

Elevation gain includes only substantial changes in altitude. No attempt is made to account for all the small ups and downs along the route. Measurements are taken from the U.S. Geological Survey topographic maps and then rounded to the nearest 100 feet.

To convert the elevation gain to meters, multiply the feet by 0.305.

## DANGER

Danger rates the extent of three major hazards: narrow trail for ridge hikes, flash flooding and rockfall for valley hikes, and altitude sickness for high mountain hikes. Those hazards have seriously injured or killed hikers in the past. For ridge hikes, the rating is based on the length and difficulty of narrow trail sections over steep slopes. For valley hikes, the rating is based on the frequency and severity of rockfall and flash floods. For high mountain hikes, the rating is based on the elevation.

The categories are low, medium, and high. A rating of low or medium does not imply that the hike is completely safe from those hazards.

## SUITABLE FOR

Use this index to determine which hikes best match your ability. The categories are novice, intermediate, and expert. Novices are beginning hikers. Experts are experienced hikers. Intermediates are those in between.

Novice hikes generally follow a short, well-graded, and marked trail with gradual elevation changes and few hazards. Expert hikes have a long, rough, sometimes obscure route with significant elevation changes and multiple hazards. Most hikes fall between those two extremes. Some are even suitable for everyone because they start out easy and then get progressively harder the farther you go.

How difficult a hike seems to you depends on your hiking experience and physical fitness. An experienced, conditioned hiker will find the novice hikes easy and the expert hikes difficult. An out-of-shape beginner may well find some of the novice hikes challenging.

Use the index only as a rough guide. Read the route description and notes to get a better feel for the hike.

Location tells the general area of the hike. Listed is the island and the nearest town or subdivision, if applicable. Also mentioned is the national park, state park, state forest reserve, or the mountain range where the hike is found.

## TOPO MAP

Topo map refers to the U.S. Geological Survey quadrangle that shows the area of the hike. All maps referenced are in the 7.5-minute topographic series with a scale of 1:24,000 and a contour interval of 20 or 40 feet, depending on the terrain.

You can purchase topographic maps online from the Geological Survey at http://www.usgs.gov. Several commercial websites offer customized topo maps and map software for Hawai'i. On O'ahu, topo maps for all the islands are available from Pacific Map Center at 94-529 Uke'e St., Unit 108, Waipahu; phone 808-677-6277.

## HIGHLIGHTS

The Highlights section briefly describes the hike and its major attractions.

## TRAILHEAD DIRECTIONS

Trailhead directions are detailed driving instructions to the start of the hike. On the Neighbor Islands, the directions begin at the town with a major airport nearest the trailhead. On O'ahu the directions start from downtown Honolulu. Included are Universal Transverse Mercator (UTM) and decimal latitude/longitude coordinates for the trailhead.

*Hike Categories*

If you are at all familiar with the Islands, these directions should be sufficient to get you to the trailhead. If not, use your GPS, Google Maps at http://maps.google.com, MapQuest at http://mapquest.com, or bring along a copy of *Bryan's Sectional Maps* for Oʻahu or James A. Bier's *Reference Maps* for the Neighbor Islands. The printed maps show the start of some of the hikes and can be purchased at local drugstores, bookstores, and tourist shops.

For some hikes, the directions stop short of the actual trailhead. There is a reason for suggesting that you do some extra road walking. In certain areas it is generally safer to park your car on a main road, rather than at the trailhead. Wherever you park, never leave valuables in your vehicle.

On Oʻahu the directions also mention the bus route number and the stop nearest the trailhead. For route and schedule information, check the The Bus website at http://www.thebus .org or phone them at 808-848-5555. The Neighbor Islands also have bus systems, but with limited routes. For the Big Island, check the Hele-on Bus website at http://www.heleonbus .org or phone them at 808–961–8744. For Kauaʻi, check the Kauaʻi Bus website at http://www.kauai.gov/transportation or phone them at 808-246-8110. For Maui, check the Maui Bus website at http://www.mauicounty.gov/bus or phone them at 808-871-4838.

## ROUTE DESCRIPTION

This section provides a detailed description of the route that the hike follows. Noted are junctions, landmarks, and points of interest. Also mentioned are specific hazards, such as a rough, narrow trail section. Out-and-back hikes are described on the way in. Loop hikes and point-to-point hikes are described in the preferred direction.

Each hike has its own map. The solid line shows the route. The letters indicate important junctions or landmarks and are keyed to the route description. For example, map point A is

always the point where you start the hike. The maps are repro-
ductions of the U.S. Geological Survey quadrangles for the
immediate area of the hike. As in the originals, the scale is
1:24,000, and the contour interval is 20 or 40 feet depending
on the terrain.

For GPS users, Universal Transverse Mercator (UTM)
and decimal latitude/longitude coordinates are provided for
the turnaround or midpoint of each hike. They are based on
the 1983 North American Datum (NAD83).

This section sometimes uses Hawaiian words to describe
the route. They are listed below with their English definition.

| | |
|---|---|
| *ʻaʻā* | rough, clinkery lava |
| *ahu* | a pile of rocks indicating the route through treeless areas; known as cairns on the mainland |
| *kīpuka* | an island of vegetated older lava surrounded by newer flows |
| *makai* | seaward; toward the ocean |
| *mauka* | inland; toward the mountains |
| *pāhoehoe* | smooth, sometimes ropy lava |
| *pali* | cliff |
| *puʻu* | hill or peak |

For Oʻahu, I have also followed the common local practice
of using place names as terms to indicate direction:

| | |
|---|---|
| ʻEwa | westward from Honolulu |
| Koko Head | eastward from Honolulu |

The word "contour" is sometimes used in the route description as a verb (that is, to contour). It means to hike roughly at
the same elevation across a slope. Contouring generally occurs
on trails that are cut into the flank of a ridge and work into and
out of each side gulch.

Visit my website at http://stuartball.aditl.com for updated
route information.

The Notes section provides additional information about the hike to make it safer and more enjoyable. Included are comments about trail conditions, major hazards, and the best time of day or year to take the hike. Also mentioned are scenic views, deep swimming holes, ripe fruit, and hungry mosquitoes. In addition, there are short notes about the plants and birds along the route and the geology, history, and legends of the area. At the end is a brief description of any alternatives to the basic route.

For hikers who enjoy botanizing and birding, I highly recommend two companion guide books, *A Hiker's Guide to Trailside Plants in Hawai'i*, by John B. Hall, and *Hawaii's Birds*, by the Hawaii Audubon Society. For more O'ahu trail history, read my book *Native Paths to Volunteer Trails: Hiking and Trail Building on O'ahu*.

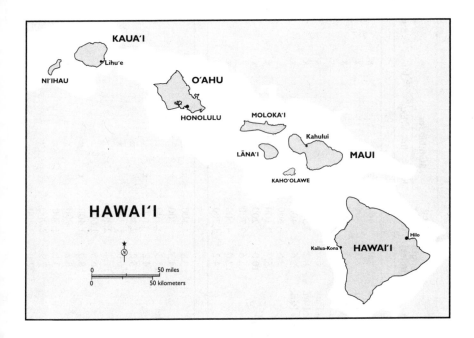

KAUA'I

NI'IHAU

Lihu'e

O'AHU

HONOLULU

MOLOKA'I

LĀNA'I

Kahului

MAUI

KAHO'OLAWE

HAWAI'I

N

0          50 miles

0          50 kilometers

Kailua-Kona

HAWAI'I

Hilo

**HIKE SUMMARY**

| Hike | Location | Length (miles) | Elev. Gain (feet) | Suitable for: Nov. | Int. | Exp. | Views | Swimming | Native Plants/ Birds | Historical Sites | Volcanic Features |
|---|---|---|---|---|---|---|---|---|---|---|---|
| **HAWAI'I (THE BIG ISLAND)** | | | | | | | | | | | |
| 1. Kilauea Iki | Volcanoes Nat Park | 4.0 | 400 | x | | | x | | x | | x |
| 2. Kilauea Crater Rim | Volcanoes Nat Park | 8.3 | 500 | x | x | | x | | x | x | x |
| 3. Makaopuhi Crater | Volcanoes Nat Park | 8.3 | 600 | x | x | | x | | x | | x |
| 4. Halapē Backpack | Volcanoes Nat Park | 15.4 | 2,700 | | x | x | x | x | | x | x |
| 5. Pu'u Koa'e | Volcanoes Nat Park | 6.6 | 200 | | x | | x | | x | | x |
| 6. Kā'aha | Volcanoes Nat Park | 8.2 | 2,300 | | x | x | x | x | | | x |
| 7. Palm Corrals | Volcanoes Nat Park | 2.6 | 400 | x | | | x | | | | |
| 8. Kalōpā Gulch | Hāmākua | 2.8 | 600 | x | | | | | x | x | |
| 9. Waipi'o Valley | Hāmākua | 5.7 | 2,100 | | x | | x | x | | x | |
| 10. Pu'u 'Ō'ō Trail | Saddle Road | 10.0 | 200 | | x | | x | | x | x | x |
| 11. Mauna Loa | Saddle Road | 12.6 | 2,700 | | | x | x | | | x | x |
| 12. Mauna Kea | Saddle Road | 12.0 | 4,600 | | | x | x | | | x | x |
| 13. Kealakekua Bay | Kona | 4.2 | 1,300 | | x | | x | x | | x | |
| **KAUA'I** | | | | | | | | | | | |
| 14. Nounou Mountain–East | Kapa'a | 3.8 | 1,100 | x | | | x | | | | |
| 15. Kuilau Ridge | Kapa'a | 4.3 | 700 | x | | | x | x | | | |
| 16. Powerline Trail | Kapa'a/Hanalei | 11.3 | 1,700 | | | x | x | | x | | |
| 17. Māhā'ulepū | Po'ipū | 4.2 | 100 | x | | | x | x | | x | |
| 18. Kukui | Kōke'e | 5.0 | 2,200 | | x | | x | x | | | |
| 19. Waimea Canyon Vista | Kōke'e | 6.0 | 700 | | x | | x | x | x | | |
| 20. Nu'alolo Cliff | Kōke'e | 11.4 | 2,200 | | | x | x | | x | | |
| 21. Awa'awapuhi | Kōke'e | 6.5 | 1,600 | | x | | x | | x | | |
| 22. Alaka'i Swamp | Kōke'e | 8.0 | 1,400 | x | x | | x | | x | | |
| 23. Kawaikōi Stream | Kōke'e | 8.2 | 900 | | x | | x | x | x | | |
| 24. 'Ōkolehao | Hanalei | 3.6 | 1,300 | | x | | x | | | x | |
| 25. Hanakāpī'ai Falls | Hanalei | 7.9 | 2,000 | | x | x | x | x | | x | |
| 26. Kalalau Backpack | Hanalei | 22.0 | 2,400 | | | x | x | x | | x | |

| Hike | Location | Length (miles) | Elev. Gain (feet) | Suitable for Nov. | Int. | Exp. | Views | Swimming | Native Plants/Birds | Historical Sites | Volcanic Features |
|---|---|---|---|---|---|---|---|---|---|---|---|
| **MAUI** | | | | | | | | | | | |
| 27. Sliding Sands–Halemau'u | Haleakalā Nat Park | 12.0 | 1,500 | | | x | x | | x | | x |
| 28. Hōlua | Haleakalā Nat Park | 7.4 | 1,700 | | x | | x | | x | | x |
| 29. Haleakalā Backpack | Haleakalā Nat Park | 19.6 | 2,400 | | x | x | x | | x | | x |
| 30. Waihou Spring | Kula | 2.4 | 400 | x | | | | | | x | |
| 31. Waiakoa Loop | Kula | 4.5 | 700 | x | | | x | | x | x | |
| 32. Polipoli Loop | Kula | 4.9 | 1,200 | x | x | | x | | x | x | |
| 33. Skyline Trail | Kula | 15.0 | 3,500 | | x | x | x | | x | | x |
| 34. Ke Ala Loa O Maui/ Pi'ilani Trail | Hāna | 4.6 | 100 | x | x | | x | x | | x | |
| 35. 'Ohe'o Gulch | Hāna | 4.0 | 900 | x | x | | | x | | x | |
| 36. Hoapili Trail | Kihei | 4.2 | 200 | x | | | x | x | | x | x |
| 37. Waihe'e Ridge | West Maui | 5.0 | 1,500 | x | x | | x | | x | | |
| 38. Lahaina Pali | West Maui | 5.0 | 1,600 | | x | | x | | x | x | |
| 39. 'Ohai Loop | West Maui | 1.2 | 100 | x | | | x | | x | | |
| **O'AHU** | | | | | | | | | | | |
| 40. Kuli'ou'ou Ridge | Honolulu | 5.0 | 1,800 | x | x | | x | | | | |
| 41. Lanipō | Honolulu | 6.7 | 2,000 | | x | | x | | x | | x |
| 42. 'Aihualama | Honolulu | 6.0 | 1,400 | x | x | | x | | | x | |
| 43. Kamananui Valley | Central O'ahu | 11.0 | 1,500 | x | x | | x | x | x | x | |
| 44. Mānana | Central O'ahu | 11.6 | 1,700 | x | x | x | x | | x | x | |
| 45. Makapu'u Point | Windward Side | 3.0 | 600 | x | x | x | x | | | x | |
| 46. Olomana | Windward Side | 5.2 | 1,600 | | x | | x | | | | x |
| 47. Maunawili | Windward Side | 7.4 | 600 | x | x | | x | x | | | |
| 48. Kahana Valley | Windward Side | 6.4 | 400 | x | x | | x | x | | x | |
| 49. Hau'ula-Papali | Windward Side | 7.4 | 1,500 | x | x | | x | | | | |
| 50. Keālia | North Shore | 6.6 | 2,000 | | x | | x | | x | x | |
| 51. Wai'anae-Ka'ala | Leeward | 8.6 | 3,500 | | x | | x | | x | | |
| 52. Ka'ena Point | Leeward | 5.8 | 100 | x | x | | x | | x | | |

The

# Hikers Guide
## to the
## Hawaiian Islands

# HAWAI‘I (THE BIG ISLAND)

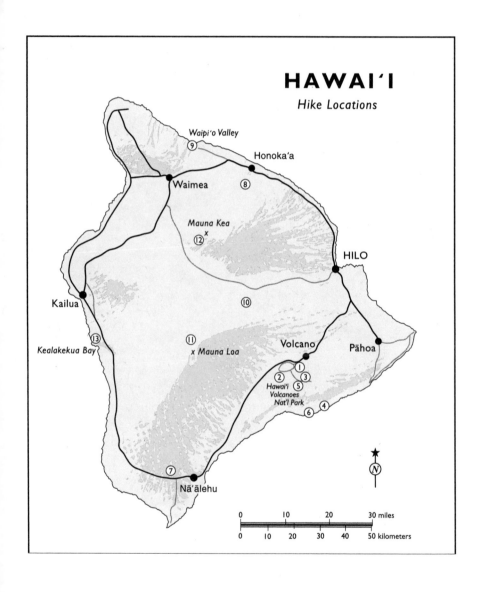

HAWAI'I

*Hike Locations*

Waipi'o Valley
⑨
Honoka'a
Waimea
⑧

*Mauna Kea*
x
⑫

HILO

Kailua
⑩

Kealakekua Bay
⑬
⑪ x *Mauna Loa*
Volcano
Pāhoa
①
② ③
⑤
*Hawai'i*
*Volcanoes*
*Nat'l Park*
⑥ ④

⑦
Nā'ālehu

★
Ⓝ

| 0 | | 10 | | 20 | | 30 miles |

| 0 | 10 | 20 | 30 | 40 | 50 kilometers |

1

# Kīlauea Iki

| | |
|---|---|
| LENGTH: | 4.0-mile loop |
| ELEVATION GAIN: | 400 feet |
| DANGER: | Low |
| SUITABLE FOR: | Novice |
| LOCATION: | Hawai'i (the Big Island): Hawai'i Volcanoes National Park |
| TOPO MAP: | Volcano, Kīlauea Crater |

## HIGHLIGHTS

Kīlauea Iki Crater was the scene of a spectacular eruption in 1959. This short loop hike crosses the crater floor past steaming vents and lava ramparts. Along the rim are scenic overlooks and lush native rain forest.

## TRAILHEAD DIRECTIONS

**DISTANCE:** (Hilo to Kīlauea Iki overlook) 30 miles
**DRIVING TIME:** 3/4 hour

From Hilo take Kanoelehua Ave. (Rte 11) to Volcano. Kanoelehua Ave. becomes Hawai'i Belt Rd. (still Rte 11). Just past Kea'au, the road narrows to two lanes.

Ascend gradually, passing the villages of Kurtistown and Mountain View.

Pass turnoffs to the village of Volcano on the right.

Enter Hawai'i Volcanoes National Park.

Shortly afterward, turn left at the sign for the park entrance.

Pay the fee at the entrance station.

Almost immediately, reach an intersection. Turn left on Crater Rim Dr. (Straight ahead on the right is Kīlauea Visitor Center with restrooms, drinking water, and trail information.)

At the stop sign turn left again, still on Crater Rim Dr.

Reach Kīlauea Iki overlook. Turn right into the lot and park there (elevation 3,874 feet) (map point A) (UTM 5Q 264475E, 2148440N) (Lat/Long N19.41644, W155.24296).

If you are starting from Kailua (Kona), you have a considerably longer drive. Take Hawai'i Belt Rd. (Rte 11) and follow it around the southern tip of the island to the National Park. Turn right at the park entrance sign and pick up the directions above. The distance to the trailhead is 98 miles, and the driving time is about 2 1/2 hours.

## ROUTE DESCRIPTION

At the overlook take the Crater Rim Trail to the left past the display case.

The gravel path hugs the rim of Kīlauea Iki Crater through native rain forest dominated by *'ōhi'a* trees and *hāpu'u* tree ferns. Ground markers identify some of the native plants in the understory.

Reach the parking lot for Thurston (Nāhuku) Lava Tube (map point B). Keep to the edge of the lot on the sidewalk.

At the crosswalk turn sharp right and down on the Kīlauea Iki Trail. (To the left across the road is the entrance to the lava tube.)

Descend, gradually at first, and then more steeply on six

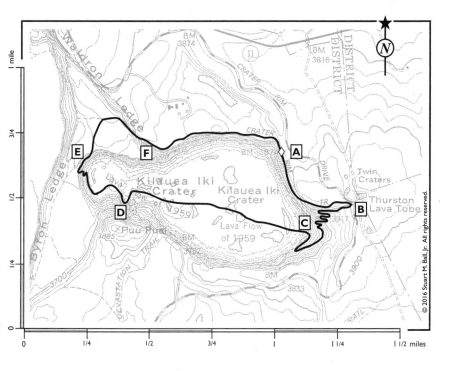

switchbacks. Look and listen for the *'oma'o,* a native bird with a slurred song.

Break out of the rain forest onto open lava. On the far side of the crater is the main vent, backed by its cinder hill, Pu'u Pua'i.

Descend briefly to the crater floor (elevation 3,520 feet) (map point C). Here small *'ōhi'a* trees, *'ōhelo* shrubs, and *'ae* ferns are gaining a foothold in the cracks and crevices of the barren lava.

Cross the crater on smooth *pāhoehoe* lava from the 1959 eruption. The route is marked by stacked rocks, called *ahu* in Hawai'i and cairns on the mainland. Watch for *'io,* the native hawk, soaring above the crater.

Pass several small steam vents.

Approaching the main vent, the trail winds through huge, desolate lava ramparts.

Bear left and ascend briefly to reach an overlook of the

vent (map point D) (UTM 5Q 263479E, 2148189N) (Lat/ Long N19.41406, W155.25241). A short side trail leads down to its lip.

Climb gradually across a rough lava flow. Watch your step on the loose, sometimes jagged rock.

Near the edge of the floor the trail ascends steeply on broken-up *pāhoehoe*.

Climb steadily out of the crater on seven switchbacks. There are rock steps in the steeper sections. Look for small *a'ali'i* trees, *pūkiawe* shrubs, and bamboo orchids on the way up.

Reach a junction near a bench (map point E). Continue straight on the Kīlauea Iki Trail. (To the left a connector trail leads to the Byron Ledge Trail and views of Kīlauea Caldera.)

Stroll through the native rain forest. Introduced *kāhili* ginger forms much of the understory here.

Reach a second junction. Keep right on the Kīlauea Iki Trail. (To the left another connector trail leads to the Byron Ledge Trail.)

Climb steadily, cross a rockfall, and pass another bench.

Reach a third junction at an overlook (map point F). Turn right on the Crater Rim Trail. (To the left the rim trail leads to Volcano House and the park visitor center.) Look back to see Kīlauea Crater with its steaming fire pit, Halema'uma'u.

Cross an indistinct trail. To the right it leads to a concrete platform, all that remains of a trolley system to lower scientific equipment to the crater floor after the 1959 eruption.

Walk along the rim of Kīlauea Iki Crater. Along the way are several overlooks.

Climb several stone stairways.

Reach Kīlauea Iki overlook (map point A).

## NOTES

The descent into Kīlauea Iki (little spewing) Crater is a breathtaking half-day introduction to hiking in Volcanoes National Park. This short loop provides a close-up look at a major eruption site and at the plants that make up the native rain forest. You can also visit Thurston (Nāhuku) Lava Tube as a side trip. The route is described clockwise so as to approach the main vent after crossing the crater floor. You can, of course, walk the loop in either direction.

Numbered points of interest along the route are detailed in an inexpensive pamphlet, called *Kīlauea Iki Trail Guide*. Pick one up at the visitor center or from the dispenser at the corner of the overlook parking lot opposite the display case. Note that the pamphlet describes the loop in a counterclockwise direction.

Before starting the hike, spend a few minutes at Kīlauea Iki overlook to get oriented. Directly below is the desolate crater, mostly covered with smooth lava. You can easily trace the hike route across the floor. On the far (south) wall is the main vent of the 1959 eruption. Behind is Puʻu Puaʻi (gushing hill), built by that eruption. In the distance to the right (west) is steaming Halemaʻumaʻu (fern house) fire pit inside Kīlauea (spewing) Caldera. In the distance looms massive Mauna Loa (long mountain).

Kīlauea Iki was the legendary home of ʻAilāʻau, the ancient Hawaiian god of fire, whose name means one who devours trees. Time and again he sent lava from his fire pits to devastate the surrounding forest and the fields of the Hawaiian people. One day, the goddess Pele arrived on the Big Island looking for a new home to build her fires. ʻAilāʻau immediately recognized her superior power and simply vanished. Pele now reigns supreme as the goddess of fire in nearby Kīlauea Caldera.

Along the rim of Kīlauea Iki Crater is the native rain forest dominated by ʻōhiʻa trees and hāpuʻu tree ferns. With their sweeping fronds, hāpuʻu form much of the understory. Their trunks consist of roots tightly woven around a small central stem. The brown fiber covering the young fronds of hāpuʻu is called *pulu*. ʻŌhiʻa trees have oval leaves and clusters of delicate red flowers. Early Hawaiians used the flowers in lei and the wood in outrigger canoes. The hard, durable wood was also carved into god images for *heiau* (religious sites).

On the descent to the crater look and listen for 'oma'o, a fairly common native forest bird found only on the Big Island. The 'oma'o has brown and gray wings, a pale gray breast, and a dark bill. Their sharp call resembles a police whistle, and their twitter is a series of jerky, slurred notes. 'Oma'o forage for fruits, berries, seeds, and insects, both on the forest floor and in the canopy.

As you emerge on to the crater floor, notice the small 'ōhi'a trees and 'ōhelo shrubs beginning to colonize the bare lava. 'Ōhelo has rounded leaves and delicious red and yellow berries, about the size of blueberries. According to legend, 'ōhelo is sacred to Pele. She changed her dead sister, Ka'ōhelo, into the shrub and named it after her.

While crossing the crater, you may spot 'io, the native Hawaiian hawk. It is dark brown all over or dark brown above and white below. The hawk soars above the forest, looking for insects, rodents, and small birds. The 'io is an endangered species found only on the Big Island and is a symbol of royalty in Hawaiian legend.

As you approach the main vent, imagine the evening of November 14, 1959. At 8:08 p.m., a fissure opened along the southwest wall of the crater. Lava cascaded down to the split-level floor from a line of fountains over a half mile long. A few days later, activity concentrated at the main vent. A single majestic fountain spewed red-orange lava, to the delight of thousands of viewers at the overlooks behind you. The fountain eventually reached a height of 1,900 feet, a world record. Cinder and ash from the fountain accumulated downwind to form the hill Pu'u Pua'i. Underneath your feet, the lava from the eruption is about 440 feet thick. The crust solidified quickly, but the core remained molten for over 35 years.

Climbing out of the crater, look for the native shrubs 'a'ali'i and pūkiawe. Pūkiawe has tiny, rigid leaves and small white, pink, or red berries. 'A'ali'i has narrow, dull green leaves and red seed capsules. Early Hawaiians used the leaves and capsules in making lei. When crushed or boiled, the capsules produced a red dye for decorating kapa (bark cloth).

# 2

# Kīlauea Crater Rim

| LENGTH: | 8.3-mile loop |
|---|---|
| ELEVATION GAIN: | 500 feet |
| DANGER: | Low |
| SUITABLE FOR: | Novice, Intermediate |
| LOCATION: | Hawai'i (the Big Island): Hawai'i Volcanoes National Park |
| TOPO MAP: | Kīlauea Crater, Volcano |

## HIGHLIGHTS

This loop hike follows a section of the rim of vast Kīlauea Caldera. Lush native rain forest alternates with barren lava and cinders. Along the way are scenic overlooks, steam vents, pit craters, lava tubes, and native birds.

## TRAILHEAD DIRECTIONS

**DISTANCE:**   (Hilo to Kīlauea Visitor Center) 29 miles
**DRIVING TIME:**   3/4 hour

From Hilo take Kanoelehua Ave. (Rte 11) to Volcano. Kanoelehua Ave. becomes Hawai'i Belt Rd. (still Rte 11). Just past Kea'au, the road narrows to two lanes.

Ascend gradually, passing the villages of Kurtistown and Mountain View.

Pass turnoffs to the village of Volcano on the right.

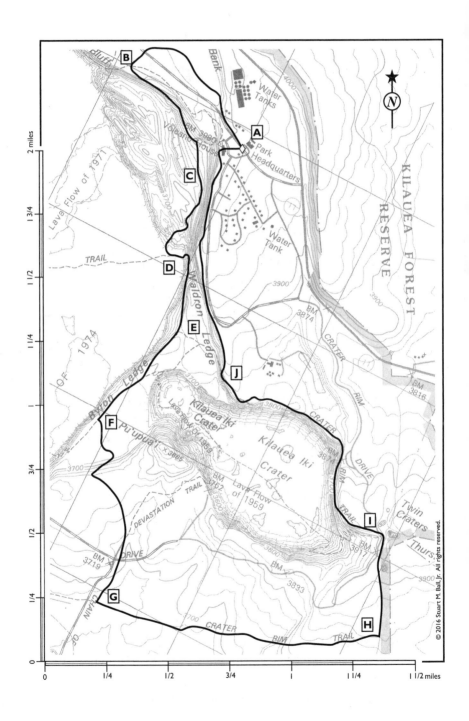

Enter Hawai'i Volcanoes National Park.

Shortly afterward turn left at the sign for the park entrance.

Pay the fee at the entrance station.

Reach Kīlauea Visitor Center. Turn right into the lot and park there (elevation 3,974 feet) (map point A) (UTM 5Q 262984E, 2149908N) (Lat/Long N19.42952, W155.25733). The visitor center has restrooms, drinking water, and trail information.

If you are starting from Kailua (Kona), you have a considerably longer drive. Take Hawai'i Belt Rd. (Rte 11) and follow it around the southern tip of the island to the National Park. Turn right at the park entrance sign and pick up the directions above. The distance to the trailhead is 97 miles, and the driving time is about 2 1/2 hours.

### ROUTE DESCRIPTION

Walk to the far end of the parking lot past the restrooms.

By the stop sign take the paved Sulfur Banks Trail, which initially parallels Crater Rim Drive.

Pass the Volcano Art Center and a hula platform on the right.

Keep right at the next junction.

Cross Sulfur Banks on a boardwalk. Along the route are several viewpoints and interpretive signs explaining the colorful sulfur crystals and other minerals in the area.

After the boardwalk ends, pass several steam vents on the left. Look for bamboo orchids.

Cross Crater Rim Drive. Watch for traffic on this short but dangerous section of the hike!

Shortly reach a signed four-way junction (map point B). Continue straight on the 'Iliahi Trail. (The Crater Rim Trail goes left to Volcano House and right to Hawaiian Volcano Observatory.)

Descend gradually into Kīlauea Caldera through native

rain forest dominated by *ʻōhiʻa* trees and *hapuʻu* ferns. Watch for a few *ʻiliahi* (sandalwood) trees on the left.

By some *ʻamaʻu* ferns reach a signed junction (map point C). Turn right and down on the Halemaʻumaʻu Trail. (To the left the trail climbs to Volcano House.)

Descend gradually toward the floor of Kīlauea Caldera. Ground markers identify some of the native plants.

Pass a small picnic shelter on the right.

Climb briefly over the tip of a rock fall from the cliff above.

Enter a dark, dense grove of introduced *faya,* a serious pest in the park.

Large boulders fallen from the crater wall line the trail.

Reach a signed junction (map point D). Keep left on the Byron Ledge Trail. (The overgrown Halemaʻumaʻu Trail to the right is closed because of an eruption in Halemaʻumaʻu fire pit.)

Reach the floor of Kīlauea Caldera. Small *ʻōhiʻa* trees are already gaining a foothold in the smooth *pāhoehoe* lava from the 1974 flow.

Hug the base of the crater wall on the left. Marking the way are stacked rocks, called *ahu* in Hawaiʻi and cairns on the mainland.

Turn left and climb out of the crater on ten mostly short switchbacks. At the rim is a bench with a panoramic view of the caldera.

Reach a signed junction just past the bench (map point E). Turn right, still on the Byron Ledge Trail. (The trail to the left connects with the Crater Rim Trail at map point J and shortens the loop considerably.)

Reach a second signed junction. Keep right on the Byron Ledge Trail. (The connector trail to the left leads to the Kīlauea Iki Trail.)

Go through a gate and continue strolling along the rim of the caldera.

Reach a third signed junction (F). Turn left, still on the Byron Ledge Trail. (Straight ahead is the overgrown extension of the Byron Ledge Trail, which is closed because of an eruption in Halemaʻumaʻu fire pit.)

Break out into the open through scattered *'ōhi'a*. Watch for *kūkaenēnē*, a crawling native shrub.

Work around the back of Pu'u Pua'i, a cinder cone formed in the Kīlauea Iki eruption of 1959.

Climb a cinder slope. Look back for a view of Halema'uma'u fire pit in the caldera and Mauna Loa and Mauna Kea in the distance.

Traverse a relatively flat section, still on cinders.

Walk through a parking lot for the Devastation Trail.

Cross Crater Rim Drive and continue straight on paved Chain of Craters Road. Watch for traffic.

By a crosswalk turn left on the Crater Rim Trail (map point G) (UTM 5Q 263379E, 2146864N) (Lat/Long N19.40208, W155.2532). (To the right the rim trail leads a short distance to some lava trees and Keanakākoi Crater.)

Pass through dark groves of introduced *faya* tree.

Enter the native rain forest with large *'ōhi'a* trees and *hāpu'u* tree ferns. Look and listen for the native birds *'apapane*, *'amakihi*, and *'oma'o*.

The trail climbs gradually.

Reach a junction with Escape Road (map point H). Turn left onto the grassy dirt road. (To the right Escape Road leads to the Mauna Ulu parking area.)

Pass a forested pit crater on the right.

Go through a gate.

Descend briefly on a wide, paved path and pass the start of the trail to Thurston (Nāhuku) Lava Tube on the right.

At the next junction turn left and cross Crater Rim Drive in the crosswalk (map point I). (Straight ahead are restrooms.)

Reach a signed junction. Turn right along the edge of the lava tube parking lot. (To the left is the Kīlauea Iki Trail.)

Climb briefly; the path is initially paved and has guardrails.

Walk along the rim of Kīlauea Iki Crater.

Reach Kīlauea Iki overlook. The trail becomes paved around the parking lot.

Cross an indistinct trail. To the right it leads to a concrete platform, all that remains of a trolley system to lower scientific equipment to the crater floor after the 1959 eruption.

Reach a signed junction (map point J). Keep right and up on the Crater Rim Trail. (To the left and down is the Kīlauea Iki Trail leading to the crater.)

Climb briefly, following the rim above Byron Ledge. Keep left at an obscure junction.

Cross an abandoned section of Crater Rim Drive and parallel it.

Jog left and then right onto the paved road. Parts of the rim trail fell into the crater during earthquakes associated with the eruptions of 1975 and 1983.

Pass the turnout for Waldron Ledge on the left.

Another paved road comes in on the right.

Reach a junction. Turn left off the road onto the paved Crater Rim Trail. (The road continues to Volcano House.)

By a small picnic shelter turn right, along the rim.

Reach the back door of Volcano House and enter the hotel. (Just ahead on the right is the site of the original Hawaiian Volcano Observatory.)

Exit through the front door and take the paved path back to the visitor center (map point A).

## NOTES

This circle hike is a grand tour of the Kīlauea (spewing) area of Hawai'i Volcanoes National Park. The varied route never fails to fascinate with its changing terrain, vegetation, and volcanic features. The loop is somewhat convoluted, so follow the narrative closely to stay on track.

After Sulfur Banks look for 'iliahi, the native sandalwood, along the appropriately named 'Iliahi Trail. The small tree has light green, leathery leaves with tiny green flowers at the branch tips. 'Iliahi is partially parasitic, with outgrowths on its roots that steal nutrients from nearby plants. Early Hawaiians ground the fragrant heartwood into a powder to perfume their *kapa.* Beginning in the late 1700s, sandalwood was indiscriminately cut down and exported to China to make incense and furniture. The trade ended around 1840 when the forests were depleted of *'iliahi.*

A short section of the loop ventures onto the floor of Kīlauea Caldera. It is a basin about 2 to 3 miles across and several hundred feet deep. The caldera was formed by successive episodes of collapse, the last one occurring in 1790. During the 1800s and early 1900s, nearly continuous eruptions created molten lava lakes that overflowed, partially filling the caldera. The eruption of 1974 produced the band of new lava on which you are walking. Look for small *'ōhi'a* trees and native shrubs colonizing the lava.

In the cinder field above the rim, watch for *kūkaenēnē,* a crawling, low-lying native shrub. It has short, narrow, dark green leaves, closely spaced along its branches. The female plants have shiny black berries relished by *nēnē,* the native goose.

Take in the awesome, eerie view from the top of the cinder slope in back of Pu'u Pua'i. Across the barren floor of Kīlauea Caldera is the steaming pit crater of Halema'uma'u, which has been active since 2008. To the left of the crater is the Southwest Rift Zone, extending into the Ka'ū Desert. On the far rim is the Hawaiian Volcano Observatory atop Uwēkahuna (wailing priest) Bluff. In the distance looms massive Mauna Loa (long mountain), the other active volcano on the Big Island.

Halema'uma'u (fern house) is the legendary home of Pele, the goddess of fire. One day she looked up from her fire pit and saw Kamapua'a, the pig god, coming to visit from O'ahu. Pele made an unfortunate remark about his appearance. Kamapua'a then taunted Pele about her fire and the destruction it caused among the Hawaiian people. An angered Pele stirred up her fire pit again and again to destroy the pig god. Each time he emerged from the flames unscathed. Finally, Kamapua'a appealed to the gods of the skies, who sent rain to cool the inferno. The rain weakened the fires but did not put them out. Pele and Kamapua'a then agreed to a truce. Because fire and water are equally powerful, the two gods decided to divide the Big Island in half. Pele kept the districts of Kaʻū, Puna, and Kona, where her fires still rage. Kamapuaʻa received the rest of the island, where rain falls and forests and gardens can grow, untouched by lava.

The short side trip along the rim trail to Keanakākoʻi (adze quarry cave) Crater is well worthwhile. Early Hawaiians shaped the dense basalt of the crater wall into stone tools. Eruptions in 1887 and 1974 poured lava into the crater and buried the adze cave. Before reaching the crater, look for some lava tree molds. They form when *pāhoehoe* lava surrounds the trunk of a tree and solidifies against it. The lava then drains downslope, leaving a shell of cooled lava around the tree. The tree burns, resulting in a hollow pillar.

After barren lava and cinders, the lush native *ʻōhiʻa-hāpuʻu* forest is a welcome sight again. With their sweeping fronds, *hāpuʻu* tree ferns form much of the understory. Their trunks consist of roots tightly woven around a small central stem. *ʻŌhiʻa* trees have oval leaves and clusters of delicate red flowers. Native birds, such as the *ʻapapane,* feed on the nectar and help in pollination.

If you're lucky, you may catch a glimpse of an *ʻapapane* in the forest canopy. It has a red breast and head, black wings and tail, and a slightly curved black bill. In flight the *ʻapapane* makes a whirring sound as it darts from tree to tree searching for insects and nectar. Another common native forest bird is the *ʻamakihi.* It is greenish yellow with a narrow black mask. The *ʻamakihi* feeds on nectar, fruits, and insects with its slightly curved gray bill.

After the solitude of barren lava and lush forest, the mob of tourists at Thurston (Nāhuku) Lava Tube comes as a shock.

If you haven't already done so, take the short walk through the tube. Then stroll the final section of the rim trail past Kīlauea Iki (little spewing) Crater and Waldron Ledge to Volcano House.

In front of the west wing of Volcano House is the original site of the Hawaiian Volcano Observatory, founded by

Thomas Jaggar in 1912. All that remains is a concrete piling that served as a base for cameras and surveying instruments. A nearby mound covers the Whitney Seismographic Vault, used to measure the size of earthquakes.

There are several variations to the route as described. You can, of course, hike the loop in reverse, if you are good at reading directions backwards. For a shorter loop, turn left at the junction by the bench (map point E), turn left again on the rim trail (map point J), and follow the narrative back to the visitor center. Total distance is 3.4 miles for the short loop.

# 3

# Makaopuhi Crater

| LENGTH: | 8.3-mile round-trip |
|---|---|
| ELEVATION GAIN: | 600 feet |
| DANGER: | Low |
| SUITABLE FOR: | Novice, Intermediate |
| LOCATION: | Hawaiʻi (the Big Island): Hawaiʻi Volcanoes National Park |
| TOPO MAP: | Makaopuhi Crater, Volcano |

## HIGHLIGHTS

This hike leads across barren lava flows to Makaopuhi Crater, a deep pit created by Kīlauea Volcano. Along the way are volcanic shields, spatter cones, lava trees, and patches of native rain forest. The view from the top of Puʻu Huluhulu is one of the best in the park.

## TRAILHEAD DIRECTIONS

| **Distance:** | (Hilo to Mauna Ulu parking area) 36 miles |
|---|---|
| **Driving Time:** | 1 hour |

From Hilo take Kanoelehua Ave. (Rte 11) to Volcano. Kanoelehua Ave. becomes Hawaiʻi Belt Rd. (still Rte 11). Just past Keaʻau, the road narrows to two lanes.

Ascend gradually, passing the villages of Kurtistown and Mountain View.

Pass turnoffs to the village of Volcano on the right.

Enter Hawaiʻi Volcanoes National Park.

Shortly afterward, turn left at the sign for the park entrance.

Pay the fee at the entrance station.

Almost immediately reach an intersection. Turn left on Crater Rim Dr. (Straight ahead on the right is Kīlauea Visitor Center with restrooms, drinking water, and trail information.)

At the stop sign turn left again, still on Crater Rim Dr.

Pass Kīlauea Iki overlook on the right and Thurston (Nāhuku) Lava Tube on the left.

Wind through a tree fern and ʻōhiʻa forest.

Pass the turnoff to Puʻu Puaʻi on the right.

At the next intersection turn left on Chain of Craters Rd.

On the right pass the turnoff to Hilina Pali overlook.

Just past Pauahi Crater turn left into the Mauna Ulu parking area. Leave your car in the lot there (elevation 3,220 feet) (map point A) (UTM 5Q 267279E, 2142714N) (Lat/Long N19.36506, W155.21557).

If you are starting from Kailua (Kona), you have a considerably longer drive. Take Hawaiʻi Belt Rd. (Rte 11) and follow it around the southern tip of the island to the National Park. Turn right at the park entrance sign and pick up the directions above. The distance to the trailhead is 112 miles, and the driving time is about 2 3/4 hours.

## ROUTE DESCRIPTION

Walk to the far end of the parking area past some cones across the road, which is blocked ahead by a large lava flow.

Shortly reach an unmarked junction. Turn left off the road onto the Nāpau Trail. (Ignore the trail signs farther down the road unless you wish to purchase the interpretive pamphlet, which is described in the Notes section.)

Immediately pass a registration stand on the right and a wooden bulletin board displaying trail maps and informa-

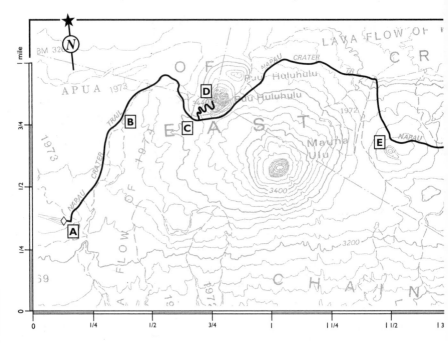

tion. Register for the hike if you plan to venture past Pu'u Huluhulu.

Cross the 1973 flow from Mauna Ulu on relatively smooth *pāhoehoe* lava. The trail is marked by stacked rocks, called *ahu* in Hawai'i and cairns on the mainland. Ground markers identify some of the native plants colonizing the barren lava flows, including *pāwale, pūkiawe,* and *'ōhelo* shrubs and *'ae* and *'ama'u* ferns.

Enter a remnant native *'ōhi'a* forest, untouched by the surrounding new lava. The huge flow on the right issued from Mauna Ulu in 1974. Watch for *'amakihi,* a greenish-yellow native bird.

Resume crossing the 1973 flow (map point B). To the right is a prehistoric spatter rampart covered with *'ōhi'a*.

Pass short, deformed lava trees, some with double or triple trunks.

Bear right through large *'ōhi'a* trees.

Break out onto the barren 1974 lava flow. Look for *pāwale,* the Hawaiian buckwheat.

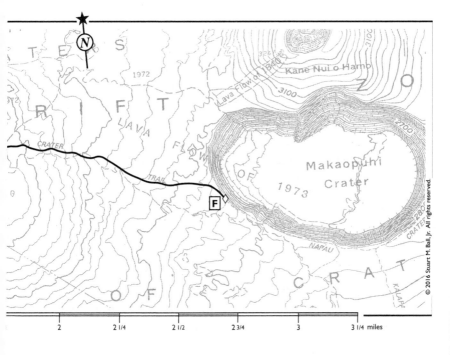

2   2 1/4   2 1/2   2 3/4   3   3 1/4 miles

Climb gradually along the edge of the flow toward Puʻu Huluhulu, a forested cone.

Bear left to the base of the cone and reach a signed junction (map point C). For now, turn left up Puʻu Huluhulu. (The main trail continues straight, to Makaopuhi Crater.)

Climb Puʻu Huluhulu on twelve short switchbacks through a remnant ʻōhiʻa forest. Look for native ʻamaʻu ferns and ʻuki, a sedge with sword-shaped leaves.

At the tenth switchback is a good view of the perched lava pond below the summit of Mauna Ulu.

Reach the top with its awesome view (elevation 3,440 feet) (map point D) (UTM 5Q 268373E, 2143385N) (Lat/Long N19.37125, W155.20524).

Backtrack down Puʻu Huluhulu and turn left on the main trail.

Initially the route hugs the base of Puʻu Huluhulu.

Descend gradually and then swing right, around Mauna Ulu. Climb the ʻAlae lava shield to a small pit crater (map point E).

Bear left and pass some steam vents.

Descend gradually toward Makaopuhi Crater on the 1973 lava flow. The hill to the left of the crater is Kānenuiohamo, an old volcanic shield similar to Mauna Ulu.

Reach the rim of Makaopuhi Crater (elevation 2,940 feet) (map point F) (UTM 5Q 271409E, 2142550N) (Lat/ Long N19.36405, W155.17625). (The Nāpau Trail continues around the rim through native *'ōhi'a-hāpu'u* forest.)

## NOTES

The hike to Makaopuhi (eye of the eel) Crater follows the upper East Rift Zone of Kīlauea (spewing) Volcano. The zone is an area of structural weakness, marked by a line of spatter cones, volcanic shields, and pit craters. The route is over mostly barren lava from the recent Mauna Ulu eruption, which has engulfed huge patches of native rain forest.

The trailhead is somewhat confusing. If you plan to hike beyond Pu'u Huluhulu, turn left by the bulletin board, sign in at the registration stand, and take the Nāpau Trail straight ahead. If you wish to buy the interpretive pamphlet, *Mauna Ulu Eruption Guide,* continue briefly along the dead-end road to the dispenser on the left. Then turn right on the signed Mauna Ulu Eruption Trail to follow the numbered points of interest. That short trail rejoins the Nāpau Trail after visiting the original fissure of the eruption.

In the remnant *'ōhi'a* forest, look for the *'amakihi,* a common native bird. It is greenish yellow with a narrow, black mask. The *'amakihi* feeds on nectar, fruits, and insects with its slightly curved gray bill.

Just past the *'ōhi'a* forest is a desolate stand of lava trees. They form when *pāhoehoe* lava surrounds the trunk of an *'ōhi'a* tree and solidifies against it. The lava then drains downslope, leaving a shell of cooled lava around the tree. The tree burns, resulting in a hollow pillar.

About a mile in, the trail hugs the base of Pu'u Huluhulu

(shaggy hill), an old forested volcanic cone. Take the side trail to its top for a bird's-eye view of the ravaged landscape. To the south is Mauna Ulu, the source of most of the lava you are walking on today. It is a volcanic shield created by an eruption lasting from 1969 to 1974. Lava poured out of several vents, completely filled two craters, and later merged to form a lava lake at the summit. Some of the flows crossed the old Chain of Craters Rd., plunged spectacularly over Hōlei Pali, and entered the ocean.

To the east lies the route of this hike to Makaopuhi Crater. Beyond the crater is Puʻu ʻŌʻō cone and vent, the scene of intermittent volcanic activity since 1983. Mauna Loa (long mountain) is the massive mountain in the distance to the west. The Civilian Conservation Corps built the rock lookout at the top in 1934. A weathered compass points out the sights, some of which were covered with lava during the Mauna Ulu eruption.

Leaving Puʻu Huluhulu, the trail climbs the ʻAlae (mudhen) lava shield and then descends gradually to Makaopuhi, the largest pit crater on Kīlauea. Makaopuhi used to have two levels, but a lava flow from Mauna Ulu filled the deep western pit and partially covered the eastern pit in 1973. The forested hill to the north is Kānenuiohamo, a volcanic shield formed about six hundred years ago.

Extending from the rim of Makaopuhi Crater is the lush native rain forest dominated by ʻōhiʻa trees and hāpuʻu tree ferns. ʻŌhiʻa colonizes recent lava flows and reaches maturity on older flows, such as this one. The trees have oval-shaped leaves and clusters of delicate red flowers.

With their sweeping fronds, hāpuʻu form a nearly continuous understory in the native forest here. Their trunks consist of roots tightly woven around a small central stem. The brown fiber covering the young fronds of hāpuʻu is called pulu. From about 1860 to 1885, pulu was harvested nearby to become pillow and mattress stuffing. A factory processed the fiber and shipped it to California from Keauhou Landing along the Kaʻū coast.

There are several attractive variations to the route as

described. For a short novice hike, climb Puʻu Huluhulu and then turn around. For a longer hike, continue to the end of the trail at Nāpau (the endings) Crater. The overlook there provides a closer view of the Puʻu ʻŌʻo cone. Total distance round-trip is 14 miles.

You can also hike the route one way if you have two cars. Park the second one at Kealakomo (the entrance path) picnic area and overlook, farther down Chain of Craters Rd. On the trail, continue around the rim of Makaopuhi Crater. At the first junction turn right on the Nāulu (the groves) Trail. At a second junction, keep right, still on the Nāulu Trail. Total one-way distance is 8.2 miles, and it's mostly downhill.

# 4

# Halapē Backpack

| LENGTH: | 2–3 days, 15.4-mile round-trip |
|---|---|
| ELEVATION GAIN: | 2,700 feet |
| DANGER: | Low |
| SUITABLE FOR: | Intermediate, Expert |
| LOCATION: | Hawai'i (the Big Island): Hawai'i Volcanoes National Park |
| TOPO MAP: | Makaopuhi Crater, Ka'ū Desert |

**HIGHLIGHTS**

This trip descends an 800-foot cliff to Halapē, an idyllic oasis along the barren, windswept Ka'ū coast. Along the shore are a secluded beach with shady palm trees, good snorkeling and tide pooling, and several historic sites.

**PLANNING**

Winter (November–April) is the best time of year to take this trip. The temperature is cooler then, and the sun is less intense. If you must do the trip in summer, use plenty of sunscreen and drink lots of water. The shelter and the palm trees provide the only shade at Halapē.

Decide how many days you want to spend along the coast. The narrative below describes a three-day trip with two nights and a layover day at Halapē. Don't even think about spending just one night there. You will be mighty sorry as you pack up and head out the second day. You can build a longer trip by following the Ka'aha day hike route and the connector trail along the coast. Check out the park's website at http://www.nps.gov /havo for other trails and campsites in the area.

Bring a tent and camp near the beach, because Halapē shelter is overrun with cockroaches and mice at night. Take a light sleeping bag or liner to ward off the early morning chill, especially in winter. *Tabis* (Japanese reef walkers) or other water footwear are perfect for exploring the slippery, rocky shoreline.

On the way to the trailhead, stop at the Backcountry Office to pick up a free camping permit, available on a first-come, first-served basis. Permits are issued from 8 a.m. to 4 p.m. daily and may be obtained one day in advance. Check on the water supply at Halapē shelter. Fill your water bottles/bladders in the restroom at the Backcountry Office or at Kīlauea Visitor Center, as the trailhead has no facilities. The phone number for the Backcountry Office is (808) 985-6178.

## TRAILHEAD DIRECTIONS

| | |
|---|---|
| **DISTANCE:** | (Hilo to Mau Loa o Mauna Ulu trailhead) 41 miles |
| **DRIVING TIME:** | 1 1/4 hours |

From Hilo take Kanoelehua Ave. (Rte 11) to Volcano.
Kanoelehua Ave. becomes Hawai'i Belt Rd. (still Rte 11).
Just past Kea'au, the road narrows to two lanes.
Ascend gradually, passing the villages of Kurtistown and Mountain View.
Pass turnoffs to the village of Volcano on the right.
Enter Hawai'i Volcanoes National Park.
Shortly afterward turn left at the sign for the park entrance.
Pay the fee at the entrance station.
Almost immediately, reach an intersection. Turn left on

Crater Rim Dr. (Straight ahead on the right is Kīlauea Visitor Center with restrooms and drinking water.)

Take the first right and park in the small lot on the left. Follow the paved path to the Backcountry Office. Get a permit for the trip and check on the water situation and trail conditions. Fill up your water bottles/bladders for the first day, as the trailhead has no water.

Drive back to Crater Rim Dr. and turn right.

Pass Kīlauea Iki overlook on the right and Thurston (Nāhuku) Lava Tube on the left.

Wind through a tree fern and *ʻōhiʻa* forest.

Pass the turnoff to Puʻu Puaʻi on the right.

At the next intersection, turn left on Chain of Craters Rd.

On the right pass the turnoff to Hilina Pali overlook.

Just past Pauahi Crater, pass the turnoff to Mauna Ulu on the left.

The road emerges from the forest onto barren lava.

Shortly afterward park at the turnout on the right for Mau Loa o Mauna Ulu. The trailhead has no facilities (elevation 2,680 feet) (map point A) (UTM 5Q 268474E, 2139559N) (Lat/Long N19.33671, W155.20382).

If you are starting from Kailua (Kona), you have a considerably longer drive. Take Hawaiʻi Belt Rd. (Rte 11) and follow it around the southern tip of the island to the National Park. Turn right at the park entrance sign and pick up the directions above. The distance to the trailhead is 117 miles, and the driving time is about 3 hours.

### DAY ONE—MAU LOA O MAUNA ULU TRAILHEAD TO HALAPĒ

**LENGTH:**         7.7 miles
**ELEVATION LOSS:**   2,700 feet

The route today is a gradual descent over lava to the Kāʻu coast. Watch your step, especially on the *pali* (cliff), as the trail is often rough and uneven. Grass may hide loose or protruding rocks and potholes in the lower section. Follow the *ahu* (stacked rocks) religiously to stay on course.

About 3 miles upslope from the Keauhou trailhead is Mauna Ulu (growing mountain), the source of the lava you are walking on initially. Mauna Ulu is a volcanic shield created by an eruption lasting from 1969 to 1974. Lava poured out of several vents, completely filled two craters, and later merged to form a lava lake at the summit. Some of the flows crossed the old Chain of Craters Rd., plunged spectacularly over Poliokeawe and Hōlei Pali, and entered the ocean.

As you descend the bare lava, look for *nēnē*, the Hawaiian goose, along the edge of the scrub *'ōhi'a* forest on the right. The *nēnē* has a black face and head and a gray-brown body. It lives on dry, rugged lava flows at high elevation and so has lost much of the webbing on its feet. Like its Canadian counterpart, the *nēnē* is a strong flyer and often honks in mid-flight. The *nēnē* is a threatened species and should be treated with respect.

In the scrub *'ōhi'a* forest, watch for the native shrubs *'a'ali'i* and *pūkiawe*. *Pūkiawe* has tiny, rigid leaves and small white, pink, or red berries. *'A'ali'i* has narrow, dull green leaves and red seed capsules. Early Hawaiians used the leaves and capsules in making lei. When crushed or boiled, the capsules produced a red dye for decorating *kapa* (bark cloth).

As you descend Poliokeawe (bosom of Keawe) Pali, keep in mind that you are traversing the Hilina (struck by wind) fault system, a highly unstable region of the Big Island. Periodically, Kīlauea (spewing) volcano injects massive amounts of magma into its East and Southwest Rift Zones, causing them to swell. The resulting stress triggers slumping along the entire south flank of the volcano. Huge sections break off and slide toward the ocean, producing the steep *pali* you see today.

On the long, gradual descent to the coast, look for the native shrub *'uhaloa*, a woody, sprawling herb. Its gray-green leaves are oval, pointed, and covered with fine hairs. Small yellow flowers with five petals emerge from the angle between the stem and the leaf stalk. Early Hawaiians used *'uhaloa* as a medicinal herb to relieve sore throats, congestion, chest pain, and asthma.

Halapē shelter is located about 1/4 mile inland near the base of Puʻu Kapukapu. The shelter has three sides, a sandy floor, and an elevated compost toilet nearby. Built into the back of the shelter is a water tank, which is fed by rainfall collected on the roof. Boil, filter, or chemically treat the water, and don't waste it, especially in summer. As mentioned before, the shelter is not a good place to spend the night because its lava rock sides are home to cockroaches and mice.

The preferred campsites are located along the line of palm trees to the left of the beach. If you have a choice, pick a site with a high rock wall to cut the wind. Don't pitch your tent right underneath a palm tree laden with coconuts!

While relaxing at your campsite, remember that Halapē is located on a fault system where local earthquakes can generate destructive tsunami (sea waves). If you feel an earthquake, move to high ground immediately. In November 1975, a large earthquake struck the Big Island beneath the coast near Kalapana. The ground at Halapē suddenly dropped 10 feet. The resulting tsunami, 50 feet high, inundated the quiet lagoon fringed with palm trees and killed two campers. You can still see a few of the tree trunks on the ocean side of the present cove.

## ROUTE DESCRIPTION

At the turnout take the Keauhou Trail past a sign with trail information.

Descend gradually on a 1974 lava flow from Mauna Ulu. Marking the route are *ahu* (stacked rocks), also known as cairns on the mainland. Small *ʻōhiʻa* trees and *ʻae* ferns are gaining a foothold in the cracks and crevices of the bare *pāhoehoe* lava.

Parallel the edge of a scrub *ʻōhiʻa* forest. Look for *nēnē*, the Hawaiian goose.

Bear right into the forest (map point B). Along the trail are the native shrubs *pūkiawe* and *ʻaʻaliʻi*.

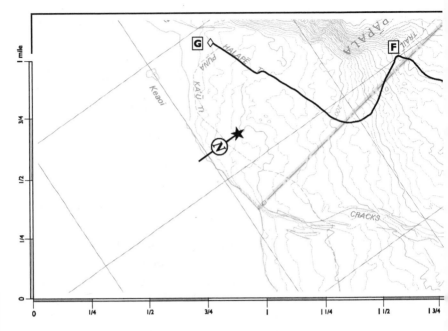

Descend gradually on older, humpy *pāhoehoe* through scattered *'ōhi'a*.

Cross a tongue of jagged *'a'ā* lava.

Go through a break in a rock wall and a derelict fence line. *Makai* (seaward) is a view of the Ka'ū coast.

Leave the scrub forest and cross a flat, grassy area dotted with *'a'ali'i*.

Reach a signed junction with a rough dirt road (map point C). Turn left, still on the Keauhou Trail. (To the right the road climbs to 'Āinahou Ranch and Chain of Craters Rd.)

Zigzag over Poliokeawe Pali and then descend more gradually on four long, lazy switchbacks (map point D). Along the coast are 'Āpua and Keauhou Points. Halapē lies below Pu'u Kapukapu on the right.

After the last switchback, descend steeply over loose rock. Watch your footing on this difficult section. On the left, the 1973 and 1974 lava flows from Mauna Ulu poured over Poliokeawe Pali.

The trail briefly works right along the base of the *pali* and then veers left toward the coast.

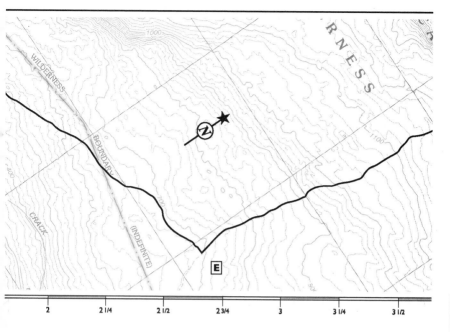

Descend gradually on old *pāhoehoe* lava covered with grass, partridge pea, and the native shrub *'uhaloa*. The trail swings from side to side to avoid rock outcrops. Follow the *ahu* marching into the distance.

Reach a signed junction (map point E). Keep right on the Puʻuʻeo Pali Trail. (To the left the Keauhou Trail continues down to Keauhou shelter and the junction with the Puna Coast Trail.)

Contour along the gradual slope, paralleling the coast.

Pass a prominent rock outcrop in the distance on the left.

Descend gradually into a broad, shallow drainage and then climb out of it. On the right is Puʻuʻeo Pali.

Cross a narrow band of clinkery *'a'ā* lava.

Reach the end of the Puʻuʻeo Pali Trail at a signed junction (map point F). Turn left and down on the Halapē Trail toward the coast. (To the right the Hilina Pali Trail ascends to Hilina Pali overlook.)

The trail descends steadily, with an occasional attempt at a switchback. Halapē finally comes into view, marked by a line of palm trees below Puʻu Kapukapu.

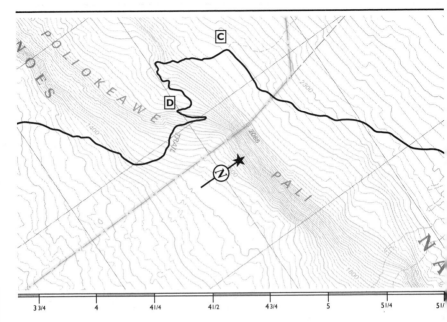

The angle of descent eases as the shoreline approaches.

Pass an elevated compost toilet on the left.

Immediately reach a signed junction in front of the Halapē shelter (elevation 40 feet) (map point G) (UTM 5Q 263141E, 2132460N) (Lat/Long N19.27198, W155.25367).

Keep right toward the beach. (To the left the Puna Coast Trail heads along the coast to Keauhou, ʻĀpua Point, and Chain of Craters Rd.)

Reach the shoreline. To the left are numerous campsites under the palm trees. To the right is a small cove and beach, where no camping is allowed.

## DAY TWO—LAYOVER AT HALAPĒ

Today enjoy the wild beauty of the Kaʻū coast. Explore the tide pools. Go swimming or snorkeling in the cove. Or take a hike.

For a short outing, walk west along the coast to Boulder

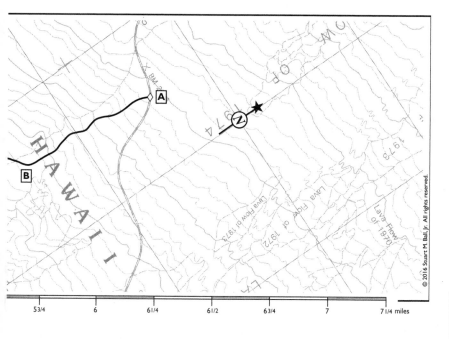

53/4    6    61/4    61/2    63/4    7    7 1/4 miles

Bay at the very foot of Pu'u Kapukapu (regal hill). Along the way are anchialine ponds in the deep lava cracks. The water in the ponds is brackish, fed by the tide, rainfall, and seepage. Just before reaching the bay is a *kōnane* playing board, etched into the rock. *Kōnane* is an ancient Hawaiian game similar to checkers. Nearby is *'ilima papa,* a low-lying native shrub with heart-shaped leaves. The yellow-orange flowers strung together have been used to make regal lei in both ancient and modern Hawai'i.

For a longer hike, head east along the Puna Coast Trail to Keauhou (new era or current) to visit a historic landing site and to go snorkeling. Pick up the trail at the last campsite by the last palm tree. The scenic route follows the rugged coastline and descends a low *pali* on a well-crafted rock staircase. At the shelter turn right toward Keauhou Point.

The Puna Coast Trail roughly follows the route of the ancient Ka'ū-Puna Trail. Hawaiian *ali'i* (chiefs), commoners, and tax collectors used the trail to travel between *ahupua'a* (land divisions). A rock altar (*ahu*) marked the division boundary. Each year the carved image of a pig (*pua'a*) was placed on top to remind the people that taxes were due.

The cove on the Halapē side of Keauhou Point is a superb snorkeling spot with plenty of colorful reef fish and coral. The fresh water entering the ocean there does make for some temperature fluctuation and fuzzy viewing, however.

Keauhou (the new era or current) was the site of an old Hawaiian fishing village destroyed by a tsunami from a local earthquake in 1868. Local entrepreneurs rebuilt a portion of the village to transship *pulu,* the brown fiber covering the young fronds of *hapu'u* (tree ferns). Workers harvested the *pulu* near Makaopuhi Crater and carted it down the Keauhou Trail to the village. The fiber was then loaded onto ships bound for California to be used for pillow and mattress stuffing.

Big Island ranchers also used Keauhou Landing to transship their cattle in the 1800s. To avoid the jagged *'a'ā* lava flows lying directly between the saddle area and Hilo, cowboys drove the cattle from pasture on Mauna Kea (white mountain) down the Pu'u 'Ō'ō–Volcano and Keauhou Trails to the coast. There the cattle were driven into the ocean and hauled on board ships bound for Hilo and Honolulu. Look for an old water tank and rock-walled corrals.

Back at Halapē, stretch out under a palm tree by the beach. Watch the waves roll in or take a nap. The native vine covering the sand is *pohuehue,* a member of the morning glory family. The leaves have a distinct notch, and the showy flowers are lavender with a deep purple throat. Early Hawaiian surfers would slap the ocean with the vine to call forth perfect waves.

Halapē means "crushed" or "missing" in Hawaiian. Sand pushed by the strong winds here would completely cover gourds growing near the beach. People passing by would not see the buried gourds and thus miss them. The old Hawaiian saying, *I Halapē aku nei paha,* refers to the location of missing items.

**LENGTH:**  7.7 miles
**ELEVATION GAIN:**  2,700 feet

Return the way you came. You can start at the crack of dawn to beat the heat or wait until mid-morning. Afternoon usually brings cooling trade winds and cloud cover *mauka* (inland) for the climb up the *pali.*

If you did not visit Keauhou yet, consider stopping by today. The detour adds about a mile to the return trip, but it is well worth it. After checking out the shoreline, return to the shelter and take the Keauhou Trail back to Chain of Craters Road.

HALAPĒ BACKPACK ⬚ HAWAI'I VOLCANOES NATIONAL PARK

# 5

# Pu'u Koa'e

| LENGTH: | 6.6-mile round-trip |
|---|---|
| ELEVATION GAIN: | 200 feet |
| DANGER: | Low |
| SUITABLE FOR: | Intermediate |
| LOCATION: | Hawai'i (the Big Island): Hawai'i Volcanoes National Park |
| TOPO MAP: | Ka'ū Desert |

## HIGHLIGHTS

This lonesome hike ventures into the stark Ka'ū Desert. Your only company is a big sky, barren lava, and blustery trade winds. At the end, tropicbirds wheel and dive above a volcanic cone with a bottomless pit.

## TRAILHEAD DIRECTIONS

| Distance: | (Hilo to Mauna Iki trailhead) 40 miles |
|---|---|
| Driving Time: | 1 1/4 hours |

From Hilo take Kanoelehua Ave. (Rte 11) toward Volcano. Kanoelehua Ave. becomes Hawai'i Belt Rd. (still Rte 11). Just past Kea'au, the road narrows to two lanes.

Ascend gradually, passing the villages of Kurtistown and Mountain View.

Pass turnoffs to the village of Volcano on the right.

Enter Hawai'i Volcanoes National Park.

Shortly afterward turn left at the sign for the park entrance. Pay the fee at the entrance station.

Almost immediately, reach an intersection. Turn left on Crater Rim Dr. (Straight ahead on the right is Kīlauea Visitor Center with restrooms, drinking water, and trail information.)

At the stop sign turn left again, still on Crater Rim Dr.

Pass Kīlauea Iki overlook on the right and Thurston (Nāhuku) Lava Tube on the left.

Wind through a tree fern and 'ōhi'a forest.

Pass the turnoff to Pu'u Pua'i on the right.

At the next intersection turn left on Chain of Craters Rd.

Pass turnoffs to Puhimau Crater on the left and Ko'oko'olau Crater on the right.

Turn right on Hilina Pali Rd. and reset your trip odometer.

Pass the turnoff to Kulanaokuaiki Campground on the right (3.6 miles).

Park in a small gravel lot on the right just past the Mauna Iki trailhead (3.9 miles) (map point A) (UTM 5Q 261043E, 2140172N) (Lat/Long N19.34137, W155.27459).

If you are starting from Kailua (Kona), you have a considerably longer drive. Take Hawai'i Belt Rd. (Rte 11) and follow it around the southern tip of the island to the National Park. Turn right at the park entrance sign and pick up the directions above. The distance to the trailhead is 113 miles, and the driving time is about 3 hours.

## ROUTE DESCRIPTION

Walk back along the road.

Shortly reach a signed junction marked by a tall *ahu* (stacked rocks) and a benchmark. Turn left on the Mauna Iki Trail.

Head into the Ka'ū Desert on old, humpy *pāhoehoe* lava through scattered 'ōhi'a trees. Look for the native shrubs *pūki-*

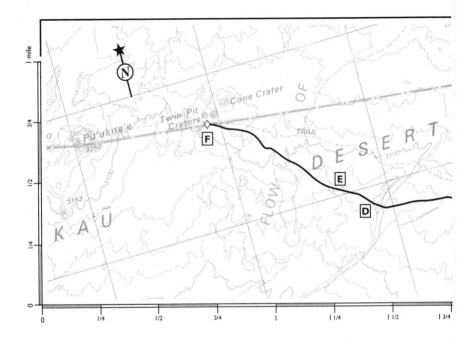

*awe* and *'a'ali'i*. In the distance is massive Mauna Loa (elevation 13,679 feet). Beyond its right flank is Mauna Kea.

Cross a shallow basin laced with small cracks. Watch for *'ama'u* ferns.

Descend briefly past several large humps. A small stand of *'ōhi'a* trees provides some shade on a winter afternoon.

As the vegetation thins, the trail parallels an escarpment on the left.

Pass a distinct hump on the left (map point B).

Descend gradually into a small sandy basin. Look for Pele's hair in crevices protected from the wind.

Pass another distinctive steep-sided hump on the left (map point C). The dark Kamakai'a Hills are downslope in the distance.

Descend gradually over mostly barren lava.

Reach an escarpment with a view of three cones (map point D). Pu'u Koa'e is the large cone in the middle. Our destination is the colorful, unnamed cone with two pit craters on the right.

Descend the *pali* on one sandy, rocky switchback. Protect your eyes from blowing sand.

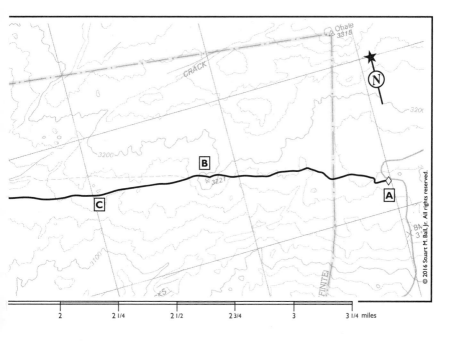

Cross *pāhoehoe* partially covered by black sand.

Bear right to follow the shiny 1974 lava flow slightly uphill (map point E). Look for *'ae* ferns colonizing the bare lava.

Cross a cinder field downwind from the unnamed cone. The trail is lined with black and red rocks.

Resume hiking on older lava.

Reach two warning signs near the two pit craters and the colorful cone (map point F) (UTM 5Q 2569230E, 2141695N) (Lat/Long N19.35463, W155.31398). Investigate the craters and cone with care because of the steep drop-offs and loose rock in the area.

## NOTES

Pu'u Koa'e is not a popular hike, probably because of the harsh, barren landscape with few points of reference or interest. Nevertheless, this serene walk is appealing because of its immense solitude and silence, broken only by your footfalls, the blustery trade winds, and the piercing cry of the tropicbird. Follow the *ahu* (stacked rocks or cairns) religiously to stay on course, as the trail is not well trod.

The route crosses an area of structural weakness, known as a rift zone, which extends southwest from the main Kīlauea (spewing) Caldera. The rift zone is marked by cracks, fault scarps, spatter cones, and pit craters, all of which you will see. Below the surface are numerous dikes, formed by upwelling lava that cooled and hardened in the fissures.

On the first section of the hike native *'a'ali'i* and *pūkiawe* shrubs, and *'ama'u* ferns are gradually colonizing the old lava. *'A'ali'i* has narrow, dull green leaves and red seed capsules. *Pūkiawe* has tiny, rigid leaves and small white, pink, or red berries. *'Ama'u* ferns have short trunks, usually 1 to 2 feet high. Their fronds are bright red when young, gradually turning green with age.

In the sandy basins, look for golden brown strands of Pele's hair. They are slender threads of viscous lava spewed into the air during an eruption and then cooled and carried downwind. The Pele's hair along the trail originated from eruptions in and around Halema'uma'u (fern house), the most active pit crater in Kīlauea Caldera.

After the escarpment the route crosses a barren, shiny lava flow. In December of 1974, fissures opened up just south of Kīlauea Caldera. The resulting flow streamed down the Southwest Rift Zone toward Pu'u Koa'e. In July of the same year, Kīlauea also erupted in the caldera itself and near Keanakākoi (the adze making cave) Crater.

At the end of the hike turn right off the trail and walk between the two pit craters. Climb the small, colorful cone and peer down into its dark, deep throat. It is difficult to see the bottom without falling in, so let's call it bottomless.

While you are investigating the cone, look for graceful *koa'e kea* (white-tailed tropicbirds) soaring overhead. They have two central tail feathers elongated into streamers. Tropicbirds feed by diving into the ocean for fish and squid. From March to October they nest in burrows or rock crevices along cliffs, such as the steep walls of these pit craters. Do not approach the craters too closely, for both your safety and the tropicbirds' peace of mind.

For a longer point-to-point hike, leave a second car at the Ka'ū Desert trailhead along Hawai'i Belt Rd. (Rte 11). From the twin pit craters, continue along the Mauna Iki Trail past Pu'u Koa'e (tropicbird hill) and Mauna Iki (little mountain). Before reaching the road, stop at the exhibit explaining nearby fossilized footprints of early Hawaiians caught in an explosive eruption of Kīlauea. Total distance across the desert is 8.8 miles.

# 6

# Ka'aha

| LENGTH: | 8.2-mile round-trip |
|---|---|
| ELEVATION GAIN: | 2,300 feet |
| DANGER: | Low |
| SUITABLE FOR: | Intermediate, Expert |
| LOCATION: | Hawai'i (the Big Island): Hawai'i Volcanoes National Park |
| TOPO MAP: | Ka'ū Desert |

## HIGHLIGHTS

This hike descends to Ka'aha, an oasis along the stark, windswept Ka'ū Coast. At a nearby cove is a small black sand beach with good swimming and snorkeling. Both out and back, you must negotiate Hilina Pali, a spectacular 1,500-foot cliff.

## TRAILHEAD DIRECTIONS

**Distance:** (Hilo to Hilina Pali overlook) 45 miles
**Driving Time:** 1 1/2 hours

From Hilo take Kanoelehua Ave. (Rte 11) toward Volcano. Kanoelehua Ave. becomes Hawai'i Belt Rd. (still Rte 11). Just past Kea'au, the road narrows to two lanes.

Ascend gradually, passing the villages of Kurtistown and Mountain View.

Pass turnoffs to the village of Volcano on the right.

Enter Hawai'i Volcanoes National Park.

Shortly afterward turn left at the sign for the park entrance.

Pay the fee at the entrance station.

Almost immediately, reach an intersection. Turn left on Crater Rim Dr. (Straight ahead on the right is Kīlauea Visitor Center with restrooms, drinking water, and trail information.)

At the stop sign turn left again, still on Crater Rim Dr.

Pass Kīlauea Iki overlook on the right and Thurston (Nāhuku) Lava Tube on the left.

Wind through a tree fern and 'ōhi'a forest.

Pass the turnoff to Pu'u Pua'i on the right.

At the next intersection turn left on Chain of Craters Rd.

Pass turnoffs to Puhimau Crater on the left and Ko'oko'olau Crater on the right.

Turn right on Hilina Pali Rd.

Pass the turnoff to Kulanaokuaiki Campground on the right (3.6 miles).

Reach the end of the road at Hilina Pali overlook and park in the small lot by a picnic shelter (elevation 2,280 feet) (map point A) (UTM 5Q 257566E, 2135130N) (Lat/Long N19.29543, W155.30703). Nearby is a fancy pit toilet.

If you are starting from Kailua (Kona), you have a considerably longer drive. Take Hawai'i Belt Rd. (Rte 11) and follow it around the southern tip of the island to the National Park. Turn right at the park entrance sign and pick up the directions above. The distance to the trailhead is 118 miles, and the driving time is about 3 1/4 hours.

## ROUTE DESCRIPTION

Take the short, paved path past the picnic shelter to reach a junction by a Backcountry Trails sign. Turn left and down on the Hilina Pali Trail. (Straight ahead is the Ka'ū Desert Trail, leading to Pepeiao Cabin.)

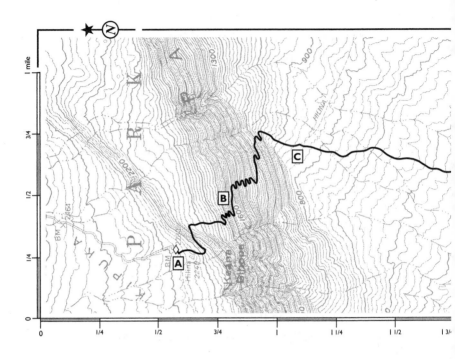

Descend gradually to the cliff edge and bear right along it. The treadway may be partially obscured by grass.

Switchback once and then go straight down as the slope angle eases momentarily.

Continue descending on a series of short switchbacks.

Cross an 'a'ā lava flow. Watch your footing on the rough, loose rock.

Pass a native *lama* and an *'ōhi'a* tree on the right.

Recross the same 'a'ā flow several times on longer switchbacks (map point B).

On the left pass a lone *'ōhi'a* tree. It's a shady spot to rest your legs.

Switchback five more times to descend straight down to the base of the cliff.

Parallel Hilina Pali briefly and then swing left toward the coast.

Reach a signed junction (map point C). Keep right on the

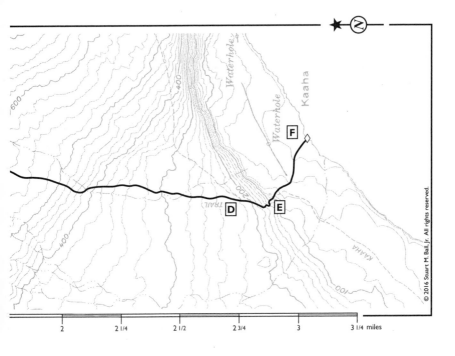

Ka'aha Trail. (To the left the Hilina Pali Trail heads down to the coast at Halapē.)

Descend gradually on old *pāhoehoe* lava covered with grass, partridge pea, and the native shrub *'uhaloa*. Follow the *ahu* (cairns) marching into the distance.

Reach a signed junction (map point D). Keep right on the Ka'aha Trail. (The trail to the left heads along the coast to Halapē.)

Pass the entrance to a lava tube on the left.

Descend a short *pali*.

Reach a signed junction (elevation 80 feet) (map point E) (UTM 5Q 257843E, 2131382N) (Lat/Long N19.26162, W155.30392). Continue straight toward the ocean. (To the left is the Ka'aha shelter and an elevated compost toilet. To the right the Ka'aha Trail continues along the coast.

Reach the shore at a cove with a small black sand beach (map point F). Look for the low-lying native shrub *naupaka kahakai* along the way.

The route to Ka'aha (the assembly) traverses the hot, dry, and rugged coastal section of Hawai'i Volcanoes National Park. Winter (November–April) is the most comfortable time of year to take this hike. If you do go in summer, be prepared for high temperatures and intense sun. The only shade along the coast is in the Ka'aha Shelter. Regardless of the season, start hiking early to beat the heat. Wait until well after lunch to start back. Late afternoon usually brings strong trade winds and heavy cloud buildup *mauka* (inland). The air then becomes cooler for the final climb up the *pali* (cliff).

Before starting the hike, spend a few minutes at the Hilina Pali (cliff struck by wind) overlook. It is a quiet, remote spot, even though accessible by car. From the picnic shelter take the short path downhill to a weathered compass, which points out the sites below. Along the coast to the left are the hump of Pu'u Kapukapu (regal hill) and Keauhou (the new era or current) and 'Āpua (fish basket) points. To the right is the cove at Ka'aha, our destination. In back is massive Mauna Loa (long mountain). Both the picnic shelter and the compass were built by the Civilian Conservation Corps in the 1930s.

Hilina Pali is a fault scarp, 12 miles long. The cliff formed when the coastal section suddenly dropped 1,500 feet during a large earthquake. The Hilina fault system is still active, producing many small temblors.

The route descends Hilina Pali on twenty-four switchbacks. Watch your step constantly because the trail is often rough and narrow, and grass may hide loose rock and potholes. The remainder of the hike is a gradual descent to the coast on old *pāhoehoe* lava covered with scrub vegetation.

The lone *lama* tree on Hilina Pali has dark green, leathery leaves. Its fruits are green, then yellow, and finally bright red when fully ripe. Lama was sacred to Laka, goddess of the hula. The early Hawaiians used the hard, light-colored wood in temple construction and in hula performances.

After descending Hilina Pali, look for the native shrub

'uhaloa, a woody, sprawling herb. Its gray-green leaves are oval, pointed, and covered with fine hairs. Small yellow flowers with five petals emerge from the angle between the stem and the leaf stalk. Early Hawaiians used 'uhaloa as a medicinal herb to relieve sore throats, congestion, chest pain, and asthma.

The route passes several lava tubes on the gradual descent to the coast. They are usually formed in *pāhoehoe* flows that are confined, such as in a gully. The top and edges of the flow cool and crust over. The lava inside continues to flow through the resulting tunnel. Eventually the flow diminishes and stops, leaving a tube. Do not enter any of the lava tubes, because their fragile ecosystems are extremely vulnerable to unintentional damage.

Ka'aha stands out as the only patch of green along the otherwise barren coast. Fresh water seeping close to the surface of the lava enters the ocean here. The green is mostly *naupaka kahakai*, a spreading, succulent, native shrub. Its flowers are white with purple streaks and appear half-formed. Its white fleshy fruits float on the ocean, helping to spread the species to other islands.

Ka'aha shelter is located about 0.25 miles inland at the foot of a small *pali*. The shelter has three sides, a sandy floor, and an elevated compost toilet nearby. Built into the back of the shelter is a water tank that is fed by rainfall collected on the roof. Filter or treat the water chemically before drinking it.

From the shelter take the makeshift trail that leads down to a small cove with the beginnings of a black sand beach. Go swimming or snorkeling; explore the tide pools; walk along the coast toward Kālu'e (hanging loose); or just sit on the beach and take in the wild beauty of the area.

The snorkeling at Ka'aha is good, but not great. The fresh water entering the cove makes for some temperature fluctuations and fuzzy viewing. Underwater are some colorful coral and a good variety of reef fish. The best area is the ocean side of the cove near the wave break.

Now that you are totally relaxed, are you ready for the climb out?

# 7

# Palm Corrals

| LENGTH: | 2.6-mile loop |
|---|---|
| ELEVATION GAIN: | 400 feet |
| DANGER: | Low |
| SUITABLE FOR: | Novice |
| LOCATION: | Hawai'i (the Big Island): Hawai'i Volcanoes National Park, Kahuku Unit |
| TOPO MAP: | Kahuku Ranch |
| ACCESS: | Open only on weekends from 9 a.m. to 3 p.m. |

## HIGHLIGHTS

This serene loop traverses ranch land acquired by Hawai'i Volcanoes National Park. Along the route are huge, remnant 'ōhi'a trees, perhaps a native bird, and a cone with a view of Ka Lae, the southernmost point in the United States.

## TRAILHEAD DIRECTIONS

**DISTANCE:** (Kailua [Kona] to the Kahuku Unit) 42 miles
**DRIVING TIME:** 1 1/4 hours

From Kailua (Kona) take Māmalahoa Hwy (Rte 11) toward Volcano.

After driving through Captain Cook, pass the turnoff (Rte 160) to Pu'uhonua o Hōnaunau National Historical Park.

Drive through Kīpāhoehoe Natural Area Reserve.

Pass the macadamia nut orchards of MacFarms.

Drive past the large subdivision of Ocean View Estates.

After mile marker 82, pass Manukā State Park on the left.

Just after mile marker 70.5, turn left into the Kahuku Unit of Hawai'i Volcanoes National Park.

Ascend gradually through a gate.

Park in the grassy lot on the left across the road from the green visitor center. The lot has a small restroom with no water, and the visitor center has trail maps and information.

After checking in at the visitor center, continue up the road, now gravel and cinder, for 2.7 miles to the signed Lower Palm trailhead on the left. Park in the grassy area on the left side of the road (map point A) (elevation 2,470 feet) (UTM 5Q 217592E, 2112504 N) (Lat/Long N19.08597, W155.68382).

If you are starting from Hilo, you have a somewhat longer drive. Take Kanoelehua Ave. (Rte 11) and Māmalahoa Hwy to Volcano, passing the main entrance to Hawai'i Volcanoes National Park. Continue along the Ka'ū Coast past the towns of Pāhala, Nā'ālehu, and Wai'ōhinu. After mile marker 70, turn right into the Kahuku Unit and pick up the directions above. The distance to the visitor center is 72 miles, and the driving time is about 1 3/4 hours.

## ROUTE DESCRIPTION

Take the Palm Trail, an old Kahuku Ranch road.

Cross the rough lava flow of 1868 through scrub native 'ōhi'a trees. Look for the native shrub *pūkiawe*.

Walk through a gap in a lava rock wall. All that remains of the gate are two 'ōhi'a posts on either side of the opening.

The road cuts straight across the grassy, rolling topography. Huge 'ōhi'a trees dot the former pastureland. If the 'ōhi'a is in bloom, look for the native 'apapane bird.

After descending briefly, reach several abandoned corrals

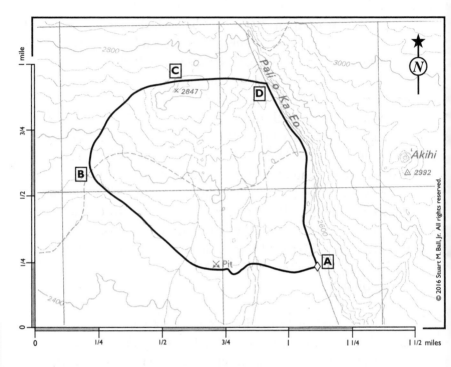

(map point B) (UTM 5Q 216177E, 2113136N) (Lat/Long N19.09148, W155.69735). Turn right following the corral railings.

Walk under a large, shady *ōhiʻa*. A lone palm tree once stood nearby and gave the trail its name.

At the corner of the last corral, turn right again on another ranch road and climb steadily.

On the right pass a grassy volcanic cone, whose slopes have been mined for cinders by the ranch (map point C) (elevation 2,847 feet). From the top of the cone is a good view *makai* (seaward) to Ka Lae, the southernmost point in the United States. On the left is Pali o Kaʻeo (cliff of Kaʻeo) and behind it is ʻAkihi Cone.

Continue along the ranch road and then descend to the signed Upper Palm trailhead (map point D).

Turn right on the main road and follow it back to your car. Look for colorful bamboo orchids along the way.

This relaxing walk follows old ranch roads through abandoned pasture land in the Kahuku Unit, the latest and largest addition to Hawai'i Volcanoes National Park. In 2003 the National Park Service purchased Kahuku Ranch from Damon Estate, doubling the size of the park. Since then the park has fenced the unit to keep out grazing animals and is gradually restoring some of the native forest with the help of volunteers. Note that the Kahuku Unit is open only on weekends from 9 a.m. to 3 p.m.

The loop winds through lava flows and past volcanic cones from the destructive 1868 eruption of Mauna Loa. In April of that year, fissures opened up in the Southwest Rift Zone and gushed lava that flowed downslope in multiple channels to the ocean. The eruption was preceded by a series of earthquakes, one of which was the most powerful temblor to hit Hawai'i. The southern section of Mauna Loa slid toward the ocean, creating a huge tsunami, which inundated the Kā'u Coast.

Native *pūkiawe* shrubs and small *'ōhi'a* trees are gradually colonizing the 1868 lava flow at the start of the loop. *Pūkiawe* has tiny, rigid leaves and small white, pink, or red berries. *'Ōhi'a* has oval leaves and clusters of delicate red flowers. Early Hawaiians used the flowers in lei and the wood in outrigger canoes. The hard, durable wood was also carved into god images for *heiau* (religious sites).

Beyond the lava flow, the *'ōhi'a* trees are mature and magnificent. If they are in bloom, you may glimpse the native *'apapane*. It has a red breast and head, black wings and tail, and a slightly curved black bill. In flight the *'apapane* makes a whirring sound as it darts from tree to tree searching for insects and nectar.

The corrals at the midpoint of the loop are named after a lone palm tree, which used to stand nearby. Kahuku was a working cattle ranch from about 1861 until 2003. The ranch produced beef, hides, and tallow and mined the red cinder in the cones for landscaping and road construction.

For a shorter walk, take the Puʻu o Lokuana Trail, which starts near the visitor center. Pick up an inexpensive interpretive pamphlet, *Puʻu o Lokuana Trail Guide,* at the trailhead. If you have a four-wheel drive vehicle, try the Glover and Kona Trails farther up the cinder road.

# HĀMĀKUA

## 8

# Kalōpā Gulch

| LENGTH: | 2.8-mile loop |
| ELEVATION GAIN: | 600 feet |
| DANGER: | Low |
| SUITABLE FOR: | Novice |
| LOCATION: | Hawai'i (the Big Island): Kalōpā Native Forest State Park and Forest Reserve near Honoka'a |
| TOPO MAP: | Honoka'a |

### HIGHLIGHTS

This short loop explores a remnant native forest above the Hāmākua Coast. The trail initially follows a rocky gulch cut into the slopes of Mauna Kea, a dormant volcano. Along the way is a good variety of native rain forest plants.

### TRAILHEAD DIRECTIONS

**Distance:** (Hilo to Kalōpā State Park) 42 miles
**Driving Time:** 1 1/4 hours

From Hilo take Māmalahoa Hwy (Rte 19) toward Waimea. Proceed along the Hāmākua Coast past a series of villages.

KALŌPĀ GULCH · HĀMĀKUA

53

Drive through Laupāhoehoe village.

Cross Laupāhoehoe and Kaʻawaliʻi Gulches.

After passing mile marker 39, drive 0.5 miles farther and turn left on Kalōpā Rd. The intersection is marked with a sign to Kalōpā State Park.

Cross two wooden bridges and pass a cemetery on the left.

Turn left on Kalaniai Rd.

Turn right, still on Kalaniai Rd.

Turn left, still on Kalaniai Rd.

Enter Kalōpā Native Forest State Park and Recreation Area.

The road forks. Keep right to the cabins and picnic area. (The left fork goes to the campground.)

Park in the small lot at the end of the road. Nearby is a bulletin board displaying park information and offering an inexpensive interpretive pamphlet for sale (elevation 2,000 feet) (map point A) (UTM 5Q244798E, 2217621N) (Lat/Long N20.03865, W155.4397).

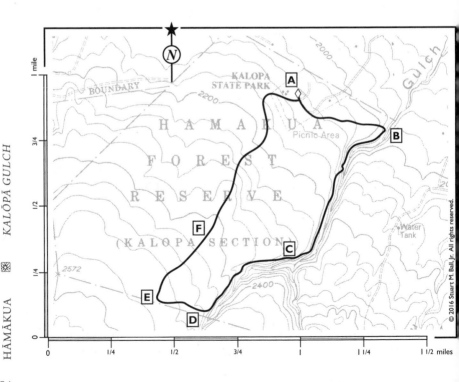

If you are starting from Kailua (Kona), you have a somewhat longer drive. Take Hawai'i Belt Rd. (Rte 190) to Waimea. Continue on the belt road (now Rte 19) past Honoka'a. Between mile markers 40 and 39, turn right on Kalōpā Rd. and pick up the directions above. The distance to the trailhead is 60 miles, and the driving time is about 1 3/4 hours.

### ROUTE DESCRIPTION

Walk back along the road toward the park entrance.

On the left pass the picnic pavilion, which has restrooms and drinking water.

Just past the fork to the campground, reach a signed junction. Turn right onto a trail, known as Robusta Lane.

Reach a signed four-way junction. Continue straight across. (To the left and right is the Perimeter Horse Trail.)

Descend gradually through a grove of tall swamp mahogany, a species of eucalyptus. *Kōpiko* and guava make up the understory.

Robusta Lane ends at the edge of Kalōpā Gulch (map point B). Turn right, up the gulch on the Gulch Rim Trail.

Climb very gradually along the gulch. Ignore a makeshift trail leading into the gulch. Look for the native *hame* trees, which grow in clumps, and *kōlea,* whose new leaves are bright pink.

Bear left and cross a rocky gully under two downed trees.

Enter a grove of blue gum trees.

Reach a signed junction. Keep left on the rim trail. (To the right, Blue Gum Lane leads to the Old Road.)

Continue the gradual ascent along the edge of the gulch.

Pass the point where the gulch splits. The trail climbs up the right gulch, called Hanaipoe.

Pass a small waterfall and pool well below in the gulch. Watch for *'ie'ie* with its tangled stems.

Immediately reach another signed junction (map point C). Continue straight on the rim trail. (To the right, Silk Oak Lane leads to the Old Road.)

Climb steeply but briefly along a gully. The trail is lined with native *hāpuʻu* tree ferns.

Reach a signed junction. Turn right on Ironwood Lane, leaving the main gulch behind (map point D).

Cross the gully.

After crossing a second gully, the trail becomes obscure. Keep right, paralleling the forest reserve boundary fence, which is occasionally visible on your left.

The trail becomes better defined through a grassy area.

Enter a grove of ironwood trees.

Reach a four-way junction (elevation 2,570 feet) (map point E) (UTM 5Q 243920E, 2216382N) (Lat/Long N20.02735, W155.44791). Turn right on an overgrown road, known as the Old Road. (To the left the road is closed off by a metal gate in the boundary fence. Beyond is private pasture land, and straight ahead is the Perimeter Horse Trail.)

Descend gradually along the dirt road.

In a stand of ironwoods, reach a signed junction (map point F). Continue straight on the road. (To the right, Silk Oak Lane leads to the Gulch Rim Trail.)

Reach another signed junction. Keep to the road. (To the right, Blue Gum Lane leads to the Gulch Rim Trail.)

The trail opens up briefly and actually becomes a road.

Reach a signed four-way junction. Continue straight on the road. (To the left and right is the Perimeter Horse Trail.)

After entering the developed area of the park, bear left on a trail toward the rental cabins by a sign for the P. Quentin Tomich Grove.

Reach the paved road and your car.

Turn left by the picnic pavilion to reach your car (map point A).

## NOTES

Kalōpā (tenant farmer) Gulch is a short, damp hike through a remnant native rain forest surrounded by pastureland. Expect to get wet, because the area receives about 100 inches of rainfall a year. After all, a rain forest should be experienced in the rain, right? If by some chance the weather is sunny, enjoy it while it lasts.

Before starting the hike, pick up the excellent trail guide at the information board across from the rental cabins. That inexpensive pamphlet has a map of the area and notes on its history and native plants.

The loop uses four different trails and has numerous junctions. All are well marked, so follow the above description closely, and you should have no navigation problems. Watch your footing on the sometimes wet, muddy, and slippery trails. Although rated novice because of its short length and low elevation gain, the loop may prove challenging for a real beginner.

On the way to the gulch, the forest understory consists of introduced guava and native *kōpiko* trees. In the 1800s, cattle grazing destroyed much of the native understory and allowed guava to come in. In 1903 the Kalōpā area became a forest reserve. With the cattle gone, the *kōpiko* seedlings thrived under the shady guava. Now the *kōpiko* trees are shading the sun-loving guava seedlings. The remaining guava trees are aging and gradually dying out.

Look for *kōpiko* along the first section of the gulch trail. The tree is a native member of the coffee family. It has leathery, oblong leaves with a light-green midrib and produces clusters of tiny white flowers and fleshy orange fruits.

Also along Kalōpā Gulch are two other native trees: *hame* and *kōlea. Hame* grows in clumps, with young trees typically ringing an old one. Its leaves are oval and glossy. Early Hawaiians used the red-purple berries as a dye for *kapa* (bark cloth). *Kōlea* has narrow, oval leaves growing at the branch tips. The leaves are bright pink when young, gradually turning dark green with age. Early Hawaiians used the light-colored wood in outrigger canoe construction and, as charcoal, to dye *kapa*.

Although the forest reserve is not large enough to support large numbers of native birds, you may catch a glimpse of an *'elepaio*. It is brown on top with a chestnut-colored breast and a dark tail, usually cocked. *'Elepaio* are very curious, which is why you can often see them.

If you are really lucky, you may spot an *'io,* the native Hawaiian hawk. It may be dark brown all over or dark brown above and white below. The hawk soars above field and forest, looking for insects, rodents, and small birds. The *'io* is an endangered species found only on the Big Island and is a symbol of royalty in Hawaiian legend.

There are several variations to the route as described. You can, of course, do the loop in reverse. For a shorter hike, take the Gulch Rim Trail and then turn right on either Blue Gum or Silk Oak Lanes. Turn right again to complete the loop. The park also has a 0.7-mile nature trail and a small arboretum of native plants.

# 9

# Waipiʻo Valley

| | |
|---|---|
| LENGTH: | 5.7-mile round-trip |
| ELEVATION GAIN: | 2,100 feet |
| DANGER: | Low |
| SUITABLE FOR: | Intermediate, Expert |
| LOCATION: | Hawaiʻi (the Big Island): Hāmākua and Kohala Forest Reserves near Honokaʻa |
| TOPO MAP: | Kukuihaele |

## HIGHLIGHTS

Waipiʻo is a deep, lush valley on the rugged Kohala Coast. This up-and-down hike descends one side of the valley and climbs the other. In between is a windswept black sand beach, framed by sheer sea cliffs.

## TRAILHEAD DIRECTIONS

**DISTANCE:** (Hilo to Waipiʻo Valley lookout) 51 miles
**DRIVING TIME:** 1 1/4 hours

From Hilo take Māmalahoa Hwy (Rte 19).
Proceed along the Hāmākua Coast past a series of villages.
Drive through Laupāhoehoe village.
Cross Laupāhoehoe and Kaʻawaliʻi Gulches.
Turn right on Honokaʻa-Waipiʻo Rd. (Rte 240) and drive through Honokaʻa town.

WAIPIʻO VALLEY ❈ HĀMĀKUA

The road jogs right and then left.

Shortly afterward reach Waipiʻo Valley Lookout (elevation 904 feet) (map point A) (UTM 5Q 229793E, 2226635N, Lat/Long N20.11799, W155.58437). Turn around and park on the side of the road. Leave the small parking lot on the right for short-term sightseers. Below the lot is the lookout, which has drinking water, restrooms, and covered picnic tables.

If you are starting from Kailua (Kona), you have a somewhat longer drive. Take Māmalahoa Hwy (Rte 190) to Waimea. Continue on the highway (now Rte 19) toward Honokaʻa. Turn left into Honokaʻa and pick up the directions above. The distance to the trailhead is 64 miles, and the driving time is about 1 3/4 hours.

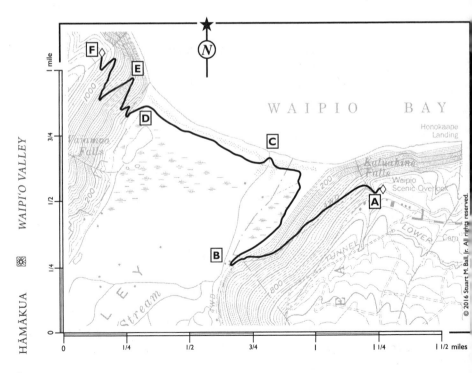

From the lookout take the one-lane paved road leading into Waipiʻo Valley.

Almost immediately, the road forks. Keep right and cross a small stream.

Descend very steeply down the side of the valley. Watch out for four-wheel-drive vehicles. Look for the lavender and purple blossoms of the Mauna Loa shrub on the ocean side of the road.

At the bottom reach a junction (map point B). Turn sharp right toward the beach. (The road on the left leads to a viewpoint of lovely Hiʻilawe Falls.)

The road becomes dirt and then sand. Huge monkeypod and *kukui* trees shade the route. Look for *ʻape* with its huge, heart-shaped leaves and *noni* with its warty fruit.

Before reaching the shore, enter a grove of ironwood trees. The road curves left and parallels the black sand beach.

Reach wide Wailoa Stream (map point C). Ford the stream at its narrow mouth near the ocean. If the current is too swift there, cross the stream just inland at its widest point. The current is much slower, but the water may be waist deep or higher. Do not attempt to cross at all if the stream is obviously swollen from recent rain or if ocean waves are riding high up the beach.

On the opposite bank pick up a wide path paralleling the beach.

Stroll through stands of ironwood and *kamani haole* (tropical almond). Near the shore is the low-lying native shrub *naupaka kahakai* with its half-formed white flowers. Look *mauka* (inland) to see Hiʻilawe Falls through the trees.

In a break in the ironwoods halfway down the beach, pass the site of Pākaʻalana Heiau, a *puʻuhonua* (place of sacred refuge).

At the far end of the beach, pass Muliwai Fishpond on the left.

Just after the pond, the path becomes rocky and then bears left away from the beach.

Reach a signed junction (map point D). Keep right onto the Muliwai Trail, which is the less-traveled route uphill. (Do not take the trail to the left that crosses private property in the valley.)

Climb the valley wall on seven long switchbacks. Look for the native shrubs *'ilima* and *'ūlei* in the sunny sections.

At the fourth switchback is a superb viewpoint (map point E). The beach and ocean are directly below. You can see well into Waipi'o Valley. The waterfall *makai* (seaward) of the road you descended is called Kaluahine.

After the fifth switchback, go through an ironwood grove. The upper switchbacks are less steep and shadier than the lower ones.

After the seventh switchback, reach the top of the ridge at a small clearing in the ironwoods (elevation 1,150 feet) (map point F) (UTM 5Q 228022E, 2227445N, Lat/Long N20.12505, W155.60142). (The trail continues across thirteen gulches to Waimanu Valley.)

## NOTES

This very scenic hike is mostly ups and downs. Initially, you descend steeply into Waipi'o (curved water) Valley on a paved road. After a stream crossing and a pleasant beach walk, the route climbs steeply out of the valley on the narrow switchbacks of the Muliwai (river) Trail. You then repeat the process in reverse on the return trip. A very attractive option is to turn around at the far end of the beach, thus eliminating over half the elevation gain.

Before starting the hike, enjoy the marvelous view from Waipi'o Lookout. The valley lies about 1,000 feet below and extends deep into the Kohala Mountains. A series of waterfalls cascades down the far wall and along the coast. You can make out the Muliwai Trail as it zigzags up the cliffs near the ocean.

In ancient times, Waipi'o (curved water) Valley was one of the major population centers on the Big Island. The fertile valley supported a thriving community based on taro farming and fish raising. Waipiʻo Valley was said to be a favorite haunt of Hawaiian royalty. Today only a few taro farmers remain.

In Waipiʻo Valley you must cross wide Wailoa (long water) Stream. The route narrative describes the best places to ford. The rocks on the bottom are very slippery, so wear tabis (Japanese reef walkers) or other water footwear. Do not attempt the crossing if the stream is obviously swollen from heavy rain in the back of the valley.

Once across the stream you can really enjoy the setting. Take in the broad sweep of the bay, framed by sheer sea cliffs. Listen for the wind soughing through the ironwoods. Watch the surf pound the black boulders and roll up the beach. Look back into the valley for lovely Hiʻilawe (lift and carry) and Hakalaoa Falls.

According to legend, a terrible whirlwind once lived in Waipiʻo Valley. He frequently flattened the houses and destroyed the crops of the Hawaiian people living there. Hiʻiaka, sister of Pele, goddess of the volcano, went on a quest to rid the Big Island of evil beings. She found the whirlwind and struck him again and again with a sacred *pāʻū* (skirt) as powerful as lightning. But the whirlwind proved elusive, twisting and turning to avoid her blows. Hiʻiaka then called upon her mighty sister for help. Pele unleashed thunder, lightning, rain, and hail to subdue the whirlwind. He crawled back to his cave and never bothered the people of Waipiʻo again.

The climb up the far wall of the valley is hot, narrow, and rocky in spots. Go at least as far as the fourth switchback with its splendid view. On the way up, look for the sprawling native shrub *ʻūlei* in the sunny sections. It has small, oblong leaves arranged in pairs, clusters of white, roselike flowers, and white fruit. Early Hawaiians ate the berries and used the tough wood for making digging sticks, fish spears, and *ʻūkēkē* (the musical bow).

The end of the hike, at the ridge top, is somewhat of an anticlimax. Ironwoods block much of the view, and the mosquitoes there encourage you to leave. From the top you can continue along the Muliwai Trail. It winds through thirteen gulches and then descends steeply to Waimanu Valley in 6.7 miles. The whole trail should really be done as an overnight trip.

For a closer view of Hiʻilawe Falls, continue straight on the paved road into the valley before climbing back to the lookout. The road initially parallels Wailoa Stream past several homesteads. Reach the best viewpoint as the road curves left by utility pole no. 24. Hiʻilawe is the larger fall on the right, with a vertical drop of over 1,000 feet, the highest in Hawaiʻi. On the left is smaller Hakalaoa Falls.

10

# Pu'u 'Ō'ō Trail

| LENGTH: | 10.0-mile round-trip |
|---|---|
| ELEVATION GAIN: | 200 feet |
| DANGER: | Low |
| SUITABLE FOR: | Intermediate |
| LOCATION: | Hawai'i (the Big Island): Mauna Loa and Upper Waiākea Forest Reserves off the Saddle Rd. |
| TOPO MAP: | Pu'u 'Ō'ō, Upper Pi'ihonua |

## HIGHLIGHTS

This pleasant hike follows the historic Pu'u 'Ō'ō–Volcano Trail, used by cattle ranchers in the 1800s and early 1900s. Along the way are *kīpuka*, islands of lush native forest surrounded by barren lava flows. You may catch a glimpse of some native birds, such as the red *'apapane* or *'i'iwi*.

## TRAILHEAD DIRECTIONS

| | |
|---|---|
| **DISTANCE:** | (Hilo to Pu'u 'Ō'ō trailhead) 23 miles |
| **DRIVING TIME:** | 3/4 hour |

From Hilo take Puainakō Ave. to Komohana St.
Turn right on Komohana St. and then immediately left on

Puainakō Extension (Rte 2000). A sign indicates Saddle Road 7 miles.

Pass Kaūmana Dr. on the right. Continue straight on Rte 2000.

Pass Old Saddle Road on the right. Puainakō Extension becomes Saddle Road (Rte 200), officially named Daniel K. Inouye Highway.

Climb gradually up Humuʻula Saddle between Mauna Loa and Mauna Kea through scrub ʻōhiʻa forest.

Pass mile marker 22.

Begin looking for the signed trailhead, which is 0.4 mile farther along the road on the left. The turnoff is identified by a yellow and black sign marked Puʻu ʻŌʻō Trail.

Turn left into a small cleared area and park near an interpretive sign (elevation 5,757 feet) (map point A) (UTM 5Q 250023E, 2177502N) (Lat/Long N19.6771, W155.38436).

If you are starting from Kailua (Kona), you have a considerably longer drive. Take Māmalahoa Hwy (Rte 190) toward Waimea. Turn right on Daniel K. Inouye Hwy (Rte 200) and drive up and partway down the saddle to mile marker 23. Look for the signed trailhead 0.6 mile farther on the right. The distance to the trailhead is 55 miles, and the driving time is about 1 1/2 hours.

## ROUTE DESCRIPTION

At the back of the cleared area, pick up the Puʻu ʻŌʻō Trail, which heads away from the road across a rough ʻaʻā lava flow.

Enter a forest of scrub ʻōhiʻa trees. Look for the native shrubs pūkiawe, ʻōhelo, and kūkaenēnē. If the ʻōhiʻa is in bloom, watch for the native birds ʻapapane and ʻiʻiwi.

Go through a dilapidated fence marking the boundary of the Upper Waiākea Forest Reserve.

Emerge onto a grassy, lumpy area lined with native koa trees (map point B). Water stands in some of the depressions along the trail. Watch for the native bird ʻamakihi.

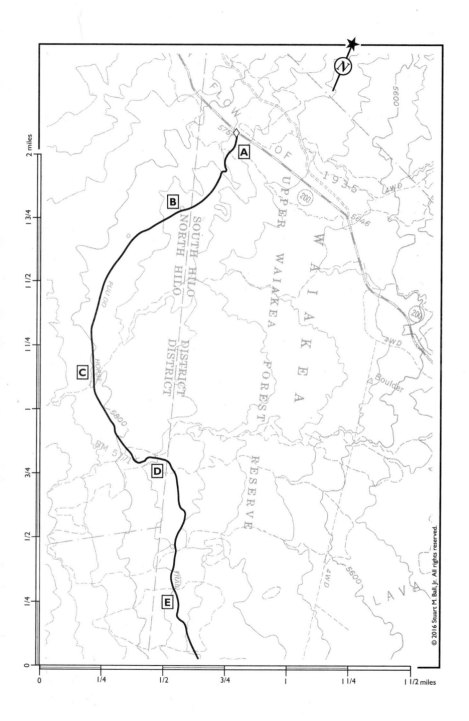

Reenter the *'ōhi'a* forest, now more open. The route is marked with small *ahu* (stacked rocks). Look for the native shrub *'a'ali'i*.

Cross another grassy area. Watch for *'ākala*, the thornless Hawaiian raspberry.

Go through a stand of koa trees and then emerge back into the open. On the left is a barren *'a'ā* lava flow from the 1855 eruption of Mauna Loa.

Enter a *kīpuka* with magnificent *'ōhi'a* and koa trees and huge *hāpu'u* tree ferns (map point C). Look for the native bird *'elepaio*.

Traverse the jagged *'a'ā* flow of 1855. Mauna Loa, the source of the lava, is in the distance to the right; Mauna Kea is to the left.

Enter an open *'ōhi'a* forest on old *pāhoehoe* lava (map point D).

Descend very gradually along a wide corridor through the woods.

The trail curves right and then crosses an arm of the 1855 flow. Small *'ōhi'a* and *'ama'u* ferns are starting to colonize the *pāhoehoe* lava. Watch for the *ahu*.

Reenter the forest (map point E).

Cross another arm of the 1855 flow.

Enter another lush *kīpuka* with old growth *'ōhi'a* and koa (map point F). Watch for the native bird *'oma'o*.

Traverse the humpy, partially vegetated lava flows of 1855 and 1881.

Skirt the right edge of a small *kīpuka* before entering it (map point G).

Emerge onto the 1881 lava flow again.

Parallel the border of the forest and then bear left to enter it (map point H).

Climb gradually and then descend.

Cross an arm of the 1855 flow once more.

Traverse the last *kīpuka*.

As the forest thins out, reach a signed junction with the dirt Kūlani Powerline Rd. (elevation 5,740 feet) (map point

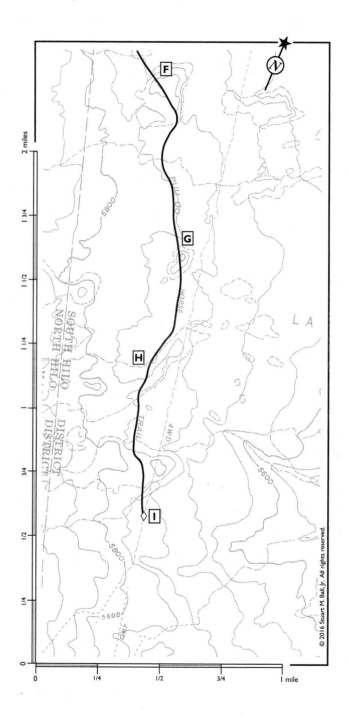

I) (UTM 5Q 252418E, 2171888N) (Lat/Long N19.62671, W155.36079). The intersection is also marked by two large *ahu* and the stump of a utility pole.

## NOTES

The Pu'u 'Ō'ō Trail is not a wildly popular hike, probably because of its lack of spectacular ocean or mountain views. If you enjoy walking through wild, remote country and/or identifying native plants and birds, take this hike. You may have it all to yourself.

Start early for the best weather. In the afternoon, clouds frequently ride up the saddle and blanket the slopes in mist and cold rain. While crossing the lava flows, watch closely for the next *ahu* (stacked rocks). Some are quite small and thus easily missed, especially when the fog rolls in. Keep at least one *ahu* in sight at all times.

The hike follows a portion of the historic Pu'u 'Ō'ō–Volcano Trail. Cattle ranchers developed that roundabout route in the 1800s to avoid the jagged *'a'ā* lava flows lying directly between the saddle area and Hilo. The ranchers drove their cattle from pasture on Mauna Kea (white mountain) over the trail to Volcano and then down the road to market in Hilo. In earlier times, the route continued south from Volcano to Keauhou (the new era) Landing along the Ka'ū Coast. There the cattle were driven into the ocean and hauled on board ships bound for Hilo and Honolulu.

The first section of the trail goes through a scrub native *'ōhi'a* forest with *kūkaenēnē, pūkiawe,* and *'ōhelo* shrubs. Creeping *kūkaenēnē* has small, narrow leaves and glossy black berries. *Pūkiawe* has tiny rigid leaves and small white, pink, or red berries. *'Ōhelo* has rounded leaves and delicious red-yellow berries, about the size of blueberries. *'Ōhi'a* trees have oval leaves and clusters of delicate red flowers. Native birds, such as the *'apapane,* feed on the nectar and help in pollination.

If the *'ōhi'a* is in bloom, you may catch a glimpse of an

'apapane or 'i'iwi in the low forest canopy. Both birds have a red breast and head, and black wings and tail. The 'i'iwi has a long, curved, salmon-colored bill for sipping 'ōhi'a nectar. The 'apapane has a slightly curved black bill. In flight the 'apapane makes a whirring sound as it darts from tree to tree searching for insects and nectar.

In the more open forest, you can see two other native shrubs: 'a'ali'i and 'ākala. 'A'ali'i has narrow, dull green leaves and red seed capsules. 'Ākala, the Hawaiian raspberry, has light-green, serrated leaves and few or no thorns. The flowers are pink to red, and the edible berries are red to purple.

The trail repeatedly crosses the 1855 and 1881 lava flows from Mauna Loa (long mountain). Both eruptions started at vents along the Northeast Rift Zone at the 9,500-foot level. As you can see, small 'ōhi'a trees and 'ama'u ferns are beginning to colonize the lava. 'Ama'u has a short trunk and fronds that are bright red when young and green when mature.

Alternating with the bare lava are wooded islands of older lava, known as kīpuka. They contain magnificent old-growth 'ōhi'a and koa trees, and hāpu'u tree ferns. Koa has sickle-shaped foliage and pale-yellow flower clusters. Hāpu'u has sweeping delicate fronds and a trunk consisting of roots tightly woven around a central stem.

In the kīpuka, you may see two other native birds: 'oma'o and 'elepaio. Found only on the Big Island, the 'oma'o has brown gray wings, a pale gray breast, and a dark bill. Their sharp call resembles a police whistle, and their twitter is a series of jerky, slurred notes. The 'elepaio is brown on top with a chestnut-colored breast and a dark tail, usually cocked. 'Elepaio are very curious, which is why you can often see them.

If the weather has turned bad, Kūlani Powerline Road makes a decent option for the return trip. The road is rough but is easier to follow than the trail and somewhat shorter. When you reach Saddle Rd., turn left and trek 0.7 miles along the busy highway back to your car. That road walk is perhaps the most dangerous part of the route.

# 11

# Mauna Loa
## (VIA THE OBSERVATORY TRAIL)

| | |
|---|---|
| LENGTH: | 12.6-mile round-trip |
| ELEVATION GAIN: | 2,700 feet |
| DANGER: | Medium |
| SUITABLE FOR: | Expert |
| LOCATION: | Hawai'i (the Big Island): Mauna Loa Forest Reserve and Hawai'i Volcanoes National Park off the Saddle Rd. |
| TOPO MAP: | Koko'olau, Mauna Loa |

## HIGHLIGHTS

Mauna Loa is the largest active volcano in the world. This demanding hike climbs to its summit, past spatter cones, pit craters, and acres of barren lava. At the top is Moku'āweoweo, a huge, desolate crater with steaming vents and fissures.

## TRAILHEAD DIRECTIONS

| | |
|---|---|
| **DISTANCE:** | (Hilo to Observatory trailhead) 45 miles |
| **DRIVING TIME:** | 1 1/2 hours |

From Hilo take Puainakō Ave. to Komohana St.

Turn right on Komohana St. and then immediately left on Puainakō Extension (Rte 2000). A sign indicates Saddle Road 7 miles.

Pass Kaūmana Dr. on the right. Continue straight on Rte 2000.

Pass Old Saddle Road on the right. Puainakō Extension becomes Saddle Road (Rte 200), officially named Daniel K. Inouye Highway.

Climb gradually up Humu'ula Saddle between Mauna Loa and Mauna Kea. The road winds through scrub 'ōhi'a forest and then barren lava flows.

Around mile marker 27, look for Pu'u Huluhulu, a wooded hill on the left near the road.

Just before reaching the hill, turn left on a one-lane paved road. The intersection is identified by a yellow and black sign marked Mauna Loa Observatory.

Ascend gradually up the lower slopes of Mauna Loa. The paved road jogs once to the left and, later on, once to the right.

Follow a power line leading up to Mauna Loa Observatory.

Park in the small public lot on the left below the observatory (elevation 11,020 feet) (map point A) (UTM 5Q 229733E, 2162375N) (Lat/Long N19.53786, W155.57557).

If you are starting from Kailua (Kona), you have a somewhat longer drive. Take Hawai'i Belt Rd. (Rte 190) toward Waimea. Turn right on Saddle Rd. (Rte 200). Drive up the saddle to mile marker 28. Turn right on the unmarked road just past Pu'u Huluhulu and pick up the directions above. The distance to the trailhead is 77 miles, and the driving time is about 2 1/2 hours.

## ROUTE DESCRIPTION

Just beyond the parking lot is a signed junction. Take the rocky dirt road straight ahead. (To the left the paved road climbs to the observatory.)

Cross two 'a'ā lava flows.

Reach a second signed junction (map point B). Turn left and up on the Observatory Trail. (The dirt road continues

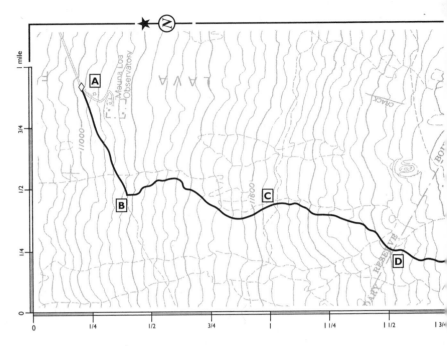

straight and then switchbacks up the mountain, crossing the trail several times.)

Climb steadily on a gray prehistoric *pāhoehoe* flow. The route is marked with *ahu* (cairns) and splotches of yellow paint on the rock. To the left is a jagged brown *'a'ā* flow, also prehistoric.

Cross the rocky dirt road (map point C).

Reach a lava tube, indicated by two tall *ahu*. A rock windbreak across the tube provides some shelter.

The trail works right and then traverses an old *'a'ā* lava flow.

Resume steady climbing on gray *pāhoehoe* lava (map point D). On the left is a prehistoric red spatter cone.

At a trail sign, turn left along the edge of the *'a'ā* flow (map point E). (The old route of the Observatory Trail continues straight up.)

At another trail sign, reach a junction. Turn right on the rocky dirt road.

The road swings left, crossing an *'a'ā* flow.

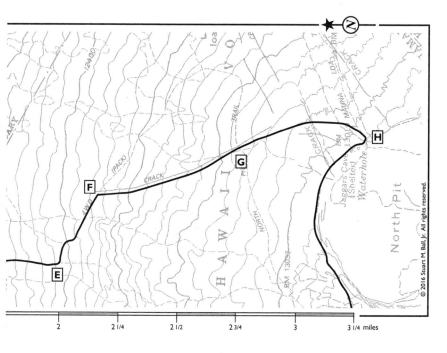

2    2 1/4    2 1/2    2 3/4    3    3 1/4 miles

By the third trail sign, reach another junction at the Hawai'i Volcanoes National Park boundary (map point F). Turn right off the road onto the Observatory Trail. (The road continues straight, through a locked gate.)

Climb alongside a brightly colored fissure. Underfoot is green, blue, orange, and black pumice. To the right is the shiny black *pāhoehoe* of the 1942 flow.

Ascend steadily across the 1942 lava flow.

Reach a second junction with the road (map point G). Continue straight across on the trail. (To the right the road leads to the original site of the Mauna Loa Observatory.)

The trail swings left and crosses the 1942 fissure.

On the right, pass a primitive toilet, strategically situated above a crack.

Reach the end of the Observatory Trail at a signed junction (map point H). Turn right on the Summit Trail. (To the left the Cabin Trail leads to the Mauna Loa Trail and Cabin.)

Shortly afterward, pass Jaggar's Cave (elevation 13,019

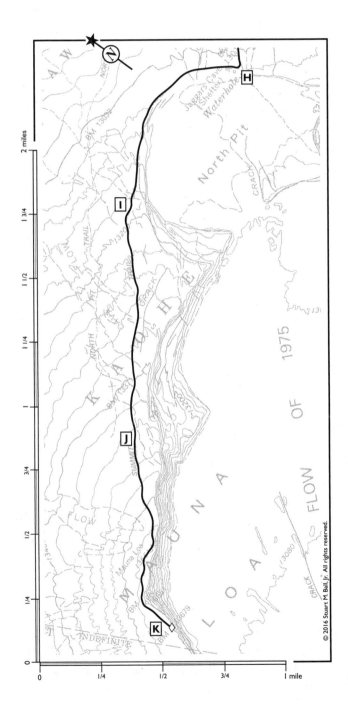

feet), marked by a monumental *ahu* on the left. The cave provides shelter from the wind and has a water hole next door.

Follow the rim of North Pit. Beyond is the summit caldera, Moku'āweoweo.

Jump over the multicolored fissure from the 1942 eruption.

Traverse prehistoric *'a'ā* and *pāhoehoe* lava flows.

Angle away from the rim and begin climbing.

Reach a signed junction (map point I). Continue straight on the Summit Trail. (To the right the old route of the Observatory Trail heads downhill.)

Climb more steeply on old *pāhoehoe* lava.

Pass a seismic station with its antenna.

Pass the original site of the observatory, downslope to the right (map point J).

Angle left toward the crater rim.

Reach the summit of Mauna Loa (elevation 13,679 feet) (map point K) (UTM 5Q 226487E, 2155516N) (Lat/Long N19.4755, W155.60549).

## NOTES

The climb to the summit of Mauna Loa (long mountain) has nothing in common with beaches, palm trees, and the rest of tourist Hawai'i. This is alpine hiking at elevations well above 10,000 feet. The thin air, long distance, high wind, and rough footing make this a climb to be reckoned with and remembered. Take this mountain seriously.

Summer (May–August) is the best time of year to climb Mauna Loa. The days are long, and the weather is usually settled. Midday temperatures range from 50 to 70 degrees F; it can feel hotter because of the intense sun or colder because of windchill. During winter (December–March), the days are shorter and the wind stronger. A sudden storm can blanket the summit area with several inches or feet of snow, burying the trail. Whatever the season, start early and bring extra layers of clothing and plenty of water and sunscreen.

Above the trailhead is the Mauna Loa Observatory, the premier research facility for collecting and monitoring data related to changes in the atmosphere. In 1958 scientist Charles Keeling began tracking the concentration of atmospheric carbon dioxide at the station. His measurements, showing rising $CO_2$ levels since then, have formed the basis for scientific studies and predictions about climate change.

In view from the parking lot are three dormant volcanoes. Across the saddle to the north is Mauna Kea (white mountain), the highest peak in the state at 13,796 feet. You can see several observatories clustered near its summit. To the left and well below is Hualālai at 8,271 feet. In the distance between those two is Haleakalā (house of the sun), the highest point on the island of Maui at 10,023 feet.

The mountain you are about to climb is a shield volcano, the largest in the world. Mauna Loa sits astride a hot spot in the earth's crust where molten rock lies close to the surface. Eruptions over many years have built the volcano from its base deep in the ocean to its present height of 13,679 feet. The latest eruption in 1984 started at the summit crater, Mokuʻāweoweo, and then shifted to the rift zone extending to the northeast above you. The resulting lava coursed down the saddle to within 5 miles of the outskirts of Hilo.

On the trail, watch closely for the *ahu* (cairns) marking the route. They are sometimes difficult to spot against a background of black lava. Keep at least one *ahu* in sight at all times, especially in bad weather. While climbing, walk at a slow but steady pace to minimize the effect of altitude. Breathe deeply, take frequent breaks, and drink plenty of water. If you have a headache, nausea, or difficulty breathing, slow down even more. Turn around if the symptoms get worse.

Before reaching Jaggar's Cave, the trail crosses a fissure and lava flow from the 1942 eruption. Volcanic activity began on the evening of April 26. A fissure opened up in the summit crater across the North Pit and along the Northeast Rift Zone. For two days, lava cascaded from small fountains in the fissure and flowed down toward the saddle. Because World War II had started, the government tried to keep the eruption secret. Some officials feared the Japanese might use the volcano as a beacon for navigation. The effort was largely unsuccessful because Tokyo Rose soon broadcast news of the eruption over Japanese radio.

Jaggar's Cave makes a good rest stop or turnaround point. The cave is actually an open pit, but it is sheltered from the wind and does have a water hole next door. (Treat the water before drinking it.) Thomas Jaggar, pioneering volcanologist and founder of the Hawaiian Volcano Observatory, used the cave on his field trips to study the mountain.

After Jaggar's Cave, the Summit Trail initially hugs the rim of North Pit. It is a shallow, circular depression covered with smooth lava from the 1984 eruption. The route then veers away from the rim and begins a rough, seemingly endless ascent to the summit. No climb lasts forever, so the top eventually heaves into sight.

The view from the summit of Mauna Loa is breathtaking. Directly below is the summit caldera, Moku'āweoweo, 2.7 miles long, 1.6 miles wide, and 600 feet deep in places. Steam still seeps from a fissure that opened the length of the crater in 1984. Lava from that eruption covers much of the floor. The tall cone in the center of the crater was built in 1940. Along the near rim to the right is the 1949 cone, colored red and green. On the far right, a gap in the crater wall leads to South Pit. North Pit is through a gap in the rim on the left. Across the crater on the far rim is Mauna Loa Cabin.

The hike down is quite pleasant, at least compared to the hike up. Just put one foot in front of the other and let gravity carry you down the slopes. Watch your footing, though, on the rough 'a'ā flows and the steep pāhoehoe sections. On the way down, enjoy the expansive views as the mountain unfolds in front of you.

# 12

# Mauna Kea

| LENGTH: | 12.0-mile round-trip |
| --- | --- |
| ELEVATION GAIN: | 4,600 feet |
| DANGER: | Medium |
| SUITABLE FOR: | Expert |
| LOCATION: | Hawaiʻi (the Big Island): Mauna Kea Forest Reserve and Mauna Kea Ice Age Natural Area Reserve off the Saddle Rd. |
| TOPO MAP: | Mauna Kea |

## HIGHLIGHTS

The dormant volcano Mauna Kea is the highest mountain in Hawaiʻi. This challenging climb follows a steep, rough trail and then a paved road to the observatories at the summit. Along the way are colorful cones, an early Hawaiian quarry, and even a glistening lake.

## TRAILHEAD DIRECTIONS

| **Distance:** | (Hilo to Visitor Information Station) 35 miles |
| --- | --- |
| **Driving Time:** | 1 hour |

From Hilo take Puainakō Ave. to Komohana St.
Turn right on Komohana St. and then immediately left on

Puainakō Extension (Rte 2000). A sign indicates Saddle Road 7 miles.

Pass Kaūmana Dr. on the right. Continue straight on Rte 2000.

Pass Old Saddle Road on the right. Puainakō Extension becomes Saddle Road (Rte 200), officially named Daniel K. Inouye Highway.

Climb gradually up Humuʻula Saddle between Mauna Loa and Mauna Kea. The road winds through scrub ʻōhiʻa forest and then barren lava flows.

After mile marker 27, look for Puʻu Huluhulu, a wooded hill on the left near the road.

Across from Puʻu Huluhulu, turn right on the paved access road to Mauna Kea.

Ascend through pasture land, gradually at first and then more steeply.

Enter Mauna Kea Forest Reserve.

Reach the Visitor Information Station of the Onizuka Center for International Astronomy (elevation 9,200 feet) (map point A) (UTM 5Q 242665E, 2186716N) (Lat/Long N19.75935, W155.45576). Turn right into the lot and park there.

Before starting, fill out a hiker registration form in the box near the front door. The box also contains trail maps and a cautionary pamphlet. The visitor station has restrooms, drinking water, and picnic tables.

If you are starting from Kailua (Kona), you have a somewhat longer drive. Take Māmalahoa Hwy (Rte 190) toward Waimea. Turn right on Daniel K. Inouye Hwy (Rte 200). Just after mile marker 28 and across from Puʻu Huluhulu, turn left on the Mauna Kea Access Rd. and pick up the directions above. The distance to the trailhead is 55 miles, and the driving time is about 1 1/2 hours.

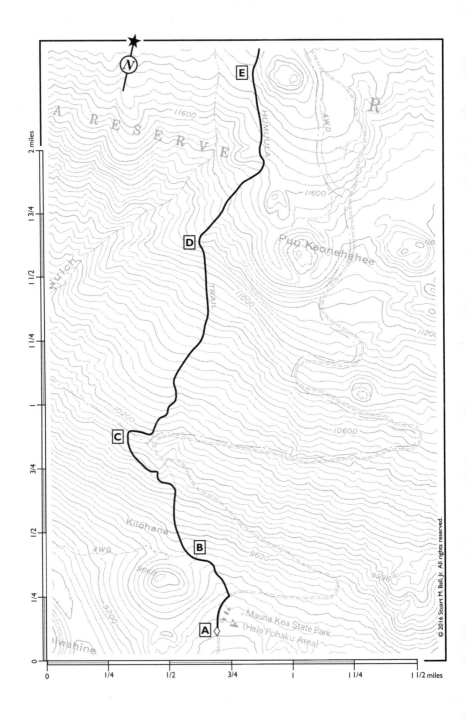

Walk back out to the main road and turn right uphill.

Pass two turnoffs to Hale Pōhaku on the right.

Reach a signed junction across from the road maintenance yard. Turn left onto a dirt road, marked Humuʻula Trail. (The access road to the summit continues straight and becomes unpaved. Only four-wheel-drive vehicles are allowed beyond this point.)

Climb steadily through scattered native *māmane* trees. On the left is a red-brown cinder cone.

The road forks (map point B). Keep right and up following the trail sign.

Pass a concrete slab on the right.

The road forks again. Keep right, but almost immediately, bear left onto the Mauna Kea-Humuʻula Trail. That signed junction is marked by several wooden posts and metal stakes.

Ascend almost straight up on brown sand and cinders.

By another trail sign, the route swings left and levels off briefly.

Angle upslope very steeply and then more gradually on black sand and cinders. Look for the native shrubs *pūkiawe* and *ʻōhelo* among the lava outcrops.

Enter Mauna Kea Ice Age Natural Area Reserve (map point C).

Ignore several side trails on the right leading to a switchback on the access road.

Resume serious climbing on gray-brown cinders. The trail is marked with rusty metal stakes.

Reach White Rock, a large boulder covered with paint and graffiti (elevation 11,200 feet) (map point D). Take a breather and look at the panoramic view.

Climb steadily on red cinder and loose rock. To the right is Keoneheʻeheʻe, a large red cinder cone. To the left is dry Waikahalulu Gulch.

Work around the base of an unnamed cone on your right (map point E).

MAUNA KEA ❋ SADDLE ROAD

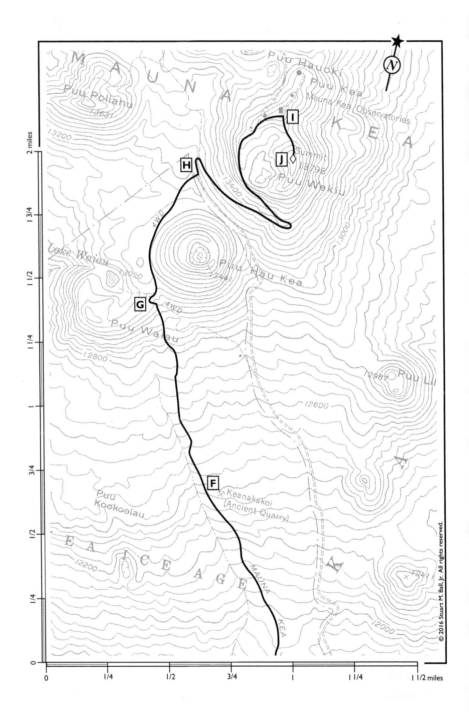

Climb up the light-colored, boulder-strewn slopes, paralleling an escarpment on your right. Enjoy the periodic easing of the angle of ascent. The trail is now marked by *ahu* (cairns) and splotches of yellow paint, as well as the metal stakes. A line of three red cinder cones on the right allows tracking of your progress toward Lake Waiau.

On the right pass Keanakākoʻi, an ancient adze quarry (elevation 12,400 feet) (map point F).

Climb steeply on loose sand and rock. The cinder cone on the left is Puʻu Waiau, and on the right across the access road is Puʻu Līlīnoe.

Reach an unmarked junction (map point G). Turn left uphill, of course. (The side trail to the right leads to a parking lot on the access road.)

Shortly afterward reach another unmarked junction. This time turn right. (The side trail to the left leads a short distance to Lake Waiau.)

Climb around the base of Puʻu Haukea on your right. To the left is a striking red-orange cone called Puʻu Poliʻahu, named after the goddess of snow.

Leave the Mauna Kea Ice Natural Area Reserve.

Shortly reach the end of the Mauna Kea-Humuʻula Trail at a junction with the access road (map point H). Climb over the guardrail and turn left and up on the paved road.

Almost immediately, switchback to the right. On the left is a side road leading to several observatories.

Switchback to the left and climb the slopes of Puʻu Wēkiu, the summit cone.

Just before a turnoff to the Keck Observatory on the left, go around the guardrail to the right and stop at a large Aloha sign.

If you wish to continue to the true summit after reading the sign, descend briefly on a makeshift trail and then climb once more.

Reach the summit of Mauna Kea by a benchmark and rock altar (elevation 13,796 feet) (map point J) (UTM 5Q 241460E, 2193524N) (Lat/Long N19.82065, W155.4682).

The ascent to the summit of Mauna Kea (white mountain) is the toughest day hike in the islands. The air is thin; the trail, rough; the route, long; and the climbing, relentless. Take this mountain seriously. Come prepared for alpine hiking at elevations well above 10,000 feet.

Summer (May–August) is the best time of year to climb Mauna Kea. The days are long, and the weather is usually settled. Midday temperatures range from 50 to 70 degrees F; it can feel hotter because of the intense sun or colder because of windchill. During winter (December–March) the days are shorter and the wind stronger. A sudden storm can blanket the summit area with snow, burying the trail. Whatever the season, start early and bring extra layers of clothing and plenty of water and sunscreen.

The mountain you are about to climb is a shield volcano, the highest in the state. Mauna Kea sits astride a hot spot in the earth's crust where molten rock lies close to the surface. Eruptions over many years have built the volcano from its base deep in the ocean to its present height of 13,796 feet. Mauna Kea has lain dormant for over two thousand years. The last series of eruptions filled the summit caldera and created a broad cap, now dotted with cinder cones.

On the trail, watch closely for the three types of route markers: metal stakes, *ahu* (stacked rocks), and yellow paint splotches on the rock. The stakes and *ahu* are sometimes difficult to spot against a background of like-colored cinders or boulders. Keep at least one marker in sight at all times, especially in bad weather. While climbing, walk at a slow but steady pace to minimize the effect of altitude. Breathe deeply, take frequent breaks, and drink plenty of water. If you have a headache, nausea, or difficulty breathing, slow down even more. Turn around if the symptoms get worse.

The initial section of the climb is incredibly steep. Take a breather at the well-known landmark White Rock. Look down for a last view of the Hale Pōhaku area. Look around for a last view of anything green. Across the saddle is massive Mauna Loa (long mountain), an active volcano with an elevation of 13,679 feet. You can clearly see the walls of its summit caldera, Mokuʻāweoweo (red fish section). To the right and well below is Hualālai, another dormant volcano, at 8,271 feet.

At the 12,400-foot level, look for Keanakākoʻi (the adze-making cave), an ancient quarry. The cave is located partway up the line of cliffs on the right. Below are piles of dark, discarded rock. Early Hawaiians mined the dense rock in the cave and shaped it into stone tools.

If you have the energy, take the short side trip to Lake Waiau (swirling water). It is a brilliant blue-green tarn nestled among red cinder hills. According to legend, the lake is bottomless, leading to the very heart of the volcano.

After leaving Lake Waiau, the trail passes a colorful cone called Puʻu Poliʻahu. It is named after Poliʻahu, the legendary snow goddess of Mauna Kea. One day she and a group of friends were sledding down the slopes on the Hāmākua side of the mountain. Out of nowhere a beautiful woman appeared and was invited to join the games. After Poliʻahu proved the faster of the two in a sled race, she noticed the ground getting warm. The beautiful stranger, now very angry, turned out to be Pele, the goddess of fire. She stoked her subterranean fires, and hot lava burst to the surface on Mauna Kea. Poliʻahu quickly retreated to the summit and then threw her mantle of snow over the whole mountain. Gradually the fires died down, and the lava cooled and hardened. Pele was forced to withdraw to her home in Kīlauea Volcano, where she lives to this day. And each winter, Poliʻahu cloaks the summit of her mountain with a blanket of snow.

The summit area with its paved road and clusters of observatories is somewhat of shock after the quiet solitude of the trail. With its legends, shrines, and burial sites, Mauna Kea is sacred ground for Native Hawaiians. They ask that you not climb the summit cone out of respect for their beliefs. In genealogical chants, the mountain is identified as Ka Mauna o Wākea, the mountain of Wākea, the original god and father of Hawaiʻi.

The hike down is quite pleasant, at least compared to the hike up. Just put one foot in front of the other and let gravity carry you down the slopes. Watch your footing, though, on the loose rock and cinder. On the way down, enjoy the expansive views as the mountain unfolds in front of you.

The access road to the summit provides several unappealing variations to the route as described. You can walk the road one way and the trail the other, or the road both ways. The road is well graded and easy to follow, but it is much longer and less interesting than the trail. Use the road as an alternate route only if the weather turns bad.

A more attractive option is to hitchhike one way. Past the visitor station, traffic is light on the access road, but your chance of getting a ride is usually good. If you have two four-wheel-drive vehicles, park one at the visitor station and the other at the end of the road near the summit. Hike up or down the mountain as you choose.

13

# Kealakekua Bay

| LENGTH: | 4.2-mile round-trip |
| --- | --- |
| ELEVATION GAIN: | 1,300 feet |
| DANGER: | Low |
| SUITABLE FOR: | Intermediate |
| LOCATION: | Hawai'i (the Big Island): Kealakekua Bay State Historical Park |
| TOPO MAP: | Hōnaunau |

The great English explorer Captain James Cook met his death at Kealakekua Bay on February 14, 1779. This hot, dry hike descends a dirt road to his monument by the shore. In the bay is some of the best snorkeling in the islands.

**TRAILHEAD DIRECTIONS**

**DISTANCE:**  (Kailua [Kona] to Captain Cook) 12 miles
**DRIVING TIME:**  1/2 hour

From Kailua (Kona) take Māmalahoa Hwy (Rte 11) toward Volcano.
Pass the junction with Rte 180 on the left.

Drive through the towns of Kainaliu and Kealakekua.

Enter the town of Captain Cook and look for a Chevron gas station on the left after mile marker 109.

Just past it, turn right on Nāpōʻopoʻo Rd. On the right a sign to Kealakekua Bay marks the intersection.

Drive 0.1 mile down the road. Look for a rock wall and three tall palm trees on the left. Just beyond is a white house on the slope above.

Park on the left shoulder of the road along the wall before the driveway leading up to the house (elevation 1,290 feet) (map point A) (UTM 5Q 193682E, 2157874N) (Lat/Long N19.49202, W155.91809).

If you are starting from Hilo, you have a considerably longer drive. Take Saddle Road and then Daniel K. Inouye Hwy (both Rte 200) to its end and then turn left on Māmalahoa Hwy (Rte

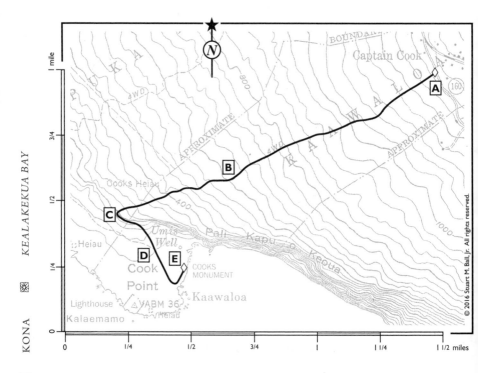

190) to Kailua (Kona) and pick up the directions above. The distance to the trailhead is 106 miles, and the driving time is about 2 3/4 hours.

ROUTE DESCRIPTION

The signed trailhead is across the street from the wall and the palms.

By an avocado tree, pick up the Ka'awaloa Trail, a dirt road lined with tall grass.

Pass a large mango tree on the right.

Descend steadily toward the coast. On the left are a rock wall and a fence, mostly hidden by the grass. Monkeypod and tamarind trees provide some welcome shade, especially on the return.

The road becomes rockier and is lined with *koa haole* trees (map point B). On the right is an old *'a'ā* lava flow.

On the right, pass Puhina o Lono Heiau, the religious site where Cook's body was taken after his death. Look for a rock-walled enclosure with a broken and rusted wire gate.

The road bends sharply to the left toward Kealakekua Bay (map point C). Across Kealakekua Bay is Ke'ei Beach and Palemanō Point. To the right along the coast is Keawekāheka Point and Bay. Look for the native shrub *'uhaloa* lining the trail.

Pass a dilapidated wooden gate just off the trail on the right.

Descend steeply over loose rock past several tamarind. Watch your footing.

Enter a forest of *koa haole* and *kiawe* trees. The angle of descent eases as you approach the bay.

A dirt road comes in on the right (map point D). Keep left toward the bay. Memorize that junction for the return trip.

The road is flanked by magnificent rock walls, all that remains of the ancient Hawaiian village of Ka'awaloa.

Enter Kealakekua Bay State Historical Park.

Reach a junction. For now, continue straight toward the water. (The path to the left through a break in the rock wall leads to the Cook Monument.)

Reach the water's edge. On the left is the concrete base for a plaque marking the approximate spot where Captain Cook met his death. Unfortunately, the plaque is missing.

Retrace your steps back to the last junction and turn right through the break in the rock wall.

The path swings right and then left to parallel the shore under *kou*, *milo*, and tamarind trees.

Go around the huge trunk of a *kiawe*.

Reach the Cook Monument at Ka'awaloa Point (map point E) (UTM 5Q 192056E, 2156713N) (Lat/Long N19.48129, W155.93337).

## NOTES

Most people arrive at Kealakekua (pathway of the god) Bay in a kayak or tour boat. If you are a landlubber or just enjoy reaching remote places the hard way, take this hot, dry hike down to the bay. Spend some time at the monument to the great English explorer Captain James Cook. Then jump in the ocean for a cooling dip and some terrific snorkeling.

Start early in the morning or late in the afternoon to avoid the sweltering heat. For clear water and good lighting, go snorkeling in the early morning. Later in the day the water near the monument is crowded with kayakers from Nāpō'opo'o and tour boats from Kailua (Kona).

As the road swings left toward the bay, look for the native shrub 'uhaloa, a woody, sprawling herb. Its gray-green leaves are oval, pointed, and covered with fine hairs. Small yellow flowers with five petals emerge from the angle between the stem and the leaf stalk. Early Hawaiians used 'uhaloa as a medicinal herb to relieve sore throats, congestion, chest pain, and asthma.

Just before reaching the shore, the road passes through the site of Ka'awaloa, an ancient Hawaiian village. All that remains are rock walls and house platforms. At the time of Cook's visit, Ka'awaloa was the royal seat of Kalani'opu'u, the chief of Kona, Ka'ū, and Puna. The village consisted of thatched houses shaded by palm trees and enclosed gardens for growing fruits and vegetables.

In the shallows at Ka'awaloa Point is the concrete base for a small metal plaque marking the approximate spot where Captain Cook died on February 14, 1779. That morning he came ashore with an armed party to retrieve a stolen ship's boat. Cook had planned to take Kalani'ōpu'u hostage and trade him for the boat. The captain, however, was unsuccessful in persuading the chief to come on board his flagship. Meanwhile, a large group of Native Hawaiians had gathered to watch the goings-on. Initially peaceful, the crowd turned hostile upon hearing that Cook's sailors had just killed a chief across the bay. Cook's party fired shots, and the natives threw stones. In the ensuing melee, Cook was stabbed and clubbed to death.

The Native Hawaiians carefully carried Cook's remains up the trail to Puhina o Lono Heiau. There they carved the body on a large flat stone and roasted the flesh and organs. Various ali'i (chiefs) received the bones, which became revered objects.

In July 1825, the British frigate HMS *Blonde* arrived at Kealakekua Bay. The ship's crew, under Captain George A. (Lord) Byron, installed a wooden capstan bar and a copper plaque at the *heiau*. In 1928, a local historical society set the post in concrete and installed another plaque and an iron gate at the site. The plaques are gone, but the post lies near the rock and concrete base, as does the gate, which is rusted and broken.

Along the shore is the Cook Monument, erected in the 1870s. It is a white obelisk, surrounded by upright cannons linked with anchor chain. The land underneath the monument belongs to Great Britain. In the pavement are plaques commemorating visits by ships of the British Commonwealth.

From the pier in front of the monument you can look across the bay to the town of Nāpō'opo'o (the holes). On the left is Pali Kapu o Keōua, a sheer cliff that contains ancient burial caves. Watch for *koa'e kea,* the white-tailed tropicbird, soaring near the cliffs.

The snorkeling at Kealakekua Bay is superb with a good variety of reef fish and coral. The monument pier offers easy access to the water. You can also get in from the fingers of lava near the site of Cook's death. If you decide to swim or snorkel, you are on your own, as there are no lifeguards at Kealakekua Bay.

For some solitude after snorkeling, walk along the shore to Kalaemamo Point and the small Nāpō'opo'o lighthouse. Along the way are several *milo,* a possible Polynesian introduction. The tree has shiny, heart-shaped leaves and pale-yellow flowers, similar to a hibiscus. Early Hawaiians carved the reddish-brown wood into bowls used for food preparation. The dried fruit, shaped like a slightly flattened globe, produced a yellow-green dye.

The return trip upslope is relatively painless, especially after an invigorating swim. Keep a slow, steady pace, drink lots of water, and take a break under a shady tamarind. Before you know it, the avocado tree at the trailhead comes into view.

# KAUA'I

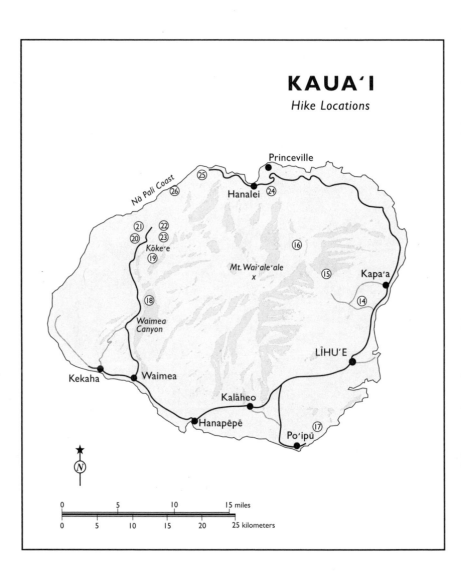

# KAUA'I

*Hike Locations*

Princeville

㉕

㉖ Na Pali Coast

Hanalei ㉔

㉑ ㉒
㉓
㉔ Kōke'e
⑲

Mt. Wai'ale'ale
x

⑯

⑮ Kapa'a

⑭

⑱

Waimea
Canyon

LĪHU'E

Kekaha

Waimea

Kalāheo

Hanapēpē

Po'ipū ⑰

★
Ⓝ

| 0 | | 5 | | 10 | | 15 miles |
|---|---|---|---|---|---|---|

| 0 | 5 | 10 | 15 | 20 | 25 kilometers |
|---|---|---|---|---|---|

14

# Nounou Mountain–East
## (SLEEPING GIANT)

| LENGTH: | 3.8-mile round-trip |
| ELEVATION GAIN: | 1,100 feet |
| DANGER: | Low |
| SUITABLE FOR: | Novice |
| LOCATION: | Kauaʻi: Nounou Forest Reserve above Wailua |
| TOPO MAP: | Kapaʻa |

### HIGHLIGHTS

In profile, Nounou Mountain resembles a sleeping giant. This steady climb to the giant's head opens up spectacular views of the eastern coast and interior mountains. At the top, white-tailed tropicbirds soar gracefully overhead.

### TRAILHEAD DIRECTIONS

**DISTANCE:** (Līhuʻe to Nounou Mountain-East trailhead) 7 miles
**DRIVING TIME:** 1/4 hour

From Līhuʻe take Kūhiō Hwy (Rte 56 north) toward Kapaʻa. Cross Wailua River on a bridge.

Pass the intersection with Kuamoʻo Rd. (Rte 580).

At the next traffic light by a Shell service station, turn left on Haleilio Rd.

Pass the intersection with Wailana Rd. on the right.

As the road curves left, turn right into a small paved lot and park there near the signed trailhead (elevation 120 feet) (map point A) (UTM 4Q 464237E, 2439656N) (Lat/Long N22.06133, W159.34662). The lot is 1.1 miles from the intersection with Route 56.

## ROUTE DESCRIPTION

Climb the embankment on the right side of the parking lot to pick up the Nounou Mountain–East Side Trail.

Ascend gradually along the slope on fourteen switchbacks through a mixed forest of *koa haole* and Christmas berry trees. Look for the native herb *ʻalaʻala wai nui* on the rocks of the upper switchbacks.

At the fourteenth switchback, reach an obscure junction. Turn sharp right and climb a short rock face. (On the left a makeshift trail leads to a lookout with a view of the giant's head. Below is the Wailua River. Beyond Līhuʻe along the coast is the massive peak of Hāʻupu, also called Hoary Head.)

The trail descends briefly to skirt a rocky cliff and then resumes climbing.

Switchback seven more times.

Gain the ridgeline and turn left up it (map point B). *Mauka* (inland) are the Makaleha Mountains.

Ascend the ridge, crossing from one side to the other on several switchbacks. Along the trail are strawberry guava and eucalyptus trees.

Pass a bench down and on the left.

Cross an eroded spot with views *makai* (seaward).

Reach an unmarked junction in a stand of *hala* trees. Keep left along the ridge. (To the right, the Nounou Mountain-West Side Trail descends to Kamalu Rd. [Rte 581]).

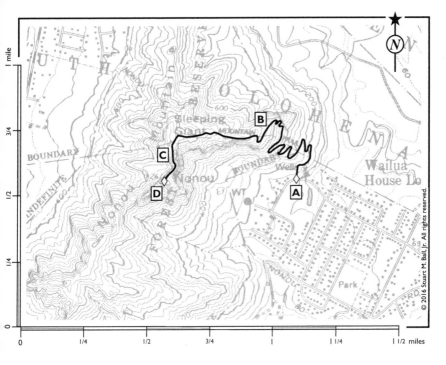

Continue climbing past some *kī* (ti) plants.

Reach a flat, grassy area (giant's chest) with a bench, two covered picnic tables, and an impressive view *mauka* (map point C). Look for *koaʻe kea* (white-tailed tropicbirds) soaring overhead.

Descend and traverse a narrow saddle in the ridge (giant's neck). Look for the native shrub *ʻakoko*.

Reach an End of Trail sign. Continue past it only if you are an intermediate or expert hiker.

Scramble up a steep slope (giant's chin). Watch your footing on the loose dirt and rock.

Reach the summit of Nounou (giant's nose) (elevation 1,241 feet) (map point D) (UTM 4Q 463372E, 2439635N) (Lat/Long N22.06112, W159.355). At the top are the remains of a triangulation station and superb views in all directions.

The climb to the chest and head of Sleeping Giant is popular with tourists and locals alike. The route is hot and steep, but the tremendous view from the top is well worth the effort. For the most part, the trail is wide and well graded. Watch your step, however, in a few rocky, narrow spots on the switchbacks.

Check the boulders on the upper switchbacks for the native herb *'ala'ala wai nui*. It grows in low mats, which cling to moss-covered rock and trees in moist, protected areas. The herb has small, succulent leaves and slender spikes bearing flowers and fruit. Early Hawaiians used the plant to make a gray-green dye and various medicines.

Strawberry guava trees (*waiawī-'ula'ula*) line the trail on the ridge. They have glossy, dark-green leaves and smooth brown bark. Their dark-red fruit is delicious, with a taste reminiscent of strawberries. The guavas usually ripen in August and September. Pickings may be slim, however, because of the popularity of the trail. The strawberry guava is a native of Brazil but was introduced to Hawai'i from China in the 1800s.

At the junction with the west side trail is a small grove of *hala* trees. They have distinctive prop roots that help support the heavy clusters of leaves and fruit on the ends of the branches. Early Hawaiians braided the long, pointed leaves, called *lau hala,* into baskets, fans, floor mats, and sails.

After the junction, look for *kī* (ti) plants. They have shiny leaves, 1–2 feet long, which are arranged spirally in a cluster at the tip of a slender stem. Early Polynesian voyagers introduced ti to Hawai'i. They used the leaves for house thatch, skirts, sandals, and raincoats. Food to be cooked in an *imu* (underground oven) was first wrapped in ti leaves. A popular sport with the commoners was *ho'he'e kī* or ti-leaf sledding. The sap from ti plants stained canoes and surfboards.

From the overlook by the picnic tables is a marvelous view *mauka* (inland). Below is the gorge of the Wailua (two waters) River. To the west is massive, flat-topped Wai'ale'ale (rippling water), the wettest spot on earth. Its summit, Kawaikini (the multitudinous water), is the highest point on the island at 5,243 feet. To the right (northwest) are the Makaleha (eyes looking about as in wonder and admiration) Mountains. Hanalei Valley lies beyond the low ridge joining Waiʻaleʻale and Makaleha.

While enjoying the view, consider this old story. A giant once lived in the hills behind Kapaʻa town. He was a gentle giant, always helping the Hawaiian people. They turned his footprints into fertile banana patches. The flattened hills where he rested became cultivated fields. The sleepy giant faithfully repaired houses knocked down by gusts from his yawn.

One day the giant yawned, laid down, and fell asleep—for hundreds of years. Over time the wind covered him with dirt, and shrubs and trees grew over his body. Who knows? Some day he may awaken, yawn, and sit up.

The novice hike ends at the picnic tables on the giant's chest. Continue to his head past the End of Trail sign only if you feel comfortable scrambling up (and down) loose rock and dirt. At the summit is the entire panorama. In addition to the *mauka* views, you can see much of the eastern coast of Kauaʻi. In back of Līhuʻe (cold chill) and the airport is the ridge culminating in Hāʻupu (recollection) peak, also called Hoary Head.

Before heading down, look for graceful *koaʻe kea* or white-tailed tropicbirds, gliding overhead. They have two central tail feathers elongated into streamers. Tropicbirds feed by diving into the ocean for fish and squid. They nest in burrows or rock crevices along cliff faces.

There are two other routes to the top of Sleeping Giant. The Nounou Mountain–West Side Trail starts from Kamalu Rd. (Rte 581) at telephone pole no. 11. The trail climbs the opposite side of the giant and joins the East Side Trail just before the picnic tables. Total distance round-trip is 3.3 miles.

The Kuamoʻo-Nounou Trail starts about 0.5 mile beyond the ʻŌpaekaʻa Falls turnout on Kuamoʻo Rd. (Rte 580). The route contours around the backside of the giant and joins the Nounou-West Side Trail. Total distance round-trip is about 6 miles. If you have two cars, you can traverse the mountain by combining the East and West Side Trails. Total distance one way is 3.5 miles.

# 15

# Kuilau Ridge

| LENGTH: | 4.3-mile round-trip |
|---|---|
| ELEVATION GAIN: | 700 feet |
| DANGER: | Low |
| SUITABLE FOR: | Novice |
| LOCATION: | Kaua'i: Līhu'e-Kōloa Forest Reserve above Wailua |
| TOPO MAP: | Wai'ale'ale, Kapa'a |

## HIGHLIGHTS

This short, pleasurable walk climbs a gentle ridge in the foothills of the Makaleha Mountains. Along the route are magnificent views of Nounou (Sleeping Giant) and massive Wai'ale'ale. The hike ends at an impressive mountain lookout.

## TRAILHEAD DIRECTIONS

**DISTANCE:** (Līhu'e to Keāhua Arboretum) 13 miles
**DRIVING TIME:** 1/2 hour

From Līhu'e take Kūhiō Hwy (Rte 56 north) toward Kapa'a.

Cross Wailua River on a bridge.

At the next traffic light turn left on Kuamo'o Rd. (Rte 580 west).

Pass the turnout for 'Ōpaeka'a Falls on the right.

KUILAU RIDGE

KAPA'A

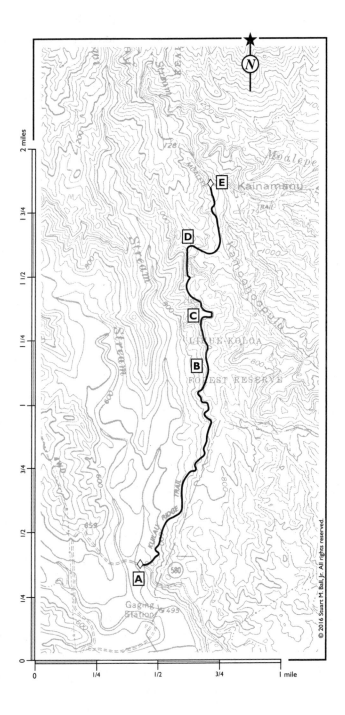

Pass the intersection with Kamalu Rd. (Rte 581).

Reach Keāhua Arboretum at the end of the paved road.

Park in the lot on the left just before the road fords Keāhua Stream (elevation 520 feet) (map point A) (UTM 4Q 456911E, 2440818N) (Lat/Long N22.07166, W159.41765). Across the stream and to the left are two pit toilets.

## ROUTE DESCRIPTION

Walk back along Kuamoʻo Rd for about 75 yards to reach the signed trailhead by a small parking lot. Turn left on a dirt road that is the Kuilau Trail.

Go through an opening in a gate blocking vehicle access to the trail.

On the left pass a bulletin board with trail information.

Climb gradually along the left side of a ridge through an introduced forest of eucalyptus and albizia. The trail is lined with grass and pest shrubs, including lantana, *Clidemia*, and *Melastoma*. Look for *kukui* trees downslope.

Gain the ridgeline (map point B), with some impressive views of the surrounding mountains through the trees. *Mauka* is massive Waiʻaleʻale. *Makai* is Nounou Mountain (Sleeping Giant). Farther along the ridge are the Makaleha Mountains.

Keep left on the main route, ignoring a hunters' trail on the right.

Reach two covered picnic tables in a flat, grassy area (map point C). Around the clearing are several native *ʻōhiʻa* trees.

At the picnic tables, turn right, following the road.

Descend briefly along a side ridge and then switchback to the left to regain the main ridge. *Kī* (ti) plants line the trail.

Switchback two more times up a steep section. From the ridge top are magnificent views in all directions.

Descend gradually along the right side of the ridge into a lush gulch with *hapuʻu* tree ferns.

Cross ʻŌpaekaʻa Stream on a wooden bridge and reach the end of the Kuilau Trail (map point D)

Climb out of the gulch on several short switchbacks of the Moalepe Trail.

Reach the top of Kamoʻohoʻopulu Ridge and turn left up it.

Stroll through a level section lined with paperbark trees and swamp mahogany.

Enter a grove of tall ironwood trees. On the left is the over-grown summit of Kainamanu hill.

As the trail starts to descend and swing right, reach a grassy overlook on the left (elevation 1,180 feet) (map point E) (UTM 4Q457556E, 2443198N) (Lat/Long N22.09318, W159.41146). Dead ahead is Kapehuaʻala (elevation 3,200 feet), the highest peak in the Makaleha Mountains. (To the right, the Moalepe Trail descends to Olohena Rd.)

## NOTES

Kuilau is a delightful hike—short, savory, and very scenic. Take your time on this one, or it will be over much too quickly. Stop every now and then to enjoy the view, take pictures, iden-tify plants, whatever.

The Kuilau Trail is actually a road built by the State Divi-sion of Forestry and Wildlife in 1971 to access a nearby fire. After the bridge, the hike follows the Moalepe Trail, con-structed by the Civilian Conservation Corps in the 1930s for reforestation. For the most part, both trails are still wide and well graded with switchbacks on the steeper sections. The route, however, may be muddy on the level stretches along Kamoʻohoʻopulu (the wet ridge). Watch out for the occasional mountain biker and a few mosquitoes.

On the trail, look and listen for the white-rumped shama. It is black on top, with a chestnut-colored breast and a long black and white tail. The shama has a variety of beautiful songs and often mimics other birds. A native of Malaysia, the shama has become widespread in introduced forests, such as this one.

Downslope from the road are *kukui* trees. Their large, pale-green leaves resemble those of the maple, with several distinct lobes. Early Polynesian voyagers introduced *kukui* into Hawai'i. They used the wood to make gunwales and seats for their outrigger canoes. The flowers and sap became medicines to treat a variety of ailments. Early Hawaiians strung the nuts together to make *lei hua* (seed or nut garlands). The oily kernels became house candles and torches for night spearfishing.

From the road and the picnic tables are some very fine views of the surrounding peaks. *Mauka* (inland) is massive, flat-topped Wai'ale'ale (rippling water), the wettest spot on earth. Its summit, Kawaikini (the multitudinous water), is the highest point on the island, at 5,243 feet. *Makai* (seaward) is Nounou, with its profile of a sleeping giant. Farther along the ridge are the Makaleha (eyes looking about as in wonder and admiration) Mountains.

Around the clearing with the picnic tables are several native '*ōhi'a* trees. They have oval leaves and clusters of delicate red flowers. Early Hawaiians used the flowers in lei and the wood in outrigger canoes. The hard, durable wood was also carved into god images for *heiau* (religious sites).

The trail ends at a sunny mountain overlook. Gaze up at imposing Kapehua'ala, the highest peak in the Makaleha Mountains. For some shade, relax under the ironwoods and listen for the wind soughing through their branches.

After finishing the hike, check out the start of the notorious Powerline Trail or just wander around the arboretum. Its lovely grounds occupy both sides of Keāhua (the mound) Stream. Along the stream are secluded picnic tables and inviting swimming holes.

As an alternative, you can take the Moalepe (chicken with comb) Trail. It starts at the end of paved Olohena Rd., off Kamalu Rd. (Rte 581), and joins the Kuilau Trail at its end. Total distance round-trip is 4.5 miles. If you have two cars, go up Kuilau and down Moalepe, or vice versa. Total distance one way is 4.4 miles.

# 16

# Powerline Trail

| LENGTH: | 11.3 miles one way |
|---|---|
| ELEVATION GAIN: | 1,700 feet |
| DANGER: | Low |
| SUITABLE FOR: | Expert |
| LOCATION: | Kaua'i: Līhu'e-Koloa Forest Reserve above Wailua and Halele'a Forest Reserve above Princeville |
| TOPO MAP: | Wai'ale'ale, Hanalei |

## HIGHLIGHTS

This awesome hike traverses the divide separating Wailua Valley and Hanalei Valley. The route follows a rough, overgrown dirt road built to service a transmission line. Along the way are intriguing native plants and unforgettable mountain views.

## TRAILHEAD DIRECTIONS

As the route is point-to-point, this hike has two trailheads, one above Wailua and the other above Princeville.

**DISTANCE:** (Līhu'e to Keāhua Arboretum) 13 miles
**DRIVING TIME:** 1/2 hour

From Līhu'e take Kūhiō Hwy (Rte 56 north) toward Kapa'a. Cross Wailua River on a bridge.

POWERLINE TRAIL

KAPA'A

At the next traffic light, turn left on Kuamoʻo Rd. (Rte 580 west).

Pass the turnout for ʻŌpaekaʻa Falls on the right.

Pass the intersection with Kamalu Rd. (Rte 581).

Reach Keāhua Arboretum at the end of the paved road.

Ford Keāhua Stream, assuming the water level is low.

Park in the lot on the right next to the stream (elevation 520 feet) (map point A) (UTM 4Q 456886E, 2440771N) (Lat/Long N22.07124, W159.41789). Across the road and up a rise are covered picnic tables and two pit toilets.

| | |
|---|---|
| **DISTANCE:** | (Līhuʻe to Kapaka St. end) 29 miles |
| **DRIVING TIME:** | 1 hour |

From Līhuʻe take Kūhiō Hwy (Rte 56 north) toward Hanalei.

Pass the turnoff to Kīlauea Lighthouse on the right and then cross a long bridge over the Kalihiwai River.

Pass Princeville Airport and Princeville Ranch on the left.

After mile marker 27, turn left on Kapaka St. across from the entrance to Church of the Pacific.

Drive 1.7 miles and park in the turnout on the right across from the driveway to the next to last house (elevation 540 feet) (map point M) (UTM 4Q 452904E, 2453545N) (Lat/Long N22.18654, W159.45686). A water tank is visible farther up the road.

## ROUTE DESCRIPTION

From the parking lot by Keāhua Stream, continue up the gravel road on foot. On the side are tangled *hau* trees. Look and listen for the white-rumped shama in the introduced forest.

As the road swings left and down, reach a signed junction (map point B). Turn right and up on a rock and gravel road that is the Powerline Trail.

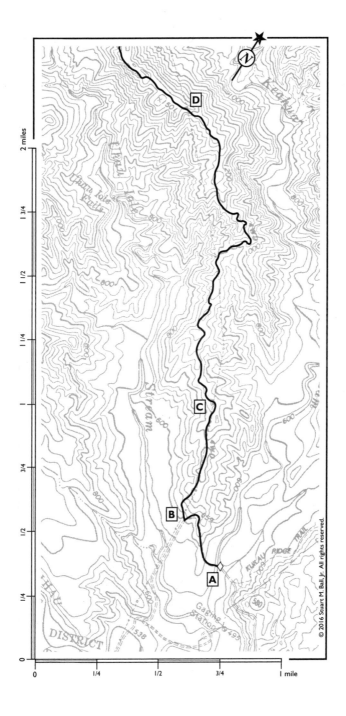

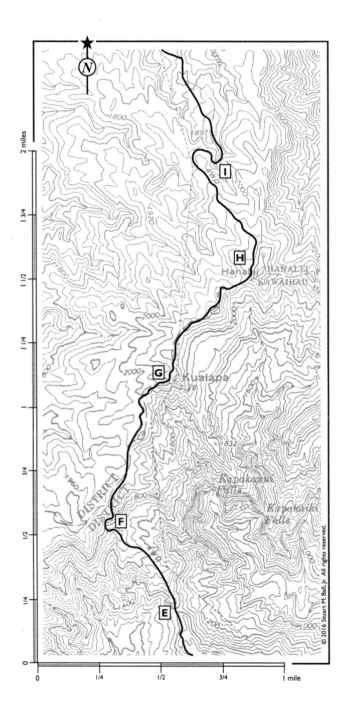

Climb steadily under white-barked albizia trees (*Paraseri-anthes lophantha*).

Pass the first of many concrete pylons supporting the powerline. On the left is massive Wai'ale'ale and on the right are the Makaleha Mountains.

The road gradually ascends a ridge, switching from one side to the other. Look for native *'ōhi'a* trees along the ridgetop. *Makai* are views of Nounou Mountain (Sleeping Giant) and Hā'upu (Hoary Head) peak beyond the airport.

Pass close to another pylon above and on the left (map point C). Ignore service roads leading left or right to the base of each pylon.

The climb steepens. Keep your eye out for *pueo,* the native owl.

Pass close to a pylon above and on the right (map point D). On the right along Keāhua Stream are two lovely waterfalls, Kapaka Nui and Kapaka Iki.

After a short level section, descend a saddle in the ridge (map point E).

Ascend steeply out of the saddle past a twin pylon.

The road curves right and climbs the side of a low ridge or divide. It separates the Wailua and Hanalei drainages by connecting Wai'ale'ale and the Makaleha Mountains.

Reach the top of the divide (elevation 1,840 feet) (map point F). Turn right along it. (On the left a short road leads to an awesome overlook of much of eastern Kaua'i.)

Stroll along the relatively level ridge past a tall rusted post.

Climb gradually, passing two pylons on the right. The second one stands on Kualapa peak (elevation 2,128 feet) (map point G) (UTM 4Q 454533E, 2444976N) (Lat/Long N22.10917, W159.44082).

Pass a structure with attached radars. Views of Hanalei Valley begin to open up.

Ignore two service roads on the left leading down to pylons. Keep right along the main ridge.

Descend into and climb out of a small saddle.

Shortly afterward the road swings left, leaving the divide for good (map point H).

Descend gradually along a side ridge toward Hanalei. The prominent peak on the right is Namahana. On the left is fortresslike Nāmolokama Mountain.

Pass a pylon close by on the left. Look for tall native *loulu* palms dwarfing the scrub *'ōhi'a* forest.

The road jogs right and then left. Underneath in a culvert is Ka'āpahu Stream (map point I).

Just before reaching a pylon on the left is a view of two waterfalls, cascading down the flank of Nāmolokama Mountain.

Jog left and then right to cross a small stream in a culvert (map point J).

The road hugs the pylons for a long stretch through thick grass (map point K). On the right is Kalihiwai Valley. Kīlauea Point comes into view along the coast.

The *'ōhi'a* trees gradually disappear, replaced by the pest shrub, Melastoma.

Curve left to cross another stream in a culvert (map point L).

On the right pass Kapaka, a wooded hill. Mountain biker trails parallel the road.

To the left is an overlook of Hanalei River and Valley. Below is a small waterfall from the stream just crossed.

Pass a hunter checking station and then two water tanks on the right.

Reach the turnout on the left by the driveway to the next to last house (map point M).

## NOTES

The Powerline Trail is actually a dirt road that crosses the divide between Wailua and Hanalei Valleys. The road originally provided access to an electric transmission line for maintenance. If your mind can blot out the pylons and powerlines, this hike becomes one of the great wilderness treks in the islands.

Unfortunately, helicopters now service the transmission

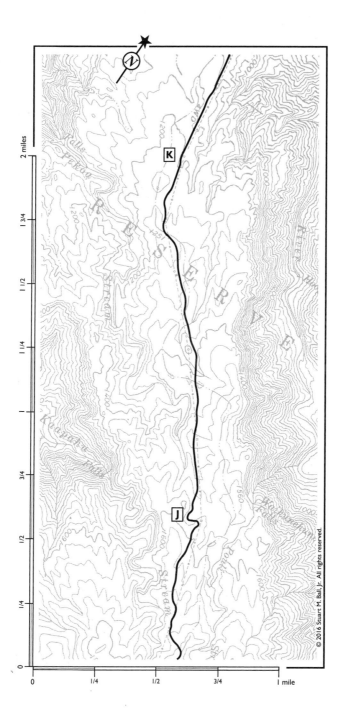

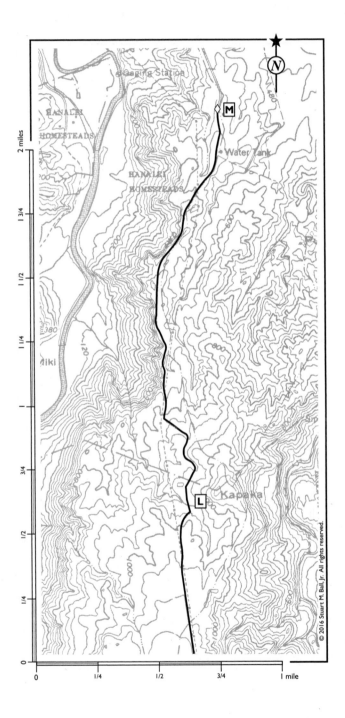

line, so this once magnificent road is no longer maintained. The route is still recognizable as a graded road in the first and last sections near the trailheads. In between, however, the road has deteriorated significantly over years of neglect. The treadway is now mostly single track—deeply rutted, heavily overgrown, and sometimes blocked by treefall. The culverts have backed up, creating flooded areas around the stream crossings after heavy rainfall. Choose a dry day in summer and start early to complete this hike in good time.

The views become incredible shortly after the hike starts. On the left is massive, flat-topped Waiʻaleʻale (rippling water), the wettest spot on earth. Its summit, Kawaikini (the multitudinous water), is the highest point on the island, at 5,243 feet. Standing guard in front of Waiʻaleʻale is a towering rock pillar, known as Pōhakupele (lava rock). On the right are the Makaleha (eyes looking about as in wonder and admiration) Mountains. *Makai* (seaward) are Nounou, with the profile of a sleeping giant, and Hāʻupu peak (Hoary Head) beyond the airport.

Along the ridgeline are native *ʻōhiʻa* trees. They have oval leaves and clusters of delicate red flowers. Early Hawaiians used the flowers in lei and the wood in outrigger canoes. The hard, durable wood was also carved into god images for *heiau* (religious sites).

You may catch a glimpse of the native owl, *pueo,* hovering above the ridge. It is brown and white with yellow eyes and a black bill. Unlike most owls, the *pueo* is active during the day, hunting birds, rodents, and insects. Early Hawaiians worshiped the owl as a god and a guardian spirit.

Along the road, look for the delicate sweeping fronds of *hāpuʻu,* the native tree fern. Its trunk consists of roots tightly woven around a small central stem. The brown fiber covering the young fronds of *hāpuʻu* is called *pulu.*

Before reaching the divide, you can see two beautiful waterfalls along Keāhua Stream to the right. The higher one on the left is called Kapaka Nui (large raindrop), and the wider one on the right is Kapaka Iki (little raindrop). After the falls overlook, the road climbs steeply to the divide. At the top, take a well-earned break and enjoy the sights. On a clear day, the view here is one of the best on the island.

The descent on the Hanalei side is gradual, but seemingly endless. While plowing through grass and slopping through flooded areas, look for native *loulu* palms standing above the scrub *'ōhi'a* forest. They have rigid, fan-shaped fronds in a cluster at the top of a ringed trunk. Early Hawaiians used the fronds for thatch. The blades of young fronds were plaited into fans and baskets.

Like the road, the views on the Hanalei side unfold gradually. On the left across the valley is fortresslike Nāmolokama (the interweaving bound fast) Mountain. Several waterfalls cascade down its flanks. On the right is Kīlauea (spewing) Point, jutting into the ocean. Eventually, you can see Hanalei River and town. Finally, the water tanks near the trailhead come into view.

As described, the route is one way from Wailua to Princeville. You can, of course, do the hike in the opposite direction. If you have only one car, start from the Keāhua Arboretum trailhead. Climb to the top of the divide and then return the way you came. Total distance round- trip is 7.4 miles.

17

# Māhā'ulepū

| LENGTH: | 4.2-mile round-trip |
| ELEVATION GAIN: | 100 feet |
| DANGER: | Low |
| SUITABLE FOR: | Novice |
| LOCATION: | Kaua'i: Southeast coast near Po'ipū |
| TOPO MAP: | Kōloa |

### HIGHLIGHTS

This marvelous hike follows the rugged shoreline from Keoneloa Bay to Māhā'ulepū Beach. Along the route are ancient sand
dunes, a fishing *heiau,* and Makauwahi Cave, an intriguing
limestone sinkhole.

### TRAILHEAD DIRECTIONS

**DISTANCE:** (Līhu'e to Shipwreck Beach) 16 miles
**DRIVING TIME:** 1/2 hour

From Līhu'e take Kaumuali'i Hwy (Rte 50) toward Waimea.
Pass Kukui Grove Center on the left and Kaua'i Community College on the right. The road then narrows to two lanes.

Turn left on Maluhia Rd. (Rte 520) toward Kōloa.

Turn left on Ala Koniki Rd. to Po'ipū.

By Po'ipū Kai Resort, turn left on Po'ipū Rd.

Pass Hyatt Regency Kaua'i Resort and Spa on the right.

By Po'ipū Bay Golf Course, turn right on Ainako Rd.

Bear right into the public lot at Keoneloa Bay and park there (elevation 10 feet) (map point A) (UTM 4Q 454843E, 241909N) (Lat/Long N21.87532, W159.4371).

## ROUTE DESCRIPTION

Walk *makai* (seaward) to Keoneloa Bay and turn left along Shipwreck Beach. Avoid the nesting area of the wedge-tailed shearwater just inland. Watch for the native shrub, *naupaka kahakai.*

At the end of the beach, angle right up a makeshift trail to the top of Makawehi Bluff.

Turn left and follow the sandy trail closest to the cliff. Farther along the coast is Punahoa Point and *mauka* (inland) is Ha'upu peak, also known as Hoary Head.

Pass a series of pinnacles, jutting out into the ocean (map point B). Look for *koa'e kea,* the white-tailed tropicbird, and humpback whales in season.

Pass a small beach with some tide pools (map point C).

Walk along the base of the rock retaining wall of the golf course.

Pass a *heiau* on the right.

Follow the golf course boundary marked by a lava rock wall.

Walk along the edge of the fairway. Watch for errant golf balls.

Bear right away from the fairway through *koa haole* around Punahoa Point (map point D).

Follow a dirt road past the resort stables.

Leave the road to follow a trail along the coast toward Māhā'ulepū Beach. Do not take the obscure fishermen's trail to the cliffs above the beach.

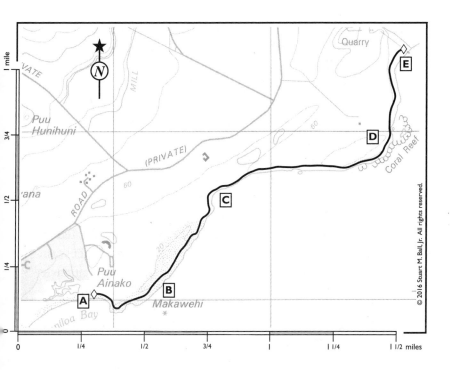

Pass a large boulder on the left and descend to the beach.
Reach Waiopili Stream (map point E) (UTM 4Q 456865E,
2420495N) (Lat/Long N21.88806, W159.41756). Turn left
upstream.

Reach the Makauwahi Cave Trail at a signed junction by
marker number 14. Keep right for the entrance to Makauwahi
Cave and a picnic area in a *milo* grove across the stream. Keep
left to view the cave sinkhole from above.

## NOTES

Māhāʻulepū (and falling together) is a beach hike, not a beach
stroll, and several suggestions and cautions are in order. Bring
water, sunscreen, and binoculars to check out the birds and
whales. Wear sturdy footwear as the route traverses uneven,
sometimes sharp, rocky sections along the shore. Stay on the

marked right-of-way along the edge of the golf course. Finally, an excellent interpretive pamphlet, *Maha'ulepu Heritage Trail*, is available online.

The hike starts at Shipwreck Beach, which got its name from a fishing boat that permanently ran aground there in the 1970s. Along the beach are ironwood trees and *naupaka kahakai*, a native low-lying shrub. It has bright-green, fleshy leaves, and half-formed white flowers with purple streaks. Its round white fruits float in the ocean, helping to spread the species to other islands.

The route initially travels over sea cliffs composed of lithified sand dunes. Chemical action over the years cemented the grains of sand together to become limestone. Rainwater washing down vertical cracks in the limestone formed the pinnacles farther along the coast.

Soaring along the cliffs are *koa'e kea* (white-tailed tropicbirds). They have two central tail feathers elongated into streamers. Tropicbirds feed by diving into the ocean for fish and squid. From March to October they nest in burrows or rock crevices along cliffs.

Scan the ocean for humpback whales. They migrate from the North Pacific to the Hawaiian Islands, arriving in October and leaving in May. The whales congregate off the leeward coast of Maui and occupy themselves calving, nursing, breeding, and generally horsing around.

The ancient *heiau* (religious site) below the golf course retaining wall is a fishing shrine. Here early Hawaiians made offerings to the gods to insure a good catch.

After reaching Māhā'ulepū Beach, cross Waiopili Stream on the bridge. At the small picnic area get a pamphlet explaining the points of interest along a trail, which visits and circles nearby Makauwahi (break through) Cave. Its most unusual feature is a sinkhole, where the limestone over the cave has collapsed.

18

# Kukui

| LENGTH: | 5.0-mile round-trip |
|---|---|
| ELEVATION GAIN: | 2,200 feet |
| DANGER: | Low |
| SUITABLE FOR: | Intermediate |
| LOCATION: | Kaua'i: Waimea Canyon State Park and Nā Pali-Kona Forest Reserve |
| TOPO MAP: | Waimea Canyon |

## HIGHLIGHTS

The Kukui Trail descends precipitously into spectacular Waimea Canyon. The scenery is stunning, with multicolored cliffs, eroded pinnacles, and cascading waterfalls. Cool off in the river before the hot return uphill.

## TRAILHEAD DIRECTIONS

**DISTANCE:** (Līhu'e to Kukui trailhead) 30 miles
**DRIVING TIME:** 1 hour

From Līhu'e take Kaumuali'i Hwy (Rte 50) toward Waimea. Pass Kukui Grove Center on the left and Kaua'i Community College on the right. The road then narrows to two lanes.

Drive through the towns of Lāwaʻi and Kalāheo.

Pass the Hanapēpē River overlook on the right.

Drive through the towns of ʻEleʻele and Hanapēpē.

Pass the Russian fort on the left and then enter Waimea town.

Pass Waimea High School on the right.

Turn right on Waimea Canyon Rd. The intersection is just past Waimea Baptist Church, with its white steeple.

Ascend gradually along the rim of Waimea Canyon.

At the stop sign turn right on Kōkeʻe Rd. (Rte 550).

Pass Kōkeʻe Hunter Check Station on the right.

After mile marker 8.5, look for the trailhead marked with a Kukui Trail sign on the right.

Park in the paved turnout on the left side of the road across from the trailhead (elevation 2,900 feet) (map point A) (UTM 4Q 431902E, 2438674N) (Lat/Long N22.0515, W159.65996).

## ROUTE DESCRIPTION

Cross the road and climb up an embankment.

Reach a signed junction just past a bench. Turn right on the Kukui Trail. (To the left a nature loop circles through a grove of native *iliau* shrubs.)

Pass several markers describing various native dryland forest plants. Look for native *ʻaʻaliʻi* and *pūkiawe* shrubs.

Keep right at a second signed junction. (To the left is the nature loop.)

On the right pass two covered picnic tables surrounded by *kī* (ti) plants.

Descend steeply on six short switchbacks. Silk oaks provide some shade.

On the left pass a lookout with a metal pole. You can now look directly into Waimea Canyon.

The trail crisscrosses a side ridge while descending on seven long switchbacks (map point B). Don't shortcut them.

Descend straight down on a narrow, eroded trail. Watch your footing on the loose rock and soil.

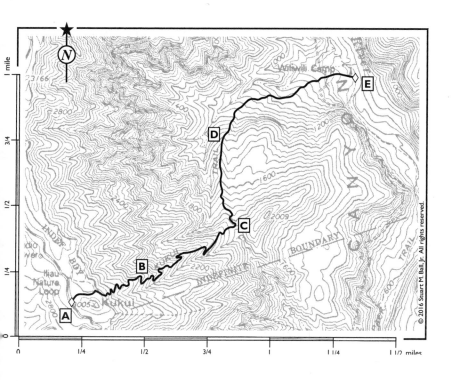

Switchback five more times and then resume heading straight down. Look for *kukui* trees with their light-green leaves on the right side of the ridge.

Pass another lookout on the right. From here is a superb view up the canyon.

Reach a signed junction in a saddle (map point C). Turn left and down on the main trail. (A side trail leads straight and up to an overlook of the canyon.)

Descend steeply on an open, eroded slope. The trail attempts to switchback at first, but soon gives up and heads straight downhill. All around you are the sheer red and green walls of the canyon.

The trail levels off briefly and then resumes the descent.

At the end of the eroded section, turn sharp right into the forest toward the canyon floor (map point D).

Continue descending a series of short, rocky switchbacks through introduced silk oak and guava trees.

Enter a grove of *kukui* trees, whose leaves and nuts litter the ground.

Angle down the slope on a gentler path.

Bear left and down along a gully. Follow the gully, first on its left and then on its right.

Contour through tall grass. The forest is now mostly *koa haole*, with an occasional native *wiliwili* tree.

Bear left to begin the final descent to the canyon bottom.

Pass a line of sisal plants with their swordlike leaves.

Walk through Wiliwili Camp, which has a pit toilet and a covered picnic table.

Reach a signed junction with the Waimea Canyon Trail (elevation 660 feet) (map point E) (UTM 4Q 433753E, 2439921N) (Lat/Long N22.06283, W159.64207). Continue straight toward the Waimea River. (To the left the Canyon Trail leads to Koai'e Canyon and Lonomea Camp. To the right the trail heads down the canyon to Waimea town.)

Reach Waimea River. Just downstream is a good swimming hole.

## NOTES

While most tourists and locals are gazing into Waimea Canyon from distant overlooks, try this adventurous hike down to the canyon floor. The steep, narrow trail, however, is not for the faint of heart. The route is short, but the elevation gain is considerable, and the footing is over loose soil and rock. As you are pounding down the trail, remember that what goes down must come up.

If possible, take the hike in the early morning or late afternoon. Besides being hot, the intense midday sun washes out the vivid canyon colors: blue sky, black lava, red earth, and green vegetation. Whenever you go, drink plenty of water and use lots of sunscreen.

Before descending into Waimea (reddish water) Canyon, take the short nature loop through a grove of *iliau,* an unusual native shrub. It has slender, swordlike leaves clustered at the top of a woody stem. After growing for many years, the shrub flowers once during the summer and then dies. The flower stalks are tall and showy with cream-colored petals. Found only on Kaua'i, *iliau* is a relative of *'āhinahina*, the silversword, found on Haleakalā and Mauna Kea.

The view from the picnic tables along the rim is breathtaking. Across Waimea Canyon is Wai'alae (mudhen water) Canyon with its lovely waterfall. To the left is Kaluahāula (reddish pit) Ridge, then Koai'e Canyon, and then Po'omau (constant source) Canyon. Farther down the trail you get a good view of the canyon floor and its red and green walls. Upstream is Po'o Kāehu, a pillar of resistant rock. Downstream is Nāwaimaka (tears) Valley with its twin falls.

Waimea Canyon is 14 miles long and up to 2,500 feet deep. Streams carved the canyon, but a massive landslide determined its north-south orientation. Notice that all the tributary canyons, such as Wai'alae, are on the far (east) side of the main canyon. Millions of years ago a slice of the island slumped, forming a north-to-south trough, known as Makaweli (fearful features) graben. Lava from Wai'ale'ale (rippling water) volcano gradually filled the graben from the east. As the volcano became extinct, streams began to erode from its summit area. The slightly higher west side of the graben blocked their normal drainage downhill. The streams diverted to the south along the graben and eventually formed Waimea Canyon.

Lining the side gulches near the canyon floor are groves of *kukui* trees. Their large, pale-green leaves resemble those of the maple, with several distinct lobes. Early Polynesian voyagers introduced *kukui* into Hawai'i. They used the wood to make gunwales and seats for their outrigger canoes. The flowers and sap became medicines to treat a variety of ailments. Early Hawaiians strung the nuts together to make *lei hua* (seed or nut garlands). The oily kernels became house candles and torches for night spear fishing.

In the forested sections you may encounter a red jungle fowl, or *moa*. It is very similar to a domestic chicken. The roosters are red-brown with a black, sickle-shaped tail. The *moa* pokes around the underbrush, looking for seeds, fruits, and insects. The early Polynesians introduced the bird to Hawai'i. It survives only on Kaua'i because of the absence of the mongoose.

Before reaching Wiliwili Camp, look for the native tree of the same name. It has heart-shaped, leathery leaflets in groups of three. Flowers appear in the spring and are usually red or orange. Early Hawaiians used the soft, light wood for surfboards, canoe outriggers, and fishnet floats. The red seeds were strung together to form *lei hua*.

Around the camp you can easily recognize sisal by its swordlike leaves. At one time, fibers from the leaves were made into rope, and the plant was introduced into Hawai'i in the late 1800s for that purpose. Sisal puts up a tall flower stalk every ten years or so, on which the baby plants form.

From the camp take the short walk to the Waimea River. Stretch out under a shady tree along the bank. Soak your feet or your whole body in the cool river water. Don't get too relaxed, because the hard part of the hike is yet to come.

There are two good variations to the route as described. For a shorter hike, take the side trail at the saddle to a canyon overlook and then return. For a longer hike, take the Waimea Canyon Trail upstream, crossing the river twice. At an unmarked junction, turn right on the Koai'e Canyon Trail and cross the river a third time. Follow Koai'e Stream to Lonomea Camp with its fine swimming hole. Total round-trip distance from the Kukui trailhead to Lonomea is 12.2 miles.

# 19

# Waimea Canyon Vista

| | |
|---|---|
| LENGTH: | 6.0-mile loop |
| ELEVATION GAIN: | 700 feet |
| DANGER: | Low |
| SUITABLE FOR: | Intermediate |
| LOCATION: | Kauaʻi: Kōkeʻe State Park and Nā Pali-Kona Forest Reserve |
| TOPO MAP: | Hāʻena, Waimea Canyon, Makaha Point |

## HIGHLIGHTS

This winding loop follows the rim of spectacular Waimea Canyon. Along the way are scenic lookouts, a lovely waterfall, and a deep swimming hole. You may even see a colorful native bird in the forest canopy.

## TRAILHEAD DIRECTIONS

**DISTANCE:** (Līhuʻe to Waineke trailhead) 41 miles
**DRIVING TIME:** 1 1/4 hours

From Līhuʻe take Kaumualiʻi Hwy (Rte 50) toward Waimea.
Pass Kukui Grove Center on the left and Kauaʻi Community College on the right. The road then narrows to two lanes.
Drive through the towns of Lāwaʻi and Kalāheo.
Pass the Hanapēpē River overlook on the right.
Drive through the towns of ʻEleʻele and Hanapēpē.

WAIMEA CANYON VISTA

※

KŌKEʻE

127

Pass the Russian fort on the left and then enter Waimea town.
Pass Waimea High School on the right.

Turn right on Waimea Canyon Rd. The intersection is just past Waimea Baptist Church, with its white steeple.

Ascend gradually along the rim of Waimea Canyon.

At the stop sign, turn right on Kōkeʻe Rd. (Rte 550).

Pass Kōkeʻe Hunter Check Station on the right.

Pass turnoffs to Waimea Canyon and Puʻu Hinahina lookouts on the right.

Enter Kōkeʻe State Park.

On the left pass the turnoff to Kōkeʻe Lodge and Museum. The lodge has restrooms and drinking water, and the museum has trail maps and guides.

Shortly afterward turn right on Waineke Rd. It's marked by a sign to Camp Sloggett.

Descend gradually on the dirt road, passing a dilapidated brown shed on the right.

Reach a junction (elevation 3,560 feet) (map point A) (UTM 4Q 432863E, 2446900N) (Lat/Long N22.12585, W159.65099). Keep left on the main road. (To the right a one-lane dirt road leads down to Camp Sloggett.)

Just past the junction, park in a signed turnout on the right side of the road.

## ROUTE DESCRIPTION

Continue along Waineke Rd. on foot.

Almost immediately, reach another junction. Turn right on a one-lane dirt road leading to the Kumuwela Trail. (Waineke Rd. continues straight to join Camp 10-Mōhihi Rd.)

Just above a ditch intake and cabin, cross ʻElekeninui Stream on a short stone bridge.

Reach a signed junction. Keep right and down on the road. (To the left the Waininiua Trail leads to Kumuwela Rd.)

Descend gradually along Kōkeʻe Stream, passing stands of *kāhili* ginger. Ignore driveways to the rustic cabins.

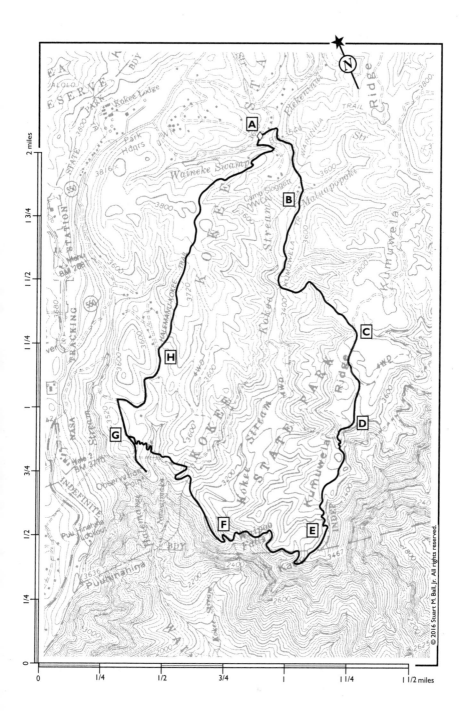

The road ends at a cabin with a stone chimney (map point B). Before reaching the cabin, turn left on the signed Kumu-wela Trail.

Continue to follow the stream through dense ginger and then dark groves of karaka nut. The trail is overgrown and obscure in spots; watch out for thorny blackberry and lantana in the sunny sections.

Climb over the foot of a side ridge and cross a short, grassy section.

At an obscure junction, bear left away from the stream. Look for the native bird 'elepaio.

Keep left at an obscure junction.

Climb straight up a ridge under silk oak and native koa trees. In the ravine on the left are some native 'ōhi'a trees, with their delicate red flowers.

The trail levels off and then ends at a signed junction with Kumuwela Rd. (map point C). Turn right onto the dirt road. (To the left the road leads to Camp 10-Mōhihi Rd.)

Descend very gradually toward the rim of Po'omau Canyon.

The road forks. Keep right on Kumuwela Rd. (To the left Waininiua Rd. provides access to the Ditch Trail.)

The road ends at the Kumuwela Lookout, which overlooks Po'omau Canyon (map point D). Turn right on the signed Canyon Trail.

Stroll through a lovely section on the canyon rim. Along the trail are koa and 'ōhi'a trees and pūkiawe shrubs. Below are Po'omau Canyon and Stream.

Climb briefly and then descend on five switchbacks.

Walk through grass in a shallow ravine and then a short section choked with lantana. Watch out for thorns.

Parallel a gulch on the left in a grove of eucalyptus trees.

Descend on three switchbacks and then swing left and climb to regain the rim.

Break out into the open. The views are panoramic from two overlooks on the left (elevation 3,467 feet) (map point E). You can see 'Āwini Falls and Kohua Ridge across Po'omau Canyon. Look for *koaʻe kea,* the white-tailed tropicbird, soaring by the cliffs.

Switchback three times on a deeply rutted trail. Native *ʻaaliʻi* shrubs line the trail.

Reach a third viewpoint. It has a round boulder with a comfortable flat top to sit on and look down into Waimea Canyon.

Traverse two wooded gulches.

Descend to Kōkeʻe Stream and turn left downstream.

Cross the stream near the top of lower Waipoʻo Falls. From the lip is a breathtaking view, 1,500 feet straight down into the canyon.

From the falls, take a makeshift trail heading up the other side of the stream.

Reach a junction (map point F) (UTM 4Q 431760E, 24444626N) (Lat/Long N22.10526, W159.66159). Turn right to the upper falls. (To the left the Canyon Trail continues along the rim.)

The short trail ends by a circular pool at the base of the short upper falls. The water is cool, clear, and inviting. Need I say more?

Backtrack to the junction and turn right on the Canyon Trail.

Climb an eroded slope on three poorly defined switchbacks.

Pass another lookout. On the left is a small arch in the canyon wall.

The trail winds through some large boulders.

Enter a *koa* forest with *ʻaaliʻi* and *pūkiawe* shrubs.

Reach a junction. Keep left on the Canyon Trail. (To the right, the Black Pipe Trail leads to Halemanu Rd.)

An irrigation ditch goes underneath the trail in a side gulch.

Climb out of the gulch on a series of short switchbacks.

Reach a signed junction with the Cliff Trail (map point G). Turn left for the Cliff lookout and one last view of Waimea Canyon.

Return to the junction and keep left on the Cliff Trail. On the left, watch for a native *hāhā lua* tree, which resembles a palm.

Take the unnamed dirt road at the trail end. (To the left is a trail to Puʻu Hinahina Lookout.)

Reach a junction. Turn right on Halemanu Rd. (To the left the road heads back to paved Kōkeʻe Rd. [Rte 550].) Ignore the sign stating No Thru Traffic.

Reach another junction. Keep left on the main road. (The dirt road on the right heads back to the Black Pipe Trail.) On the left is a plum grove.

On the right pass a cabin with a line of evergreen trees in front.

On the right pass a second row of evergreen trees in front of a palatial cabin with an expansive front lawn.

At the far end of the lawn, reach a signed junction (map point H). Turn right on the Halemanu-Kōkeʻe Trail. (The road continues straight to connect with the Unnamed Trail to Faye Rd. and Kōkeʻe Rd.)

Climb steeply up a ridge through grass.

The trail levels off, ascends, and then levels off again past groves of karaka nut and then ʻōhiʻa.

Descend gradually, switchbacking once.

Reach the end of the trail at a signed junction with a dirt road. Turn left on it. (To the right the road leads to Camp Sloggett.)

Reach the familiar junction with Waineke Rd. where your car is parked. (map point A).

## NOTES

This scenic, intricate loop is pieced together from eight different trails and dirt roads near Waimea (reddish water) Canyon. Follow the route description religiously. The junctions come fast and furiously, and several are less than obvious. Some trail sections may be partially overgrown with ginger, blackberry, or lantana. The loop is described clockwise. You can, of course, walk the opposite way, if you are good at reading directions in reverse.

Two native trees, 'ōhi'a and *koa*, predominate along much of the loop. 'Ōhi'a has oval leaves and clusters of delicate red flowers. Native birds, such as the 'apapane, feed on the nectar and help in pollination. Early Hawaiians used the flowers in lei and the wood in outrigger canoes. The hard, durable wood was also carved into god images for *heiau* (religious sites). *Koa* has sickle-shaped foliage and pale-yellow flower clusters. Early Hawaiians made surfboards and outrigger canoe hulls out of the beautiful red-brown wood. Today it is made into fine furniture.

The view from the lookouts on the Canyon Trail is spectacular. Po'omau (constant source) Canyon lies directly below. Across the canyon is Kohua Ridge and 'Āwini Falls. Farther along the rim you can look into Waimea Canyon, which descends all the way to the ocean. On the right are the twin cascades of Waipo'o Falls. Keep your eye out for feral goats scrambling on the cliffs and *koa'e kea*, the white-tailed tropicbird, soaring on the warm canyon air.

Waimea Canyon is 14 miles long and up to 2,500 feet deep. Streams carved the canyon, but a massive landslide determined its north-south orientation. Notice that all the tributary canyons, such as Po'omau, are on the left (east) side of the main canyon. Millions of years ago a slice of the island slumped, forming a north-to-south trough, known as Makaweli (fearful features) graben. Lava from Wai'ale'ale (rippling water) volcano gradually filled the graben from the east. As the volcano became extinct, streams began to erode from its summit area. The slightly higher west side of the graben blocked their normal drainage downhill. The streams diverted to the south along the graben and eventually formed Waimea Canyon.

Along the canyon rim are the native dryland shrubs *pūkiawe* and 'a'ali'i. *Pūkiawe* has tiny, rigid leaves and small white, pink, or red berries. 'A'ali'i has narrow, shiny leaves and red seed capsules that the early Hawaiians used in lei making and for *kapa* (bark cloth) dye.

Spend some time at Waipo'o Falls. From the lip of the lower falls is a heart-stopping view, straight down. At the base of the upper falls is a lovely circular pool backed by cliffs and *koa* trees. The idyllic setting brings to mind an old Hawaiian legend about a beautiful maiden and a waterfall in Waimea Canyon.

On a dark, rainy night a baby was born, and the mother called her Ua, rain. She lived in a village along the rugged Nāpali Coast. While climbing a rope ladder above the ocean, the father accidently dropped his baby daughter. The god of waterfalls suddenly appeared out of a rainbow, caught the baby in midair, and carried her back to Waimea Canyon, where she grew up.

One day the son of a chief from Waimea village walked into the canyon to select a *koa* tree to build a canoe. He spotted a lovely maiden coming out of the mist in front of a waterfall. The man called to her softly, saying that he loved her. She was surprised and then pleased, but asked to be called by her real name if he was to win her love.

The chief's son returned to his village and asked all the *kahuna* (priests) for the name of the maiden of the mist. No one could tell him. Finally, he talked to his grandmother, who had heard the story of Ua, the baby carried on a rainbow to a canyon waterfall. The man rushed back to the waterfall and called the maiden by her name. Together the couple returned to his village, were married, and lived happily for many years.

Look for a native *hāhā lua* at the junction with the short trail to the Cliff lookout. The tall tree resembles a palm and is found only on Kaua'i. Native honeycreepers, such 'apapane and 'i'iwi, sip nectar from the purple, tube-shaped flowers.

On the Halemanu-Kōke'e Trail watch for 'apapane and 'elepaio. The 'elepaio is gray-brown on top and has a white breast splotched with gray and black. Its dark tail is usually cocked. The 'apapane has a red breast and head, black wings and tail, and a slightly curved black bill. In flight the 'apapane makes a whirring sound as it darts from tree to tree searching for insects and nectar.

Dense, dark groves of karaka nut line portions of the Halemanu-Kōkee and Kumuwela Trails. A native of New Zealand, karaka nut was first planted at Halemanu about 1880. In 1929 the Territorial Forestry broadcast seeds from an airplane to reforest open areas in the Kōkeʻe area. The orange flesh of the fruit is edible, but the nut is poisonous.

For a shorter hike to the Cliff lookout and Waipoʻo Falls, park in the large turnout on the left between mile markers 14 and 15 on Kōkeʻe (to bend) Road. Take the rutted dirt road on the right marked Halemanu (bird house) Valley. The road descends into the valley, swings right, and then climbs. At the first junction, turn right on an unnamed dirt road. Pick up the route description in reverse at the start of the Cliff Trail. A second option starts at the Puʻu Hinahina Lookout. Park in the large lot there and take the Puʻu Hinihina Trail to the start of the Cliff Trail. Both options are about 3 miles round-trip.

# 20

# Nuʻalolo Cliff

| LENGTH: | 11.4-mile loop |
|---|---|
| ELEVATION GAIN: | 2,200 feet |
| DANGER: | Low |
| SUITABLE FOR: | Expert |
| LOCATION: | Kauaʻi: Kōkeʻe State Park and Nā Pali-Kona Forest Reserve |
| TOPO MAP: | Hāʻena, Mākaha Point |

## HIGHLIGHTS

This splendid loop hike winds above the sheer cliffs in back of Nuʻalolo, a deep canyon descending to the Nāpali Coast. Along the way are cascading waterfalls, awe-inspiring lookouts, and some narrow trail sections. You may also encounter *nēnē*, the endangered Hawaiian goose, and *iliau*, a distinctive shrub found only on Kauaʻi.

## TRAILHEAD DIRECTIONS

**DISTANCE:** (Līhuʻe to Nuʻalolo trailhead) 40 miles
**DRIVING TIME:** 1 1/4 hours

From Līhuʻe take Kaumualiʻi Hwy (Rte 50) toward Waimea. Pass Kukui Grove Center on the left and Kauaʻi Community College on the right. The road then narrows to two lanes.

Drive through the towns of Lāwaʻi and Kalāheo.

Pass the Hanapēpē River overlook on the right.

Drive through the towns of ʻEleʻele and Hanapēpē.

Pass the Russian fort on the left and then enter Waimea town.

Pass Waimea High School on the right.

Turn right on Waimea Canyon Rd. The intersection is just past Waimea Baptist Church, with its white steeple.

Ascend gradually along the rim of Waimea Canyon.

At the stop sign, turn right on Kōkeʻe Rd. (Rte 550).

Pass Kōkeʻe Hunter Check Station on the right.

Pass turnoffs to Waimea Canyon and Puʻu Hinahina Lookouts on the right.

Enter Kōkeʻe State Park.

On the left pass four driveways leading to the Kōkeʻe cabins.

After the last driveway, turn left onto a dirt road marked with a Nuʻalolo Trail sign.

Almost immediately, park in a gravel lot by the trailhead (elevation 3,680 feet) (map point A) (UTM 4Q 431963E, 2447305N) (Lat/Long N22.12947, W159.65973). If you have only one car, start hiking. If you have two cars, drop off people, if necessary, and continue along Kōkeʻe Rd.

Just up the road on the left is Kōkeʻe Lodge and Museum. The lodge has restrooms and drinking water, and the museum has trail maps and guides.

Pass Kōkeʻe campground on the left and then ascend gradually on three switchbacks.

Just after mile marker 17, look for a parking lot on the left with an Awaʻawapuhi Trail sign. Just before the lot is a dirt road with a yellow gate on the right.

Turn left into the lot and park one car there by the Awaʻawapuhi trailhead (elevation 4,120 feet) (map point N) (UTM 4Q 433111E, 244861N) (Lat/Long N22.14131, W159.64865). Backtrack to the Nuʻalolo trailhead in the other car and leave it there. The distance between the two trailheads is about 1.7 miles.

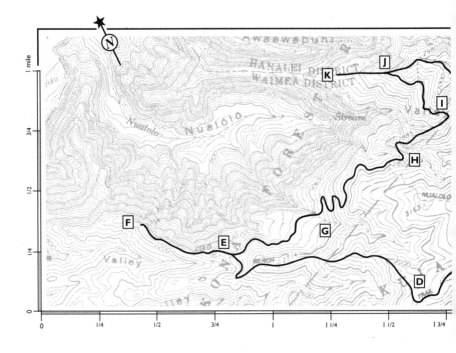

## ROUTE DESCRIPTION

Take the Nuʻalolo Trail from the left side of the parking lot.

Climb steeply at first on two switchbacks, and then more gradually. The forest consists of native ʻōhiʻa and *koa* trees with an understory of introduced strawberry guava and karaka nut.

Begin descending on a wide trail. On the forest floor are huge *koa* trunks downed by hurricane ʻIwa.

Enter Kuia Natural Area Reserve and pass a fenced enclosure on the left.

Descend into a long, shallow gulch (map point B). *Kahili* ginger and thorny blackberry may overgrow the trail. Leave the gulch periodically to cross over small side ridges.

Traverse an uneven meadow covered with scattered lantana shrubs.

Climb out of the gulch to the right and then bear left down

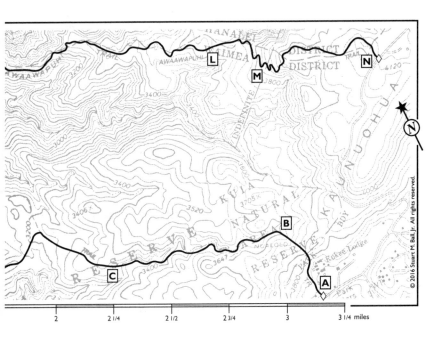

a broad ridge (map point C). The ocean comes into view as the forest opens up.

Veer to the left side of the ridge. Watch for the native dryland shrubs *pūkiawe, ʻaʻaliʻi,* and *naupaka kuahiwi* with its white half-flowers. You can also see *ʻiliahi* (sandalwood), with its droopy leaves, and *olomea,* with its red veins and stems.

The trail descends over a series of small knobs, each with a lookout (map point D). In the distance are the islands of Niʻihau and Lehua. Along the trail are native *iliau* shrubs.

Descend steeply on two switchbacks through strawberry guava.

Shortly afterward reach a signed junction (map point E). For now, continue straight on the Nuʻalolo Trail. (To the right is the Nuʻalolo Cliff Trail, the return route.)

Below on the left is a deer-proof fence.

Descend steeply on a deeply rutted trail.

Go around to the left of an eroded hump in the ridge.

The ridge becomes narrow and eroded. On the right is a sheer drop to the floor of Nuʻalolo Valley. In back is a cascading waterfall. Look for *koaʻe kea*, the white-tailed tropicbird, soaring by the cliffs.

The official trail ends at a railing near the Lolo benchmark (elevation 2,234 feet) (map point F) (UTM 4Q 428159E, 2449632N) (Lat/Long N22.15034, W159.69672).

Descend a short distance past a second benchmark for a better view of the awesome Nāpali Coast.

Backtrack to the junction with the Nuʻalolo Cliff Trail (map point E) and turn left on it. (Straight ahead is the way you came in.)

Descend steadily off the ridge line on eight switchbacks. Watch your footing.

Contour through a stand of guava.

Switchback two more times and then resume contouring around the back of Nuʻalolo Valley.

Pass a covered picnic table on the right. Look for *nēnē* (Hawaiian goose).

Enter a lush gulch (map point G). Watch for the native birds *ʻelepaio* and *ʻapapane* in the tall *ʻōhiʻa* trees.

Climb out of the gulch on five switchbacks.

Amble through a level shady section.

Work into and out of another gulch with a tiny stream (map point H).

Enter the large gulch at the very back of Nuʻalolo Valley. Watch for native *lama* trees. In the cliff above is a nesting area for the tropicbirds.

Cross Nuʻalolo Stream below a small waterfall (map point I). Lower down the stream becomes the large waterfall seen from the Lolo benchmark.

Reach a signed junction with the Awaʻawapuhi Trail (map point J). For now, turn left on it. (To the right is the return route.)

Reach the end of the Awaʻawapuhi Trail at the double overlook (elevation 2,520 feet) (map point K)

(UTM 4Q 430360E, 2449810N) (Lat/Long N22.15203, W159.67538).

Retrace your steps to the junction with the Nuʻalolo Cliff Trail (map point J). This time, continue straight on the Awaʻawapuhi Trail. (To the right is the way you came in.)

Ascend steadily through a lush gully and then climb to the top of a ridge on two switchbacks (map point L).

The trail mostly stays on the right side of the ridge through native dryland forest.

Go through a stand of strawberry guava and then switchback once.

The vegetation gradually changes from dryland shrubs to rain forest.

Climb more steeply on a series of S curves (map point M).

The angle of ascent eases. On the forest floor are huge *koa* trunks downed by hurricanes ʻIwa and Iniki.

Descend briefly to reach the parking lot on Kōkeʻe Rd. (elevation 4,120 feet) (map point N). If your only car is parked at the museum, turn right onto the road.

Walk the 1.7 miles back to your car (map point A).

## NOTES

Nuʻalolo Cliff is certainly the best day hike on Kauaʻi, and it may be the best in the islands. The winding route provides a bird's-eye view of the spectacular Nāpali (the cliffs) Coast. Along the ridges and ravines leading down to Nuʻalolo and Awaʻawapuhi (ginger valley) are some unusual plants and wildlife. The hike also provides a challenge with its down-and-up, sometimes narrow route. Get an early start because of the high mileage and many points of interest.

The Nuʻalolo Cliff Trail, which connects Nuʻalolo and Awaʻawapuhi, is a high-maintenance trail that is sometimes closed for repairs. Check its status at the museum, where trail conditions and closures are posted on a bulletin board by the front door. If the cliff trail is closed, hike Awa'awapuhi or Nu'alolo and return the way you came. Awa'awapuhi is the shorter, easier, and more popular of the two outings and has its own chapter in this guide.

The Nu'alolo Trail winds through the Kuia Natural Area Reserve, established by the State Department of Land and Natural Resources in 1981. The 1,636-acre preserve protects five native plant communities from wet forest to dry shrubland and a number of bird species that live there. Over fifty of the plant species and one of the bird species are considered rare, so tread lightly in this magnificent resource.

Native 'ōhi'a trees predominate in the wet upper section of the Nu'alolo Trail. They have oval leaves and clusters of delicate red flowers. Native birds, such as the 'apapane, feed on the nectar and help in pollination. Early Hawaiians used the flowers in lei and the wood in outrigger canoes. The hard, durable wood was also carved into god images for *heiau* (religious sites).

In the drier middle section of the trail, native *koa* gradually replaces 'ōhi'a as the dominant tree. *Koa* has sickle-shaped foliage and pale-yellow flower clusters. Early Hawaiians made surfboards and outrigger canoe hulls out of the beautiful red-brown wood. Today it is made into fine furniture.

Farther down the ridge the native dryland shrubs *pūkiawe* and 'a'ali'i make an appearance. *Pūkiawe* has tiny, rigid leaves and small white, pink, or red berries. 'A'ali'i has narrow, shiny leaves and red seed capsules that early Hawaiians used in lei making and for *kapa* (bark cloth) dye.

Before reaching the two switchbacks, watch for the native shrub *iliau*. It has slender, swordlike leaves clustered at the top of a woody stem. After growing for many years, the shrub flowers once during the summer and then dies. The flower stalks are tall and showy with cream-colored petals. Found only on Kaua'i, *iliau* is a relative of 'āhinahina, the silversword, found on Haleakalā and Mauna Kea.

Past the second benchmark is a magnificent view of the rugged Nāpali Coast. Far below lies Nu'alolo Valley, backed by steep cliffs and a cascading waterfall. To the right (north) is Kalalau (the straying) Beach and Valley. In the distance, the Nāpali Coast ends at Kēʻē (avoidance) Beach near Kaʻīlio (dog) Point. Look for feral goats perched on the cliffs and white-tailed tropicbirds soaring above them.

Along the cliff trail you may see *nēnē*, the Hawaiian goose. The *nēnē* has a black face and head and a gray-brown body. It lives in dry upland areas, so has lost much of the webbing on its feet. Like its Canadian counterpart, the *nēnē* is a strong flyer and often honks in mid-flight. The *nēnē* is an endangered species and should be treated with respect.

In the gulches look for the native birds *ʻelepaio* and *ʻapapane*. The *ʻelepaio* is gray-brown on top and has a white breast splotched with gray and black. Its dark tail is usually cocked. The *ʻapapane* has a red breast and head, black wings and tail, and a slightly curved black bill. In flight the *ʻapapane* makes a whirring sound as it darts from tree to tree searching for insects and nectar.

At the very back of Nuʻalolo Valley is the native tree *lama*. Its oblong, pointed leaves are dark green and leathery. The fruits are green, then yellow, and finally bright red when fully ripe. Lama was sacred to Laka, goddess of the hula. Early Hawaiians used the hard, light-colored wood in temple construction and in hula performances.

The view from the double overlook at the end of Awaʻawapuhi Trail is breathtaking. On the left is the Lolo benchmark ridge extending from the sheer Nuʻalolo cliffs. Far below on the right is Awaʻawapuhi, a narrow canyon with a meandering stream leading to the ocean. Between the overlooks is a knife-edge ridge dividing the two valleys. Spend some time watching the interplay of sun and clouds on ocean, ridge, and canyon. Don't get too comfortable, however, because the route is all uphill from here.

Although the loop is described clockwise, you can, of course, walk it in either direction. For a similar but shorter hike, try Awaʻawapuhi, which forms the return portion of the Nuʻalolo Cliff loop.

# Awa'awapuhi

| LENGTH: | 6.5-mile round-trip |
|---------|---------------------|
| ELEVATION GAIN: | 1,600 feet |
| DANGER: | Low |
| SUITABLE FOR: | Intermediate |
| LOCATION: | Kaua'i: Kōke'e State Park and Nā Pali-Kona Forest Reserve |
| TOPO MAP: | Hā'ena, Mākaha Point |

## HIGHLIGHTS

This hike descends to an awesome overlook of the Nāpali Coast. Far below lies Awa'awapuhi, a slot canyon leading to the ocean. Along the route are many varieties of native rain forest and dryland plants.

## TRAILHEAD DIRECTIONS

**DISTANCE:** (Līhu'e to Awa'awapuhi trailhead) 42 miles
**DRIVING TIME:** 1 1/2 hours

From Līhu'e take Kaumuali'i Hwy (Rte 50) toward Waimea.
Pass Kukui Grove Center on the left and Kaua'i Community College on the right. The road then narrows to two lanes.
Drive through the towns of Lāwa'i and Kalāheo.
Pass the Hanapēpē River overlook on the right.
Drive through the towns of 'Ele'ele and Hanapēpē.

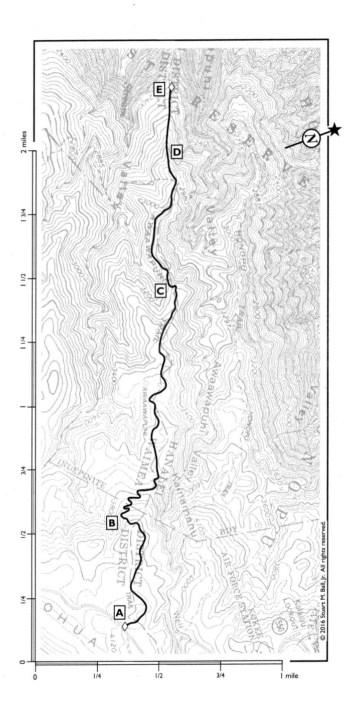

Pass the Russian fort on the left and then enter Waimea town.
Pass Waimea High School on the right.

Turn right on Waimea Canyon Rd. The intersection is just past Waimea Baptist Church, with its white steeple.

Ascend gradually along the rim of Waimea Canyon.

At the stop sign, turn right on Kōke'e Rd. (Rte 550).

Pass Kōke'e Hunter Check Station on the right.

Pass turnoffs to Waimea Canyon and Pu'u Hinahina Lookouts on the right.

Enter Kōke'e State Park.

Drive by Kōke'e Lodge and Museum on the left. The lodge has restrooms and drinking water, and the museum has trail maps and guides.

Pass Kōke'e Campground on the left and then ascend gradually on three switchbacks.

After mile marker 17, look for a parking lot on the left with an Awa'awapuhi Trail sign. Just before the lot is a dirt road with a yellow gate on the right.

Turn left into the lot and park there (elevation 4,120 feet) (map point A) (UTM 4Q 433111E, 244861N) (Lat/Long N22.14131, W159.64865).

## ROUTE DESCRIPTION

Take the Awa'awapuhi Trail from the left side of the parking lot.

Climb briefly and then descend gradually along a broad side ridge. Signs identify some of the native plants.

The trail levels off through native rain forest recovering from hurricanes 'Iwa and Iniki. Look for small 'ōhi'a trees and *naupaka kuahiwi* shrubs with their white half-flowers.

Descend steeply on a series of S curves (map point B). Watch for the native birds 'elepaio and 'apapane in the forest canopy.

The angle of descent eases. On the forest floor are huge *koa* trunks downed by the hurricanes.

Climb briefly and pass an overlook with the first view of the ocean.

Switchback once and descend through a stand of strawberry guava.

The forest opens up as the vegetation gradually changes to dryland. Predominating are *koa* trees and *pūkiawe* and *'a'ali'i* shrubs.

Go around to the left of an eroded knob. The trail stays mostly on the left side of the ridge from here on.

Descend into a lush gully on two switchbacks. At the first switchback are several native *'iliahi* (sandalwood) (map point C).

Go through a patch of scratchy lantana shrubs and then look for a native *hala pepe* tree on the left.

Reach a signed junction (map point D). Continue straight on the Awa'awapuhi Trail. (To the left the Nu'alolo Cliff Trail leads to the Nu'alolo Trail.)

Reach the end of the Awa'awapuhi Trail at a double overlook (elevation 2,520 feet) (map point E) (UTM 4Q 430360E, 2449810N) (Lat/Long N22.15203, W159.67538).

## NOTES

If you have time for only one hike in the Kōke'e (to bend) area, make it Awa'awapuhi. The trail is straightforward, well graded, and of reasonable length. On the way down, you start in native rain forest and finish in dryland scrub. At the end is a view worth sweating for. The only catch is the climb back up.

On the upper section of the trail, watch for the native birds *'elepaio* and *'apapane*. The *'elepaio* is gray-brown on top and has a white breast splotched with gray and black. Its dark tail is usually cocked. The *'apapane* has a red breast and head, black wings and tail, and a slightly curved black bill. In flight the *'apapane* makes a whirring sound as it darts from tree to tree searching for insects and nectar.

Also along the trail are well over fifty different species of native rain forest and dryland plants. Some are identified by small signs; a few of the white numbered markers keyed to the *Awa'awapuhi Botanical Trail Guide* are still along the trail, but the pamphlet is out of print. The notes below describe a few of the more easily identified native plants.

'Ōhiʻa trees predominate in the wet upper section of the trail. They have oval leaves and clusters of delicate red flowers. Native birds, such as the 'apapane, feed on the nectar and help in pollination. Early Hawaiians used the flowers in lei and the wood in outrigger canoes. The hard, durable wood was also carved into god images for heiau (religious sites).

In the drier middle section of the trail, koa gradually replaces 'ōhiʻa as the dominant tree. Koa has sickle-shaped foliage and pale-yellow flower clusters. Early Hawaiians made surfboards and outrigger canoe hulls out of the beautiful red-brown wood. Today it is made into fine furniture.

To build a canoe, the master canoe maker (kahuna kalai waʻa) first selected a tall, straight koa tree, preferably near water. After felling the tree, he waited for Lea, the goddess of canoe builders, to appear in the form of a small native bird, the 'elepaio. If the bird walked along the entire trunk without stopping, the wood was sound and could be used for the canoe. If, however, the 'elepaio stopped and pecked at the bark, the master knew that the tree was riddled with insects and must be discarded.

Farther down the ridge, the native dryland shrubs pūkiawe and 'aʻaliʻi make their appearance. Pūkiawe has tiny, rigid leaves and small white, pink, or red berries. 'Aʻaliʻi has narrow, shiny leaves and red seed capsules that early Hawaiians used in lei making and for kapa (bark cloth) dye.

At the next to last switchback, look for 'iliahi, the native sandalwood tree. Its small leaves are dull green and appear wilted. 'Iliahi is partially parasitic, having outgrowths on its roots that steal nutrients from nearby plants. Early Hawaiians ground the fragrant heartwood into a powder to perfume their kapa. Beginning in the late 1700s, sandalwood was indiscriminately cut down and exported to China to make incense and furniture. The trade ended around 1840 when the forests were depleted of 'iliahi.

Just after the patch of lantana shrub, watch for a lone native *hala pepe* tree. It has a thin trunk topped with a thatch of long, slender leaves. Early Hawaiians used the showy yellow flowers in lei and placed a cluster of flowers on the altar in the *hula halau* (long house) to honor Laka, goddess of the hula.

The view from the double overlook at the end of the trail is truly awesome. On the left are the sheer cliffs of Nuʻalolo Valley. Far below on the right is Awaʻawapuhi (ginger valley), a narrow canyon with a meandering stream leading to the ocean. Between the overlooks is a knife-edge ridge dividing the two valleys. Look for feral goats perched on the cliffs and *koaʻe kea*, the white-tailed tropicbird, soaring above them. Spend some time watching the interplay of sun and clouds on ocean, ridge, and canyon. Life doesn't get much better than this.

The Hawaiian name for the valley may be Awawāpuhi (eel valley), rather than Awaʻawapuhi (ginger valley). Nearby is Kaluapuhi (eel pit), whereas the valley has no ginger.

The Awaʻawapuhi Trail is also the return leg of the Nuʻalolo Cliff loop. If you have a whole day and are an experienced hiker, try that 11.4-mile loop instead.

# 22

# Alaka'i Swamp

| | |
|---|---|
| LENGTH: | 8.0-mile round-trip |
| ELEVATION GAIN: | 1,400 feet |
| DANGER: | Low |
| SUITABLE FOR: | Novice, Intermediate |
| LOCATION: | Kaua'i: Kōke'e State Park, Nā Pali-Kona Forest Reserve and Alaka'i Wilderness Preserve |
| TOPO MAP: | Hā'ena |

## HIGHLIGHTS

A scenic stroll along the rim of Kalalau Valley turns into a wet, wild tramp through the Alaka'i Swamp. Follow the boardwalk to misty Kilohana, a lookout over Hanalei Bay. Along the route is an incredible variety of native rain forest plants and birds.

## TRAILHEAD DIRECTIONS

**DISTANCE:** (Līhu'e to Pu'u o Kila lookout) 44 miles
**DRIVING TIME:** 1 1/2 hours

From Līhu'e take Kaumuali'i Hwy (Rte 50) toward Waimea.
Pass Kukui Grove Center on the left and Kaua'i Community College on the right. The road then narrows to two lanes.
Drive through the towns of Lāwa'i and Kalāheo.
Pass the Hanapēpē River overlook on the right.
Drive through the towns of 'Ele'ele and Hanapēpē.

Pass the Russian fort on the left and then enter Waimea town.

Pass Waimea High School on the right.

Turn right on Waimea Canyon Rd. The intersection is just past Waimea Baptist Church, with its white steeple.

Ascend gradually along the rim of Waimea Canyon.

At the stop sign, turn right on Kōkeʻe Rd. (Rte 550).

Pass Kōkeʻe Hunter Check Station on the right.

Pass turnoffs to Waimea Canyon and Puʻu Hinahina Lookouts on the right.

Enter Kōkeʻe State Park.

Drive by Kōkeʻe Lodge and Museum on the left. The lodge has restrooms and drinking water, and the museum stocks trail maps and guides and posts trail conditions.

Pass Kōkeʻe Campground on the left and then ascend gradually on three switchbacks.

Pass Headquarters, Hawaii National Guard, on the left.

The road forks. Keep right for Puʻu o Kila lookout. (To the left is Kalalau Lookout.)

Park in the large lot at the end of the paved road (map point A) (UTM 4Q 434881E, 2449305N) (Lat/Long N22.14765, W159.63152).

## ROUTE DESCRIPTION

From the parking area, walk up the paved path to Puʻu o Kila lookout (elevation 4,176 feet).

Pick up the Pihea Trail, an eroded dirt road following the rim of Kalalau Valley.

Descend initially through a native ʻōhiʻa forest. On the left are several more lookouts; ahead along the rim is the peak of Pihea.

Traverse a series of small ups and downs. Look for ʻamaʻu ferns along the route. In the forest canopy you may see the native birds ʻapapane and ʻiʻiwi, when the ʻōhiʻa is in bloom.

The road narrows to a rough and rooty trail.

Cross a muddy area and then climb steeply on a deeply

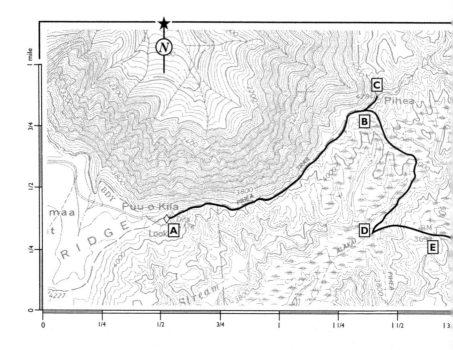

rutted trail. Watch for native ʻōlapa trees, with their fluttering leaves, and hāpuʻu tree ferns.

Reach a signed junction (map point B). For now, continue straight to the Pihea vista. (To the right the Pihea Trail leads into the Alakaʻi Swamp.)

Climb steeply to the summit of Pihea (elevation 4,284 feet) (map point C). From the top you can now see the left side of Kalalau Valley. Ringing the lookout are ʻōlapa trees and pūʻahanui (kanawao) shrubs, with their delicate pink flowers.

Retrace your steps to the junction (map point B) and turn left on the Pihea Trail. (Straight ahead is the way you came in.) The trail roughly parallels a fence line on your left.

After descending steeply down a side ridge, the muddy trail becomes a dry boardwalk passing through an amazing assemblage of native rain forest plants. ʻŌhiʻa and hāpuʻu still predominate; however, look for ʻōhā wai, with its curved purple-and-white flowers and yellow berries, and lapalapa, with its round, fluttering leaves.

| 2 | 2 1/4 | 2 1/2 | 2 3/4 | 3 | 3 1/4 miles |

The boardwalk descends more gradually and then levels off in a flat area. Watch for *alani,* with its curled-up leaves and purple stems. Also, look for the native birds 'elepaio and 'anianiau in the forest canopy.

Reach a signed four-way junction with another boardwalk (map point D) (UTM 4Q 436290E, 2449188N) (Lat/Long N22.14664, W159.61785). Turn left on the Alaka'i Swamp Trail. (The Pihea Trail continues straight, to Kawaikōī Camp. To the right the Alaka'i Swamp Trail heads back to Camp 10-Mōhihi Rd.)

Descend steeply on wooden stairs. The route follows a telephone line built during World War II. Most of the poles have rotted, but you can still see a few standing or lying on the ground.

The boardwalk ends as the angle of descent eases.

Cross a tributary of Kawaikōī Stream (map point E). The boardwalk resumes briefly.

Climb steadily up a ridge.

Go around to the right of a hump in the ridge. On the left are views of Pihea peak and the rim of Kalalau Valley.

The boardwalk reappears across a flat, swampy area (map point F). The vegetation, mostly 'ōhi'a and 'ōlapa, is stunted.

As the slope changes, drier, more vegetated sections alternate with standing water.

Descend into and climb out of a small lush gully. Watch for native 'ohe naupaka, with its yellow, tube-shaped flowers.

The boardwalk swings left, away from the phone line (map point G).

Rejoin the phone line.

Descend gradually through a more vegetated section.

Reach Kilohana Lookout, with a small bench and wooden platform (elevation 4,022 feet) (map point H) (UTM 4Q 438805E, 2450186N) (Lat/Long N22.15575, W159.5935).

## NOTES

This unusual hike follows an elevated boardwalk through the Alaka'i (to lead) Swamp. The boardwalk has seen better days, so watch out for loose planks and partially missing sections. With a little acrobatic skill, however, you can still walk through the bog without getting your feet wet. Fall off the boardwalk, though, and you're up to your knees or thighs in mud. Good luck.

Summer (May–October) is the best time of year to hike in the swamp. Rainfall is lighter, and the temperature is higher then. Start early in the morning for the best views and bird watching. Later in the day the clouds usually roll in and blanket the swamp in mist and light rain. Whenever you go, bring a good rain jacket and an extra layer of warm clothing.

Before starting, take in the magnificent view from Pu'u o Kila Lookout. Far below lies the broad expanse of Kalalau (the straying) Valley, with its sheer, fluted cliffs. *Mauka* (inland) is our destination, the featureless Alaka'i Swamp. In back the ground slopes upward to cloud-draped Wai'ale'ale (rippling water), the wettest spot on earth.

The hike initially follows a dirt road along the rim of Kalalau Valley. The road is a remnant of an ill-conceived scheme to build a paved highway from Kōke'e (to bend) to Hanalei. A lack of money and the rough terrain and wet conditions soon forced the project to a halt.

Because the forest canopy is at eye level, the road is a good place to spot native birds, such as the 'apapane and 'i'iwi. Both of those birds have a red breast and head and black wings and tail. The 'i'iwi has a long, curved, salmon-colored bill, whereas the 'apapane has a slightly curved black bill. In flight the 'apapane makes a whirring sound as it darts from tree to tree searching for insects and nectar.

Along the trail are well over fifty different species of native plants that prefer a wet mountain habitat. All are identified and illustrated in the pamphlet *Pihea Trail Native Plant Guide,* available online. The notes below describe a few of the more distinctive native plants.

Ringing the Pihea vista are native 'ōlapa trees. The leaves are opposite, oblong, and flutter in the slightest wind. In a special hula stance named after the tree, dancers mimic the exquisite movements of the leaves. Early Hawaiians used the bark, leaves, and purple fruit to make a blue-black dye to decorate their *kapa* (bark cloth).

On the initial boardwalk section, look for the native lobelia 'ōhā wai. It has narrow, serrated leaves and branches arranged like a candelabra. The showy curved flowers are purple outside and cream colored within. Native honeycreepers, such as the 'apapane and 'i'iwi, use their curved bills to feed on the nectar.

Around the four-way boardwalk junction, you may catch a glimpse of two other native birds, 'elepaio and 'anianiau. The 'elepaio is gray-brown on top and has a white breast splotched with gray and black. Its dark tail is usually cocked. Found only on Kaua'i, the 'anianiau is yellow-green on top and bright yellow underneath with a short, slightly curved bill. Both birds are very curious, which is why you can often see them.

After the short ridge section, watch for the native shrub 'ohe naupaka. It has narrow, pointed leaves growing in clumps at the end of the branches. The distinctive tube-shaped flowers are bright yellow-orange.

The route through the swamp follows a telephone line put up by the U.S. Army in World War II. Most of the poles have fallen over or been cut down at the base. In the bog, the vegetation is stunted because of the high wind and soggy soil. In some areas the rain has washed away the colorful minerals, leaving gray clay, rich in titanium.

Walking in the swamp is a dark, eerie experience. Clouds blot out the sun. Mist settles over the bog and swirls over the dwarf trees and standing water. Then the rain begins to fall, every day of the year.

The boardwalk ends at Kilohana (lookout point). If you are very, very lucky, you may get a spectacular, if fleeting, view. Wainiha (unfriendly water) Valley and Bay lie 4,000 feet below. Along the coast are Hanalei (crescent) Bay and Kīlauea (spewing) Point. Along the ridge to the left is Pali 'Ele'ele (black cliff). To the right Wainiha Pali leads to Wai'ale'ale, the wettest spot on earth, at 5,080 feet.

# 23

# Kawaikōī Stream

| LENGTH: | 8.2-mile loop |
| --- | --- |
| ELEVATION GAIN: | 900 feet |
| DANGER: | Low |
| SUITABLE FOR: | Intermediate |
| LOCATION: | Kauaʻi: Kōkeʻe State Park and Nā Pali-Kona Forest Reserve |
| TOPO MAP: | Hāʻena |

## HIGHLIGHTS

Follow the spectacular rim of Kalalau Valley to perhaps the most lovely stream walk in the islands. Along the varied route are intriguing native plants, colorful native birds, and a short section of the Alakaʻi Swamp.

## TRAILHEAD DIRECTIONS

**DISTANCE:** (Līhuʻe to Puʻu o Kila lookout) 44 miles
**DRIVING TIME:** 1 1/2 hours

From Līhuʻe take Kaumualiʻi Hwy (Rte 50) toward Waimea.

Pass Kukui Grove Center on the left and Kauaʻi Community College on the right. The road then narrows to two lanes.

Drive through the towns of Lāwaʻi and Kalāheo.

Pass the Hanapēpē River overlook on the right.

Drive through the towns of 'Ele'ele and Hanapēpē.

Pass the Russian fort on the left and then enter Waimea town.

Pass Waimea High School on the right.

Turn right on Waimea Canyon Rd. The intersection is just past Waimea Baptist Church, with its white steeple.

Ascend gradually along the rim of Waimea Canyon.

At the stop sign, turn right on Kōke'e Rd. (Rte 550).

Pass Kōke'e Hunter Check Station on the right.

Pass turnoffs to Waimea Canyon and Pu'u Hinahina Lookouts on the right.

Enter Kōke'e State Park.

Drive by Kōke'e Lodge and Museum on the left. The lodge has restrooms and drinking water, and the museum stocks trail maps and guides and posts trail conditions.

Pass Kōke'e Campground on the left and then ascend gradually on three switchbacks.

Pass Headquarters, Hawaii National Guard, on the left.

The road forks. Keep right for Pu'u o Kila Lookout. (To the left is Kalalau Lookout.)

Park in the large lot at the end of the paved road (map point A) (UTM 4Q 434881E, 2449305N) (Lat/Long N22.14765, W159.63152).

**ROUTE DESCRIPTION**

From the parking area, walk up the paved path to Pu'u o Kila Lookout (elevation 4,176 feet).

Pick up the Pihea Trail, an eroded dirt road following the rim of Kalalau Valley.

Descend initially through a native 'ōhi'a forest. On the left are several more lookouts; ahead along the rim is the peak of Pihea.

Traverse a series of small ups and downs. In the forest canopy you may see the native birds 'apapane and 'i'iwi, when the 'ōhi'a is in bloom.

The road narrows to a rough and rooty trail.

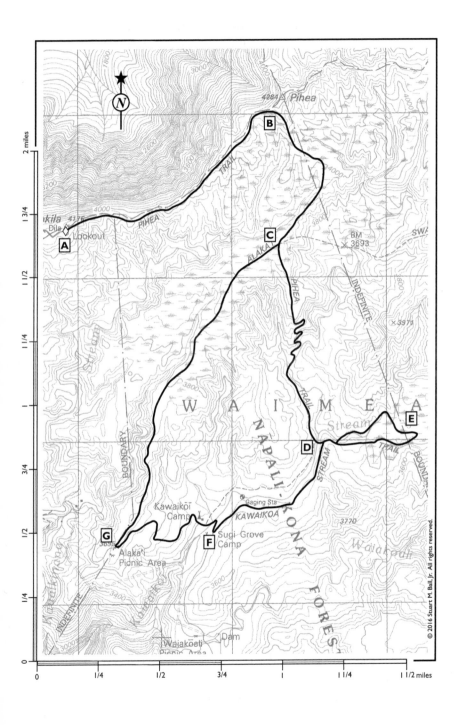

Cross a muddy area and then climb steeply on a deeply rutted trail. Reach a signed junction (map point B). Turn right on the Pihea Trail. (To the left a short, steep trail leads to the summit of Pihea.)

Descend steeply along a side ridge. The trail roughly parallels a fence line on your left.

The muddy, slippery trail becomes a dry boardwalk passing through an amazing assemblage of native rain forest plants. *'Ōhi'a* and *hāpu'u* still predominate; however, look for *'ōhā wai*, with its curved purple-and-white flowers and yellow berries, and *'ohe naupaka*, with its yellow, tube-shaped flowers.

The boardwalk descends more gradually and then levels off in a flat area. Watch for the native birds *'elepaio* and *'anianiau* in the forest canopy.

Reach a signed four-way junction with another boardwalk (map point C) (UTM 4Q 436290E, 2449188N) (Lat/Long N22.14664, W159.61785). Continue straight on the Pihea Trail toward Kawaikōī Camp (To the left the Alaka'i Swamp Trail leads to Kilohana Lookout. To the right the swamp trail heads down to Camp 10–Mōhihi Rd. and is the return portion of the hike).

The boardwalk soon ends.

On the right pass several overlooks. In the distance is the rim of Waimea Canyon. Watch for *pueo*, the native owl, gliding above the *'ōhi'a* forest.

Descend gradually along the side ridge passing huge *'ōhi'a* trunks uprooted by hurricanes 'Iwa and Iniki.

Switchback nine times on the descent into the Kawaikōī drainage. *Kahili* ginger and scratchy *uluhe* ferns may overgrow the lower switchbacks.

Approach a large tributary of Kawaikōī Stream and turn right, heading downstream.

Cross a small side stream.

Climb briefly and contour well above the stream.

Descend gradually to the stream and pass a covered picnic table on the left.

The tributary joins Kawaikōī Stream on the left.

Reach a signed junction (elevation 3,450 feet) (map point D) (UTM 4Q 436516E, 2447878N) (Lat/Long N22.13482, W159.61561). Turn left and rock hop across the stream. (The Pihea Trail continues downstream to Kawaikōī Camp.)

On the far bank, turn left on the Kawaikōī Stream Trail (To the right the Stream Trail leads back to Sugi Grove and Camp 10–Mōhihi Rd.)

Stroll along the deep, dark stream. *'Ama'u* ferns line the banks. Watch for two native waterfowl, *'alae ke'oke'o,* the Hawaiian coot, and *koloa,* the Hawaiian duck. Look for native *olomea* shrubs with their red-veined leaves.

Reach another signed junction with the loop portion of the trail. Keep right and up. (The trail on the left along the stream is the return route.)

The trail climbs away from the stream and then levels off. Cross a side stream.

Climb steadily, working back toward the stream.

Pass two stream overlooks on the left. Near the second one is a native *lapalapa* tree, with its round, fluttering leaves.

Descend to the stream on one switchback and ford it (map point E). On the left is a deep swimming hole.

Proceed downstream right next to the water.

Pass a towering *'ōhi'a* tree on the right.

Traverse a narrow, slippery ledge just above the stream. Watch your footing.

Contour above the stream and cross two marshy areas on a series of planks. Water drips from the cliff on the right.

Ford Kawaikōī Stream once again.

Shortly afterward, reach the familiar loop junction. Keep right, heading downstream.

Cross a side stream on a plank.

Enter a grove of sugi cedars, planted by the Civilian Conservation Corps in the 1930s.

Cross two wet gullies on a short boardwalk.

Swing left through a second stand of sugi cedars.

Reach a signed junction (map point F). Turn right onto the Camp 10–Mōhihi Rd. (Straight ahead is Sugi Grove Camp.

To the left the road leads to Camp 10 and the Mōhihi-Waialae Trail.)

Descend briefly and cross Kawaikōī Stream for the last time. On the right pass Kawaikōī Camp, which has covered picnic tables and a composting toilet.

Ascend gradually along the Camp 10 Rd. to a signed junction in a grassy, open area (map point G) (UTM 4Q 435229E, 2447354N) (Lat/Long N22.13004, W159.62806). Turn right on another dirt road, which is the Alakaʻi Swamp Trail. (The Camp 10-Mōhihi Road continues straight and down, to Kōkeʻe Lodge and Museum. The road on the left leads a short distance to the Alakaʻi Picnic Area, which has a covered table, pit toilet, and a superb view down Poʻomau Canyon.)

Go around a barrier blocking vehicle access.

The road narrows to a trail, and the trail becomes a boardwalk through the Alakaʻi Swamp. Watch for *lehua makanoe,* a dwarf native shrub with red blossoms similar to an *ʻōhiʻa.*

Reach the familiar four-way junction to complete the large loop (map point C). Turn left on the Pihea Trail and retrace your steps back to Puʻu o Kila Lookout.

## NOTES

The Kawaikōī (flowing water) Stream hike is for lovers—plant lovers, bird lovers, lovers of solitude, and lovers of softly murmuring streams. All the outings in the Kōkeʻe area are superb, but this one is special. Don't miss it.

The route initially follows the Pihea Trail, which passes over fifty different species of native plants that prefer a wet mountain habitat. All are identified and illustrated in the pamphlet, *Pihea Trail Native Plant Guide,* available online. Two of the most distinctive are *ʻohe naupaka* and the lobelia *ʻōhā wai. ʻOhe naupaka* has narrow, pointed leaves growing in clumps at the end of the branches. The distinctive tube-shaped flowers are bright yellow orange. *ʻŌhā wai* has narrow, serrated leaves and branches arranged like a candelabra. The showy curved flowers are purple outside and cream colored within. Native honeycreepers, such as the 'apapane and 'i'iwi, use their curved bills to feed on the nectar.

Around the four-way boardwalk junction, you may catch a glimpse of two other native birds, 'elepaio and 'anianiau. The 'elepaio is gray-brown on top and has a white breast splotched with gray and black. Its dark tail is usually cocked. Found only on Kaua'i, the 'anianiau is yellow-green on top and bright yellow underneath with a short, slightly curved bill. Both birds are very curious, which is why you can often see them.

On the descent to Kawaikōī Stream, look for pueo, the native owl, gliding above the forest. The pueo is brown and white with yellow eyes and a black bill. Unlike most owls, the pueo is active during the day, hunting birds, rodents, and insects. Early Hawaiians worshiped the owl as a god and a guardian spirit.

Watch your footing while rock hopping across Kawaikōī Stream. If the rocks are submerged, do not ford the stream, as the water is well above your knees. Skip the stream loop by continuing along the Pihea Trail at map point D. At Kawaikōī Camp, turn right on Camp10-Mōhihi Rd. and pick up the narrative there.

The walk beside stream is lovely and serene. Deep, placid pools alternate with shallow, noisy riffles. The water flowing by is dark and mysterious, colored a rich brown by tannin from swamp vegetation. Soft grass and native ferns line the banks of the stream. Savor this walk; don't rush it.

While strolling quietly along the stream, keep your eye out for two native waterfowl, 'alae ke'oke'o, the Hawaiian coot, and koloa, the Hawaiian duck. The coot is black, except for a white bill and forehead. The duck is mottled brown, similar to a female mallard. Both birds eat freshwater vegetation, mollusks, and insects. 'Alae ke'oke'o is prominent in Hawaiian mythology.

At a secluded overlook before the second stream ford is a large native lapalapa tree. Its roundish leaves are arranged in groups of three and flutter in the slightest wind. Early Hawaiians used the bark, leaves, and purple fruit to make a blue-black dye to decorate their *kapa* (bark cloth). The leaves also make a distinctive lei.

On the way back, the route traverses a section of the Alakaʻi (to lead) Swamp. Along the boardwalk look for the short native shrub *lehua makanoe* (misty-eyed *lehua*), growing in clumps. It has narrow, pointed leaves closely spaced along the stem. The delicate blossoms are large and red, similar to an *ʻōhiʻa*. Many bog plants are dwarfs because of the waterlogged soil.

The Camp 10–Mōhihi Road provides an alternate access to Kawaikōī Stream for four-wheel-drive vehicles. Follow the trailhead directions for the Waimea Canyon Vista hike and then continue along the main dirt road to Sugi Grove Camp. Roundtrip distance on the road is about 7.5 miles. The stream loop then becomes about 2.2 miles. If the road is dry and well graded, you may be able to take a two-wheel-drive vehicle over the first two miles. Park in the large lot on the left just before a steep downhill section.

24

# 'Ōkolehao

| LENGTH: | 3.6-mile round-trip |
| --- | --- |
| ELEVATION GAIN: | 1,300 feet |
| DANGER: | Low |
| SUITABLE FOR: | Intermediate |
| LOCATION: | Hanalei National Wildlife Refuge and Haleleʻa Forest Reserve above Hanalei |
| TOPO MAP: | Hanalei |

This steep climb follows a ridge route established by bootleggers during prohibition. Along the way are delicious strawberry guava, as well as the kī (ti) plants used to make the liquor 'ōkolehao. From several overlooks you can see Hanalei River and Bay and the peaks surrounding the valley.

TRAILHEAD DIRECTIONS

**DISTANCE:**     (Līhuʻe to 'Ōkolehao trialhead) 29 miles
**DRIVING TIME:**  1 hour

From Līhuʻe take Kūhiō Hwy (Rte 56 north) toward Hanalei.

Cross Wailua River on a bridge.

Drive through the town of Kapaʻa.

Continue on Kūhiō Hwy along the windward coast.

Pass the turnoff to Kīlauea Lighthouse on the right and then cross a long bridge over the Kalihiwai River.

Pass Princeville Airport on the left and Princeville Center on the right.

Descend into Hanalei Valley and cross the river on a one-lane bridge.

Immediately after the bridge, turn left on narrow but paved ʻŌhiki Rd.

Parallel Hanalei River, passing wetland *kalo* (taro) fields and Haraguchi Rice Mill on the right.

Enter Hanalei National Wildlife Refuge.

Park in a small dirt lot on the left (elevation 20 feet) (map point A) (UTM 4Q 451293E, 2455231N) (Lat/Long N22.20172, W159.47254). Across the road from the lot is a wooden bridge spanning an irrigation ditch. The lot is 0.6 mile from the main highway.

## ROUTE DESCRIPTION

Take the wooden bridge across China Ditch, an old irrigation channel that delivers river water to the taro fields at the front of the valley.

Walk through strawberry guava thickets on a path paved with stones.

Swing right through a wet, muddy area.

Turn left on a dirt road heading uphill.

Angle steeply up the side of a ridge through native *koa* and introduced eucalyptus and paperbark trees.

Switchback once to the right.

Reach the ridgeline near a powerline pylon in a grove of Cook pines (map point B). Turn sharp left up the ridge.

Ascend gradually through a corridor of pines, strawberry guava, and eucalyptus. Look for *hala* trees with their prop

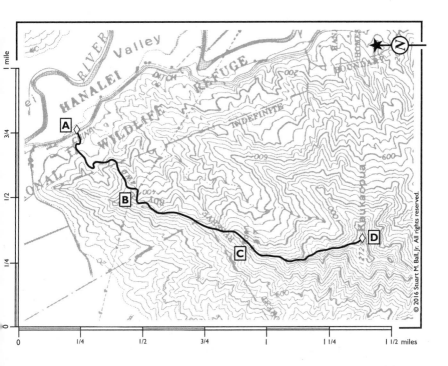

roots. Through openings in the forest, you can see Hanalei Valley and the surrounding mountains.

Leave the ridgeline briefly to the left and then ascend to the right to regain it.

Climb steeply but briefly to a scenic overlook with a bench and a cluster of *kī* (ti) plants (map point C). The overlook was once the site of a triangulation station called Roan.

Ascend gradually and then steeply to an indistinct knob along the ridge. Watch for *'awapuhi* (shampoo ginger) along the narrow, sometimes overgrown trail.

Descend briefly and then resume the steady ascent.

Reach a broad peak, known as Kauka'ōpua (elevation 1,272 feet) (map point D) (UTM 4Q 450544E, 2453386N) (Lat/Long N22.18503, W159.47975), where a long side ridge comes in on the left. Keep right to find a small clearing with good views *mauka*. The overlook is just before the trail drops steeply.

While the tourist legions are marching to Hanakāpī'ai, try this nearby but less-traveled hike. The route follows a very scenic ridge that separates Hanalei (crescent bay) and Wai'oli (joyful water) Valleys. The trail is not graded, though, so the climb is often steep and rough.

While driving to the trailhead along the river, watch for two native waterfowl, 'alae ke'oke'o, the Hawaiian coot, and 'alae 'ula, the Hawaiian moorhen. The coot is grayish black, except for a white bill and forehead, while the moorhen is mostly gray with a red bill and forehead. Both birds periodically dive underwater looking for vegetation, mollusks, and insects. Both are also prominent in Hawaiian mythology.

Look for native *koa* trees on the climb to the ridgetop. They have sickle-shaped foliage and pale-yellow flower clusters. Early Hawaiians made surfboards and outrigger canoe hulls out of the beautiful red-brown wood. Today it is made into fine furniture.

Strawberry guava trees (*waiawī-'ula'ula*) line the trail along the ridge. They have glossy, dark-green leaves and smooth brown bark. Their dark-red fruit is delicious, with a taste reminiscent of strawberries. The guavas usually ripen in late summer (July–September). The tree is a native of Brazil but was introduced to Hawai'i from China in the 1800s.

Also found along the ridge trail are *kī* (ti) plants. They have shiny leaves, 1–2 feet long, that are arranged spirally in a cluster at the tip of a slender stem. Early Polynesian voyagers introduced ti to Hawai'i. They used the leaves for house thatch, skirts, sandals, and raincoats. Food to be cooked in the *imu* (underground oven) was first wrapped in ti leaves. A popular sport with the commoners was *ho'he'e kī*, or ti-leaf sledding. The sap from ti plants stained canoes and surfboards.

The ti plant also had a more modern use. During prohibition in the 1920s local moonshiners distilled a liquor, *'ōkolehao*, from ti roots. 'Ōkolehao means iron bottom, referring to

'ŌKOLEHAO ❖ HANALEI

the iron try-pot stills used by the bootleggers. They established this ridge route to cultivate and harvest the plants.

From overlooks along the ridge are marvelous views of Hanalei River, Bay, and town. Along the coast to the east is Kīlauea (spewing) Point and, to the west, Wainiha (unfriendly water) Pali. *Mauka* (inland) is fortresslike Nāmolokama Mountain (the interweaving bound fast). Several waterfalls cascade down its flanks.

Near the indistinct knob are patches of *'awapuhi,* or shampoo ginger, which is an herb with long, pointed leaves. Leaf stalks arise from a network of knobbed, underground stems. In late summer the plant sends up a flower stalk with an oblong head. Small yellow flowers emerge from the head, one at a time. Squeeze the flower head to get a sudsy, fragrant sap. Like early Hawaiians, you can use it to wash your hands or shampoo your hair.

The final section of the trail becomes increasingly rough and overgrown. Watch your footing as the vegetation may conceal holes and drop-offs. On the far side of Kauka'ōpua (the horizon clouds alight) is a lookout that makes a good lunch spot and turnaround point.

# 25

# Hanakāpīʻai Falls

| | |
|---|---|
| LENGTH: | 7.9-mile round-trip |
| ELEVATION GAIN: | 2,000 feet |
| DANGER: | Medium |
| SUITABLE FOR: | Intermediate, Expert |
| LOCATION: | Kauaʻi: Nā Pali Coast State Park |
| TOPO MAP: | Hāʻena |

## HIGHLIGHTS

This popular hike winds above vertical sea cliffs along the rugged Nā Pali Coast. Midway is an idyllic cove with a white sand beach. At the end is lovely Hanakāpīʻai Falls, cascading into a wide, circular pool.

## TRAILHEAD DIRECTIONS

**DISTANCE:** (Līhuʻe to Kēʻē Beach) 37 miles
**DRIVING TIME:** 1 1/4 hours

From Līhuʻe take Kūhiō Hwy (Rte 56 north) toward Hanalei.

Cross Wailua River on a bridge.

Drive through the town of Kapaʻa.

Continue on Kūhiō Hwy along the windward coast.

Pass the turnoff to Kīlauea Lighthouse on the right and then cross a long bridge over the Kalihiwai River.

Pass Princeville Airport on the left and Princeville Center on the right. Route 56 becomes Route 560 west.

Descend into Hanalei Valley and cross the river on a one-lane bridge.

Drive through Hanalei town.

Cross a series of short one-lane bridges.

Enter Hā'ena State Park.

Reach the end of the road at Kē'ē Beach (map point A) (UTM 4Q 439959E, 2457364N) (Lat/Long N22.22064, W159.58257). Park on either side of the road. The state park has restrooms, drinking water, and outdoor showers. If all the parking spaces are taken, drive back to the overflow lot on the left.

## ROUTE DESCRIPTION

Take the Kalalau Trail that starts on the left just before the end of the paved road across from mile marker 10.

Pass some interpretive signs on the left and a bulletin board displaying trail maps and information on the right.

Climb steadily along the Makana cliffs above Kē'ē Beach. The trail is very rocky and slippery when wet. Some sections are paved with smooth stones. Look for the native shrub, *naupaka kahakai*, with its white half-flowers.

Work into and out of two small ravines. The first is dotted with *hala* trees and the second with *kukui* trees and *kī* (ti) plants.

Around the corner from the second ravine is the first good view of the Nā Pali Coast.

Work into and out of two more gulches. The last one has a small stream.

The trail straightens out for a while (map point B). Water seeps from the cliffs above.

Descend gradually through another ravine. On the left is a cleared area used for emergency helicopter landings.

Descend into a double gulch on a series of eroded switchbacks.

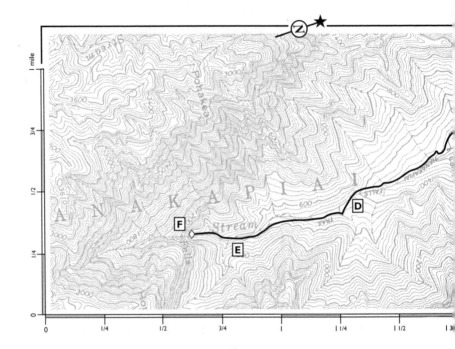

Cross two streams and climb out of the gulch.

Descend into Hanakāpīʻai Valley on two switchbacks.

Cross Hanakāpīʻai Stream by rock hopping or wading. As always, do not ford the stream if the water is much above your knees (map point C).

Climb the opposite bank and reach a signed junction. Turn sharp left upstream. (The trail to the right leads to the beach.)

Shortly afterward, reach a second signed junction near a lone ironwood tree in a grove of *hala*. Turn left on the Hanakāpīʻai Falls Trail. (To the right the Kalalau Trail continues along the coast. Just up that trail is an elevated compost toilet.)

Walk across an open area used as an emergency helipad.

Ascend gradually up Hanakāpīʻai Valley well above the stream.

Cross two side gullies. In between are several bamboo stands and huge mango trees. Watch for the white-rumped shama.

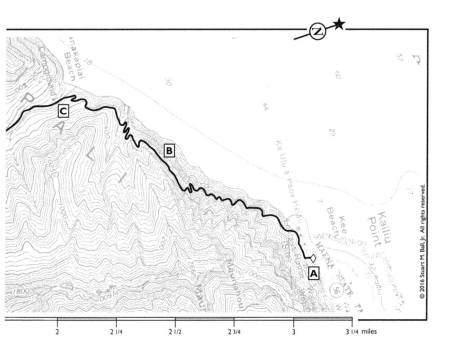

The trail levels off through groves of coffee, mountain apple, and fragrant yellow ginger.

Walk past *lo'i,* rock-walled terraces for growing *kalo* (taro).

Turn right along a small channel of the main stream and climb briefly up a rocky gully. Ignore side trails leading down to the stream.

Turn left and ford the main channel of the stream (map point D).

Cross an island in midstream and then ford a second smaller channel.

Climb gradually along the left bank of Hanakāpī'ai Stream through *lo'i* and coffee and mountain apple groves.

Ford two side streams and pass more terraces and bamboo.

Reach an obscure junction. Turn left and climb well above the stream. Through the trees is the first view of Hanakāpī'ai Falls.

Negotiate a rough, narrow section with some slippery ledges.

Descend steeply back to the main stream. Watch your footing.

Ford the main stream once again to work around an inviting swimming hole (map point E). If the water is low, you may be able to continue along the ledges above the pool without crossing the stream.

Cross the main stream for the last time.

Reach a broad open basin (elevation 1,000 feet) (map point F) (UTM 4Q 438688E, 2453562N) (Lat/Long N22.18624, W159.59476). At the back, lovely Hanakāpīʻai Falls cascades into a wide circular pool. White-tailed tropicbirds soar above the falls along the surrounding cliffs.

## NOTES

Hanakāpīʻai Falls is the classic hike in the islands. It visits both an idyllic white sand beach and a cascading mountain waterfall. What more could you possibly want? Those twin attractions, however, make the hike popular with tourists and locals alike. If you don't like crowds, go during the week and start early.

Summer (May–October) is the best time to take this hike. Hanakāpīʻai Stream is usually lower then and thus easier to ford. The surf and the offshore current along the beach are not as strong in summer. Also, the beautiful white sand goes out to sea during winter, leaving an uninviting jumble of rock.

Several cautions are in order for this hike. Do not ford Hanakāpīʻai stream when the water is much above your knees. If you are caught in the valley by rapidly rising water, wait for the stream to go down. It is far better to be stranded for half a day than to get swept away. Never make any evening commitments that might encourage you to cross the stream during high water.

The trail along the coast is slippery and eroded in spots. The route to the falls is usually muddy and mosquitoey, sometimes narrow, and occasionally hard to follow. Look for surveyor ribbon marking the route. If possible, wear tabis (Japanese reef walkers) or other water footwear for more secure footing. Finally, if you decide to swim, you are on your own, as there are no lifeguards at the beach.

Before starting the hike, walk to Kēʻē (avoidance) Beach. A short stroll along the beach to the right leads to a good first view of Nā Pali (the cliffs) Coast. To the left below the cliffs are the remains of a *heiau* (religious site) and a *hālau* hula platform where the ancient hula was performed.

The hike initially follows the Kalalau Trail, an old Hawaiian route connecting the valleys along the coast. The trail was improved in the 1800s and the 1930s. The stone paving on the first section dates from that last upgrade.

Look for *hala* trees on the way to Hanakāpīʻai Stream. They have distinctive prop roots that help support the heavy clusters of leaves and fruit on the ends of the branches. Early Hawaiians braided the long, pointed leaves, called *lau hala,* into baskets, fans, floor mats, and sails.

About a half mile in is the first spectacular view of Nā Pali Coast. Deep valleys alternate with vertical sea cliffs. Rainfall runoff created the valleys and wave action the cliffs. Where stream erosion has proceeded faster than sea erosion, the stream flows into the ocean at sea level, as at Hanakāpīʻai. The reverse situation creates a hanging valley with a waterfall cascading into the ocean, as at Hanakoa (bay of warriors), farther along the coast. From the viewpoint you can also see the islands of Lehua and Niʻihau in the distance.

After crossing the stream, take the short side trip to the beach. It is crescent shaped, with small caves at each end. In back of the beach is the native low-lying shrub *naupaka kahakai.* It has bright-green, fleshy leaves, and white half-flowers with purple streaks. Its round white fruits float in the ocean, helping to spread the species to other islands.

Hanakāpīʻai (bay sprinkling food) is the first valley along the Nā Pali Coast to be settled by early Hawaiians. They lived near the beach and grew *kalo* (taro) and other crops in *loʻi* (irrigated terraces) back in the valley. You can still see the rock walls of *loʻi* on the way to the falls.

In the late 1800s, Hanakāpī'ai was the site of a coffee plantation, complete with a mill. The falls trail passes the wild descendants of the original trees. They have glossy, dark-green leaves and white flowers. Their fruit is red, drying to black or brown. Coffee is still commercially grown on the Big Island, where it is sold as Kona coffee.

In the forest, look and listen for the white-rumped shama. It is black on top with a chestnut-colored breast and a long black-and-white tail. The shama has a variety of beautiful songs and often mimics other birds. A native of Malaysia, the shama has become widespread in introduced forests, such as this one.

Also along the falls trail are extensive groves of mountain apple ('ōhi'a 'ai). They have dark, oblong, shiny leaves. In spring their purple flowers carpet the trail. The delicious pink or red fruit usually ripens in late July or early August. If none are in reach, shake the tree gently and try to catch the apples as they come down. The species is native to Malaysia and was brought over by early Polynesians.

Hanakāpī'ai Falls is a welcome sight after the muddy slog up the valley. Step out on the ledges near the stream to view the falls from a distance. As the trail finally peters out, you emerge from the forest into a vast amphitheater at the back of the valley. At center stage is a dark-green, circular pool. Above, the waterfall cascades from a narrow notch in the valley wall. On the sides, the towering, fluted cliffs rise over 2,000 feet to Pōhākea (white stone) peak and Hono o Nāpali (brow of the cliffs).

Take the long swim to the base of the falls. Look for koa'e kea, the white-tailed tropic bird, soaring overhead. Or just sit and enjoy the wild, rugged beauty of this remote spot.

Instead of taking the falls trail, you can continue on the Kalalau Trail. A good turnaround place is the highest point on the trail, marked by a huge boulder overlooking Ho'olulu Valley. Total distance round-trip for that option is 6.5 miles. The entire coastal trail is 11 miles long one way and makes a memorable backpack, described under Kalalau, the next hike.

# 26

# Kalalau Backpack

| LENGTH: | 2–5 days, 22.0-mile round-trip |
|---|---|
| ELEVATION GAIN: | 2,400 feet |
| DANGER: | Medium |
| SUITABLE FOR: | Intermediate, Expert |
| LOCATION: | Kauaʻi: Nā Pali Coast State Park, Hono O Nā Pali Natural Area Reserve |
| TOPO MAP: | Hāʻena |

## HIGHLIGHTS

Kalalau is the classic tourist backpack in Hawaiʻi. The route winds along the rugged Nā Pali Coast past vertical sea cliffs and into deep, lush gulches. Along the way are rushing streams, cascading waterfalls, and the surging ocean below. At the end is a wide sandy beach backed by the towering, fluted walls of Kalalau Valley.

## PLANNING

Summer (May–October) is the best time of year to take this trip. The weather is usually drier then, the streams are easier to cross, and the beaches have lots of sand. Whenever you go, be prepared for hot sun, rain, and high water.

Decide how many days you want to spend along the coast. The narrative below describes a leisurely four-day trip with a night at Hanakoa and two nights and a layover day at

Kalalau Beach. The minimum stay is two days, one in and one out, but don't even think of doing the trip in that short a time. You are going to be very tired and very disappointed that you didn't spend an extra day at Kalalau.

Bring a tent and put all your gear in plastic bags. Pack a light sleeping bag or liner because the nights can be chilly, especially in winter. Take mosquito repellent if you plan to camp at Hanakoa. The dry, windy campsites at Kalalau Beach are relatively free of the pest. Tabis (Japanese reef walkers) or other water footwear are perfect for crossing the streams and exploring the slippery, rocky shoreline.

Pick up a copy of *On the Nā Pali Coast* by Kathy Valier. It provides a detailed and fascinating look at the geology, plants, and historical sites along the route. The book is available online and in tourist shops and bookstores in Honolulu and on Kauaʻi.

This trip requires an overnight permit issued by the Division of State Parks. To make a reservation online, visit their website at http://dlnr.hawaii.gov/dsp/hiking/kauai/kalalau-trail. You can also obtain permits in person at the State Parks offices in Honolulu and Līhue. Check the appendix for their address and phone number. The maximum stay is currently five nights, and camping is only allowed at Hanakoa Valley and Kalalau Beach. This backpacking trip is very popular, especially in summer, so get your permits well in advance.

The trailhead at Kēʻē Beach has restrooms, outside showers, and a water fountain where you can fill your water bottles. Do not leave a car overnight there, as break-ins are a common occurrence. If you must, don't leave any valuables in your car. As an alternative, check online for companies offering shuttle service to the trailhead.

Be forewarned that Kalalau is a wilderness Waikīkī. It's crowded, noisy, and a bit trashy, but still great fun. If you are looking for a coastal trip with more solitude, try Halapē on the Big Island.

**Distance:** (Līhuʻe to Kēʻē Beach) 37 miles
**Driving Time:** 1 1/4 hours

From Līhuʻe take Kūhiō Hwy (Rte 56 north) toward Hanalei.
Cross Wailua River on a bridge.
Drive through the town of Kapaʻa.
Continue on Kūhiō Hwy along the windward coast.
Pass the turnoff to Kīlauea Lighthouse on the right and then cross a long bridge over the Kalihiwai River.
Pass Princeville Airport on the left and Princeville Center on the right. Route 56 becomes Route 560 west.
Descend into Hanalei Valley and cross the river on a one-lane bridge.
Drive through Hanalei town.
Cross a series of short one-lane bridges.
Enter Hāʻena State Park.
Reach the end of the road at Kēʻē Beach (map point A) (UTM 4Q 439959E, 2457364N) (Lat/Long N22.22064, W159.58257). The state park has restrooms, drinking water, and outdoor showers.

## DAY ONE—KĒʻĒ BEACH TO HANAKOA VALLEY

**Length:** 6.0 miles
**Elevation Gain (Loss):** 1,200 (750) feet

The route today is not long, but it does involve two major stream crossings and numerous elevation changes. The trail to Hanakāpīʻai Valley is wide, rutted, and well used by day hikers. Beyond the valley, the trail becomes rough and narrow but also less crowded.

Before starting the hike, walk to Kēʻē (avoidance) Beach. A short stroll along the beach to the right leads to a good first

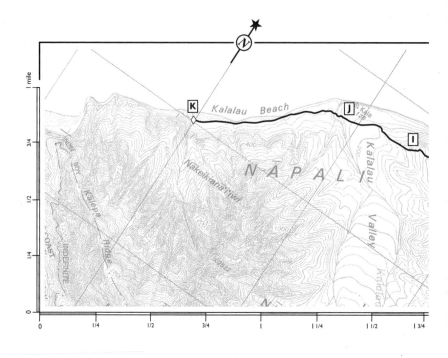

view of Nā Pali (the cliffs) Coast. To the left below the *pali* are the remains of a *heiau* (religious site) and a *hālau* hula platform where the ancient hula was performed.

The Kalalau Trail was originally an old Hawaiian route connecting the valleys along the coast. The trail was improved in the 1800s and the 1930s. The stone paving on the first section dates from that last upgrade.

About a half mile in is the first spectacular view of the Nā Pali Coast. Deep valleys alternate with vertical sea cliffs. Rainfall runoff created the valleys and wave action the cliffs. Where stream erosion has proceeded faster than sea erosion, the stream flows into the ocean at sea level, as at Hanakāpī'ai and Kalalau. The reverse situation creates a hanging valley with a waterfall cascading into the ocean, as at Hanakoa. From the viewpoint you can also see the islands of Lehua and Ni'ihau in the distance.

The first valley you reach is Hanakāpī'ai (bay sprinkled food). It has a curved white sand beach in summer and a long side trail leading into the valley to a lovely waterfall. Hanakāpī'ai

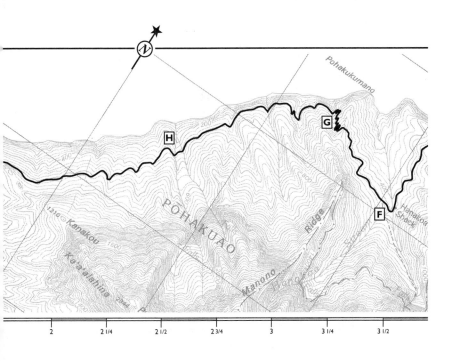

Stream is fast flowing and can rise suddenly. Do not cross if the water is much above your knees.

The early Hawaiians did settle in Hanakāpī'ai Valley. They lived near the beach and grew *kalo* (taro) in *lo'i* (rock terraces) back in the valley. In the late 1800s Hanakāpī'ai was the site of a coffee plantation, complete with a mill.

After climbing steeply out of Hanakāpī'ai Valley, the trail reaches its highest point above a small cove. The route then works into and out of two hanging valleys, Ho'olulu (protected bay) and Waiahuakua. The latter has several terraced sites near the trail but no signs of permanent habitation.

While entering Waiahuakua Valley, look for the native *lama* tree. Its oblong, pointed leaves are reddish when young and then dark green and leathery when mature. The fruits are green, then yellow, and finally bright red when fully ripe. *Lama* was sacred to Laka, goddess of the hula. Early Hawaiians used the hard, light-colored wood in temple construction and in hula performances.

The damp campground at Hanakoa (warrior bay) lies deep

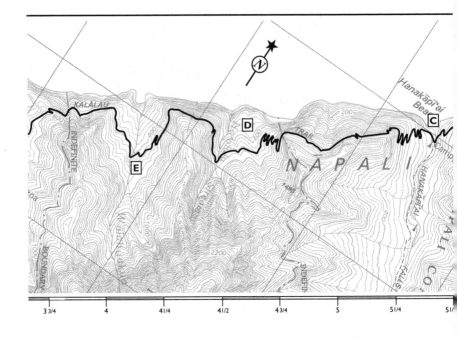

3 3/4     4     41/4     41/2     43/4     5     51/4     51/

in the valley, well away from the coast. The best tent sites are located in a terraced area near the picnic shelter on the far side of the stream. Wherever you camp, expect to be harassed by the resident mosquito population.

Water is from Hanakoa Stream and should be boiled, filtered, or chemically treated. Above and below the trail crossing are small swimming holes. If you have time and energy after setting up camp, take the half-mile hike to idyllic Hanakoa Falls. The route starts at a signed junction just before the shelter.

The back of Hanakoa Valley resembles a huge amphitheater. At the center is a circular pool, perhaps the largest in the state. Ringing the pool are four vertical waterfall chutes. Hanakoa Falls cascades down the chute on the right, which is usually the only one with water. Try the long swim to the base of the falls. Look for *koaʻe kea*, the white-tailed tropicbird, as it soars along the cliffs above. Enjoy the wild, rugged beauty of this remote spot.

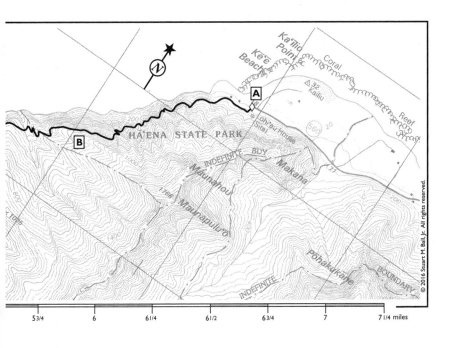

| | | | | | | |
|---|---|---|---|---|---|---|
| 5 3/4 | 6 | 6 1/4 | 6 1/2 | 6 3/4 | 7 | 7 1/4 miles |

## ROUTE DESCRIPTION

Take the Kalalau Trail that starts on the left just before the end of the paved road across from mile marker 10.

Pass some interpretive signs on the left and a bulletin board displaying trail maps and information on the right.

Climb steadily along the Makana cliffs above Kēʻē Beach. The trail is very rocky and slippery when wet. Some sections are paved with smooth stones. Look for the native shrub, *naupaka kahakai,* with its white half-flowers.

Work into and out of two small ravines. The first is dotted with *hala* trees and the second with *kukui* trees and *kī* (ti) plants.

Around the corner from the second ravine is the first good view of the Nā Pali Coast.

Work into and out of two more gulches. The last one has a small stream.

The trail straightens out for a while (map point B). Water seeps from the cliffs above.

Descend gradually through another ravine. On the left is a cleared area used for emergency helicopter landings.

Descend into a double gulch on a series of eroded switchbacks.

Cross two streams and climb out of the gulch.

Descend into Hanakāpīʻai Valley on two switchbacks.

Pass a faded brown-and-yellow tsunami marker.

Cross Hanakāpīʻai Stream by rock hopping or wading. As always, do not ford the stream if the water is much above your knees (map point C).

Climb the opposite bank and reach a signed junction. Turn sharp left upstream. (The trail to the right leads to the beach.)

Shortly afterward reach a second signed junction near a lone ironwood tree in a grove of *hala*. Keep right on the Kalalau Trail. (To the left, the Hanakāpīʻai Falls Trail heads up Hanakāpīʻai Valley to the falls.)

Immediately pass an elevated compost toilet on the right.

Pass another faded tsunami marker on the right.

Climb out of Hanakāpīʻai Valley on eleven switchbacks. Along the trail are superb views of the beach and the valley.

Switchback six more times and then contour along the coast beneath dark cliffs.

Pass a tiny pool at the base of a rock wall in a ravine. This area is known as Keanuenue.

Resume climbing on four short switchbacks.

Enter Hono o Nā Pali Natural Area Reserve.

Shortly reach the high point on the trail by a huge boulder overlooking Hoʻolulu Valley (elevation 800 feet) (map point D). The sharp peak on the left is Pōhākea.

Descend into Hoʻolulu Valley on ten switchbacks.

Cross three intermittent tributaries of Hoʻolulu Stream.

Cross rocky, intermittent Hoʻolulu Stream.

Climb out of Hoʻolulu Valley.

Contour below near-vertical rock cliffs. Along the trail are good views back toward Kēʻē Beach.

Reach an overlook of Waiahuakua Valley.

Initially, climb into the valley and then descend on two switchbacks. Look for a remnant forest of native *lama* trees.

Cross three intermittent tributaries of Waiahuakua Stream.

Cross Waiahuakua Stream itself (map point E).

Cross two more intermittent tributaries.

Leaving the valley behind, climb steadily along sheer sea cliffs.

Ascend on two switchbacks.

Reach an overlook of Hanakoa Valley and Falls.

Descend very gradually into the valley.

On the right, pass a large mango tree and then a cleared area used by helicopters.

Pass a picnic shelter on the left and an elevated compost toilet on the right.

Ford the two forks of Hanakoa Stream (elevation 450 feet) (map point F) (UTM 4Q 436014E, 2454087N)) (Lat/Long N22.19089, W159.62072).

Shortly, reach a signed junction with the Hanakoa Falls Trail. Set up camp at one of the sites on the left near the junction and another picnic shelter.

## DAY TWO—HANAKOA VALLEY TO KALALAU BEACH

**LENGTH:** 5.0 miles
**ELEVATION LOSS:** 450 feet

The hike today to Kalalau Beach is very scenic and a bit scary. After leaving Hanakoa Valley, the route becomes drier and more open, with breathtaking views all around. However, the trail has some very narrow and eroded sections over loose rock and dirt. Watch your footing religiously; don't hike and sightsee at the same time.

While climbing out of the gulch with the small waterfall, watch for *'iliahi*, the native sandalwood tree. Its small leaves are dull green and appear wilted. *'Iliahi* is partially parasitic, with outgrowths on its roots that steal nutrients from nearby plants. Early Hawaiians ground the fragrant heartwood into a powder to perfume their *kapa*. Beginning in the late 1700s, sandalwood was indiscriminately cut down and exported to China to make incense and furniture. The trade ended around 1840 when the forests were depleted of *'iliahi*.

In the next gulch you can easily recognize sisal by its sword-like leaves. They were once made into rope, and the plant was introduced into Hawai'i in the late 1800s for that purpose. Sisal puts up a tall flower stalk every ten years or so where the baby plants form.

From Pu'ukula Lookout is the first spectacular view of Kalalau (the straying) Beach and Valley. Look *mauka* (inland) for feral goats, which are responsible for the denuded hillsides nearby. From the lookout, descend steadily to Kalalau Stream on the loose red dirt, partially contained by plastic steps. The stream is fast flowing and can rise suddenly. As always, do not cross if the water is much above your knees.

The campsites at Kalalau are strung along the half-mile beach from the helipad to the waterfall. At the near end of the beach past the first toilet are some pleasant sites in a *milo* grove. Toward the middle of the beach the sites are more exposed and sociable. The sites below the cliffs near the waterfall look attractive, but sometimes they get bombarded with small and not so small rocks. Wherever you camp, make sure you have some nearby shade, as the afternoon sun can be hot.

The campground has two elevated compost toilets spaced evenly behind the beach. Water is available from Kalalau Stream or from Ho'ole'a Falls near the far end of the beach. Boil, filter, or chemically treat the water, as usual. The waterfall also makes an excellent shower.

Swim in the ocean only in summer. Even then, be careful, as the waves and currents are very powerful. Keep in mind that the Nā Pali Coast is subject to tsunami (sea waves) generated by earthquakes. If you feel one or if the ocean starts to recede, move to high ground immediately.

Climb gradually out of Hanakoa Valley.

Cross over the end of Manono Ridge. A short path leads to a spectacular lookout with views along the coast in both directions; Kalalau, however, remains hidden by the intervening cliffs.

Descend into a gulch on ten precarious switchbacks (map point G). The narrow trail hugs the cliff above the ocean. Watch your footing constantly over the loose dirt and rock.

Work into and out of two more gulches. In the second one, cross a tiny stream and switchback several times. Look for dikes in the exposed rock.

Reach a windy, open overlook.

Descend into and climb out of another gulch. The trail crosses a stream and is deeply eroded in some sections.

After passing another lookout, traverse a narrow, eroded, and crumbly section. Watch for feral goats upslope.

On the left, pass a shady but illegal campsite with a helicopter landing area in front.

Descend into and climb out of a deep ravine with a fast-flowing stream.

Contour through scrub guava and lantana. Look for a sea arch below.

Descend into a deep, lush gulch with native *lama* (map point H).

While climbing out of the gulch, pass the rock walls of an ancient *lo'i* (taro terrace) on the left.

Cross a hot, dry gulch dotted with sisal.

Contour around the back of two small ravines.

Descend into a larger gulch and cross a stream. Turn left uphill, paralleling the stream.

By a small waterfall, switchback to the right and climb out of the gulch. On the way up, look for *'iliahi,* the native sandalwood tree.

Reach another superb overlook. Below is a rock with a

double hole, and beyond is Secret Beach. Above are the rocky, turreted ridges of the Nā Pali Coast.

Contour around the back of a deep, narrow ravine.

Work into and out of a gulch lined with *kukui* trees.

Reach another lookout. The narrow ridges above are nearly vertical.

Traverse a series of small, ill-defined gulches.

Reach a grassy, eroded overlook known as Puʻukula near the end of Kaʻaʻalahina Ridge (map point I). In front is the broad expanse of Kalalau Valley with its white sand beach. Above is massive Kanakou peak.

Descend a red, eroded slope, gradually at first and then more steeply. Some sections have plastic steps, but the trail is washed out in spots and deeply grooved in others.

At the bottom of the slope, bear left, skirting a grassy area.

The trail winds through a forest of Java plum.

Descend steeply to Kalalau Stream.

Ford the stream where it splits to form an island.

Turn right downstream.

Climb the bank, angling away from the stream.

Reach a signed junction (map point J) (UTM 4Q 432801E, 2452618N) (Lat/Long N22.1775, W159.65183). Turn right, toward the beach. (To the left is the Kalalau Valley Trail, which leads into the valley.)

Reach the shore and turn left along the vegetation line.

Cross a small gully.

Begin passing turnoffs to the camping area in the trees on the left.

Pass an open, grassy area used by helicopters.

Pass a side trail to an elevated compost toilet.

The trail splits (map point K). The left fork leads to a second helipad, a storage cabin, another toilet, several campsites below the cliffs, and Hoʻoleʻa waterfall. The right fork goes straight to the beach.

| | |
|---|---|
| **Length:** | 4.5 miles |
| **Elevation Gain (Loss):** | 1,500 (1,500) feet |

The hike today up valley involves some elevation gain, but the climb is gradual. The route to Big Pool is wide open and easy to follow. The trail to Waimakemake Falls is narrow, rough, and obscure in spots.

Retrace your steps to the junction just before Kalalau Stream (map point J) and keep right on the Kalalau Valley Trail. On the left, pass an eroded, rocky slope, which provides a superb view of the entire valley. After crossing a side stream, the trail splits. Turn sharp right for Big Pool. (The left fork leads to a series of swimming holes, called Outlaw Pools.) Cross Kalalau Stream and then negotiate a narrow trail to Big Pool.

Big Pool is not all that big, but it is deep, and the water is cool and inviting. Its setting is idyllic, nestled below two miniature waterfalls and the towering west wall of the valley. The rock slabs next to the pool are perfect for stretching out on.

Along the way to Big Pool, you pass through several *lo'i* (rock terraces), now overgrown with Java plum and other introduced trees. The rock walls originally enclosed *kalo* (taro) patches, cultivated by the Hawaiians. They transported their crop by canoe along the coast to trade for other staples. The Hawaiians used the wood from the tangled *hau* trees along the trail to make the outriggers for their narrow canoes.

After a refreshing dip at Big Pool, backtrack down the valley trail for about five minutes to an obscure junction with the falls trail. On the left, look for a collapsed rock wall and a downed guava log with some hand-painted directions. Turn right to get to the falls.

Waimakemake consists of two upper falls and one lower one. The trail reaches the base of the lower cascade with its tiny pool. The falls are fed by springs in the cliffs above. Vertical rock dikes trap water in the porous lava and release it over the falls. Waimakemake is also known as Davis Falls, named

KALALAU BACKPACK ❊ HANALEI

after Richard H. Davis, mountain man and explorer from the Hawaiian Trail and Mountain Club on Oʻahu.

On the way back to your campsite, take a short side trip to a *heiau* (religious site) on the bluff between Kalalau Stream and Beach. Just after the signed junction with the coast trail, turn right and up on a faint trail through some boulders. Climb gradually to a grass-covered plateau with the remains of the *heiau* just below. To get back to the beach, descend the front of the plateau and turn left.

Back at the beach, make the most of the rest of the afternoon. Take a swim or a snooze. Enjoy the stunning view of blue ocean, white sand, and red, black, and green cliffs. In the evening, watch the sun set over the Pacific Ocean and the stars come out. Life doesn't get much better than this!

## DAY FOUR—KALALAU BEACH TO KĒʻĒ BEACH

| | |
|---|---|
| **Length:** | 11.0 miles |
| **Elevation Gain (Loss):** | 1,200 (1,200) feet |

Retrace your steps to Kēʻē Beach. Start early to avoid the hot sun during the steep climb out of Kalalau Valley.

Down the mountain, Mauna Loa in back. Mauna Kea hike, Hawaiʻi. *(Photo by Lynne Masuyama)*

Waipiʻo Bay and Valley. Waipiʻo Valley hike, Hawaiʻi. *(Photo by Deborah Uchida)*

Through the native rain forest. Kīlauea Crater Rim hike, Hawai'i.
*(Photo by John Hoover)*

Idyllic beach fringed with palm trees. Halapē backpack, Hawai'i. *(Photo by Deborah Uchida)*

Crossing the crater. Kīlauea Iki hike, Hawai'i. *(Photo by Kelvin Lu)*

Down Hilina Pali. Ka'aha hike, Hawai'i. *(Photo by Kelvin Lu)*

Hanakāpīʻai Falls. Hanakāpīʻai Falls hike, Kauaʻi. *(Photo by Lynne Masuyama)*

RIGHT: At Kilohana Lookout.
Alakaʻi Swamp hike, Kauaʻi.
*(Photo by John Hoover)*

LEFT: Kawaikōi Stream.
Kawaikōi Stream hike, Kauaʻi.
*(Photo by Deborah Uchida)*

RIGHT: Up the ridge.
Kuilau Ridge hike, Kauaʻi.
*(Photo by Lynne Masuyama)*

ABOVE: Strolling along Kalalau Beach. Kalalau backpack, Kauaʻi.
*(Photo by Kelvin Lu)*

BELOW: Double rainbow over the Nā Pali coast. Kalalau backpack, Kauaʻi.
*(Photo by Kelvin Lu)*

OPPOSITE PAGE, TOP: Waiʻaleʻale in the clear. Powerline Trail, Kauaʻi.
*(Photo by Lynne Masuyama)* MIDDLE: Overlooking the canyon. Waimea
Canyon Vista hike, Kauaʻi. *(Photo by Kelvin Lu)* BOTTOM: Leaving Kalalau
Valley. Kalalau backpack, Kauaʻi. *(Photo by Kelvin Lu)*

ABOVE: Climbing out of Kalalau Valley. Kalalau backpack, Kauaʻi.
*(Photo by Kelvin Lu)*

LEFT: Along the Kanaio coast. Hoapili Trail hike, Maui.
*(Photo by Lynne Masuyama)*

OPPOSITE PAGE, TOP: Down the switchbacks. Haleakalā backback, Maui.
*(Photo by Deborah Uchida)*

BOTTOM: Clouds riding up Koʻolau Gap. Sliding Sands–Halemauʻu hike, Maui.
*(Photo by Deborah Uchida)*

ABOVE: Strolling through the pine forest. Waihou Spring hike, Maui.
(Photo by Joyce Oka)

LEFT: Waimoku Falls.
ʻOheʻo Gulch hike, Maui.
(Photo by Lynne Masuyama)

ABOVE: Along the Hāna coast. Ke Ala Loa O Maui/Piʻilani Trail, Maui. *(Photo by Lynne Masuyama)*

BELOW: Walking the sea cliffs. ʻŌhai Loop, Maui. *(Photo by Lynne Masuyama)*

ABOVE: Kulana'ahane Trailhead. Kamananui (Moanalua) Valley hike, O'ahu.
*(Photo by Nathan Yuen)*

RIGHT: Heading for the summit through native *koa* forest. Mānana hike, O'ahu.
*(Photo by Nathan Yuen)*

Second and third peaks. Olomana hike, Oʻahu. *(Photo by Lynne Masuyama)*

ABOVE: Crossing Kahawainui Stream. Kahana Valley hike, Oʻahu.
*(Photo by Lynne Masuyama)*

OPPOSITE PAGE: Koʻolau cliffs and waterfall chutes. Maunawili hike, Oʻahu.
*(Photo by Deborah Uchida)*

Tide pools along the rugged leeward coast. Kaʻena Point hike, Oʻahu.
*(Photo by Nathan Yuen)*

# MAUI

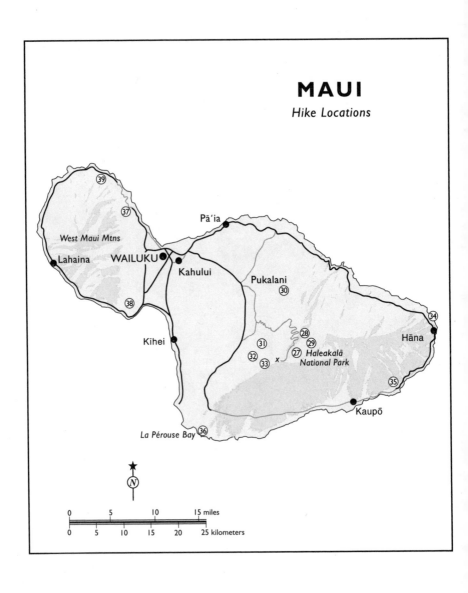

# MAUI

*Hike Locations*

39

37

Pā'ia

West Maui Mtns

Lahaina

WAILUKU

Kahului

Pukalani

30

38

34

Kīhei

28

31

29

Hāna

32

33

x

27 Haleakalā
National Park

35

Kaupō

La Pérouse Bay 36

*N*

| 0 | | 5 | | 10 | | 15 miles |
| 0 | 5 | 10 | 15 | 20 | 25 kilometers |

27

# Sliding Sands–Halemau'u

| | |
|---|---|
| LENGTH: | 12.0-mile loop |
| ELEVATION GAIN: | 1,500 feet |
| DANGER: | Low |
| SUITABLE FOR: | Expert |
| LOCATION: | Maui: Haleakalā National Park |
| TOPO MAP: | Kilohana, Nāhiku |

## HIGHLIGHTS

This magnificent loop hike winds through the vast, eroded crater of Haleakalā, a once active volcano. Along the way are towering cliffs and colorful cinder cones. Much in evidence are two threatened species, *nēnē*, the Hawaiian goose, and *'āhinahina,* the Haleakalā silversword.

## TRAILHEAD DIRECTIONS

**DISTANCE:** (Kahului to Haleakalā Visitor Center) 37 miles
**DRIVING TIME:** 1 1/4 hours

From Kahului take Hāna Hwy (Rte 36).
At the first major intersection, turn right on Haleakalā Hwy (Rte 37).

Ascend gradually through sugarcane fields.

Pass turnoffs to Pukalani on the right and Makawao on the left.

Turn left on Rte 377 (still Haleakalā Hwy).

Climb steadily through lush pastureland and stands of fragrant eucalyptus trees.

Pass Kula Lodge on the right.

Turn left on Haleakalā Crater Rd. (Rte 378).

Ascend steeply on a series of short switchbacks through pasture belonging to Haleakalā Ranch.

Enter Haleakalā National Park and pay the fee at the entrance station.

Pass Park Headquarters Visitor Center on the right. It has restrooms, drinking water, and trail information.

Ascend steadily on a series of long switchbacks.

On the left by the fourth switchback, pass the parking area for Halemau'u trailhead, where the hike ends (elevation 7,990 feet) (map point M) (UTM 4Q 788596E, 2297211N) (Lat/Long N20.75232, W156.2285).

Pass Leleiwi and Kalahaku Overlooks, both on the left.

Turn left into the parking area for Haleakalā Visitor Center. Leave your car in the near right corner of the lot close to a horse-loading ramp (elevation 9,740 feet) (map point A) (UTM 4Q 786359E, 2292986N) (Lat/Long N20.71453, W156.25065). If you have two cars, drop off people and packs and shuttle one car back to Halemau'u trailhead. The visitor center has restrooms.

## ROUTE DESCRIPTION

The Sliding Sands Trail starts by a wooden bulletin board next to the horse-loading ramp.

Briefly parallel the paved road leading to Pu'u'ula'ula (Red Hill), the summit of Haleakalā at 10,023 feet.

Bear left away from the road around Pā Kao'ao, also known as White Hill.

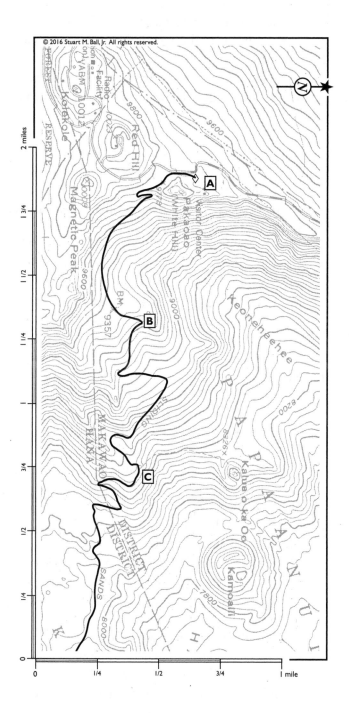

Reach the rim of the crater and the first of many awesome views. On the horizon to the right is the peak of Mauna Kea on the Big Island.

Descend gradually on five long, lazy switchbacks. The trail crosses an area of gray-brown and then red-brown cinders known as Keonehe'ehe'e.

Begin looking for native 'āhinahina (silverswords) on the right. The only other vegetation along the trail is the native shrubs pūkiawe and kūpaoa, also known as na'ena'e.

Reach an unmarked junction (map point B). Turn right between two boulders. The side trail straight ahead leads down to a view into Ka Lu'u o ka 'Ō'ō cone.

Continue the descent on three switchbacks. The trail briefly crosses rough 'a'ā lava. Watch your footing on the loose rock.

Cross a relatively flat area covered with red cinder. Silverswords line the trail. Kama'oli'i and Pu'u o Māui cones are on the left at a distance.

Climb briefly past Pu'u o Pele, a red cinder cone close by on the left.

Descend to the crater floor on two switchbacks through kīlau (bracken) ferns (map point C).

Reach a signed junction by a hitching post and a māmane tree (map point D). Turn left on a side trail across the crater. (The Sliding Sands Trail continues straight, to Kapalaoa Cabin.)

Cross an old 'a'ā flow partially buried by cinders.

Pass a small patch of silverswords. Also in this area are native 'ōhelo and kūkaenēnē shrubs.

Climb steadily up the left side of Ka Moa o Pele cone on red cinders. Dead ahead, at the top of the saddle, is Halāli'i cone. In the distance along the rim is Hanakauhi peak (elevation 8,907 feet).

Descend briefly to a signed four-way junction (map point E). Continue straight, around Halāli'i cone in a counterclockwise direction to Kawilinau. (The trail to the left is a shortcut to Hōlua. The trail to the right heads back across the crater to

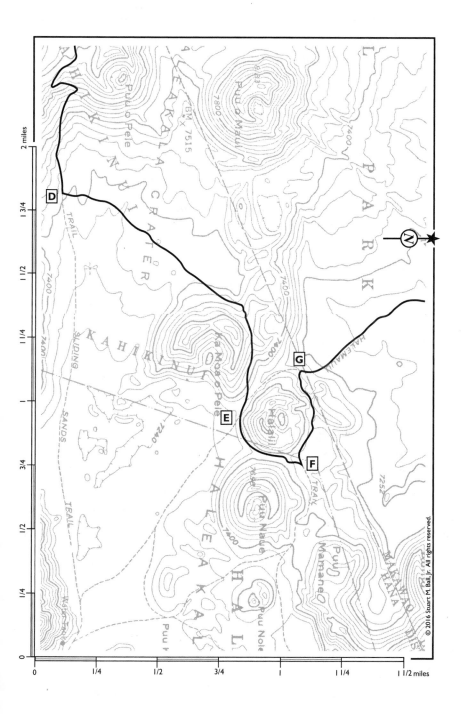

Kapalaoa Cabin.) The colorful, rectangular, spatter rampart on the left is informally known as Pele's Pigpen.

Circle Halāli'i cone. On the right is a large red-gray cone known as Pu'u Naue. Look for Kapalaoa Cabin at the foot of the crater wall.

Reach a signed junction at Kawilinau, formerly known as Bottomless Pit (map point F) (UTM 4Q 792002E, 2293826N) (Lat/Long N20.72124, W156.19638). Turn left on the Halemau'u Trail toward Hōlua. (To the right the trail leads to Palikū Cabin.)

Continue to circle the base of Halāli'i cone. At its far side are views down Ko'olau Gap and across the crater to Kalahaku Pali and Leleiwi Pali.

Reach a signed junction (map point G). Bear right to Hōlua. (The left fork is the shortcut mentioned previously.)

Descend briefly and cross a basin covered with black sand, cinders, and lava rock.

Climb out of the basin on red cinders.

Shortly afterward, reach a signed junction (map point H). Turn right on Silversword Loop. (The main trail continues straight, to Hōlua.)

Wind through red-brown cinders dotted with silverswords.

Reach a signed junction with the main trail and turn right on it. Just ahead on the left is a native *'iliahi* (sandalwood tree).

Cross an old *'a'ā* flow partially covered with native vegetation. Look for *māmane* trees and *'a'ali'i, 'ōhelo, kūkaenēnē,* and *pūkiawe* shrubs. In the distance you can see Hōlua Cabin nestled against the crater wall.

Descend briefly on a rough trail.

Reach a signed junction near Hōlua Cabin (map point I). Turn right on the main trail. (The side trail straight ahead leads to the cabin and campground.)

Descend Ko'olau Gap, gradually at first and then more steeply through ridges of jumbled-up *'a'ā* lava.

Work left toward the crater wall as the angle of descent eases.

Cross a meadow covered with evening primrose.

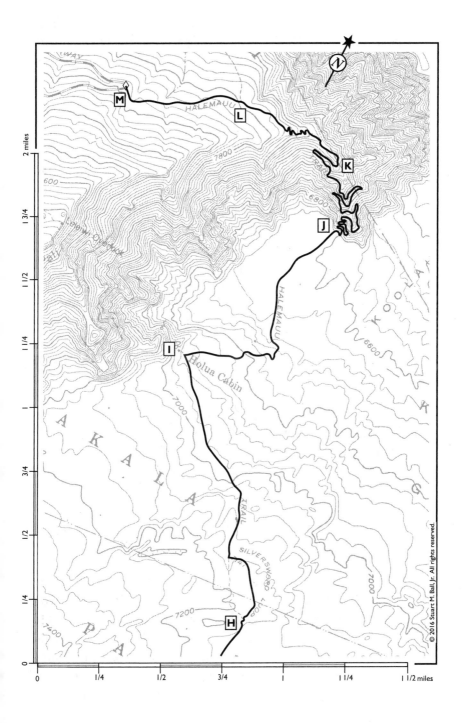

Reach the base of the cliff by a wooden gate and a hitching post (map point J). Go through the gate, closing it behind you. Begin climbing the crater wall on seven short switchbacks. The views back into the crater are spectacular. On the way up, look for 'ama'u ferns, whose young fronds are bright red.

Switchbacks eight through twelve are much longer and repeatedly cross a prominent side ridge in the cliff. After the twelfth zigzag is a particularly fine overlook. Below, Ko'olau Gap drops steeply to the ocean. Across the gap is Hanakauhi peak and the north rim of the crater. Upslope are several of the cones you passed by earlier in the hike.

After the twelfth switchback, briefly follow the level side ridge (map point K).

As the slope steepens, resume climbing on a series of short switchbacks. On the right is the park boundary fence.

After the last switchback (yes!), reach a signed junction (map point L). Keep left on the main trail. (The supply trail to the right leads down to Hosmer Grove Campground.)

Ascend gradually along the outer slope of Haleakalā on a rough, rocky trail. Look for *hinahina*, a native geranium with toothed, silvery leaves.

Reach Halemau'u trailhead and parking lot (elevation 7,990 feet) (map point M) (UTM 4Q 788596E, 2297211N) (Lat/Long N20.75232, W156.2285). Nearby is a fancy pit toilet. If your only car is parked at Sliding Sands trailhead, hitchhike back up to it.

## NOTES

The Sliding Sands–Halemau'u loop is the best day hike on Maui. The winding route provides a close-up look at the volcanic features of Haleakalā (house of the sun) crater and at the plants and birds that live there. The route also provides a challenge, starting with a long descent on loose cinders and ending with a steep climb on narrow switchbacks. Get an early start because of the high mileage and the many points of interest.

Leaving the visitor center parking lot, you quickly reach the crater rim with its panoramic view. To the left (northeast) are Kalahaku (proclaim the lord) Pali (cliff) and Leleiwi (bone altar) Pali. Beyond is Koʻolau (windward) Gap, descending to the north coast of Maui. To the east at the far end of the crater lies green Palikū (vertical cliff). To the right of Palikū and out of sight is Kaupō (landing at night) Gap, descending to the south coast of the island.

Haleakalā is a dormant volcano, but its "crater" is not really a volcanic one. The vast double amphitheater before you is more the result of wind and water erosion than volcanic activity. From opposite sides of the island, two streams eroded headward and met to form a "crater." Lava from vents near the summit partially filled both deep valleys to create the wide Koʻolau and Kaupō Gaps. More recent volcanic activity produced the colorful cinder cones dotting the crater floor. Haleakalā last erupted in 1790, when two small flows from the southwest rift zone outside the crater reached the ocean.

Much of the loop hike becomes visible as you start the descent to the crater floor. Look for the Sliding Sands Trail in front and below. Try to pick out the Halemauʻu (grass house) Trail as it emerges from a jumble of cones and traverses Koʻolau Gap to Hōlua (sled) Cabin. Beyond the cabin are the switchbacks climbing the crater wall.

As you are sliding down the sand and cinder, watch for the park's signature plant, ʻāhinahina, the Haleakalā silversword. It has narrow silver green leaves and a tall flower stalk. The leaves are covered with tiny hairs to conserve moisture and protect the plant from the intense sun. Other adaptations include a deep taproot to anchor the plant in high winds and a wide network of surface roots to collect water. The silversword usually grows for fifteen to twenty years before flowering. The flower stalks usually appear in summer or early fall and have purple blossoms. After the seeds develop, the entire plant dies. Silverswords are endemic to Hawaiʻi, meaning they are found nowhere else. Don't approach mature plants too closely, and don't step on the baby ones.

Also on the trail is the native shrub *kūpaoa* or *na'ena'e*. It has woody, erect stems and stiff leaves shaped like rounded triangles. Notice that *kūpaoa* and *'āhinahina* have crossed to form several hybrid plants with green swords and an upright posture.

The middle section of the route meanders through a group of large cinder cones dotted with silverswords. According to Hawaiian legend, the cones are the handiwork of Pele, the goddess of fire. She stopped at Haleakalā on her way to the Big Island, where she currently resides in Kīlauea (spewing) Volcano. Pele created the cinder cones and Kawilinau, formerly known as Bottomless Pit, with her magic digging tool, Pā'oa.

After walking Silversword Loop, check out the small native *'iliahi* (sandalwood tree). It has stiff, olive-green leaves and red buds becoming cream-colored flowers. *'Iliahi* is partially parasitic, with outgrowths on its roots that steal nutrients from nearby plants. This particular species is found only in Haleakalā.

The native dryland vegetation at the far side of Ko'olau Gap is a welcome site after the colorful but desolate cones. The plants have taken hold on an older *'a'ā* flow that receives some moisture from the clouds advancing up the gap. Look for *māmane* trees and *'a'ali'i*, *pūkiawe*, and *'ōhelo* shrubs. *Māmane* has downy, oblong leaflets and clusters of bright yellow flowers. *'A'ali'i* has narrow, shiny leaves and red seed capsules. *Pūkiawe* has tiny, rigid leaves and small white, pink, or red berries. *'Ōhelo* has rounded leaves and juicy red-yellow berries, about the size of blueberries.

The area around Hōlua (sled) Cabin makes a good rest stop before the climb out of the crater. Just beyond the cabin are a pit toilet, a water faucet, and the Hōlua Campground. The water should be filtered or chemically treated. The cabin is solely for the use of overnight hikers with reservations. Check the Halaekalā Backpack chapter for information about staying there.

At Hōlua Cabin you may see *nēnē*, the Hawaiian goose. The *nēnē* has a black face and head and a gray-brown body. It lives on dry, rugged lava flows at high elevation and so has lost much of the webbing on its feet. Like its Canadian counterpart, the *nēnē* is a strong flyer and often honks in mid-flight. The *nēnē* is a threatened species and should be treated with respect. Don't feed them.

The Halemauʻu Trail climbs out of the crater on more than twenty switchbacks. The path is graded, although narrow in spots. While ascending, maintain a slow but steady pace. Stop to rest occasionally and admire the view, if there is any. In the early afternoon, clouds frequently ride up Koʻolau Gap and shroud the cliffs in swirling mist and cold rain.

The hike ends at Halemauʻu trailhead, which is about 6 miles from and 1,800 feet below the start of the loop. If your only car is at Sliding Sands trailhead, you could walk up the road—that is, if you have any energy left. A better alternative is to hitchhike, as rides are usually easy to catch with fellow hikers or tourists driving to the summit.

# Hōlua

| | |
|---|---|
| LENGTH: | 7.4-mile round-trip |
| ELEVATION GAIN: | 1,700 feet |
| DANGER: | Low |
| SUITABLE FOR: | Intermediate |
| LOCATION: | Maui: Haleakalā National Park |
| TOPO MAP: | Kilohana |

## HIGHLIGHTS

This awesome hike descends a sheer *pali* (cliff) into the crater of Haleakalā, a once active volcano. The destination is Hōlua Cabin and Campground at the top of Koʻolau Gap. By the cabin you may encounter *nēnē,* the endangered Hawaiian goose.

## TRAILHEAD DIRECTIONS

**DISTANCE:** (Kahului to Halemauʻu trailhead) 31 miles
**DRIVING TIME:** 1 hour

From Kahului take Hāna Hwy (Rte 36).

At the first major intersection, turn right on Haleakalā Hwy (Rte 37).

Ascend gradually through sugarcane fields.

Pass turnoffs to Pukalani on the right and Makawao on the left.

Turn left on Rte 377 (still Haleakalā Hwy).

HŌLUA

HALEAKALĀ NATIONAL PARK

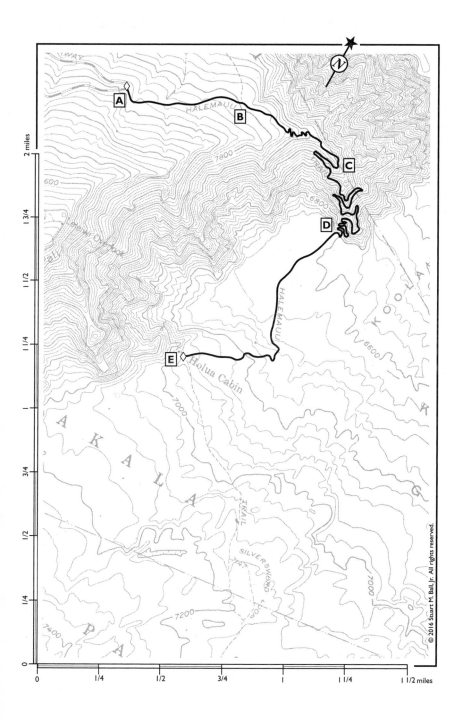

Climb steadily through lush pastureland and stands of fragrant eucalyptus trees.

Pass Kula Lodge on the right.

Turn left on Haleakalā Crater Rd. (Rte 378).

Ascend steeply on a series of short switchbacks through pasture belonging to Haleakalā Ranch.

Enter Haleakalā National Park and pay the fee at the entrance station.

Pass Park Headquarters Visitor Center on the right. It has restrooms, drinking water, and trail information.

Ascend steadily on a series of long switchbacks.

At the fourth switchback, turn left to the Halemau'u trailhead.

Park in the large lot there (elevation 7,990 feet) (map point A) (UTM 4Q 788596E, 2297211N) (Lat/Long N20.75232, W156.2285). Nearby is a fancy pit toilet.

## ROUTE DESCRIPTION

Pick up the Halemau'u Trail at the far end of the parking lot by a bulletin board with trail information.

Descend gradually along the outer slope of Haleakalā on a rough, rocky trail. Look for *hinahina,* a native geranium with toothed, silvery leaves.

Reach a junction (map point B). Keep right on the main trail. (The supply trail to the left leads down to Hosmer Grove Campground.)

Descend a series of short switchbacks as the slope steepens. The trail roughly parallels the park boundary fence on the left.

Briefly follow a prominent side ridge down the *pali* (map point C).

As the trail leaves the side ridge, watch for a particularly fine lookout on the left. Below is Ko'olau Gap, which drops steeply to the ocean. Across the gap is Hanakauhi peak and the north rim of the crater. Upslope is the crater interior dotted with cones.

Descend on five long switchbacks that repeatedly cross the side ridge. Look for native *'ama'u* and *kīlau* (bracken) ferns and *'ōhelo* and *pūkiawe* shrubs along the trail.

Continue the steep descent on seven shorter switchbacks. In the distance is Hōlua Cabin nestled below Leleiwi Pali.

By a wooden gate and a hitching post, reach the crater floor (map point D). Go through the gate, closing it behind you.

Cross a meadow covered with evening primrose.

Work left, away from the crater wall and begin to climb.

Ascend steadily through ridges of jumbled-up *'a'ā* lava.

Reach a signed junction (elevation 6,900 feet) (map point E) (UTM 4Q 789705E, 2296035N) (Lat/Long N20.74153, W156.21805). To the right a short trail leads to Hōlua Cabin and Campground. Look for *nēnē* hanging around the cabin.

## NOTES

The Hōlua (sled) hike follows a steep, spectacular route to the floor of Haleakalā (house of the sun) crater. Watch your footing on the narrow switchbacks; don't look and walk at the same time. Start early to ensure good views on the way down. In the early afternoon, clouds frequently ride up Ko'olau (windward) Gap and shroud the cliffs in swirling mist and cold rain.

On the initial descent of the outer slopes of the volcano, look for *hinahina*, a native geranium. The compact shrub has silvery, toothed leaves about 1 inch long. The attractive flowers are white, often with purple veins or throat.

The Halemau'u (grass house) Trail soon reaches the crater rim and the first of many breathtaking views. To the left (north), Ko'olau (windward) Gap descends abruptly toward the windward coast. Beyond is green Ke'anae (the mullet) Valley, ending at a peninsula and village of the same name. To the east across the gap is Hanakauhi (the cover bay) peak (eleva-

HŌLUA ⊠ HALEAKALĀ NATIONAL PARK

tion 8,907 feet). To the south is the crater floor, covered with colorful volcanic cones and backed by sheer Leleiwi (bone altar) Pali.

In Hawaiian, Haleakalā means "House of the Sun." According to legend, the sun traveled so quickly across the sky that the farmers and fisherman did not have enough time to plant crops and catch fish before night fell. The demigod Māui went to Haleakalā, where the sun's rays first struck the island. There Māui snared the sun with sixteen great ropes. In return for his freedom, the sun promised to travel more slowly across the sky during summer. Māui let the sun go but left some ropes tied to the sun to remind him of his promise. The people now had more time to catch fish and grow their crops. At sunset you can still see the white ropes trailing through the sky.

In addition to views, you can see various native shrubs and ferns along the switchbacks. *Pūkiawe* has tiny, rigid leaves and small white, pink, or red berries. *'Ōhelo* has rounded leaves and delicious red yellow berries, about the size of blueberries. *'Ama'u* ferns have short trunks, usually 1 to 2 feet high. Their fronds are bright red when young, gradually turning green with age.

Near Hōlua Cabin you may see *nēnē*, the Hawaiian goose. The *nēnē* has a black face and head and a gray-brown body. It lives on dry, rugged lava flows at high elevation and so has lost much of the webbing on its feet. Like its Canadian counterpart, the *nēnē* is a strong flyer and often honks in mid-flight. The *nēnē* is an endangered species and should be treated with respect. Do not feed them.

Just beyond the cabin are a pit toilet, a water faucet, and the Hōlua Campground. The water should be filtered or chemically treated. The cabin is solely for the use of overnight hikers with reservations. Check the Halaekalā Backpack chapter for information about staying there.

If you have time and energy after reaching the cabin, continue along the Halemau'u Trail to Silversword Loop. The loop winds through red-brown cinders dotted with *'āhinahina,* the Haleakalā silversword. It has narrow, silver green leaves and a tall flower stalk. The silversword is a threatened species and is found only on Maui and the Big Island. This side trip adds about 2.5 miles to the hike.

The climb back out of Haleakalā crater is not as bad as it looks. While ascending, maintain a slow but steady pace. Stop to rest occasionally and admire the view, if there is any. Before you know it, you are on top, and the parking lot is in sight.

# Haleakalā Backpack

| | |
|---|---|
| LENGTH: | 2–4 days, 19.6-mile loop |
| ELEVATION GAIN: | 2,400 feet |
| DANGER: | Low |
| SUITABLE FOR: | Intermediate, Expert |
| LOCATION: | Maui: Haleakalā National Park |
| TOPO MAP: | Kilohana, Nāhiku |

## HIGHLIGHTS

Haleakalā (house of the sun) is a once-active volcano with a vast eroded crater, much like an amphitheater. On this loop trip through the crater, you see towering cliffs, colorful spatter cones, and deep pit craters. Much in evidence are two threatened species: *nēnē,* the Hawaiian goose, and *'āhinahina,* the Haleakalā silversword.

## PLANNING

Take this trip any time during the year. Winter (November–April) is predictably rainier and colder than summer (May–October). Be prepared for large temperature swings, especially at Hōlua Campground. At night the temperature may drop to the thirties in winter and forties in summer. On a sunny day, the crater quickly warms up to the seventies or eighties.

Decide how many days you want to spend in the crater. The maximum stay is three nights, with up to two nights at any one campground. The narrative below describes a three-day trip with overnights at Palikū and Hōlua Campgrounds. If you only have only two days, skip Hōlua, but you will regret it. You can build a two-day trip around Hōlua using the Sliding Sands–Halemau'u or Hōlua day hikes.

If you have extra time, spend a layover day at Palikū or Hōlua, as both areas have some superb side trips. From Palikū, take the unmaintained Lau'ulu Trail, which starts in back of the pit toilet and climbs steadily to the north rim. For ocean views, follow the Kaupō Trail, which descends Kaupō Gap to the park boundary. From Hōlua, try the service trail across Ko'olau Gap to the Waikau Cabin site. That unmaintained route starts by the hitching post at the bottom of the Halemau'u switchbacks. On all of the side trips just mentioned, hike as far as you want and then return the way you came. A final option from Palikū is to descend Kaupō Gap to Kaupō town on the south coast of the island. The hike is a foot-pounding, knee-jarring descent of about 6,000 feet in 6.8 miles. The trail is maintained but is rough and rocky in spots. The main problem with this option is the complicated 100-mile shuttle necessary to leave a car at Kaupō. If possible, arrange to have someone pick you up at the trailhead. Otherwise, it's a long hitchhike back to the National Park.

On the way to the trailhead, stop at the Headquarters Visitor Center to pick up a free camping permit, available on a first-come, first-served basis. Provide a photo ID and watch a short orientation video. Permits are issued from 8 a.m. to 3 p.m. daily and may be obtained one day in advance. Fill your water bottles/bladders there, as the trailhead has a limited supply. The visitor center also has an inexpensive booklet, *Hiking in Haleakalā National Park*, which describes the backpacking route.

The trip narrative assumes you are staying at the campgrounds each night. There are, however, three cabins in the crater at Kapalaoa, Palikū, and Hōlua. Each has twelve bunks with mattresses and a table and chairs. The kitchen area has running water, cooking utensils, and propane and wood-burning stoves. Outside is a nearby pit toilet. The cabins are very comfortable and very popular. Visit the Haleakalā National Park website at http://www.nps.gov/hale for cabin reservations and the latest camping and trail information.

## TRAILHEAD DIRECTIONS

**Distance:** (Kahului to Haleakalā Visitor Center)
37 miles

**Driving Time:** 1 1/4 hours

From Kahului take Hāna Hwy (Rte 36).

At the first major intersection, turn right on Haleakalā Hwy (Rte 37).

Ascend gradually through sugarcane fields.

Pass turnoffs to Pukalani on the right and Makawao on the left.

The highway narrows to two lanes.

Turn left on Rte 377 (still Haleakalā Hwy).

Climb steadily through lush pastureland and stands of fragrant eucalyptus trees.

Pass Kula Lodge on the right.

Turn left on Haleakalā Crater Rd. (Rte 378).

Ascend steeply on a series of short switchbacks through pasture belonging to Haleakalā Ranch.

Enter Haleakalā National Park and pay the fee at the entrance station.

On the right, stop at Park Headquarters Visitor Center to get a backcountry permit for the trip. Check on the water situation and trail conditions. Fill up your water bottles/bladders for the first day, as the trailhead has only a limited supply of water.

Ascend steadily on a series of long switchbacks.

On the left by the fourth switchback pass the parking area for Halemau'u trailhead, where the trip ends (elevation 7,990 feet) (map point M) (UTM 4Q 788596E, 2297211N) (Lat/Long N20.75232, W156.2285).

Pass Leleiwi and Kalahaku overlooks, both on the left.

Turn left into the parking area for Haleakalā Visitor Center near the summit. Park your car in the near right corner of the lot close to a horse-loading ramp (elevation 9,740 feet) (map point A) (UTM). If you have two cars, drop off people and packs and shuttle one car back to the Halemau'u trailhead. The visitor center has restrooms.

## DAY ONE—HALEAKALĀ VISITOR CENTER TO PALIKŪ

**LENGTH:**  9.2 miles
**ELEVATION LOSS:**  3,400 feet

Start early today so you have plenty of time to enjoy the scenic Sliding Sands Trail. Built by the Civilian Conservation Corps in the mid-1930s, the path is well designed and graded—and all downhill. The initial high altitude should not cause any major problems because of the quick descent to a much lower elevation.

Leaving the visitor center parking lot, you quickly reach the crater rim, with its panoramic view. To the left (northeast) are Kalahaku (proclaim the lord) Pali (cliff) and Leleiwi (bone altar) Pali. Beyond is Ko'olau (windward) Gap, descending to the north coast of Maui. To the east at the far end of the crater lies green Palikū (vertical cliff), our destination today. To the right of Palikū and out of sight is Kaupō (landing at night) Gap, descending to the south coast of the island.

Haleakalā is a dormant volcano, but its "crater" is not really a volcanic one. The vast double amphitheater before you is more the result of wind and water erosion than volcanic activity. From opposite sides of the island two streams eroded headward and met to form a "crater." Lava from vents near the summit partially filled both deep valleys to create the wide Ko'olau and Kaupō Gaps. More recent volcanic activity produced the colorful spatter cones dotting the crater floor. Haleakalā erupted for perhaps the last time in 1790, when two small

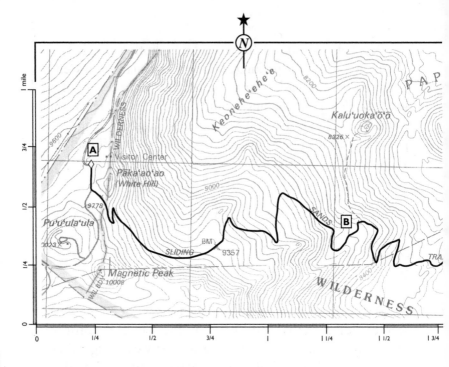

flows from the southwest rift zone outside the crater reached the ocean.

As you are sliding down the sand and cinder, watch for the park's signature plant, 'āhinahina, the Haleakalā silversword. It has narrow silver green leaves and a tall flower stalk. The leaves are covered with tiny hairs to conserve moisture and protect the plant from the intense sun. Other adaptations include a deep taproot to anchor the plant in high winds and a wide network of surface roots to collect water. The silversword usually grows for fifteen to twenty years before flowering. The flower stalks usually appear in summer or early fall and have purple blossoms. After the seeds develop, the entire plant dies. Silverswords are endemic to Hawai'i, meaning they are found nowhere else. Don't approach mature plants too closely, and don't step on the baby ones.

Also on the trail is the native shrub kūpaoa or na'ena'e. It has woody, erect stems and stiff leaves shaped like rounded triangles. Notice that kūpaoa and 'āhinahina have crossed to

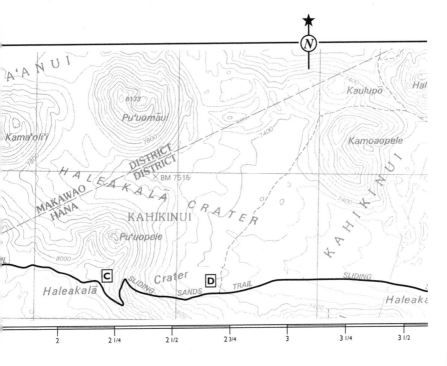

form several hybrid plants with green swords and an upright posture.

At Kapalaoa Cabin you may see *nēnē*, the Hawaiian goose. Some like to hang around the cabins, so look for them at Palikū and Hōlua, too. The *nēnē* has a black face and head and a gray-brown body. It lives on dry, rugged lava flows at high elevation and so has lost much of the webbing on its feet. Like its Canadian counterpart, the *nēnē* is a strong flyer and often honks in mid-flight. The *nēnē* is a threatened species and should be treated with respect.

The native dryland vegetation between Kapalaoa and Palikū Cabins is a welcome site after the colorful but desolate cones. The plants have taken hold on an older *'a'ā* flow that receives some moisture from the clouds advancing up the gap. Look for *māmane* trees and *'a'ali'i, pūkiawe,* and *'ōhelo* shrubs. *Māmane* has downy, oblong leaflets and clusters of bright yellow flowers. *'A'ali'i* has narrow, shiny leaves and red seed capsules. *Pūkiawe* has tiny, rigid leaves and small white, pink, or red berries. 'Ōhelo has rounded leaves and juicy red-yellow berries, about the size of blueberries.

Near the trail on the right is a lone native 'iliahi (sandalwood tree). It has stiff, olive green leaves, and red buds becoming cream-colored flowers. 'Iliahi is partially parasitic, with outgrowths on its roots that steal nutrients from nearby plants. This particular species is found only in Haleakalā.

The idyllic campground at Palikū is backed by a towering pali and overlooks a lush pasture. The water supply is from a faucet on the trail to the nearby cabin. Boil, filter, or chemically treat the water. The pit toilet is behind the cabin and can be reached from the back of the campground.

In the 'ōhi'a and māmane trees near the cabin watch for 'amakihi and 'apapane, two colorful native birds. The 'amakihi is yellowish green with a slightly curved gray bill and feeds on nectar, fruits, and insects. The 'apapane has a red breast and head, black wings and tail, and a slightly curved black bill. In flight the 'apapane makes a whirring sound as it darts from tree to tree searching for insects and nectar.

In the pasture you may catch a glimpse of pueo, the native owl. It is brown and white with yellow eyes and a black bill. Unlike most owls, the pueo is active during the day, hunting birds, rodents, and insects. Early Hawaiians worshiped the owl as a god and a guardian spirit.

Evenings at Palikū are magical. Watch the lingering color of the sunset on the cliffs and clouds above Kaupō Gap. Listen for the honk of a pair of nēnē making their last flight of the evening. Look for the moon rising through a notch in the crater wall. Can life get any better than this?

If you have wisely planned to spend an extra day at Palikū, two scenic side trips await you tomorrow. For ocean views, take the Kaupō Trail, which descends Kaupō Gap to the park boundary. For crater views, follow the unmaintained Lau'ulu Trail, which starts in back of the pit toilet and climbs steadily to the north rim. On both trips, return the way you came.

The Sliding Sands Trail starts by a wooden bulletin board next to the horse-loading ramp.

Briefly parallel the paved road leading to Puʻuʻulaʻula (Red Hill), the summit of Haleakalā at 10,023 feet.

Bear left away from the road around Pā Kaoʻao, also known as White Hill.

Reach the rim of the crater and the first of many awesome views. On the horizon to the right is the peak of Mauna Kea on the Big Island.

Descend gradually on five long, lazy switchbacks. The trail crosses an area of gray-brown and then red-brown cinders known as Keoneheʻeheʻe.

Begin looking for native *ʻāhinahina* (silverswords) on the right. The only other vegetation along the trail is the native shrubs *pūkiawe* and *kūpaoa,* also known as *naʻenaʻe.*

Reach an unmarked junction (map point B). Turn right between two boulders. The side trail straight ahead leads down to a view into Ka Luʻu o ka ʻŌʻō cone.

Continue the descent on three switchbacks. The trail briefly crosses rough *ʻaʻā* lava. Watch your footing on the loose rock.

Cross a relatively flat area covered with red cinder. Silverswords line the trail. Kamaʻoliʻi and Puʻu o Māui cones are on the left at a distance.

Climb briefly past Puʻu o Pele, a red cinder cone close by on the left.

Descend to the crater floor on two switchbacks through *kīlau* (bracken) ferns (map point C).

Reach a signed junction by a hitching post and a *māmane* tree (map point D). Continue straight on the Sliding Sands Trail. (The side trail to the left leads across the crater to Halemauʻu Trail and Hōlua Cabin and Campground.)

Pass more silverswords on the left. Well behind them is Ka Moa o Pele, a large red cinder cone.

Walk through fields of *kīlau* fern and then native bunchgrass on a wide, sandy trail.

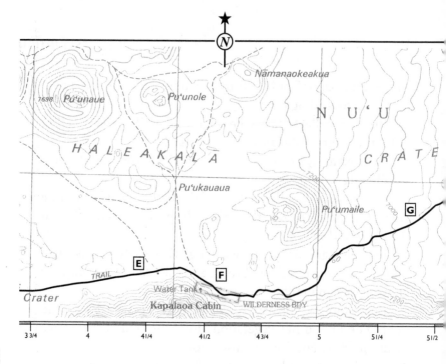

Reach a signed junction (map point E). Again, continue straight toward Kapalaoa Cabin. (The side trail to the left leads across the crater to Halemau'u Trail and Hōlua Cabin and Campground.)

Reach another signed junction. Continue straight on the Sliding Sands Trail. (The side trail to the left leads across the crater to Halemau'u Trail and Hōlua Cabin and campground.)

Almost immediately, reach Kapalaoa Cabin (map point F) (UTM 4Q 793328E, 2292224N) (Lat/Long N20.70657, W156.18389). Tent camping is not allowed at the cabin, but water is available from a tank in back. Boil, filter, or chemically treat the water.

After leaving the cabin, the vegetation gradually reappears. Watch for *māmane* trees and *pūkiawe, 'ōhelo, 'a'ali'i,* and *pilo* shrubs.

Wind through an *'a'ā* flow past heaps of broken-up lava. The trail parallels an eroded gully on the right.

Work left toward Pu'u Maile, a vegetated cone, and then swing right.

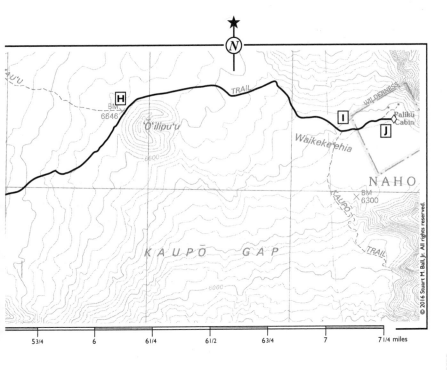

Descend steadily on rough 'a'ā lava (map point G). Watch for loose rock on the trail. Look for a lone 'iliahi (sandalwood) on the right.

Cross a mostly barren 'a'ā flow. Look right to see Mauna Kea and Mauna Loa.

Go left around a vegetated cone, known as 'Ō'ilipu'u.

Reach a signed junction with the Halemau'u Trail (map point H). Turn right on it toward Palikū. (To the left is the route tomorrow to Hōlua Campground.)

Continue around the base of the cone.

Descend gradually on old pāhoehoe lava through grass, 'a'ali'i, and 'ōhelo.

Reach a signed junction (map point I). Keep left to Palikū. (The trail to the right leads down Kaupō Gap to the park boundary and the town of Kaupō along the south coast.)

Reach Palikū Campground and Cabin (elevation. 6,380 feet) (map point J) (UTM 4Q797653E, 2293544N) (Lat/Long N20.7178, W156.14222).

**Length:** 6.7 miles
**Elevation Gain:** 1,000 feet

If you wish, linger at Palikū for awhile this morning. The hike today does not require a crack-of-dawn start, as the mileage is low, and the trail is well marked and groomed. The route climbs gradually to Kawilinau, formerly known as Bottomless Pit, and then descends gradually to Hōlua Campground.

The route to Hōlua traverses the crater along its northern side. You see several of the large cones and deep pits up close, rather than from a distance as you did the first day. The vegetation pattern begins with native dryland shrubs near Palikū, switches to ʻāhinahina (silverswords) among the cones, and reverts to native shrubs near Hōlua.

Along the route are two remnants of a bygone era when cattle and goats grazed in the crater. On the left just before the low *pali* is a fenced enclosure used to measure the recovery of the native plants inside without grazing pressure from goats. As a result of this and other study areas, the park service completed a fence in 1986 to exclude goats from the crater. Past Mauna Hina on the right is a long rock wall perpendicular to the trail. The wall corralled cattle on their way to pasture at Palikū in the 1800s and early 1900s.

Hōlua (sled) Campground enjoys a spectacular setting at the top of Koʻolau Gap and at the foot of Leleiwi Pali. Among the *pūkiawe* and grass are numerous flat tent sites. Water is available from a faucet below the campground near the cabin. As always, boil, filter, or chemically treat the water. The campground has a pit toilet across from a dilapidated ranger's retreat, affectionately known as the Hōlua Hilton.

In the evening, enjoy the wild, stark beauty of the crater. Watch the clouds retreat down Koʻolau Gap. As the shadows lengthen, look for the sun's last rays hitting Hanakauhi peak across the gap. Feel the temperature plummet because of the clear skies and high elevation.

In Hawaiian, Haleakalā means "House of the Sun." According to legend, the sun traveled so quickly across the sky that the farmers and fisherman did not have enough time to plant crops and catch fish before night fell. The demigod Māui went to Haleakalā, where the sun's rays first struck the island. There Māui snared the sun with sixteen great ropes. In return for his freedom, the sun promised to travel more slowly across the sky. Māui let the sun go but left some ropes tied to the sun to remind him of his promise. The people now had more time to catch fish and grow their crops. At sunset you can still see the white ropes trailing through the sky.

## ROUTE DESCRIPTION

Retrace your steps along the Halemauʻu Trail.

Reach the signed junction near ʻŌʻilipuʻu cone (map point H). Turn right to Hōlua.

Ascend gradually through a grassy area with scattered *māmane, pūkiawe,* and *ʻaʻaliʻi.*

The grass narrows to a strip between two barren *ʻaʻā* flows. The flow on the right issued from Kalua Awa vent on the crater wall. The trail follows or parallels several rocky gullies.

The grassy strip widens. On the right is a broad gully and on the left is an old fenced enclosure.

Bear left and climb a low *pali* (map point K).

On the left, pass Honokahua, a vegetated cinder cone.

Cross a short, flat, grassy section with an *ʻaʻā* flow on the left.

On the right pass Mauna Hina, a steep cone covered with grass.

Cross several fingers of *ʻaʻā* lava from a vent near Mauna Hina.

On the right is a lava rock wall perpendicular to the trail.

Pass close to Nā Mana o ke Akua, an old vegetated cone on the left.

On the far side of the cone reach a signed junction (map point L). Keep right for Hōlua. (The trail to the left leads to Kapalaoa Cabin.)

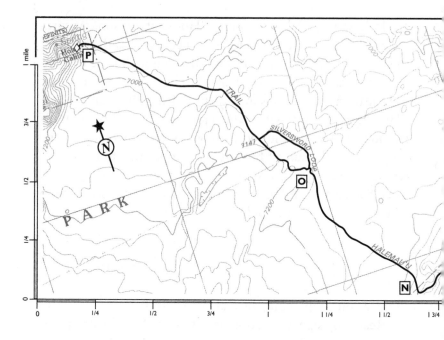

The vegetation thins. Underfoot are dark sand and cinders.

Partway up the ridge on the right is a series of huge rock dikes. They have eroded to look like the dorsal fins on a fish.

On the left pass Puʻu Nole, a brown-black cone dotted with silverswords near the top.

Reach a signed junction (map point M). Continue straight on the Halemauʻu Trail. (The trail to the left leads to Kapalaoa Cabin.)

Ascend gradually around the right side of Puʻu Naue cone, which is colored red and gray and dotted with silverswords.

Almost immediately, reach an obscure junction. Continue straight on the main trail.

Descend briefly to reach another junction at Kawilinau, formerly known as Bottomless Pit, which is surrounded by a fence. Continue straight, to Hōlua. (The trail to the left leads across the crater to Sliding Sands Trail. An unmaintained trail to the right just before the pit leads down Koʻolau Gap to the Waikau Cabin site.)

Go around the base of Halāliʻi cone. At its far side are views

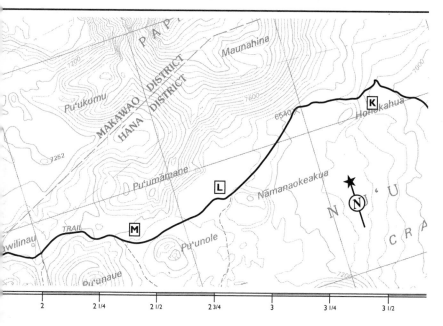

down Koʻolau Gap and across the crater to Kalahaku and Lele-iwi Pali.

Reach a signed junction (map point N). Bear right to Hōlua. (The left fork leads back to Sliding Sands Trail.)

Descend briefly and cross a basin covered with black sand, cinders, and lava rock.

Climb out of the basin on red cinders.

Reach a signed junction (map point O). Turn right on Silversword Loop. (The main trail continues straight, to Hōlua.)

Wind through red-brown cinders dotted with silverswords.

Reach a signed junction with the main trail and turn right on it. Just ahead is another *iliahi* (sandalwood tree).

Cross an old *ʻaʻā* flow partially covered with native vegetation. Look for *māmane* trees and *ʻaʻaliʻi, ʻōhelo, kūkaenēnē,* and *pūkiawe* shrubs. In the distance you can see Hōlua Cabin nestled against the crater wall.

Descend briefly on a rough trail.

Reach a signed junction near Hōlua Cabin (map point P) (UTM 4Q 789705E, 2296035N) (Lat/Long N20.74153,

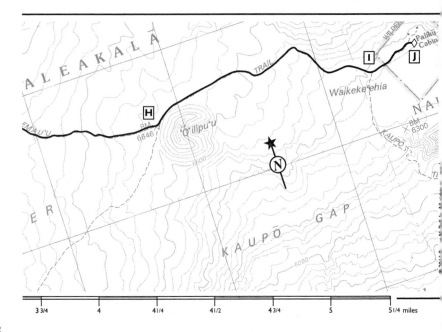

W156.21805). Continue straight to the cabin. (The trail to the right is the route out tomorrow.)

At the front lawn of the cabin, turn left past a water faucet.

Climb briefly, but steeply, to Hōlua Campground (elevation 6,940 feet).

## DAY THREE—HŌLUA TO HALEAKALĀ CRATER ROAD

**LENGTH:**             3.7 miles
**ELEVATION GAIN:**     1,400 feet

Today you gain back some of the elevation you lost the first day. The Halemauʻu Trail climbs out of the crater on more than twenty switchbacks. Built by the Civilian Conservation Corps in the mid-1930s, the path is well designed and graded, although narrow in spots. While ascending, maintain a slow but steady pace and stop to rest occasionally and admire the view, if there is any. In the early afternoon, clouds frequently ride up Koʻolau Gap and shroud the cliffs in swirling mist and cold rain, so get an early start.

On the way up watch for *ʻamaʻu* ferns, as well as the familiar native dryland shrubs. The ferns have short trunks, usually 1 to 2 feet high. Their fronds are bright red when young, gradually turning green with age.

On the gradual ascent of the outer slopes of the volcano, look for *hinahina*, a native geranium. The compact shrub has silvery, toothed leaves about 1 inch long. The attractive flowers are white, often with purple veins or throat.

The hike ends at Halemauʻu trailhead, which is about 6 miles from and 1,800 feet below the start of the loop. If your only car is at Sliding Sands trailhead, you could walk up the road—that is, if you have any energy left. A better alternative is to hitchhike, as rides are usually easy to catch with fellow hikers or tourists driving to the summit.

## ROUTE DESCRIPTION

Walk back to the junction in front of the cabin (map point P). Turn left on the Halemauʻu Trail. (The trail also continues straight, which is the way you came in yesterday.)

Descend Koʻolau Gap, gradually at first and then more steeply through ridges of jumbled-up *ʻaʻā* lava.

Work left toward the crater wall as the angle of descent eases.

Cross a meadow covered with evening primrose.

Reach the base of the cliff by a wooden gate and a hitching post (map point Q). Go through the gate, closing it behind you. (To the right an unmaintained trail leads across Koʻolau Gap to the Waikau Cabin site.)

Begin climbing the crater wall on seven short switchbacks. The views back into the crater are spectacular. On the way up look for *ʻamaʻu* ferns, whose young fronds are bright red.

Switchbacks eight through twelve are much longer and repeatedly cross a prominent side ridge in the cliff. After the twelfth zigzag is a particularly fine overlook. Below Koʻolau

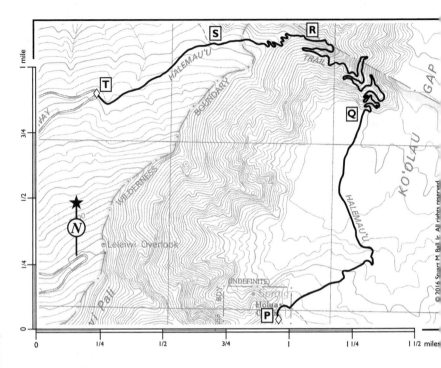

Gap drops steeply to the ocean. Across the gap is Hanakauhi peak and the north rim of the crater. Upslope are several of the cones you passed by earlier in the trip.

After the twelfth switchback, briefly follow the level side ridge (map point R).

As the slope steepens, resume climbing on a series of short switchbacks. On the right is the park boundary fence.

After the last switchback (yes!), reach a signed junction (map point S). Keep left on the main trail. (The supply trail to the right leads down to Hosmer Grove Campground.)

Ascend gradually along the outer slope of Haleakalā on a rough, rocky trail. Look for *hinahina,* a native geranium with toothed, silvery leaves.

Reach Halemau'u trailhead and parking lot (elevation 7,990 feet) (map point T) (UTM 4Q 788596E, 2297211N) (Lat/Long N20.75232, W156.2285). Nearby is a fancy pit toilet. If your only car is parked at Sliding Sands trailhead, walk or hitchhike back up to it.

30

# Waihou Spring

| | |
|---|---|
| LENGTH: | 2.4-mile round-trip |
| ELEVATION GAIN: | 400 feet |
| DANGER: | Low |
| SUITABLE FOR: | Novice |
| LOCATION: | Maui: Waihou Spring Forest Reserve above Makawao |
| TOPO MAP: | Kilohana |

## HIGHLIGHTS

This short, pleasant hike crosses reforested pastureland en route to a perennial spring on the west slope of Haleakalā. Along the way are a few remnant native plants.

## TRAILHEAD DIRECTIONS

**DISTANCE:**  (Kahului to Waihou Spring trailhead) 17 miles
**DRIVING TIME:**  1/2 hour

From Kahului take Hāna Hwy (Rte 36).

At the first major intersection, turn right on Haleakalā Hwy (Rte 37).

Ascend gradually through sugarcane fields.

Pass a turnoff to Pukalani on the right.

At the second traffic light, turn left on Makawao Ave.

At the stop sign in the center of Makawao town, turn right on Olinda Rd. Reset your trip odometer.

After ascending for about 4.6 miles, pass the Maui Bird Conservation Center and the Maui Forest Bird Recovery Project, both on the left.

Just past the recovery project sign, look for the signed trailhead gate on the right. Park at an angle to a barbed wire fence just downhill of the gate (elevation 3,730 feet) (map point A) (UTM 4Q 783154E, 2303062N) (Lat/Long N20.80596, W156.27977).

## ROUTE DESCRIPTION

Go around the gate to the right and pass a sign explaining the managed Waihou Spring Forest Reserve.

Stroll along a wide dirt road through a pine forest with evenly spaced trees.

After passing an open gate, reach a junction. Continue straight on the main road. (The left fork is a private road.)

On the left, pass an open grassy area, the site of a lumber mill.

Descend gradually through eucalyptus trees and cross a gulch.

Reach a signed junction and the start of the loop portion (map point B). Turn right to walk the loop counterclockwise.

Reach another signed junction. For now, turn right to the overlook and spring. (To the left is the continuation of the loop.)

Descend gradually to the overlook, where trees have blocked most of the view. Look for the native shrub *pukiawe* and a lone native *koa* tree, which is marked by a small plaque.

At the far edge of the overlook clearing, turn right onto a narrow trail and descend into deep Kailua Gulch on thirteen short switchbacks.

Reach Waihou Spring at an end of trail sign (elevation 3,320 feet) (map point C) (UTM 4Q 782404E, 2302971N) (Lat/Long N20.80526, W156.28698).

Backtrack out of the gulch to the main loop and turn right (map point B).

Climb gradually though tropical ash trees to reach the top of the loop.

Descend gradually to complete the loop and turn right to exit the forest reserve.

**NOTES**

Waihou (new water) Spring is a popular hike because of its low mileage and its proximity to Makawao and Pukalani towns. The route follows an old tree plantation road through a state forest reserve. A short but steep descent leads to a perennial spring with some water diversion tunnels.

In 1909 the Territory of Hawai'i established the forest reserve to protect the sources of Waihou Spring. Workers planted evenly spaced mainland pines and eucalyptus to help retain moisture and control erosion. Previously the reforested area had been overgrown pasture. The spring itself had been used to water livestock well before the forest reserve was created. Short tunnels cut into the rock diverted water through pipes to the pastures of Haleakalā Ranch farther down the slopes.

In the introduced forest, look for a few native *pūkiawe* shrubs and *koa* trees. *Pūkiawe* has tiny, rigid leaves and small white, pink, or red berries. *Koa* has sickle-shaped foliage and pale-yellow flower clusters. Early Hawaiians made surfboards and outrigger canoe hulls out of the beautiful red-brown wood. Today it is made into fine furniture.

# 31

# Waiakoa Loop

| | |
|---|---|
| LENGTH: | 4.5-mile loop |
| ELEVATION GAIN: | 700 feet |
| DANGER: | Low |
| SUITABLE FOR: | Novice |
| LOCATION: | Maui: Kula Forest Reserve above Kula |
| TOPO MAP: | Kilohana |

## HIGHLIGHTS

This short, very pleasant walk loops through introduced forest on the slopes of Haleakalā, a dormant volcano. Along the way are dry, rocky gulches lined with native ʻōhiʻa trees. You may also see some native birds, such as ʻalauahio, the Maui creeper.

## TRAILHEAD DIRECTIONS

**DISTANCE:** (Kahului to Waiakoa trailhead) 24 miles
**DRIVING TIME:** 1 hour

From Kahului take Hāna Hwy (Rte 36).

At the first major intersection, turn right on Haleakalā Hwy (Rte 37).

Ascend gradually through sugarcane fields.

Pass turnoffs to Pukalani on the right and Makawao on the left.

After the highway narrows to two lanes, reach the first intersection with Rte 377 to Haleakalā. Continue straight on Kula Hwy (still Rte 37).

At the second intersection with Rte 377, turn left on Haleakalā Hwy. Reset your trip odometer.

Turn right on Waipoli Rd. (0.3 mile). It's the first road on the right with a stop sign.

Ascend steadily through a eucalyptus forest.

After going over a cattle grate, the road becomes Polipoli Access Rd.

Switchback steadily through pastureland.

Reach a hunter check-in station on the left (5.4 miles). Park well off the road on the left just below the station (elevation 6,020 feet) (map point A) (UTM 4Q 781090E, 2293299N) (Lat/Long N20.71816, W156.30115).

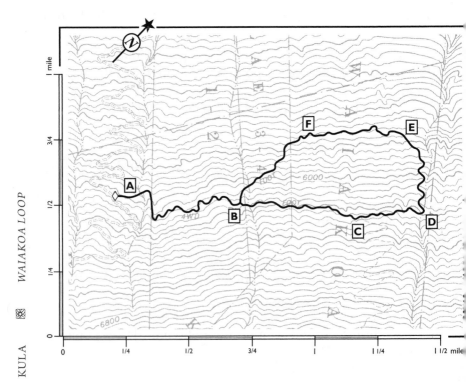

Just past the hunter check-in station, take the dirt road on the left through a gate.

Descend briefly and cross Ka'ono'ulu Gulch.

The road jogs right, climbs steadily, and then jogs left.

Contour through open eucalyptus and pine forest. Ignore side roads up- and downslope. To the left you can see the West Maui Mountains.

Reach the end of the road and the signed start of the Waiakoa Loop Trail. Orient yourself using the colorful trail map etched in wood.

Proceed through a gate in a barbed wire fence.

Continue to contour through pines, crossing a gully.

Reach the loop portion of the hike at a trail fork (map point B). Keep right and up to start the loop in a counterclockwise direction.

Contour gradually through introduced black wattle trees. Look for the 'amakihi, a yellowish-green native bird.

Cross Nā'alae Gulch and then several others. One has an inviting slide and pool, but rarely any water! Another has a nearby comfortable bench. All the gulches are lined with native 'ōhi'a trees.

Reach a signed junction (elevation 6,250 feet) (map point C). Continue straight on the loop trail. (To the right the Waiakoa Trail connects with the Māmane and Skyline Trails.)

After contouring through more black wattle, bear left and begin to descend.

Cross Keāhuaiwi Gulch (map point D) (UTM 4Q 782395E, 2294689N) (Lat/Long N20.73051, W156.28841), switchback once, and recross it. Look for native māmane trees and pūkiawe shrubs in this section.

Descend steadily on five switchbacks and reenter the pine forest.

Continue to descend, first on switchbacks and then straight down.

Reach an unmarked junction (map point E). Turn left on a grassy dirt road.

Shortly cross a gulch. On the left, a side trail leads to a lovely 'ōhi'a and fern grotto.

Contour again, crossing several small gulches. The forest here is mostly introduced Monterey pine.

Leave the road briefly to traverse a steep gully.

Bear left off the road (map point F) and climb steadily on six switchbacks. Look for the small, yellow-green native bird called 'alauahio (Maui creeper).

Reach the familiar fork, completing the loop (map point B).

Backtrack to the hunter check-in station (map point A).

## NOTES

The Waiakoa (water used by warriors) Loop is a gem of a hike—short, scenic, and absolutely delightful. Savor this walk; don't rush it. Look for native birds, identify some of the trees and shrubs, and enjoy the crisp mountain air.

Take this hike in the morning. Later in the day, clouds frequently roll in and blanket the slopes in mist and light rain. The loop is described counterclockwise. You can, of course, walk the route in either direction.

The loop passes through country that was once covered with a native forest of koa, 'ōhi'a, and māmane trees. In the 1800s, cattle and goat grazing and logging for firewood and fence posts destroyed much of the original forest. You can still see some remnant 'ōhi'a, lining the rocky gulches. The trees have oval, dull-green leaves and clusters of delicate red flowers.

In the forest canopy, watch for the 'amakihi, a yellowish-green native bird. It has a slightly curved gray bill and feeds on nectar, fruits, and insects. If the 'ōhi'a are in bloom, you may glimpse the 'apapane. It has a red breast and head, black wings and tail, and a slightly curved black bill. In flight the 'apapane makes a whirring sound as it darts from tree to tree searching for insects and nectar.

On the descent, look for native *māmane* trees and *pūkiawe* shrubs. *Māmane* has downy, oblong leaflets and clusters of bright yellow flowers. *Pūkiawe* has tiny, rigid leaves and small white, pink, or red berries.

The return portion of the loop goes through a forest of introduced pines, planted for watershed protection. One of the species represented is a native of California, the Monterey pine. It has 4-inch needles arranged in bunches of three. The cones are lopsided at the base; the outer side has greatly swollen scales tipped with a short point.

In the pine groves you may see *'alauahio*, the native Maui creeper. It is a small, yellow-green bird with a short, straight bill. Creepers move about the forest understory, taking insects from the vegetation. They frequently travel in small family groups.

# 32

# Polipoli Loop

| | |
|---|---|
| LENGTH: | 4.9-mile loop |
| ELEVATION GAIN: | 1,200 feet |
| DANGER: | Low |
| SUITABLE FOR: | Novice, Intermediate |
| LOCATION: | Maui: Polipoli Springs State Recreation Area and Kula Forest Reserve above Kula |
| TOPO MAP: | Luala'ilua Hills, Mākena |

## HIGHLIGHTS

The Polipoli Loop is a mainland-style hike with a touch of local color. The route winds through dense stands of pine, redwood, and other introduced evergreens on the slopes of Haleakalā. In the clearings you may catch a glimpse of some of the flashy native birds.

## TRAILHEAD DIRECTIONS

DISTANCE: (Kahului to Polipoli State Park) 29 miles
DRIVING TIME: 1 1/2 hours

From Kahului take Hāna Hwy (Rte 36).
At the first major intersection, turn right on Haleakalā Hwy (Rte 37).
Ascend gradually through sugarcane fields.
Pass turnoffs to Pukalani on the right and Makawao on the left.

After the highway narrows to two lanes, reach the first intersection with Rte 377 to Haleakalā. Continue straight on Kula Hwy (still Rte 37).

At the second intersection with Rte 377, turn left on Haleakalā Hwy. Reset your trip odometer.

Turn right on Waipoli Rd. (0.3 mile). It's the first road on the right with a stop sign.

Ascend steadily through a eucalyptus forest.

After going over a cattle grate, the road becomes Polipoli Access Rd.

Switchback steadily through pastureland.

Pass a hunter check-in station on the left (5.2 miles).

The pavement ends (6.0 miles).

Go over another cattle grate and pass a signed junction with the Boundary Trail on the right (6.5 miles).

Pass a signed junction with the Waihouli Trail on the right (8.2 miles).

The dirt road forks (9.2 miles). Bear right and down. (The left fork climbs to the Skyline switchback.)

Reach the end of the road at Polipoli Springs State Recreation Area (9.8 miles). Park in the small lot there (elevation 6,160 feet) (map point A) (UTM 4Q 778166E, 2288758N) (Lat/Long N20.67761, W156.32992). The Polipoli area has drinking water, a toilet, covered picnic tables, and a small campground. Nearby is a lone housekeeping cabin.

## ROUTE DESCRIPTION

Walk across the grassy picnic and camping area toward a colorful trail map.

Just past the map, pick up the Polipoli Trail.

Walk through deadfall left by several intense windstorms. The area used to be mature forest of Monterey pine and cypress. Look for a small yellow-green native bird, called 'alauahio (Maui creeper).

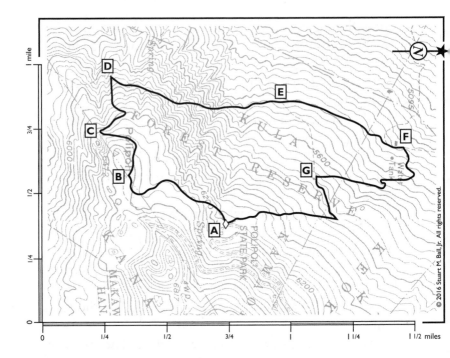

Climb gradually through uprooted stumps and trunks cut by the State Park trail crews.

Shortly afterward reach a signed junction with the Haleakalā Ridge Trail (map point B). Turn right on it. (To the left, the ridge trail climbs to the start of the Skyline Trail at the Skyline switchback.)

Descend steadily around Polipoli Peak (elevation 6,472 feet) through eucalyptus and introduced evergreens.

As the main trail switchbacks to the right, reach an obscure junction (map point C). For now, take the makeshift trail to the left.

The side trail splits. The left fork descends briefly to a cool, damp cave in a cinder cone. The right fork leads to a spectacular overlook of the leeward coast. Across ʻAlenuihāhā Channel is the Big Island, with its four volcanic peaks. From left to right they are Mauna Kea, Kohala, Mauna Loa, and Hualālai. Look for the native shrub *pūkiawe* in back of the overlook.

Retrace your steps to the main trail and continue down the broad ridge. Switchback once on wooden steps. Look for the native bird *'i'iwi.*

The trail veers right across the ridge.

Shortly afterward reach a signed junction at the end of the ridge trail (map point D). Turn right on the Plum Trail.

Descend gradually, across slopes planted with cedar and cypress.

Cross several dry gullies. Through the trees are views of the West Maui Mountains.

The trail enters a more open stand of tropical ash.

Go through a fence as the trail narrows.

Reach a signed junction (map point E) (UTM 4Q 777395E, 2289126N) (Lat/Long N20.68104, W156.33726). Continue straight on the Plum Trail. (To the right the Tie Trail connects with the Redwood Trail.)

Walk through alternating groves of tropical ash and introduced evergreens.

On the left, pass a dilapidated bunkhouse built by the Civilian Conservation Corps. Look for the inscribed names of some of the CCC workers on the left side of the short causeway just before the next junction.

Reach a signed junction (map point F). Continue straight and up on the Redwood Trail. (To the left and down is the Boundary Trail, which leads to the Waiohuli Trail and Polipoli Access Rd.)

Shortly pass an abandoned rangers cabin on the right. The trail is lined with hydrangea.

Begin climbing through a grove of tall, straight redwoods.

Switchback three times to gain elevation comfortably.

By a spreading cedar, reach another signed junction (map point G). Keep left, still on the Redwood Trail. (To the right the Tie Trail leads back to the Plum Trail.)

Bear left to keep a small shelter on your right.

Ascend gradually on two long switchbacks through introduced evergreens.

The Redwood Trail widens briefly and then ends at a cabin. Walk up the road from the cabin.

Go around a yellow gate to reach Polipoli Access Rd. Turn right to return to the parking lot (map point A).

## NOTES

The Polipoli Loop looks and feels just like a forest walk on the mainland. Groves of tall redwood trees remind you of northern California. Stands of pine and ash are reminiscent of the Appalachian Mountains. Only from the overlook, with the ocean below and the Big Island in the distance, is it clear you are actually on Maui.

Morning is the best time to take this hike. Later in the day, clouds frequently roll in and envelop the slopes in mist and light rain. A late afternoon walk through the redwoods makes for a dark, eerie experience.

The drive to the trailhead is long and a bit rough. The last 4 miles are over a dusty dirt road. Although rocky in spots, the road is passable for two-wheel-drive vehicles under dry conditions. If the dirt road is muddy from a heavy rainstorm, try the Waiakoa Loop hike instead.

If not crowded, the picnic area is actually a good place to birdwatch. Look for the native 'apapane high in the forest canopy. It has a red breast and head, black wings and tail, and a slightly curved black bill. In flight the 'apapane makes a whirring sound as it darts from tree to tree searching for insects and nectar. Other birds that may frequent the area are the yellow-green 'amakihi and the red-billed leiothrix.

At the back of the camping area, check out the route on the colorful trail map. The Polipoli Loop is pieced together from four separate trails, the Polipoli, Haleakalā (house of the sun) Ridge, Plum, and Redwood. All four are well graded, and the junctions are well marked. As the route is described clockwise, you take the right fork at each major intersection.

The hike passes through country that was once covered

with a native forest of *koa, ʻōhiʻa,* and *māmane* trees. In the 1800s, cattle and goat grazing and logging for firewood and fence posts destroyed much of the original forest. In 1912 the Polipoli area became part of the Kula Forest Reserve. To restore the watershed, the Division of Forestry began to plant trees in the 1920s. Over the next decade, the Civilian Conservation Corps (CCC) continued the project, planting over 1,000 acres in introduced pines, cedar, cypress, redwoods, and tropical ash. The route goes by one of the old CCC work camps.

On the trail, look for one of the introduced trees, the Monterey pine from California. It has 4-inch needles arranged in bunches of three. The cones are lopsided at the base; the outer side has greatly swollen scales tipped with a short point. Many of the pines were toppled recently by strong windstorms. Trail crews from State Parks spent many days clearing the first section of the loop.

In the pine groves and deadfall, look for *ʻalauahio,* the native Maui creeper. It is a small, yellow-green bird with a short, straight bill. Creepers move about the forest understory, taking insects from the vegetation. They frequently travel in small family groups.

If you're lucky, you may catch a glimpse of the native *ʻiʻiwi* on the lower section of the Haleakalā Ridge Trail. The striking bird has a red breast and head and black wings and tail. It sips nectar with a long, curved, salmon-colored bill. Its squeaky call is very distinctive, similar to a rusty hinge.

The return portion of the loop winds through dark, damp stands of towering redwood trees. Their bark is red-brown, soft, and heavily furrowed. They have narrow leaves, about 3/4-inch long. Underneath is a prominent midrib with whitish bands on either side.

Although the loop is described clockwise, you can, of course, walk it in either direction. To shorten the loop, take the Tie Trail. For a longer hike, check the trail map. The Polipoli area has ten different trails; you could easily spend several enjoyable days walking all of them.

# 33

# Skyline Trail

| LENGTH: | 15.0-mile round-trip |
|---|---|
| ELEVATION GAIN: | 3,500 feet |
| DANGER: | Low |
| SUITABLE FOR: | Intermediate, Expert |
| LOCATION: | Maui: Kula and Kahikinui Forest Reserves above Kula, and Haleakalā National Park |
| TOPO MAP: | Lualaʻilua Hills, Kilohana |

## HIGHLIGHTS

This arduous climb follows the Southwest Rift Zone of Haleakalā, a dormant volcano. The goal is Puʻu ʻUlaʻula (Red Hill), the true summit at 10,023 feet. Along the way are native dryland vegetation, colorful cinder cones, deep pit craters, and a possible headache from the high altitude.

## TRAILHEAD DIRECTIONS

**Distance:** (Kahului to Skyline switchback) 29 miles
**Driving Time:** 1 1/2 hours

From Kahului take Hāna Hwy (Rte 36).
At the first major intersection, turn right on Haleakalā Hwy (Rte 37).
Ascend gradually through sugarcane fields.
Pass turnoffs to Pukalani on the right and Makawao on the left.

After the highway narrows to two lanes, reach the first intersection with Rte 377 to Haleakalā. Continue straight on Kula Hwy (still Rte 37).

At the second intersection with Rte 377, turn left on Haleakalā Hwy. Reset your trip odometer.

Turn right on Waipoli Rd. (0.3 mile). It's the first road on the right with a stop sign.

Ascend steadily through a eucalyptus forest.

After going over a cattle grate, the road becomes Polipoli Access Rd.

Switchback steadily through pastureland.

Pass a hunter check-in station on the left (5.2 miles).

The pavement ends (6.0 miles).

Go over another cattle grate and pass a signed junction with the Boundary Trail on the right (6.5 miles).

Pass a signed junction with the Waihouli Trail on the right (8.2 miles).

The dirt road forks (9.2 miles). Bear left and up. (The road to the right leads down to Polipoli Springs State Recreation Area. It has drinking water, a toilet, covered picnic tables, and a small campground.)

Reach the Skyline switchback, where the road crests the ridge and turns sharp left (9.9 miles). Park there in a small lot on the right (elevation 6,560 feet) (map point A) (UTM 4Q 778137E, 2288263N) (Lat/Long N20.67314, W156.33027). Nearby is the signed junction with the Haleakalā Ridge Trail, which heads down to Polipoli Springs State Recreation Area.

## ROUTE DESCRIPTION

On foot, continue along the road, now called the Skyline Trail, which climbs the Southwest Rift Zone of Haleakalā. Watch out for the occasional four-wheel-drive vehicle.

Enter a grove of eucalyptus trees.

As the ridge narrows and levels briefly, pass a water tank and catchment on the right.

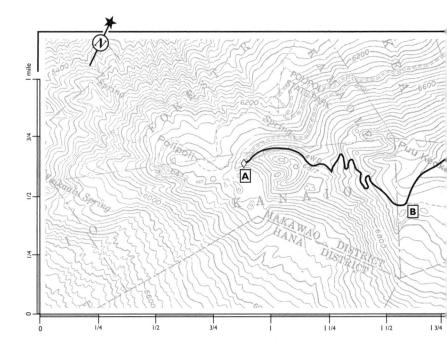

Climb steadily on five switchbacks. The road is rocky and rutted. On the right the massive leeward slopes of Haleakalā drop steadily to the ocean. Look for Lualaʻilua Hills, a pair of eroded cinder cones downslope.

Near a flat grassy area, reach a fork, known as Ballpark Junction (map point B). Keep left along the ridge. (To the right, Kahua Rd. leads to the Kahikinui Trail.)

Ascend gradually through an open forest of native *māmane* trees, *pūkiawe* and *ʻōhelo* shrubs, and *kīlau* (bracken) ferns. Superb views of West Maui start to open up on the left.

Reach a signed junction. Keep right on the Skyline Trail. (To the left, the Māmane Trail loops back to Polipoli Access Rd.)

Reach another junction. Keep right on the main road. (The dirt road on the left provides access for hunters.)

Climb more steeply on two switchbacks (map point C).

Switchback twice again to ease the elevation gain.

Work left around the base of Kanahau, a large, partially vegetated cinder cone. Look for the native shrub *aʻaliʻi*.

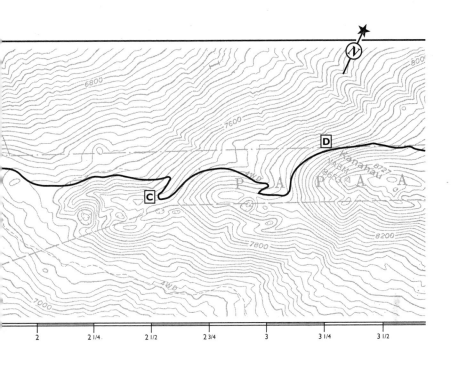

Go around a locked yellow gate, blocking vehicle access (map point D).

Ascend gradually on two switchbacks. The *māmane* disappear, and the shrubs hunker down. Look for evening primrose with its yellow flowers. You may also see some feral goats in this area.

Climb steadily on five lazy switchbacks. The *pūkiawe* and *kīlau* gradually thin and then disappear.

On the left, pass a low mound of red cinders known as Kalepeamoa (map point E).

On the left is a fenced enclosure to protect a planting of *'āhinahina,* the Haleakalā silversword.

Another dirt road comes in on the left. Continue straight on the Skyline Trail.

On the right, pass two pit craters, the second one larger than the first.

Go through a gate, closing it behind you.

Cross over to the right side of the ridge (map point F) and continue climbing. The view is now of the leeward slopes of

Haleakalā. In the distance are the summits of Mauna Kea and Mauna Loa on the Big Island.

Go around a locked gate, blocking vehicle access.

Shortly afterward, reach the end of the Skyline Trail at a signed junction with a paved road (map point G). Turn right on it toward the summit of Haleakalā. (To the left the road leads to an FAA radar installation.)

Pass a communication facility on the left.

Reach a second junction. Keep right on the main road. (The paved road to the left leads to Science City, an astronomy center.)

Enter Haleakalā National Park.

Reach a third junction (map point H). This time turn left and up. (The main road continues straight to the Haleakalā Visitor Center, 0.7 miles distant.) To the right is Magnetic Peak.

Walk through a parking lot and climb some stairs to reach the top of Puʻu Ulaʻula (Red Hill), the summit of Haleakalā (elevation 10,023 feet) (map point I) (UTM 4Q 786155E, 2292468N) (Lat/Long N20.70989, W156.2527). At the

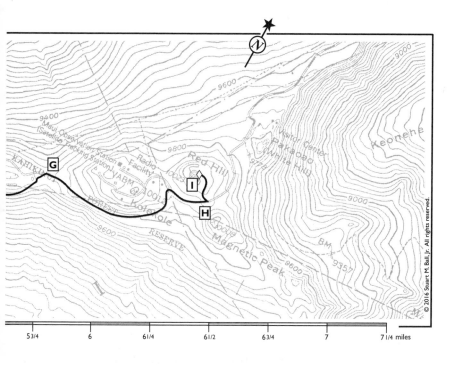

enclosed summit lookout is a breathtaking view into Haleakalā crater.

## NOTES

Most hikers drive to the top of Haleakalā (house of the sun) and then walk down into the crater. If you want to climb the volcano, take the Skyline Trail. The trail is actually a rough dirt and cinder road. It ascends 6.5 miles from the Skyline switchback to a paved road leading to the summit of Haleakalā. The upper section is closed to vehicles to keep the air free of dust for the astronomy complex just below the top. The footing on the road is generally good, and the climbing is steady but not steep. Start early because of the long mileage and large elevation gain.

Like the hike itself, the drive to the trailhead is long and a bit rough. The last 4 miles are over a dusty dirt road. Although rocky in spots, the road is passable for two-wheel-drive vehicles under dry conditions. Do not attempt to drive the dirt portion during or after a heavy rainstorm. In a four-wheel-drive vehicle, you may get as far as the locked gate (map point D). From there the hike becomes a 9-mile round-trip.

On the trail, you climb steadily to an intersection by a flat, grassy area, locally known as Ballpark Junction. In the 1930s, members of the Civilian Conservation Corps played softball there during their time off. While working, they planted many of the introduced evergreens you see on the drive along the dirt road.

Beyond Ballpark Junction, the Skyline Trail ascends through native dryland vegetation. Look for *māmane* trees and *pūkiawe* and *'ōhelo* shrubs. *Māmane* has downy, oblong leaflets and clusters of bright yellow flowers. *Pūkiawe* has tiny, rigid leaves and small white, pink, or red berries. *'Ōhelo* has rounded leaves and delicious red-yellow berries, about the size of blueberries.

To the west are superb views of West Maui. Downslope are upcountry Kula and the resort areas of Wailea (water of Lea) and Kīhei (cloak) along the coast. Across the isthmus you can see the West Maui Mountains and Kahului (the winning) and Wailuku (water of destruction) towns. Across 'Alalākeiki (child's wail) Channel is the island of Kaho'olawe (the carrying away), and across 'Au'au (bathe) Channel lies the island of Lāna'i (day of conquest).

After you pass through the locked gate, the vegetation gradually disappears, revealing a moonscape of cinder cones and pit craters. The trail follows the Southwest Rift Zone of Haleakalā. Rift zones are areas of structural weakness extending from the summit of a shield volcano. They are laced with cracks, providing passageway for rising molten rock, called magma. Two prehistoric eruption cycles, known as the Kula and the Hāna Series, produced the line of cones and craters you are slowly walking by.

The Skyline Trail reaches the 9,000-foot level at Kalepeamoa (rooster's comb), a low mound of red cinder on the left. Above that elevation many people start to feel the altitude. If you have a headache, nausea, or difficulty breathing, slow your pace. Breathe deeply, rest often, and drink plenty of water. Remember you can turn around any time you feel like it.

The summit area, with its radars, observatories, and paved roads, is somewhat of an anticlimax, but not for long. Climb the steps to the enclosed lookout on Puʻu ʻUlaʻula (Red Hill) and take in the awesome view of Haleakalā crater. Check out the exhibits on early Hawaiian use of the area and on the ʻuaʻu, a dark-rumped petrel that nests near the summit.

Needless to say, the hike down is a breeze. Just put one foot in front of the other and let gravity carry you down the slopes. On the way, enjoy the expansive views as the mountain unfolds in front of you.

As just described, the route is a long round-trip climb. You can, of course, hike the trail one way, either up or down. Unfortunately, that option requires a complicated four-hour shuttle to place and retrieve cars at each end. To get to the summit trailhead, follow the directions in the Haleakalā Backpack. Perhaps the best alternative is for a friend to drop you off at either trailhead and pick you up at the other.

34

# Ke Ala Loa O Maui/ Pi'ilani Trail

| | |
|---|---|
| LENGTH: | 4.6-mile round-trip |
| ELEVATION GAIN: | 100 feet |
| DANGER: | Low |
| SUITABLE FOR: | Novice, Intermediate |
| LOCATION: | Maui: Wai'ānapanapa State Park near Hāna |
| TOPO MAP: | Hāna |

## HIGHLIGHTS

This hike follows an ancient Hawaiian path along the rugged windswept Hāna coast. En route are sea arches, tide pools, a *heiau* (religious site), and a black sand beach. The walk ends under a shady tree at lovely Ka'inalimu Bay.

## TRAILHEAD DIRECTIONS

| | |
|---|---|
| **DISTANCE:** | (Kahului to Wai'ānapanapa State Park) 49 miles |
| **DRIVING TIME:** | 2 1/4 hours |

From Kahului take Hāna Hwy (Rte 36). Reach the intersection with Haleakalā Hwy (Rte 37). Continue straight on Hāna Hwy.

Drive through Lower Pāʻia, a plantation town, and pass Hoʻokipa Beach Park, with its pounding surf.

Just past the last turnoff to Makawao (Kaupakulua Rd.), the road becomes Rte 360.

For the next 35 miles, the narrow road winds into and out of numerous lush gulches along the windward coast of Maui. At the back of each gulch is a stream, sometimes a waterfall, and a one-lane bridge to cross them.

On the right, pass Kaumahina State Wayside, which has restrooms and a scenic overlook of Keʻanae Peninsula.

Pass Keʻanae Arboretum on the right.

On the left, pass Puaʻakaʻa State Wayside, which has restrooms and a short walk to a lovely pool across the road.

Pass the junction with the road to Hāna Airport.

About a mile past the airport road, turn left on a Honokalani St. to Waiʻānapanapa State Park.

By the park headquarters, turn left again toward Paʻiloa Point and the camping and picnic areas.

Park in the lot at the end of the road (elevation 40 feet) (map point A) (UTM 4Q 811870E, 2301666N) (Lat/Long N20.78877, W156.00442). Waiʻānapanapa State Park has drinking water, restrooms, outdoor showers, picnic tables, rental cabins, and a campground.

**ROUTE DESCRIPTION**

From the parking lot, walk *makai* (seaward) past several interpretive signs to an overlook of Paʻiloa Bay. Below is a black sand beach and to the right a sea arch carved out of a spit jutting into the ocean.

At the overlook, turn right on a paved path along the coast. (To the left the path becomes a short loop trail to Waiʻānapanapa Cave.)

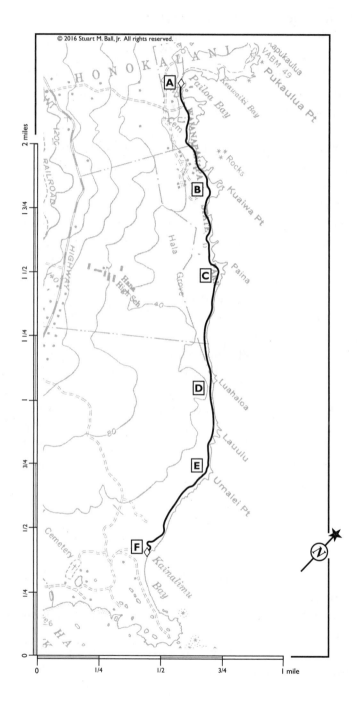

Go through a break in a rock wall. Underfoot are the large seeds of the *kamani haole* (tropical almond) tree.

Reach a junction by another overlook. Keep right along the cliff. (The path to the left leads down to the black sand beach.)

On the right, pass Honokalani Cemetery and the state park campground. On the left is a craggy islet frequented by *noio* (black noddy). Look for *milo* trees, with their heart-shaped leaves.

As the railing ends, reach a signed junction. Continue straight on a wide, grassy path by the cemetery. (On the left the paved path descends to another overlook.)

Walk along the rugged shoreline made up of black, clinkery *'a'ā* lava. The native shrub *naupaka kahakai* spills down the cliff, almost touching the water. *Mauka* (inland) is a grove of *hala* trees.

Pass the state park cabins on the right. Ignore the paths leading to them.

A dirt road comes in on the right (map point B). *Makai* is Kuaiwa Point, with a three-hole blowhole.

Cross a sea arch; the sea surges underneath.

Descend a small cliff. Tide pools dot the wave-swept ledges. Along the rock face to the right is a faded Hawaiian pictograph.

Reach Ohala Heiau (religious site), which has several platforms and massive rock walls.

The treadway follows a line of smooth stones.

Cross a flat, grassy area near Pa'ina Point (map point C).

Just past a grove of ironwood trees, another grassy dirt road comes in on the right. In the distance *mauka* lie the slopes of Haleakalā, dotted with old cinder cones of the Hāna Series of prehistoric eruptions.

Pass a rock shelter on the left and traverse jumbled-up *'a'ā* lava covered with lichen. Smooth stones underfoot make the going easier.

Walk along a sheer cliff pounded by the surf through scattered ironwood trees. The footing is rough and rocky.

On the right, pass Luahaloa Fishing Hale, a weathered shelter used by local fishermen (map point D).

Cross the base of twin Lauʻulu Point. Here the smooth wave-washed cliffs are topped by an unruly mop of ʻaʻā. At the waterline is a colorful band of pink corraline algae.

Pass Umalei Point on the left (map point E). Small rocks line the trail to mark the way. You can see Kaʻinalimu Bay and Nānuʻalele Point farther along the coast. In back of them is Kaʻuiki Head, covered with ironwoods. It is a prehistoric cinder cone and the legendary home of Māui, demigod and trickster.

Descend briefly through a shady grove of *kamani* trees. *Lauaʻe* ferns carpet the ground.

Emerge on to the rocky beach at Kaʻinalimu Bay (map point F) (UTM 5Q 189237E, 2299307N) (Lat/Long N20.76767, W155.98454).

## NOTES

In the Hāna area, most hikers take the popular trail up ʻOheʻo (gathering of pools) Gulch. While they are all jostling for space at Waimoku Falls, try this less-traveled coastal walk instead. After you pass the campground and cabins, you and a few local fishermen have this wild coast all to yourselves.

If possible, take this hike in the early morning or late afternoon. The air is cooler then, and the colors are vivid and contrasting: blue sky and sea, green vegetation, black lava, and white coral and driftwood.

Before you start the hike, a few cautions are in order. The route traverses a rocky, windswept coastline exposed to powerful currents and surf. While exploring, remember the old saying: never turn your back on the ocean. At the beaches, there are no lifeguards. If you decide to swim, you are on your own.

After you pass the campground, look for the native low-lying shrub *naupaka kahakai*. It has bright-green, fleshy leaves and white half-flowers with purple streaks. The unusual appearance of the flowers has given rise to several unhappy legends. According to one, a Hawaiian maiden believed her lover unfaithful. In anger she tore all the *naupaka* flowers in half. She then asked him to find a whole flower to prove his love. He was, of course, unsuccessful and died of a broken heart.

On the *makai* side of the cemetery are several *milo*, a possible Polynesian introduction. The tree has shiny, heart-shaped leaves and pale-yellow flowers, similar to a hibiscus. Early Hawaiians carved the reddish-brown wood into bowls used for food preparation. The dried fruit, shaped like a slightly flattened globe, produced a yellow-green dye.

On the islet in Pa'iloa Bay, look for *noio* (black noddy), a member of the tern family and a year-round resident. The *noio* has black plumage with a white cap and a yellow bill. In flight the noddy resembles a swallow with quick turns and movements. *Noio* skim along the ocean to catch small fish, often brought to the surface by schools of larger fish.

Near the cabins are groves of *hala* trees. They have distinctive prop roots that help support the heavy clusters of leaves and fruit on the ends of the branches. Early Hawaiians braided the long, pointed leaves, called *lau hala,* into baskets, fans, floor mats, and sails.

Farther along the route is Ohala Heiau, a place of worship for early Hawaiians. The site has several platforms and massive rock walls. Beyond the *heiau,* smooth stepping-stones make the walking easier. They are the remnants of an old Hawaiian footpath, known as the King's Highway. *Ali'i* (chiefs), commoners, and tax collectors used the highway to travel between *ahupua'a* (land divisions) along the coast.

Without the stepping-stones, the trail becomes rough and obscure in spots. Watch your footing on the loose *'a'ā* lava. Look for small rocks lining the route. You can hardly get lost, but the walking is a lot easier if you stay on the trail.

The hike ends under a shady beach heliotrope tree partway along Ka'inalimu (seaweed procession) Bay. Find a comfortable spot and stretch out. Take in the broad sweep of the bay. Listen for the growl from the rocks as the surf rubs them together.

There are several variations on this hike. For a short 1-mile walk, go as far as the *heiau* and then turn around. For a longer hike, continue around Ka'inalimu Bay to Nānu'alele (the altar heaps) Point. You can also hike the coastal trail in the other direction for about 0.7 miles. At the overlook in the state park, turn left past Wai'ānap'anapa (glistening water) Cave. The route passes two small beaches and ends at Hāna Airport. Be sure to visit the cave; its haunting secret is retold on a nearby wooden sign.

# 35

# 'Ohe'o Gulch

| LENGTH: | 4.0-mile round-trip |
|---|---|
| ELEVATION GAIN: | 900 feet |
| DANGER: | Low |
| SUITABLE FOR: | Novice, Intermediate |
| LOCATION: | Maui: Haleakalā National Park, Kīpahulu area near Hāna |
| TOPO MAP: | Kīpahulu |

## HIGHLIGHTS

This hike leads into a lush, steep-walled gulch, known as 'Ohe'o. Along the route are lovely streams, early Hawaiian rock walls, and dense bamboo groves. At the end is powerful Waimoku Falls, cascading down a fern-covered cliff.

## TRAILHEAD DIRECTIONS

**DISTANCE:** (Kahului to Kīpahulu Ranger Station) 61 miles
**DRIVING TIME:** 2 3/4 hours

From Kahului take Hāna Hwy (Rte 36).
Reach the intersection with Haleakalā Hwy (Rte 37). Continue straight on Hāna Hwy.
Drive through Lower Pā'ia, a plantation town, and pass Ho'okipa Beach Park, with its pounding surf.

'OHE'O GULCH ⊠ HĀNA

Just past the last turnoff to Makawao (Kaupakulua Rd.) the road becomes Rte 360.

For the next 35 miles, the narrow road winds into and out of numerous lush gulches along the windward coast of Maui. At the back of each gulch is a stream, sometimes a waterfall, and a one-lane bridge to cross them.

On the right, pass Kaumahina State Wayside, which has restrooms and a scenic overlook of Ke'anae Peninsula.

Pass Ke'anae Arboretum on the right.

On the left, pass Pua'aka'a State Wayside, which has restrooms and a short walk to a lovely pool across the road.

On the left, pass the roads leading to Hāna Airport and Wai'ānapanapa State Park.

At the fork in Hāna village, keep right on Rte 360.

Pass Travaasa Hotel Hāna and Hasegawa General Store on the left.

Just outside Hāna, Rte 360 becomes Pi'ilani Hwy (Rte 31).

The road winds into and out of numerous gulches.

After mile marker 42, enter Haleakalā National Park, Kīpahulu Area.

Cross 'Ohe'o Gulch on a white bridge.

Shortly turn left and pay the fee at the entrance station (elevation 140 feet) (map point A) (UTM 4Q 807912E, 2287550N) (Lat/Long N20.66205, W156.04487).

After passing the campground on the right, park in one of the two lots and take the stairs down to the visitor center. Nearby are restrooms, drinking water, and picnic tables.

## ROUTE DESCRIPTION

From the visitor center, take the paved path toward a bulletin board displaying trail warnings.

Shortly reach a signed junction. Turn left onto the Pīpīwai Trail. (To the right a path leads down 'Ohe'o Gulch past several swimming holes to Kūloa Point.). Behind the junction is Hale Kū'ai, a replica of a Hawaiian storage and trading house.

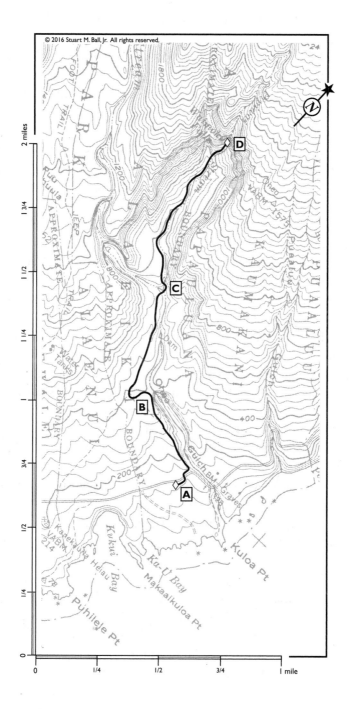

Bear left through a break in the wall and cross the highway.

The trail jogs right, paralleling the highway and then left toward the mountains.

Ascend gradually through Java plum and *hala* trees. Note that the Park Service has placed warning signs on many of the side trails leading down into 'Ohe'o Gulch.

The trail goes along the edge of a pasture overgrown with grass and guava trees.

Enter a grove of Christmas berry trees. *Laua'e* ferns carpet the ground.

Reach an overlook of Makahiku Falls at a rock wall (map point B).

Shortly go through a gate in a fence, closing it after you.

Pass the remains of a rock wall by a spreading banyan tree. Along the trail are the tangled branches of *hau* trees, with their yellow flowers.

Pass a large mango tree. On the right is an overlook of a double waterfall pouring into a deep pool.

Cross 'Ohe'o Stream on a bridge (map point C). The stream splits above the crossing, forming several waterfalls. To the left is Palikea Stream, which drains the eastern side of Kīpahulu Valley. To the right is Pīpīwai Stream.

Walk through bamboo briefly and then cross Pīpīwai Stream on another bridge.

Pass several huge mango trees. Look for bird's-nest ferns nestled in the trunks and branches.

Climb gradually through a bamboo forest on a series of boardwalks.

Keep left and up as the trail forks.

Descend to Pīpīwai Stream and follow it upstream. The trail becomes rough, narrow, and wet.

After one last boardwalk, look through the trees for a glimpse of three waterfalls cascading down the cliffs ahead. Waimoku is the middle and most impressive fall.

Ford a stream flowing from the waterfall on the left.

Reach the base of Waimoku Falls (elevation 1,000 feet)

(map point D) (UTM 4Q 806628E, 2289271N) (Lat/Long N20.67779, W156.05688).

'Ohe'o (gathering of pools) Gulch is a very popular tourist hike, and deservedly so. The short, well-maintained Pīpīwai (sprinkling water) Trail follows a wild stream to a stunning waterfall. If you want to miss the crowd, take the walk in the early morning or late afternoon. If you want to miss the mosquitoes, keep moving.

While you are hiking, keep in mind that the streams are subject to flash flooding. 'Ohe'o Gulch drains much of Kīpahulu (fetch from exhausted gardens) Valley, a huge watershed. A heavy rainstorm back in the valley can trigger a rapid increase in stream flow. If the water level rises suddenly, move to high ground immediately. The Park Service reports that 'Ohe'o Stream can rise 4 feet in 10 minutes; I don't doubt them.

The trail initially climbs alongside the gulch through a mixed forest of Java plum, guava, Christmas berry, and *hala* trees. In the late 1800s to the early 1900s, this area was planted in sugarcane and then pineapples. The sugar mill and plantation village were just down the road in Kīpahulu. Early Hawaiians also cultivated the area, as evidenced by the rock walls.

One of the trees the Hawaiians found useful was the *hala*. It has distinctive prop roots that help support the heavy clusters of leaves and fruit on the end of the branches. The early Hawaiians braided the long, pointed leaves, called *lau hala,* into baskets, fans, floor mats, and sails.

Near the rock walls are some tangled *hau* trees. They have large, heart-shaped leaves. Their flowers are bright yellow with a dark-red center and resemble those of a hibiscus. Early Hawaiians used the wood for kites and canoe outriggers, the bark for sandals, and the sap as a laxative.

'Ohe'o Stream forks at the twin bridges. The trail continues up the right fork, Pīpīwai Stream. The left fork, Palikea (white

'OHE'O GULCH ⌗ HĀNA

cliff) Stream, penetrates deep into Kīpahulu Valley, a biological reserve closed to the general public. The valley contains a vast *koa* and *'ōhi'a* rain forest that provides habitat for many native birds, including the endangered *nukupu'u* and Maui parrotbill.

In the upper section of the streams live *'o'opu,* small native fishes in the goby family. After birth, the young fish swim all the way down to the ocean. To mature fully, the *'o'opu* must return to the fresh water of the upper streams. The fish climbs the waterfalls by using a suction cup evolved from its lower front fins to cling to the wet rocks.

Waimoku Falls is both powerful and delicate. A wall of white water free-falls from cliff to canyon bottom. Behind and to the side, rivulets cascade down the banded rock. The falling water creates its own breeze, laden with a fine mist. If the sun is shining, a rainbow forms across the shallow pool at the base.

After returning from the gulch hike, take the short loop walk *makai* (seaward) of the visitor center. The path descends to Kūloa Point and then returns along 'Ohe'o Stream. The stream drops to the ocean in a series of pools separated by small waterfalls. Pick a pool and take a cooling dip.

36

# Hoapili Trail

| LENGTH: | 4.2-mile round-trip |
| --- | --- |
| ELEVATION GAIN: | 200 feet |
| DANGER: | Low |
| SUITABLE FOR: | Novice |
| LOCATION: | Maui: Southwest coast beyond Mākena |
| TOPO MAP: | Mākena |

## HIGHLIGHTS

This hike follows an ancient Hawaiian footpath to the dry Kanaio coast. Along the way are historic sites, tide pools, pocket-size beaches, and the last lava flow from Haleakalā. The walk ends at a secluded cove shaded by contorted *kiawe* trees.

## TRAILHEAD DIRECTIONS

DISTANCE: (Kahului to La Perouse Bay) 23 miles
DRIVING TIME: 3/4 hour

From Kahului take Puʻunēnē Ave (Rte 311).
Near the sugar mill in Puʻunēnē town, bear right on Mokulele Hwy (still Rte 311) toward Kīhei.

HOAPILI TRAIL    KĪHEI

The road swings left along the leeward coast and becomes Piʻilani Hwy (Rte 31).

Pass sprawling Kīhei on the right.

Rte 31 ends abruptly. Turn right on Wailea Iki Rd. into the Wailea resort area.

At the road end by the shops at Wailea, turn left on Mākena Alanui Rd.

The road narrows to two lanes and passes Makena State Park.

The road narrows some more, and the pavement becomes bumpy and uneven.

Drive through ʻĀhihi-Kīnaʻu Natural Area Reserve.

As the pavement ends, pass the La Pérouse Monument on the left. Turn right on a rough road toward the shore. Park near the beach (map point A) (UTM 4Q 768903E, 2279946N) (Lat/Long N20.59942, W156.42011).

## ROUTE DESCRIPTION

At the beach, take the trail along the shore of Keoneʻōʻio Bay, also known as La Pérouse Bay.

Immediately pass the site of Paʻalua Heiau (religious site).

A dirt road comes in on the left (map point B). Continue straight to follow the road along the coast.

Walk barren ʻaʻā lava from the 1790 eruption of Haleakalā. To the left and back is Puʻu o Kanaloa cone; farther upslope is Puʻu Naio. Both are prehistoric cinder cones.

Stroll under shady *kiawe* trees past old rock walls.

Pass a small beach with tide pools in the rocks nearby. On the right, look for a native *milo*, with its heart-shaped leaves.

The road forks, just past a vehicle turnaround (map point C). Keep left, briefly paralleling a wire fence. (The right fork hugs the shore and ends at a small cove.)

The road winds through clinkery red ʻaʻā lava.

Reach a junction near a grove of *kiawe* (map point D). Turn left through a vehicle barrier of cemented lava rock. (The road continues straight to a beacon at the tip of Cape Hanamanioa.)

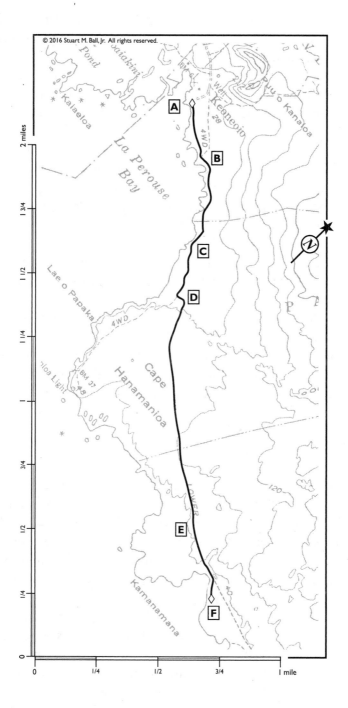

Shortly afterward, reach a signed junction. Turn right on the Hoapili Trail. (To the left a trail leads back to the main dirt road at the wire fence.)

The Hoapili Trail heads straight across the base of Cape Hanamanioa. Beautifully constructed rock causeways smooth out the dips in the lava flow. Watch your step on the loose rock, however.

At the top of the first rise, look *makai* (seaward) across ʻAlalākeiki Channel to see the islands of Kahoʻolawe and Lānaʻi. In front of Lānaʻi is the islet of Molokini. Upslope is Puʻu Pūmoe, a prehistoric cone named after a demigod who lived in the sea.

Cross the base of Kamanamana Point (map point E). On the left you can look all the way up to the astronomy complex near the top of Haleakalā. In front of you extends the Kanaio coast.

Descend steeply off the lava flow to a lovely cove backed by *kiawe* (map point F) (UTM 4Q 771283E, 2278062N) (Lat/ Long N20.58207, W156.39758). Look for the native shrubs *naupaka kahakai* and *naio*. Beyond is a tiny white sand beach and rock shelves with tide pools.

## NOTES

The Hoapili Trail traverses a short section of the hot, dry south-west coast. Winter (November–April) is the most comfortable time of year to take this hike. If you go in summer (May–October), start early in the morning or late in the afternoon. Besides being hot, the intense midday sun washes out the vivid coastal colors: blue sea and sky, green vegetation, black lava, and white coral and driftwood.

Leeward coasts, such as this one, generally have less-powerful surf and currents than windward coasts, especially in summer. Nevertheless, remember the old saying: never turn your back on the ocean. At the beaches, there are no lifeguards. If you decide to swim, you are on your own.

The hike starts at Keoneʻōʻio (the sandy place with bone-fish) Bay, also named La Pérouse after the French explorer. On May 29, 1786, he sailed along this coast in command of two frigates, *La Boussole* and *L'Astrolabe*. The expedition was met by about 150 canoes laden with trading goods. The next morning, La Pérouse and a well-armed party went ashore nearby and exchanged gifts with the Hawaiian natives.

The route initially crosses a jagged *ʻaʻā* flow from Haleakalā (house of the sun) Volcano. In 1790, lava erupted from two vents *mauka* (inland) and poured into the ocean, creating Cape Kīnaʻu (flaw) on the western side of the bay. The date of the lava flow was estimated by comparing maps of the coastline drawn by the La Pérouse expedition of 1786 and the Vancouver expedition of 1793. The eruption in 1790 may not have been the last for Haleakalā, which is still classified as a dormant volcano.

The *heiau* (religious site) and rock walls along the way are evidence of ancient Hawaiian use of the area. At the first small beach is a native *milo*, a possible Polynesian introduction. The tree has shiny, heart-shaped leaves and pale-yellow flowers, similar to a hibiscus. Early Hawaiians carved the reddish-brown wood into bowls used for food preparation. The dried fruit, shaped like a slightly flattened globe, produced a yellow-green dye.

The Hoapili Trail roughly follows an old Hawaiian foot-path, known as the King's Highway. *Aliʻi* (chiefs), commoners, and tax collectors used the highway to travel between *ahupuaʻa* (land divisions). Hoapili, governor of Maui, had the route reconstructed in the early 1800s and gave it his name. The trail was restored by volunteers under the direction of Na Ala Hele, a state program involved in trail maintenance and access. The route resembles a Roman road with its straight, graded alignment.

At the end of the trail is a secluded cove and beach. Plop down underneath a shady *kiawe* tree and take a well-earned rest. If ambition gets the better of you, check out the tide pools or go swimming. In winter look for migratory shorebirds, such as *ʻūlili*, the wandering tattler, with its yellow legs.

HOAPILI TRAIL ▨ KĪHEI

267

This stretch of coast is named Kanaio, after the *naio* tree. It has narrow, pointed leaves and tiny white flowers. Early Hawaiians used the hard, heavy wood for house posts and rafters and in tools for making fishnets. They also burned it as a torch for night fishing. As the wood dries, it has a fragrance similar to *'iliahi* (sandalwood), but the smell doesn't last as long. When the sandalwood trade with China declined in the middle 1800s, *naio* was offered as a substitute, but the Chinese wouldn't buy it.

You can explore farther along the Kanaio coast. A rough road leads to more coves, beaches, tide pools, and a blowhole. Other options include a side trip to the beacon at Cape Hanamanioa. On the return you can proceed straight at the signed junction, taking the trail that parallels the dirt road and ends at the wire fence.

37

# Waihe'e Ridge

| | |
|---|---|
| LENGTH: | 5.0-mile round-trip |
| ELEVATION GAIN: | 1,500 feet |
| DANGER: | Low |
| SUITABLE FOR: | Novice, Intermediate |
| LOCATION: | Maui: West Maui Forest Reserve near Waihe'e |
| TOPO MAP: | Wailuku |

### HIGHLIGHTS

This incredible hike leads deep into the wet and wild West Maui Mountains. Along the way is a rich variety of native rain forest plants. From the summit picnic table, you may glimpse the deep gorges and massive ridges leading to Pu'u Kukui, one of the wettest areas on earth.

### TRAILHEAD DIRECTIONS

**DISTANCE:** (Kahului to Waihe'e Ridge trailhead) 10 miles
**DRIVING TIME:** 1/2 hour

From Kahului take Ka'ahumanu Ave (Rte 32) toward Wailuku.
Turn right on Kahului Beach Rd. (Rte 3400).

*WAIHE'E RIDGE*

*WEST MAUI*

Pass the harbor on the right and Maui Community College on the left.

Turn right on Waiehu Beach Rd. (still Rte 3400).

At the road end, turn right on Kahekili Hwy (Rte 340).

Drive through Waiheʻe village and cross Waiheʻe River on a bridge.

The road narrows and curves in and out of several gulches.

Pass mile marker 6.

At 0.9 miles past the marker, turn left on a paved road to Camp Maluhia, a Boy Scout camp. The intersection is across from the Mendes Ranch gate.

After driving 0.8 miles, pass the signed trailhead on the left and park in the large gravel lot on the right (elevation 1,069 feet) (map point A) (UTM 4Q 756605E, 2318951N) (Lat/Long N20.95325, W156.53229). The parking area has a portable toilet, but no other facilities.

## ROUTE DESCRIPTION

Walk back down the road to the trailhead and turn right around a gate onto a dirt road.

Ascend steeply on the one-lane road, now paved.

Just before the road ends at a water tank, bear left on the Waiheʻe Ridge Trail.

Enter a small gulch, filled with *kukui* and guava trees.

Go around a second gate through a stile.

Pass a grove of Cook pines on the left.

Work right, out of the gulch, through eucalyptus trees.

As the trail switchbacks to the left, reach an overlook with a bench. To the right is a waterfall along Makamakakaʻole Stream. Straight ahead is Kānoa Ridge, our destination. Nearby are several small native ʻōhiʻa trees with yellow flowers.

Cross over to the left side of Kānoa Ridge (map point B). The view is now of Waiheʻe Valley and River. In the distance you can see Wailuku and Kahului towns and the slopes of Haleakalā.

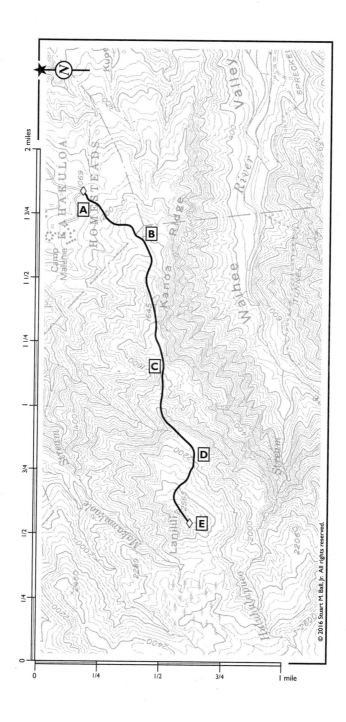

Stroll through a lovely open stretch lined with *uluhe* ferns.

Look for the native bird, *'apapane,* flitting among the *'ōhi'a.*

Pass a second bench near a lone Cook pine.

Go through a stile in a wire fence. The trail narrows.

Ascend steadily on a double series of short switchbacks. Watch for native *kōpiko* trees and listen for the distinctive call of the Japanese bush warbler (*uguisu*).

At the back of a small gulch, the trail levels briefly and then resumes climbing (map point C).

After passing a stand of paperbark trees, bear right across a flat, marshy area (map point D). To the right is a hanging gulch leading down to Makamakaka'ole Stream.

Climb Lanilili Hill on a series of switchbacks. Look for *hāpu'u* and *'ama'u* ferns and stunted *'ōhi'a* with red, yellow, and salmon-colored blossoms.

Reach the flat top of Lanilili (elevation 2,563 feet) (map point E) (UTM 4Q 754607E, 2318194N) (Lat/Long N20.9467, W156.55161).

The trail ends at a picnic table with a superb view of the West Maui Mountains.

## NOTES

Waihe'e (octopus liquid) Ridge is a misty hike through a native rain forest. Expect to get wet, and you won't be disappointed. After all, a rain forest should be experienced in the rain, right? If the weather just happens to be sunny and clear, count yourself lucky.

The ridge trail is well graded and maintained. The climbing is steady but rarely steep. Hike as far as you want and then turn around; even going partway is worthwhile.

Along the trail are well over fifty different species of native plants that prefer a wet mountain habitat. All are identified and illustrated in the pamphlet, *Waihe'e Ridge Trail Native Plant Guide,* available from the State Division of Forestry and Wildlife in Wailuku. The address is in the appendix. The pamphlet may also be available online. The notes below describe a few of the more easily identified native plants.

After the overlook of Makamakaʻoleʻole (without friends) Stream, begin looking for native ʻōhiʻa. When first seen along Kānoa (bowl) Ridge, they are good-sized trees. By the end of the hike, they have become small shrubs, stunted by the exposed conditions higher up. ʻŌhiʻa has oval, dull-green leaves and clusters of delicate red, yellow, or salmon-colored flowers. Native birds, such as the ʻapapane, feed on the nectar and help with pollination.

You may catch a glimpse of an ʻapapane in the forest canopy. It has a red breast and head, black wings and tail, and a slightly curved black bill. In flight the ʻapapane makes a whirring sound as it darts from tree to tree searching for insects and nectar.

On the series of short switchbacks look for kōpiko, a native member of the coffee family. It has leathery, oblong leaves with a light-green midrib. Turn the leaf over to see a row of tiny holes (piko [navel]) on either side of the midrib. The kōpiko produces clusters of tiny white flowers and fleshy, orange fruits.

Also, on the switchbacks listen for the Japanese bush warbler (uguisu), a bird often heard but rarely seen. Its distinctive cry starts with a long whistle and then winds down in a series of notes. The bush warbler is olive brown on top with a white breast and a long tail.

On the upper section are two native ferns, ʻamaʻu and hāpuʻu. You can tell them apart by the structure of their fronds. Those of ʻamaʻu branch once before the green segments are attached to the stem. The fronds are red when young, gradually turning green with age. Hāpuʻu fronds branch several times before the green segments. Their fronds have a lacy, delicate appearance.

From the summit picnic table is a view not easily forgotten, perhaps because it is so rare. All around lies the convoluted topography of the West Maui Mountains. Massive ridges alternate with deeply dissected valleys. Below and to the west is Huluhulupueo (owl feathers) Stream, which flows into Waiheʻe River. Beyond the stream to the right is

Keahikauō (the dragged fire), a hill rising from a swamp. The broad ridge to the southwest climbs to ʻEke Crater (elevation 4,480 feet), a flat-topped volcanic dome with a bog on top. Beyond the crater, the mountains rise steadily to Puʻu Kukui (candlenut hill) (elevation 5,788 feet), one of the wettest areas on earth.

# 38

# Lahaina Pali

| LENGTH: | 5.0 miles one way |
|---------|-------------------|
| ELEVATION GAIN: | 1,600 feet |
| DANGER: | Low |
| SUITABLE FOR: | Intermediate |
| LOCATION: | Maui: West Maui Mountains near Māʻalaea Harbor |
| TOPO MAP: | Māʻalaea |

## HIGHLIGHTS

This hot, dry, but very scenic hike follows a historic horse and foot trail built in the early 1800s. Numbered signs along the route explain various points of interest. From lookouts along the cliffs you may see humpback whales in the ocean below.

## TRAILHEAD DIRECTIONS

As the route is point-to-point, this hike has two trailheads: one near Māʻalaea Harbor and the other near Ukumehame Beach Park.

**DISTANCE:** (Kahului to Ukumehame trailhead) 12 miles
**DRIVING TIME:** 1/2 hour

From Kahului take Puʻunēnē Ave. (Rte 350) toward Puʻunēnē.

Turn right on Kūihelani Hwy (Rte 380).

At the road end, turn left on Honoapiʻilani Hwy (Rte 30) toward Lahaina.

At the next traffic light, continue straight through the intersection with Kīhei Rd. (Rte 31).

To get to Māʻalaea trailhead, turn right onto a dirt road about 0.2 miles beyond the Kīhei intersection. The turn is marked by a Lahaina Pali Trail sign.

Immediately drive through the unlocked gate on the right, closing it behind you.

Drive through a second unlocked gate and turn left onto a wide gravel road.

Bear right off the road into a small lot and park there (elevation 200 feet) (map point G) (UTM 4Q 758876E, 2302829N) (Lat/Long N20.8074, W156.51287).

To get to Ukumehame trailhead, continue on Honoapiʻilani Hwy (Rte 30) toward Lahaina.

On the left, pass several turnoffs to the aquarium and Māʻalaea Harbor.

Drive by the scenic lookout at Papawai Point, also on the left.

Go through a tunnel.

About 0.4 miles beyond the tunnel, turn right into a dirt area shaded by *kiawe* trees and park there (elevation 10 feet) (map point A) (UTM 4Q 753602E, 2301018N) (Lat/Long N20.79178, W156.56377). If necessary, drop off people and packs and shuttle one car back to Māʻalaea trailhead.

## ▩ ROUTE DESCRIPTION

At the back of the parking area, take the trail past some information plaques.

Climb briefly up Manawaipueo Gulch and then turn right on an old *pali* (cliff) road.

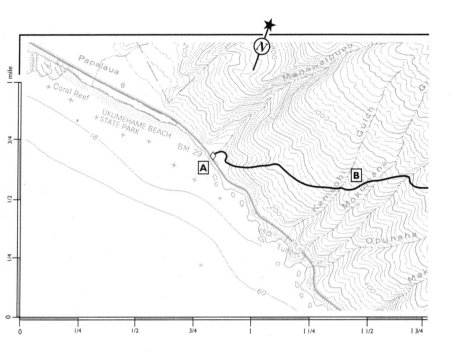

Shortly reach a signed junction. Turn left off the road onto the Lahaina Pali Trail.

Ascend steadily through grass-covered lava, roughly paralleling the coast. Some sections still have the original rock pavement. Watch for graffiti cut in the rock by travelers long ago.

The trail levels briefly by a shady *kiawe* tree above the tunnel portal. Look back to see Lahaina town and the island of Lānaʻi across ʻAuʻau Channel.

Cross Kamaohi Gulch (map point B). The trail gradually works *mauka* (inland).

Climb steeply alongside Mokumana Gulch and then cross it.

Cross Ōpūnahā Gulch (map point C).

Cross shallow Makahuna and Kaʻalaina Gulches.

Descend gradually into rocky Manawainui Gulch (map point D) and climb steeply out of the gulch on three switchbacks.

Cross a line of wind turbines and their gravel access road. Interpretive signs explain the wind energy generation facility.

Contour across a grassy area known as Kaheawa Pastures to the highest point along the trail (elevation 1,600 feet). To

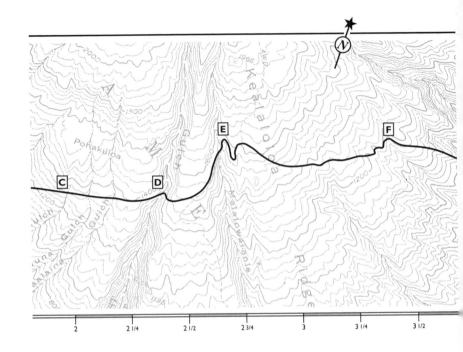

the east, Haleakalā dominates the view. To the south are the islet of Molokini and the island of Kahoʻolawe across ʻAlalākeiki Channel.

After descending some stone stairs, reach a signed junction. Turn left on dirt McGregor Point Rd.

Cross Malalowaiaole Gulch on the road (map point E).

As the road swings sharp left up Kealaloloa Ridge, turn right and down on the Lahaina Pali Trail.

Descend gradually along broad Kealaloloa Ridge, traversing a series of small gullies. Watch for two native shrubs, ʻilima and ʻiliahialoʻe, the coastal sandalwood.

Bear right and descend steadily down a side ridge (map point F). The path usually hugs the right side of the ridge. On steeper sections, however, the trail slaloms back and forth across the ridge.

A gulch appears on the right. Look for the native shrub ʻaʻaliʻi in this stretch. Along the coast are views of Māʻalaea Harbor, Keālia Fishpond, and Kīhei town. To the left in the distance is Kahului town.

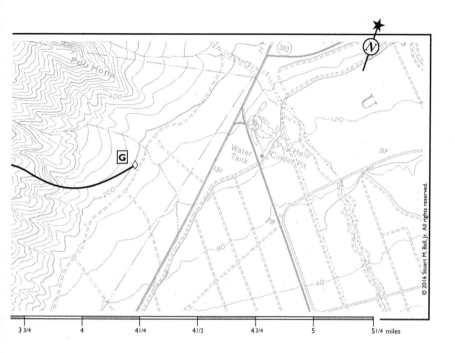

3 3/4    4    4 1/4    4 1/2    4 3/4    5    5 1/4 miles

Swing left away from the gulch and descend more gradually through scattered *kiawe* trees.

Reach the small gravel lot (map point G).

## NOTES

This hot, dry hike is well named; *Pali* means "cliff," and Lāhainā means "cruel sun" in its old pronunciation. Take this climb during the winter (November–April) when the temperature is cooler and the sun less intense. If you must do the hike in summer, drink lots of water and use plenty of sunscreen. Whether in summer or winter, start early to avoid the heat or start very late and just go partway.

In the early 1800s, the Lahaina Pali Trail was constructed across the southern slopes of the West Maui Mountains. The trail provided a more direct route between the Wailuku (water of destruction) and Lahaina Districts. In 1900, prison laborers built a winding dirt road at the base of the *pali* near the coast.

The trail fell into disuse, as travelers preferred the ease of the dirt road and then the paved highway, constructed in 1951. The Lahaina Pali Trail was rebuilt by volunteers under the direction of Na Ala Hele, a state program involved in trail maintenance and access.

The renovated route is well marked but rough and steep in some spots. Along the way are signs explaining the points of interest. The signs are keyed to a pamphlet, *Maui History and Lore from the Lahaina Pali Trail.* If possible, pick one up at the Division of Forestry and Wildlife in Wailuku before starting the hike. The address is in the appendix. The pamphlet may also be available online.

After the initial climb, scan the ocean for humpback whales. They migrate from the North Pacific to Maui, arriving in October and leaving in May. While in the Maui area, they occupy themselves calving, nursing, breeding, and generally horsing around.

While descending broad Kealaloloa (the long pathway) Ridge, watch for two native shrubs, 'ilima and 'iliahialo'e, the coastal sandalwood. 'Ilima has oblong, serrated leaves, about 1 inch long. The yellow-orange flowers strung together have been used to make a regal lei, both in ancient and modern Hawai'i. 'Iliahialo'e has oval, gray-green leaves about 1 to 2 inches long and tiny white star-shaped flowers. 'Iliahialo'e is partially parasitic, with outgrowths on its roots that steal nutrients from nearby plants. Early Hawaiians ground the fragrant heartwood into a powder to perfume their *kapa.*

Look for another native shrub, 'a'ali'i, in Kaheawa Pastures and lower down by the last gulch. It has shiny, narrow leaves and red seed capsules. Early Hawaiians used the leaves and capsules in making lei. When crushed, the capsules produced a red dye for decorating *kapa* (bark cloth).

As described, the route is one way from Ukumehame to Mā'alaea. You can, of course, do the hike in the opposite direction. If you have only one car, start at either trailhead, climb to the top of Kealaloloa Ridge, and return the same way. If you do not want to drive the dirt road to Māʻalaea trailhead, park on Honoapiʻilani Hwy (Rte 30) near the tall utility pole. Follow the driving instructions on foot and add about 1 mile to the one-way hike mileage.

# 39

# 'Ōhai Loop

| | |
|---|---|
| LENGTH: | 1.2-mile loop |
| ELEVATION GAIN: | 100 feet |
| DANGER: | Low |
| SUITABLE FOR: | Novice |
| LOCATION: | Maui: West Maui above Papanalahoa Point |
| TOPO MAP: | Kahakuloa |

## HIGHLIGHTS

This short loop winds above the sea cliffs of West Maui. Along the way are some spectacular coastal views and a good variety of native dryland plants.

## TRAILHEAD DIRECTIONS

**DISTANCE:** (Kahului to 'Ōhai Loop trailhead) 42 miles
**DRIVING TIME:** 1 1/4 hours

From Kahului take Pu'unēnē Ave. (Rte 350) toward Pu'unēnē.

Turn right on Kūihelani Hwy (Rte 380).

At the road's end, turn left on Honoapi'ilani Hwy (Rte 30) toward Lahaina.

Pass Lahaina town and the resort villages of Kā'anapali, Nāpili, and Kapalua.

Past Kapalua the road narrows significantly and winds into and out of numerous gulches. Begin looking for mile markers. Pass mile marker 40.

Just after mile marker 40.5, park in a small paved lot on the left. The trailhead is signed but has no facilities, other than a handicapped parking stall (elevation 280 feet) (map point A) (UTM 4Q 751899E, 2325839N) (Lat/Long N21.01608, W156.57652).

## ROUTE DESCRIPTION

From the parking lot, walk *makai* (seaward) along a paved path.

Almost immediately, pass a signed junction. For now, continue up the path to an overlook. (To the right is the 'Ōhai Trail.) Watch for the native shrub *naupaka kahakai*.

Reach a very scenic lookout. Along the coast to the left is Pō'elua Bay. Across Pailolo Channel is the island of Moloka'i. Kahakuloa is the massive headland that juts out along the coast to the right. See if you can spot Nākālele blowhole spouting from the point across Pō'elua Bay.

Retrace your steps to the signed junction and turn left on the 'Ōhai Trail. Native *'ūlei* shrubs line the trail.

Shortly reach another junction and the start of the loop portion (map point B). Bear right to walk the loop counterclockwise.

Wind above the cliffs, crossing several small gullies. Look for native *'a'ali'i* shrubs and *alahe'e* trees among the introduced lantana and Christmas berry.

Cross a flat, eroded area. Rocks line the trail for easier navigation.

Reach an obscure junction. Keep left on the main trail. (To the right, a short side trail leads to an overlook of Kahakaloa Head.)

The loop swings left and returns along the coast (map point C) (UTM 4Q 752548E, 2325775N) (Lat/Long N21.01542, W156.57029).

Pass a sign identifying some of the topography of the West

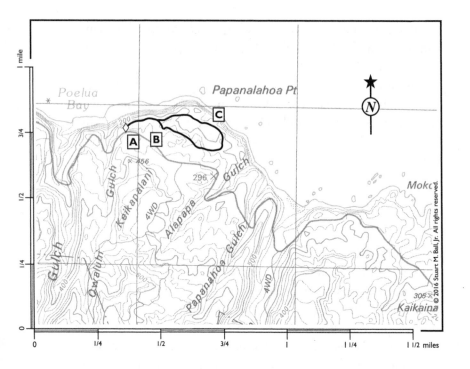

Maui Mountains. On a rare cloudless day, you can see all the way to ʻEke, a flat-topped crater with a bog at the summit.

Reach a plant interpretive sign. Look for low-lying native ʻōhai and the crawling vine pāʻū o Hiʻiaka.

Pass a comfortable bench on the right. Just beyond is a second plant interpretive sign.

Climb briefly to reach the end of the loop and then backtrack to your car.

## NOTES

This short hike is a hidden gem well worth the long drive from central Maui. The loop features windswept headlands and sea cliffs, whale watching in season, and a surprising selection of native coastal vegetation. The Sierra Club provided volunteers to help build the trail a number of years ago.

ʻŌHAI LOOP

WEST MAUI

Lining much of the trail is the sprawling native shrub *'ūlei*. It has small, oblong leaves arranged in pairs; clusters of white, roselike flowers; and white fruit. Early Hawaiians ate the berries and used the tough wood for making digging sticks, fish spears, and *'ūkēkē* (the musical bow).

Also along the loop are the native shrub *a'ali'i* and the native tree *alahe'e*. *'A'ali'i* has shiny, narrow leaves and red seed capsules. Early Hawaiians used the leaves and capsules in making lei. When crushed or boiled, the capsules produced a red dye for decorating *kapa* (bark cloth). *Alahe'e* has oblong leaves that are shiny and dark green. Its fragrant white flowers grow in clusters at the branch tips. Early Hawaiians fashioned the hard wood into farming tools and hooks and spears for fishing.

On the *makai* (seaward) section of the route, scan the ocean for humpback whales. They migrate from the North Pacific to the Hawaiian Islands, arriving in October and leaving in May. The whales congregate off the leeward coast of Maui and occupy themselves calving, nursing, breeding, and generally horsing around.

Behind the first plant identification sign is the low-lying native shrub *'ōhai*, which gave the trail its name. *'Ōhai* has low-lying silver-green leaflets and scarlet winged and clawed flowers. Nearby is *pā'ū o* Hi'iaka, a crawling vine with thick, elliptical leaves and pale-blue bell-shaped flowers. The name means "skirt of Hi'iaka" and derives from a legend about the fire goddess Pele and her baby sister, Hi'iaka. One day, Pele went out to fish, leaving the baby asleep on the beach. When the goddess returned to shore, she found Hi'iaka draped with a vine protecting her from the hot sun.

# O‘AHU

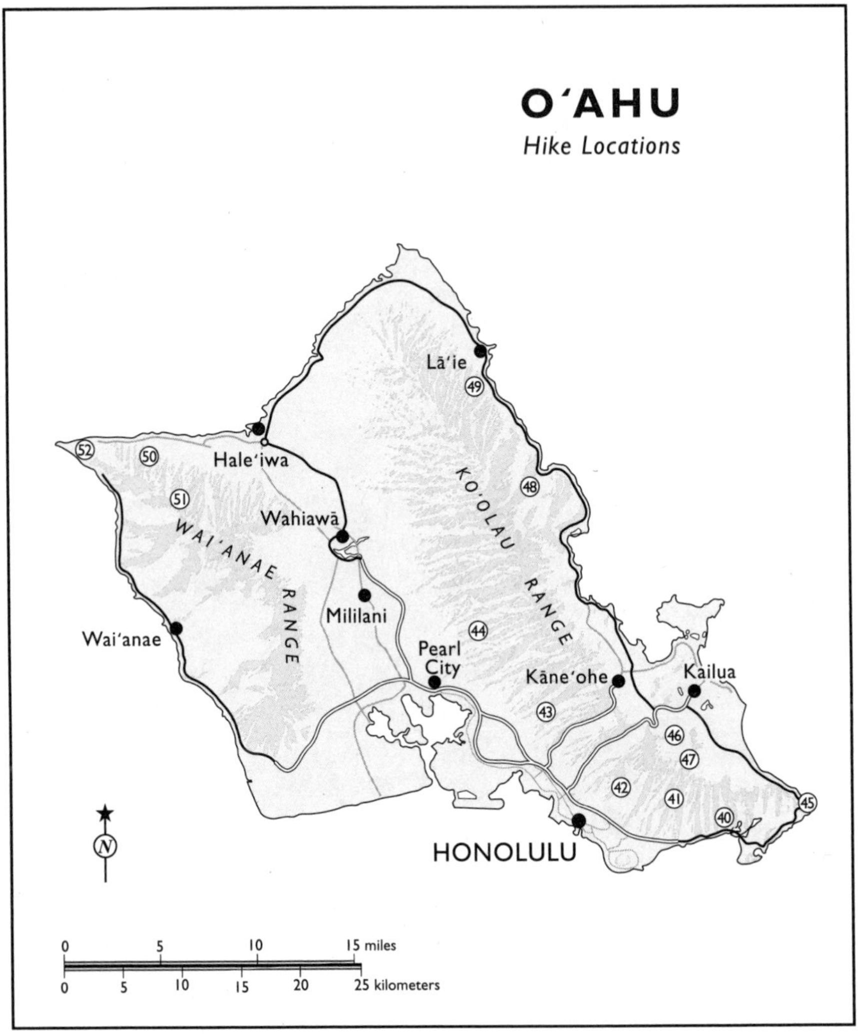
O'AHU
Hike Locations
Lā'ie
(49)
Hale'iwa
(52)
(50)
(51)
KO'OLAU RANGE
(48)
Wahiawā
WAI'ANAE RANGE
Mililani
Wai'anae
(44)
Pearl City
Kāne'ohe
Kailua
(43)
(46)
(47)
(42)
(41)
(40)
(45)
HONOLULU
N
0 5 10 15 miles
0 5 10 15 20 25 kilometers

## 40

# Kuliʻouʻou Ridge

| | |
|---|---|
| LENGTH: | 5.0-mile round-trip |
| ELEVATION GAIN: | 1,800 feet |
| DANGER: | Low |
| SUITABLE FOR: | Novice, Intermediate |
| LOCATION: | Oʻahu: Kuliʻouʻou Forest Reserve above Kuliʻouʻou |
| TOPO MAP: | Koko Head |

### HIGHLIGHTS

This popular hike climbs a dry, shady ridge to the top of the Koʻolau Range. Along the way are some native plants and a stately forest of Cook pines. From the summit lookout are superb views of the windward coast.

### TRAILHEAD DIRECTIONS

**DISTANCE:** (Downtown Honolulu to Kālaʻau Pl.) 11 miles
**DRIVING TIME:** 1/2 hour

At Ward Ave. get on Lunalilo Fwy (H-1) Koko Head bound (east).

As the freeway ends, continue straight on Kalanianaʻole Hwy (Rte 72).

*KULIʻOUʻOU RIDGE* ❊ HONOLULU

289

Drive by ʻĀina Haina and Niu Valley Center on the left.

Pass Holy Trinity Catholic School and Church on the right.

Turn left on Kuliʻouʻou Rd. and head into Kuliʻouʻou Valley.

At the stop sign, turn left and then right, still on Kuliʻouʻou Rd.

Pass Kuliʻouʻou Neighborhood Park on the right. The park has restrooms and drinking water.

At the Dead End sign, turn right on Kālaʻau Pl.

Park on the street just before it ends at a turnaround circle (elevation 260 feet) (map point A) (UTM 4Q 632325E, 2356251N) (Lat/Long N21.3033, W157.72426).

**BUS:** Route 1 on weekends or route 1L on weekdays to Kalanianaʻole Hwy and Kuliʻouʻou Rd. Walk 1.3 miles along Kuliʻouʻou Rd. and Kālaʻau Pl. to the trailhead.

## ROUTE DESCRIPTION

At the back of the circle, go around a yellow gate and take the one-lane, paved road on your left leading down to Kuliʻouʻou Stream.

Before crossing the stream, bear right on a grassy road by the second utility pole.

Register at the hunter/hiker check-in mailbox on the left.

The road narrows and becomes the Kuliʻouʻou Valley Trail. Cross a small gully.

Contour above the intermittent stream through an introduced forest of Christmas berry, *koa haole,* and guava. Look for the low-lying native shrub *ʻūlei* in the open sections.

Reach a signed junction by some small boulders and a patch of *lauaʻe* ferns (map point B). Turn sharp right and up on the Kuliʻouʻou Ridge Trail. (The valley trail continues straight.) Just after the junction, watch for *noni,* a small tree with large, shiny green leaves and warty fruits.

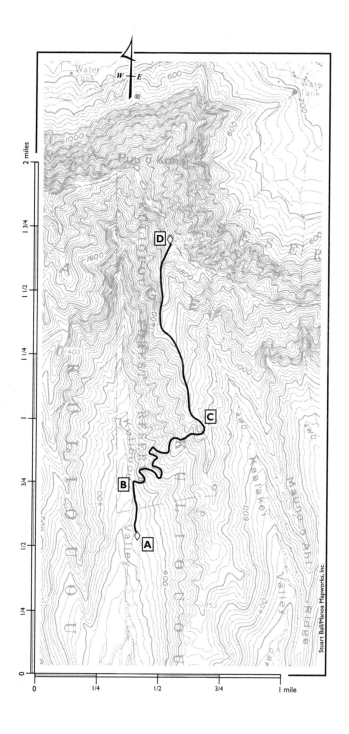

Climb gradually up the side of the valley through groves of Formosa *koa* and logwood on long switchbacks. Look and listen for the red-billed leiothrix.

After the first switchback are good views of Kuliʻouʻou Valley.

After the eighth one, the trail enters a grove of ironwood trees.

After the tenth one, ascend straight up a side ridge briefly.

Bear right off the side ridge and continue climbing via two short switchbacks.

Just before the top, work up a gully lined with ironwoods.

Reach the ridgeline (map point C) and turn left up the ridge. Memorize that junction for the return trip.

Climb steadily up the ridge on its right side.

After regaining the ridgeline, wind through a stand of large Cook pines.

Skirt to the right of an eroded spot.

Shortly afterward, pass two covered picnic tables on the right.

The trail climbs steeply and then levels off briefly in a lovely area lined with stately pines.

Ascend steadily along the left side of the broad ridge through Cook pines and ironwoods.

After passing a bench on the left, break out into the open. To the left you can see the sheer walls of Kuliʻouʻou Valley. Along the route are the native trees *ʻōhiʻa* and *lama*.

The ridge narrows, and the trail becomes rough and eroded in spots. The steep sections have plastic steps. Look to the left for an unusual view of the backside of Diamond Head (Lēʻahi). To the right are Koko Crater (Kohelepelepe) and Koko Head (Kuamoʻo Kāne) overlooking Hawaiʻi Kai and Maunalua Bay.

Climb steeply on plastic staircase.

Reach the Koʻolau summit at an eroded hill and an End of Trail sign (elevation 2,028 feet) (map point D) (UTM 4Q 632430E, 2358156N) (Lat/Long N21.3205, W157.72309).

Kuliʻouʻou Ridge is a popular route to the summit of the Koʻolau Range. The hike is reasonably short, mostly shady, and usually mud free. Novices can climb the graded switchbacks to the picnic tables. More experienced hikers can head for the summit lookout with its superb view of the windward coast.

Before you start the hike, a few cautions are in order. Look out for mountain bikers and trail runners on the switchback section. Beyond the picnic tables, the trail becomes steep and eroded in spots. Watch your footing, especially on the descent. In the worst areas, plastic steps have been installed to slow the erosion and stabilize the trail.

On the switchbacks, look and listen for the red-billed leiothrix, a songbird introduced from China in 1918. The leiothrix is olive green above with an orange-yellow throat and underside. It is frequently seen on the ground, foraging for insects, fruits, and seeds.

The switchbacks pass through a section reforested in 1934–1935 by the Civilian Conservation Corps (CCC). CCC crews planted hundreds of Formosa koa and thousands of logwood trees along the slopes of Kuliʻouʻou Valley to reduce water runoff and thus erosion. The workers undoubtedly built a rudimentary trail network to access the planting areas, but volunteers and the staff of Na Ala Hele, the state trail program, constructed the current alignment in 1991–1992.

In 1935, CCC crews also planted the groves of tall Cook pines along the ridge near the picnic tables. Named after Captain James Cook, the pines are native to New Caledonia's Isle of Pines in the South Pacific between Fiji and Australia. They are columnar in shape and have overlapping, scalelike leaves about 1/4-inch long, rather than true needles.

Beyond the pines, the trail climbs through a more open native forest of ʻōhiʻa and lama trees. ʻŌhiʻa has oval leaves and clusters of delicate red flowers. Early Hawaiians used the flowers in lei and the wood in outrigger canoes. The hard, durable wood was also carved into god images for *heiau* (religious sites).

*Lama* has oblong, pointed leaves that are dark green and leathery. Its fruits are green, then yellow, and finally bright red when fully ripe. *Lama* was sacred to Laka, goddess of the hula. Early Hawaiians used the hard, light-colored wood in temple construction and in hula performances.

Along the open ridge, listen for the Japanese bush warbler (*uguisu*), a bird often heard but rarely seen. Its distinctive cry starts with a long whistle and then winds down in a series of notes. The bush warbler is olive brown on top with a white breast and a long tail.

After the steep final climb, relax on the summit and take in the magnificent view. In front of you is the broad sweep of Waimānalo (potable water) Bay. To the right, the sheer summit ridge ends at Makapuʻu (bulging eye) Point. Offshore is Mānana Island, a seabird sanctuary. Along the coast to the left is Kailua (two seas) Bay, stretching to Mōkapu (taboo district) Peninsula. Puʻu o Kona (hill of leeward) is the flat-topped peak on the summit ridge to the left.

Kuliʻouʻou means "sounding knee," referring to the sound made by the *pūniu* (knee drum). Early Hawaiians made the drum out of a coconut shell. They cut off the top portion and covered it with the stretched skin of *kala,* the surgeonfish. The *pūniu* was tied to the right thigh of the player, just above the knee.

The Kuliʻouʻou Valley Trail is an attractive alternative for beginning hikers. Instead of turning right on the ridge trail, continue into the valley. Walk until the graded trail ends in 0.6 miles and then turn around. A few mosquitoes lurk by the intermittent stream in the valley.

# 41

# Lanipō

| LENGTH: | 6.7-mile round-trip |
|---|---|
| ELEVATION GAIN: | 2,000 feet |
| DANGER: | Low |
| SUITABLE FOR: | Intermediate |
| LOCATION: | Oʻahu: Honolulu Watershed Reserve above Maunalani Heights |
| TOPO MAP: | Honolulu, Koko Head |

## HIGHLIGHTS

This early Hawaiian route follows the crest of Mauʻumae Ridge to the Koʻolau summit. Along the up-and-down trail are a rich variety of native plants and a hidden volcanic crater. From the summit lookout is a splendid view of much of the windward coast.

## TRAILHEAD DIRECTIONS

**DISTANCE:** (Downtown Honolulu to Maunalani Circle) 7 miles

**DRIVING TIME:** 1/4 hour

At Ward Ave. get on Lunalilo Fwy (H-1) Koko Head bound (east).

Take the Koko Head Ave. exit (26A) in Kaimukī.

At the top of the off-ramp, turn left on Koko Head Ave.

LANIPŌ ⊠ HONOLULU

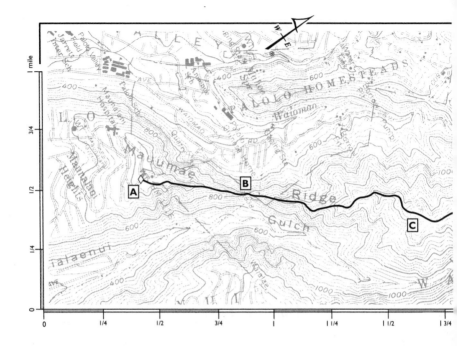

Cross Wai'alae Ave.

At the first stop sign, turn left, still on Koko Head Ave.

At the next stop sign, turn right on Sierra Dr.

Switchback up the ridge to Maunalani Heights.

Pass Maunalani Community Park on the right and Maunalani Nursing Center on the left. The park has restrooms and drinking water.

At the end of Sierra Dr. by a stop sign and the last bus stop, bear right and up on Maunalani Circle.

The road swings left in a broad arc.

On the right, look for a chain-link fence enclosing a Board of Water Supply tank.

Park on the street next to the fence (elevation 1,040 feet) (map point A) (UTM 4Q 625975E, 2355535N) (Lat/Long N21.29729, W157.78552).

BUS: Route 14 to the end of Sierra Dr. Walk 0.2 miles up Maunalani Circle to the trailhead.

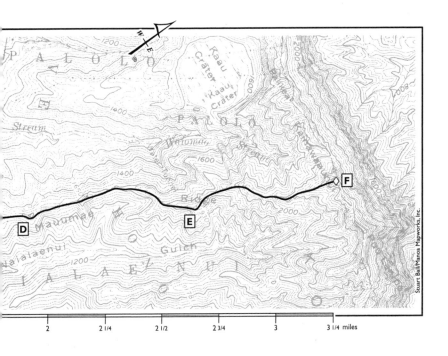

Stuart Ball/Manoa Mapworks, Inc.

| | | | | | |
|---|---|---|---|---|---|
| 2 | 2 1/4 | 2 1/2 | 2 3/4 | 3 | 3 1/4 miles |

## ROUTE DESCRIPTION

Walk back down the road to a signed junction at the corner of the fence. Turn left on the Mauʻumae Ridge Trail, which follows a narrow right-of-way between two chain-link fences. The passageway is directly across from the garage of 4970 Maunalani Circle.

At the end of the fences, keep left through a small grove of ironwood trees.

Reach the crest of Mauʻumae Ridge and bear right along it.

Descend moderately along the mostly open ridge, which has a short rocky section. Along the trail are Formosa *koa* trees and the native dryland shrubs *ʻūlei, ʻaʻaliʻi,* and *ʻilima.*

Pass a utility pole on the left (map point B). Ignore a side trail leading down into Pālolo Valley on the left.

Begin a long climb interspersed with two dips. On the left is a memorial bench. To the right is Waiʻalae Nui Gulch.

After the second dip, ascend steeply through native *koa* trees. The ridge is massive and well forested.

The trail levels out briefly through ironwood and native *alahe'e* trees.

Climb steeply again on a badly eroded trail. Avoid the worst part by taking a bypass trail on the right.

Stroll through a lovely stretch of native *koa* and *'iliahi* (sandalwood) trees.

Ascend a flat, grassy knob with a 360-degree view (map point C). Look behind you for an unusual view of the backside of Diamond Head (Lē'ahi). Along the coast to the left are Maunalua Bay and Koko Head.

The vegetation gradually changes from dryland to rain forest. Native *'ōhi'a* trees form a loose canopy, and *uluhe* ferns cover the ground. Look for two native birds, the red *'apapane* and the yellowish-green *'amakihi*.

Climb a second, shady knob topped by three Cook pines (map point D).

Traverse a long, relatively gentle section underneath magnificent *koa*, *'iliahi*, and *'ōhi'a* trees. Look for native *kōpiko* trees and maile and *naupaka kuahiwi* shrubs in the understory. The trail drops below the ridgeline several times.

As the trail resumes serious climbing, reach a small, grassy lookout by a *koa* skeleton. Across Pālolo Valley is Ka'au Crater, nestled below the Ko'olau summit ridge. A waterfall cascades from the lip of the crater.

The ridge narrows, and the vegetation thins.

After a stiff ascent, reach a flat, open knob with a view of the final climb (map point E).

Descend off the knob, passing a spindly Cook pine on the right.

Ascend steeply on a rutted trail past *kōpiko* and other native shrubs to a broad hump.

Descend the backside of the hump and then begin the final climb to the summit along the open, windswept ridge.

As the top nears, the trail steepens and becomes severely eroded.

Reach the Ko'olau summit at a peak called Kainawa'auika (elevation 2,520 feet) (map point F) (UTM 4Q 628289E,

2359394N) (Lat/Long N21.33199, W157.76292). To the right is a lone 'ōhi'a 'āhihi tree with its fluttering leaves.

Lanipō is the classic O'ahu ridge hike. It offers a challenging climb, breathtaking windward views, and a surprising variety of native plants. As a bonus, you get to see a little-known volcanic crater and a lovely waterfall.

The hike follows Mau'umae (wilted grass) Ridge, an early Hawaiian route once used by bird catchers, maile collectors, and sandalwood cutters. In 1910, the Kaimuki Land Company began to develop Palolo Hill (now Maunalani Heights), a tract on the lower part of the ridge. The following year, the company partnered with the Hawaiian Trail and Mountain Club to reopen the ridge route above the subdivision to the Ko'olau summit. Club stalwarts rode the Kaimukī streetcar line to its end along Wai'alae Road and then climbed up Wilhelmina Rise to reach the current trailhead.

Start early to avoid the hot sun in the open lower section of the trail. Watch your footing constantly because the ungraded route is often rough, sometimes muddy, and occasionally narrow. The middle section of the trail may be overgrown with grass and scratchy uluhe ferns. The cool and wet upper section is slippery and deeply rutted in spots. Test any ropes you find before using them.

Some hikers are put off by the initial rocky descent, which, of course, must be climbed on the way back in the hot afternoon. Don't be discouraged! The native plants and the spectacular views farther in are well worth the extra effort.

On the lower part of the trail, look for the native dryland shrubs 'a'ali'i and 'ilima. 'A'ali'i has shiny, narrow leaves and red seed capsules. Early Hawaiians used the leaves and capsules in making lei. When crushed or boiled, the capsules produced a red dye for decorating kapa (bark cloth). 'Ilima has oblong, serrated leaves, about 1 inch long. The yellow-orange flowers strung together have been used to make regal lei, both in ancient and modern Hawai'i.

In the dry section of the trail, *koa* is the most common native tree. It has sickle-shaped foliage and pale-yellow flower clusters. Early Hawaiians made surfboards and outrigger canoe hulls out of the beautiful red-brown wood. Today it is made into fine furniture.

Less common along the route is *'iliahi,* the native sandalwood tree. Its small leaves are dull green and appear wilted. *'Iliahi* is partially parasitic, with outgrowths on its roots that steal nutrients from nearby plants. Early Hawaiians ground the fragrant heartwood into a powder to perfume their *kapa.* Beginning in the late 1700s, sandalwood was indiscriminately cut down and exported to China to make incense and furniture. The trade ended around 1840 when the forests were depleted of *'iliahi.*

In the wetter middle section of the trail, native *'ōhi'a* gradually replaces *koa* as the dominant tree. *'Ōhi'a* has oval leaves and clusters of delicate red flowers. Early Hawaiians used the flowers in lei and the wood in outrigger canoes. The hard, durable wood was also carved into god images for *heiau* (religious sites).

Underneath the *'ōhi'a,* look for *kōpiko,* a native member of the coffee family. It has leathery, oblong leaves with a light-green midrib. Turn the leaf over to see a row of tiny holes (*piko* or navel) on either side of the midrib. The *kōpiko* produces clusters of little white flowers and fleshy, orange fruits.

In the forest canopy, watch for the *'amakihi,* the most common native forest bird on O'ahu. It is yellowish green with a slightly curved gray bill and feeds on nectar, fruits, and insects. If the *'ōhi'a* are in bloom, you may glimpse the scarce *'apapane.* It has a red breast and head, black wings and tail, and a slightly curved black bill. In flight the *'apapane* makes a whirring sound as it darts from tree to tree searching for insects and nectar.

From the grassy lookout you can see Ka'au (forty), a circular crater on the left at the base of the Ko'olau summit ridge. The crater was probably formed by steam explosions, as rising molten rock encountered groundwater. Both Ka'au and Diamond Head Craters are remnants of the last volcanic activity on O'ahu, known as the Honolulu Series.

According to Hawaiian legend, the demigod and trickster Māui wanted to join all the islands together. From Ka'ena (the heat) Point, he threw a great hook toward Kaua'i, hoping to snare the island. Initially the hook held fast, and Māui gave a mighty tug on the line. A huge boulder, known as Pōhaku o Kaua'i, dropped at his feet. The hook sailed over his head and fell in Pālolo Valley, forming Ka'au Crater. The crater may have been named after Ka'auhelemoa, a supernatural chicken that lived in the valley.

From the summit lookout on Kainawa'auika (also known as Kainawa'anui) are some impressive windward views. In front is Olomana (forked hill) with its three peaks. On the right is a portion of Waimānalo (potable water) Bay. Farther along the coast are Kailua (two seas) and Kāne'ohe (bamboo husband) Bays, separated by Mōkapu (taboo district) Peninsula. To the left along the sheer Ko'olau (windward) summit ridge are Mount Olympus (Awāwaloa) and twin-peaked Kōnāhuanui (large fat testicles). Lanipō is the broad peak close by on the right.

# 42

# 'Aihualama
## (VIA MĀNOA FALLS)

| | |
|---|---|
| LENGTH: | 6.0-mile round-trip |
| ELEVATION GAIN: | 1,400 feet |
| DANGER: | Low |
| SUITABLE FOR: | Novice, Intermediate |
| LOCATION: | O'ahu: Honolulu Watershed Reserve above Mānoa |
| TOPO MAP: | Honolulu |
| ACCESS: | Open, for groups of twelve or less; for larger groups, obtain a special-use permit. See the appendix for more information |

## HIGHLIGHTS

This hike climbs the west side of Mānoa Valley through mostly introduced forest. Along the way is lovely Mānoa Falls, and at the end is a windy overlook of Nu'uanu Valley and Pali.

## ⊠ TRAILHEAD DIRECTIONS

| | |
|---|---|
| **DISTANCE:** | (Downtown Honolulu to Wa'akaua St.) 5 miles |
| **DRIVING TIME:** | 1/4 hour |

Get on S. King St. Koko Head bound (east).

Turn left on Punahou St.

Pass Punahou School on the right and enter Mānoa Valley.

The road splits and narrows to two lanes. Take the left fork onto Mānoa Rd.

At the stop sign, proceed straight across the intersection on a much wider Mānoa Rd.

Pass Mānoa Elementary School on the right.

Park on Mānoa Rd. just before it narrows at the intersection with Waʻakaua St. (elevation 280 feet) (map point A) (UTM 4Q 624236E, 2358812N) (Lat/Long N21.32701, W157.80204).

**BUS:** Route 5 to Mānoa Rd. and Kumuone St. Walk 0.5 mile to the start of the hike.

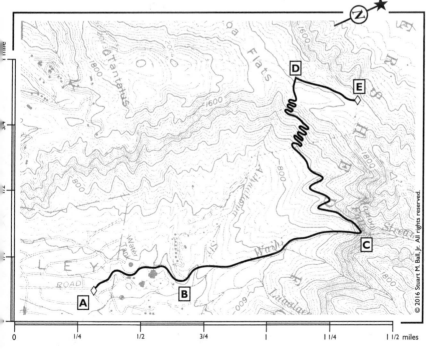

ʻAIHUALAMA (VIA MĀNOA FALLS) ❊ HONOLULU

Continue along Mānoa Rd. on foot.

Walk underneath a pedestrian overpass leading to Tree-tops Restaurant in Paradise Park.

Follow the main road as it curves left and then right around the lower parking lot. Hiker parking is available there for a fee.

As the paved road turns left to Harold L. Lyon Arboretum, proceed straight on a gravel road through a chain-link gate (map point B).

Pass compost toilets on the left.

At the road's end, cross 'Aihualama Stream on a bridge.

Swing left and up on the Mānoa Falls Trail and then descend briefly to ford a small side stream. Look and listen for the white-rumped shama.

Angle across a flat, damp section toward Waihī Stream. The trail is graveled and lined with plastic planks. Stay on the defined path to minimize trampling and erosion.

Ascend gradually along the stream. On the left is a *hau* tree tangle. Above are introduced Paraserianthes (albizia) trees with their whitish bark and layered branches. The path is paved with rocks in several spots.

Climb more steeply as the valley narrows. The trail is often rooty, muddy, and rocky.

Go through a bamboo grove on raised plastic steps.

Just before the falls, reach a signed junction with the 'Aihualama Trail in a grove of mountain apple trees. For now, continue a short distance to a rock platform to view lovely Mānoa (Waihī) Falls (map point C).

Backtrack to the signed junction. Turn right and up on the 'Aihualama Trail. The path is narrow and rocky at first but soon widens.

Work in and out of three gulches through bamboo groves and past huge banyan trees. Look for yellow ginger and red heliconia along the way. Ignore side trails heading up the gulches.

Climb the side of Mānoa Valley on fourteen switchbacks (count 'em, but don't cut 'em). *Kī* (ti) plants line the trail. After the eighth switchback are two concrete posts. Between nine and thirteen, a dense stand of cinnamon trees blots out much of the light.

At the top of the ridge, enter a bamboo forest and turn right on a muddy, rooty trail.

Reach a signed junction with the Pauoa Flats Trail (map point D). Turn right on it. (To the left, the Pauoa Flats Trail leads to the Nuʻuanu, Kalāwahine, and Mānoa Cliff Trails.) Memorize that junction for the return trip.

Walk through dark cinnamon trees on a muddy trail.

Reach windy Nuʻuanu Valley Overlook and a memorial bench (elevation 1,640 feet) (map point E) (UTM 4Q 623787E, 2360851N) (Lat/Long N21.34302, W157.80624). Nearby are some native ʻōhīʻa ʻāhihi trees, their leaves fluttering in the wind.

## NOTES

The ʻAihualama hike combines a pleasant walk in Mānoa (vast) Valley with a steady climb to a scenic viewpoint. The short stroll to the falls at the back of the valley is popular with tourists and locals alike, especially on weekends. Few people go beyond the falls because of the long ascent to the ridgetop.

The trails making up this hike are generally well graded, although muddy and rooty in spots. The ʻAihualama (eat *lama* fruit) Trail climbs out of the valley on long, lazy switchbacks. Because of the heavy traffic, the wet and eroded sections of the Mānoa Falls Trail have been improved with gravel, plastic steps, and wooden walkways. The upgraded trail allows you to keep just ahead of the hungry mosquitoes along the stream.

The ʻAihualama area has a long and colorful past. The first scene of the grisly Hawaiian legend of Kahalaopuna takes place along ʻAihualama Stream. In 1895, royalist rebels fleeing government forces used an old Hawaiian trail along the stream as an escape route after a skirmish at the back of Mānoa Valley. The royalists had tried to overthrow the recently founded

Republic of Hawai'i and return Queen Lili'uokalani to the throne.

In 1919, the Hawaiian Sugar Planters' Association (HSPA) established a small station, later known as Lyon Arboretum, in the 'Aihualama area to carry out reforestation projects. For easier access to the *mauka* (inland) section, HSPA crews built a trail that switchbacked up the steep slope to Pauoa Flats. In 1978, volunteers under the direction of the Sierra Club, Hawai'i Chapter, restored the deteriorated arboretum switchbacks and built a new contour route connecting them with the Mānoa Falls Trail.

The falls trail passes several groves of tangled *hau* trees with large, heart-shaped leaves. Their flowers are bright yellow with a dark-red center and resemble those of a hibiscus. Early Hawaiians used the wood for kites and canoe outriggers, the bark for sandals, and the sap as a laxative.

Along the way, look and listen for the white-rumped shama. It is black on top with a chestnut-colored breast and a long black-and-white tail. The shama has a variety of beautiful songs and often mimics other birds. A native of Malaysia, the shama has become widespread in introduced forests such as this one.

Mānoa Falls makes a refreshing rest stop or a good turn-around point for novice hikers. Early Hawaiians aptly named the falls Waihī (trickling water). Stay on the viewing platform to lower the risk of being hit by rocks falling from the cliffs. If it's late July, you may get some delicious mountain apples (*'ōhi'a 'ai*) from the grove in front of the falls.

Lining the middle switchbacks of the 'Aihualama Trail are *kī* (ti) plants. They have shiny leaves 1–2 feet long that are arranged spirally in a cluster at the tip of a slender stem. Early Polynesian voyagers introduced ti to Hawai'i. They used the leaves for house thatch, skirts, sandals, and raincoats. Food to be cooked in the *imu* (underground oven) was first wrapped in ti leaves. A popular sport with the commoners was *ho'ohe'e kī* or ti-leaf sledding. The sap from ti plants stained canoes and surfboards.

From the windy overlook at the end of the Pauoa Flats Trail, you can look down into Nuʻuanu (cool height) Valley. The massive peak across the valley is Lanihuli (turning royal chief). The saddle to the right of Lanihuli is Nuʻuanu Pali (cliff). You can see the windward coast through the gap in the Koʻolau (windward) summit ridge. To the right of the Pali is mist-shrouded Kōnāhuanui (large fat testicles) (elevation 3,105 feet), the highest point in the Koʻolau Range.

Near the overlook are several native ʻōhiʻa ʻāhihi trees found only on Oʻahu. They have narrow, pointed leaves with red stems and midribs. Their delicate red flowers grow in clusters and are similar to those of the more common ʻōhiʻa. Queen Liliʻuokalani mentioned the ʻāhihi lehua (blossom) in her haunting love song, "Aloha ʻOe."

The Mānoa Falls and ʻAihualama Trails are part of the Honolulu mauka trail system. You could easily spend a week hiking all eighteen trails in the complex. One option from the same trailhead is the climb of Tantalus (Puʻu ʻŌhiʻa; elevation 2,013 feet). From the ʻAihualama Trail, turn left on the Pauoa Flats Trail. At its end, turn left on the Mānoa Cliff Trail. At the next junction, turn sharp right on the Puʻu ʻŌhʻia Trail. Reach a one-lane paved road and follow it to the summit. Total distance round-trip is 7.7 miles.

43

# Kamananui (Moanalua) Valley

| | |
|---|---|
| LENGTH: | 11.0-mile round-trip |
| ELEVATION GAIN: | 1,500 feet |
| DANGER: | Low |
| SUITABLE FOR: | Novice, Intermediate |
| LOCATION: | O'ahu: Honolulu Watershed Forest Reserve above Moanalua |
| TOPO MAP: | Kāne'ohe |

## HIGHLIGHTS

This classic stream hike winds through a lovely valley rich in historical sites and legends. Along the way are a small swimming hole, a boulder covered with petroglyphs, and over forty stream crossings. Near the end a short climb leads to a windward overlook on the Ko'olau summit ridge.

## TRAILHEAD DIRECTIONS

| | |
|---|---|
| **DISTANCE:** | (Downtown Honolulu to Moanalua Valley Park) 7 miles |
| **DRIVING TIME:** | 1/4 hour |

At Punchbowl St. get on Lunalilo Fwy (H-1) heading 'ewa (west).

Near Middle St., keep left on Moanalua Fwy (H-201) to 'Aiea.

Take the exit marked Moanalua Valley–Red Hill.

From the off-ramp, turn right on Ala Aolani St., heading into Moanalua Valley.

The road ends at Moanalua Valley Park. The park has restrooms and drinking water.

Park on the street just before the park entrance (elevation 240 feet) (map point A) (UTM 4Q 616028E, 2363929N) (Lat/Long N21.37378, W157.88082).

BUS: Route 16 to Ala Aolani and Ala Lani Streets on weekday mornings and afternoons only. Walk 0.4 miles along Ala Aolani St. to the park.

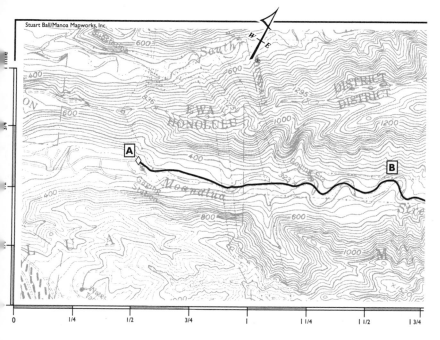

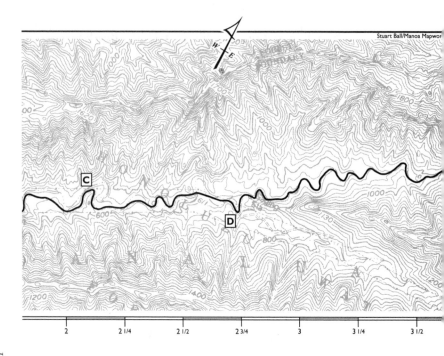

## ROUTE DESCRIPTION

Enter Moanalua Valley Park and proceed along Kamananui Valley Road, the one-lane dirt/gravel track at the back of the parking lot.

Walk around a locked green gate.

On your left by a huge monkeypod tree, pass a muddy driveway leading to the Douglas Damon house site (marker no. 3 and sign).

Cross Kamananui Stream seven times on stone bridges. Look and listen for the white-rumped shama in the introduced forest.

On the right under a mango tree at the seventh crossing is Pōhakukaluahine, a large boulder covered with petroglyphs (map point B) (marker no. 10 and sign).

Around the bend from the petroglyph rock and before the next stream crossing, reach a junction (marker no. 11). Con-

CENTRAL O'AHU ⊠ KAMANANUI (MOANALUA) VALLEY

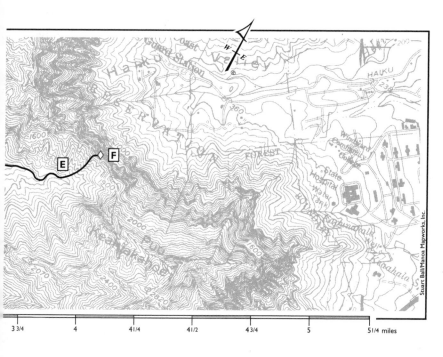

tinue straight on the dirt road. (To the right a short loop trail leads up to the May Damon house site and a view up the valley.)

Ford the stream four times. Along the stream are *kukui* trees and tangled groves of *hau*.

Reach an obscure junction by marker no. 12 in a grove of strawberry guava. Continue straight on the dirt road. (To the right a steep route climbs out of the valley to Kauakaulani Ridge above Tripler Hospital.)

Ascend gradually to a wide vehicle turnaround area (map point C). On the right a short trail leads up to another overlook of the entire valley.

Cross the stream six more times.

After the sixth ford and as the road curves right, look for two boulders on the left and a large *koa* tree on the right.

Just past the second boulder, reach a signed junction. Turn left off the road onto Kulana'ahane Trail (map point D). (The road continues to the back of the valley.)

Cross the right fork of Kamananui Stream immediately, climb the embankment, and turn left again.

Under a *hau* tangle, skirt the foot of Keanaakamanō, the middle ridge, which divides the valley into two drainages.

Pass a stream gaging station on the left.

The trail gradually ascends to the head of the valley while fording the left fork of Kamananui Stream twenty-three times.

Just before the second crossing, reach an obscure junction. Keep right and ford the stream. (To the left the Godek-Jaskulski route ascends the valley wall to the ridgeline above Red Hill.)

After the sixth crossing is a small but delightful pool on the left and another petroglyph rock on the right. Look and listen for the *'elepaio,* an endangered native bird.

Starting at the seventh ford is a series of dense *hau* groves. Turn sharp right under the *hau* to reach the eighth crossing and turn sharp right again just after the ninth crossing. Keep your head down!

After the eighteenth crossing is a short open stretch with native *hapu'u* tree ferns on the right and a lone native *loulu* palm on the left. Along the stream, watch for wreckage from a plane crash farther up the valley.

After the nineteenth ford, go over the foot of a small side ridge and around an old Hawaiian house site.

Walk under another *hau* tangle around the twentieth crossing.

After the twenty-first ford, cross an intermittent side stream.

The stream splits in two. The trail generally hugs the main (left) channel on the island created by the two braids. Lining the route are Chinese ground orchids, which bloom in winter.

The twenty-third ford with a tiny pool and waterfall is a good rest stop before the final climb.

Between the twenty-third and twenty-fourth crossings is a grove of *'ōhi'a 'āhihi* trees.

At the twenty-fifth crossing, reach an End of Maintained Trail sign. Bear left and up on a rough route that leaves the stream for good (map point E). Listen for the Japanese bush warbler.

Climb steeply up a spur ridge through *uluhe* ferns and *'ōhi'a 'āhihi* trees. To the right is a waterfall chute at the head of the stream.

Reach the Ko'olau summit at a saddle with an overlook of Ha'ikū Valley (elevation 1,660 feet) (map point F) (UTM 4Q 621001E, 2366818N) (Lat/Long N21.39955, W157.83266). On the left behind an End of Trail sign, an *'ōhi'a 'āhihi* and a citrus tree provide some shade.

## NOTES

Kamananui (Moanalua) Valley is a classic combination hike that includes a valley stroll, a stream walk, and a ridge climb. Along the valley road are some historical sites. By the stream is a delightful small swimming hole. At the ridgetop are native plants and windward views. What more could you want?

Interpretive signs and numbered wooden posts mark points of interest along the road. In 1884, Bernice Pauahi Bishop willed the entire *ahupua'a* (land division) of Moanalua (two camps) to her husband's business partner, Samuel M. Damon. His son, Douglas, built a luxurious mountain house (marker no. 3) in the valley, which was originally known as Kamananui (great spiritual power). A cobbled carriage road crossed seven ornate bridges and ended at the house of his daughter, May Damon (marker no. 11). For a detailed explanation of those and other sites, pick up the booklet *A Walk into the Past* from Moanalua Gardens Foundation, whose address is listed in the appendix.

Along the road, look and listen for the white-rumped shama. The bird is black on top with a chestnut-colored breast and a long black-and-white tail. The shama has a variety of beautiful songs and often mimics other birds. A native of Malaysia, the shama has become widespread in introduced forests such as this one. Until the 1920s, the owners grazed cattle in the valley, resulting in the destruction of much of the original native vegetation.

At marker no. 10 is Pōhakukaluahine (rock of the old woman), a sacred boulder covered with ancient petroglyphs. Most of the carvings are human stick figures, although a few resemble birdmen. Also on the boulder are a *kōnane* game board and a winding groove suggesting Kamananui Stream.

Pōhakukaluahine received its name from an old story. Many years ago, a small child cried during the consecration of a *heiau* (religious site) in the lower valley. As such an offense to the gods was punishable by death, the grandmother rushed up the valley with the child and hid behind a large boulder. The *mana* (supernatural power) of the rock protected the two from the pursuing warriors. When the noise *kapu* (taboo) was lifted, the grandmother returned the child safely to its parents.

After the vehicle turnaround, start counting stream crossings to home in on the junction with the trail. After the sixth ford, look for the twin boulders and the trail sign on the left. On the trail, watch your footing while rock-hopping across the stream. If necessary, slosh through the water. Your boots are eventually going to get wet anyway. As always, do not ford the stream if the water gets much above your knees. Finally, look out for a few wayward mosquitoes.

The stream trail frequently tunnels through tangled *hau* trees with large, heart-shaped leaves. Their flowers are bright yellow with a dark-red center and resemble those of a hibiscus. Early Hawaiians used the wood for kites and canoe outriggers, the bark for sandals, and the sap as a laxative.

While walking along the stream, watch for the *'elepaio*, a small native bird. It is brown on top and white underneath with a black throat and a dark tail, usually cocked. The bird roams the forest understory catching insects on the fly or on vegetation. *'Elepaio* are territorial and very curious, which is why you can sometimes see them.

After the last *hau* tangle, look for the Chinese ground or nun's orchid in winter. Its lovely flowers have tapered petals, which are white on the outside and reddish brown within. The lowest petal is a cream-colored tube with purple marking.

Toward the back of the valley, listen for the Japanese bush warbler (*uguisu*), a bird often heard but rarely seen. Its distinctive cry starts with a long whistle and then winds down in a series of notes. The bush warbler is olive brown on top with a white breast and a long tail.

On the climb to the saddle, the trail is lined with native ʻōhiʻa ʻāhihi trees found only on Oʻahu. They have narrow, pointed leaves with red stems and midribs. Their delicate red flowers grow in clusters and are similar to those of the more common ʻōhiʻa. Queen Liliʻuokalani mentioned the ʻāhihi lehua (blossom) in her haunting love song, "Aloha ʻOe."

From the saddle along the Koʻolau (windward) summit, the *pali* (cliff) drops straight down into Haʻikū (sharp break) Valley, where the H-3 Freeway runs. The long side ridges enclosing the valley constrict the view somewhat, but you can still see Kāneʻohe (bamboo husband) Bay extending to Mōkapu (taboo district) Peninsula. On the steep side ridge to the right are the Haʻikū Stairs, climbing to a small radar installation on top of Puʻu Keahi a Kahoe (hill of Kahoe's fire).

A short side trip leads to the site of a plane crash on September 2, 1948. To get there, leave the trail at the last stream crossing (no. 23) and walk up the streambed. At a fork, keep right, following the main channel. The wreckage of the F-47N Thunderbolt is strewn along the stream just below an intermittent waterfall with a shallow pool at it base. The Hawaiʻi Air National Guard pilot parachuted to safety from his disabled fighter, whose engine had caught fire. He then hiked out of the valley and was picked up at Moanalua Golf Course.

# 44

# Mānana

| LENGTH: | 11.6-mile round-trip |
|---|---|
| ELEVATION GAIN: | 1,700 feet |
| DANGER: | Low |
| SUITABLE FOR: | Novice, Intermediate, Expert |
| LOCATION: | O'ahu: 'Ewa Forest Reserve above Pacific Palisades |
| TOPO MAP: | Waipahu, Kāne'ohe |

## HIGHLIGHTS

This long, splendid ridge hike leads deep into the wild Ko'olau Mountain Range. Along the way is an incredible variety of native dryland and rain forest plants. Lofty lookouts, en route and at the summit, provide stunning views of leeward and windward O'ahu.

## TRAILHEAD DIRECTIONS

| DISTANCE: | (Downtown Honolulu to end of Komo Mai Dr.) 15 miles |
|---|---|
| DRIVING TIME: | 1/2 hour |

At Punchbowl St. get on Lunalilo Fwy (H-1) heading 'ewa (west).

Near Middle St., keep left on Moanalua Fwy (H-201) to 'Aiea.

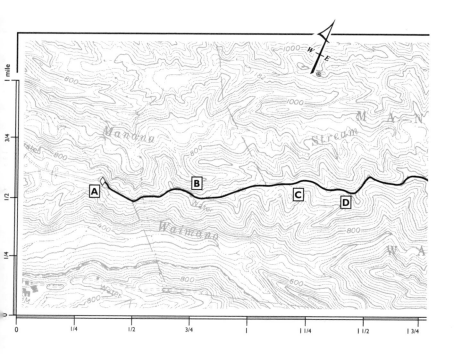

By Aloha Stadium, bear right to rejoin H-1 to Pearl City.
Leave the freeway at exit 10, marked Pearl City-Waimalu.
Turn right on Moanalua Rd. at the end of the off-ramp.
At the third traffic light, turn right on Waimano Home Rd.
At the third traffic light and just before the road narrows to two lanes, turn left on Komo Mai Dr.

The road descends into Waimano Valley and then climbs the next ridge.

Drive through Pacific Palisades subdivision to the end of the road.

Park on the street just before a turnaround circle (elevation 960 feet) (map point A) (UTM 4Q 609966E, 2370131N) (Lat/Long N21.43019, W157.93888).

**BUS:** Route 53 to Komo Mai Dr. and 'Auhuhu St. Walk 0.4 miles along Komo Mai Dr. to the trailhead.

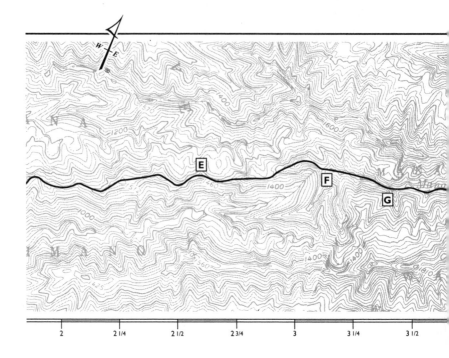

## ROUTE DESCRIPTION

At the back of the circle, walk through an opening in the fence next to a gate.

Register at the hunter/hiker check-in mailbox on the right.

Proceed up the one-lane paved road through a grove of ironwood trees.

On the right, pass a water tank at the road end (map point B).

Continue straight on the Mānana Trail through a eucalyptus forest.

Pass a utility tower on the left.

Stroll through a pleasant level section on top of the ridge.

As the trail splits, keep left, avoiding the small grassy area on the right.

In a rooty clearing, keep left and down to continue on the main ridge. Ignore the trail leading down a side ridge on the right.

While contouring to the right of a small hump in the ridge, the trail forks. Keep left on the upper trail (map point C).

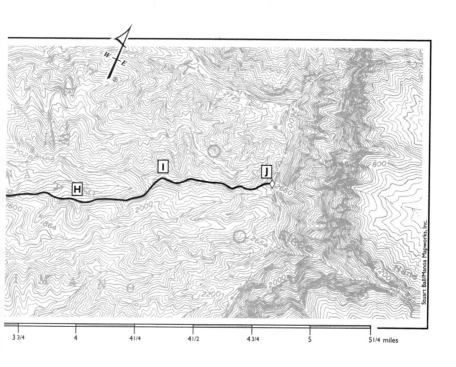

3 3/4     4     4 1/4     4 1/2     4 3/4     5     5 1/4 miles

Shortly afterward, reach a signed junction. Keep left around the hump on the main ridge. (The right fork leads down a side ridge into Waimano Valley to a waterfall and two swimming holes.)

Climb gradually through a grove of brush box trees.

The trail forks in another rooty area. Bear left and down to stay on the ridgetop (map point D).

Break out into the open. *Mauka* (inland) is a view of the entire ridge to be climbed.

Traverse a narrow, eroded stretch with plastic steps. Watch your footing, especially if the ground is wet.

The trail becomes a grassy avenue lined with introduced pines and the stumps of paperbark trees. Look for native *koa* and *'iliahi* (sandalwood) trees and the native shrub *naupaka kuahiwi*.

On the left a side trail climbs to a small knob and then rejoins the main route.

Descend a steep, eroded section to the right of a flat, grassy viewpoint.

Pass a covered picnic table on the right.

Stroll through a lovely, rolling ridge section with more *koa* and *'iliahi* trees.

Climb steeply to the first really distinct knob in the ridge (map point E).

Descend the next dip and ascend steeply to the next hump. The native vegetation gradually changes from dryland to rain forest. Along the route are *'ōhi'a* and *kōpiko* trees and *hāpu'u* tree ferns.

Cross a short level section.

Climb very steeply to another knob, where a long side ridge comes in on the right (map point F).

The trail narrows and becomes rough and rooty.

Cross another level section, descend briefly, and then ascend a flat, cleared hill used occasionally as a helipad (map point G). There is a view in all directions. To leeward is Pearl Harbor (Pu'uloa) and the Wai'anae Range. On the left is a native *lapalapa* tree with its fluttering leaves.

Traverse a long series of small but steep knobs in the ridge.

Cross a level muddy section.

Ascend steeply to a large hill with a small clearing on top (map point H). From there is a commanding view of the ridge ahead.

Swing left and climb steadily. The vegetation becomes stunted, and the wind picks up.

Curve right toward the Ko'olau summit as a long side ridge comes in on the left (map point I).

The main ridge narrows significantly.

Traverse a series of small humps. On the left are several native *loulu* palms.

The ridge broadens and levels briefly through low-lying sedge.

Cross a second series of humps on the narrow ridge.

Pass a waterfall chute down and on the right.

Climb steadily through increasing vegetation.

Reach the Ko'olau summit at a massive knob (elevation

2,660 feet) (map point J) (UTM 4Q 616532E, 2373093N)
(Lat/Long N21.45653, W157.87533).

The Mānana hike offers some of the finest ridge walking on the
island. Along the route are some intriguing native plants and
a chance at glimpsing some native birds. The last mile of the
open, windswept ridge is wild and wonderful. Mist frequently
settles over the summit area, reducing visibility and creating a
dark, eerie atmosphere.

The 6-mile trail was a project of Charles (Charlie)
Nakamura and several friends, all members of the Hawaiian
Trail and Mountain Club. In 1965, they started clearing the
ridge route *mauka* (inland) of the recently built Pacific Palisades subdivision. The group finally reached the Ko'olau summit in 1969. Named after the stream and *ahupua'a* (land division) north of the ridge, the new Mānana Trail quickly became
popular with hikers of all abilities. Novices strolled to the picnic table. Intermediate hikers continued to the helipad, and
experts headed for the summit.

Although not graded, the trail is wide and clear to the distinct knob beyond the picnic table. Watch your step, however,
on the two eroded sections. Farther *mauka* the route becomes
rough, steep, narrow, and muddy, although rarely all at the same
time. Between the helipad and the final climb, the trail may be
overgrown with scratchy *uluhe* ferns and *Clidemia* shrubs.

On the initial trail section, remember to keep left along the
main ridge. Ignore the side trails leading down into Waimano
(many waters) Valley on the right. Also, watch for mountain
bikers, especially in the afternoon. Portions of the trail in
this section are lined with strawberry guava (*waiawī-'ula'ula*)
trees, whose tasty, dark-red fruit usually ripens in August and
September.

After leaving the introduced forest, the route winds
through a lovely open stretch still recovering from a fire in

MĀNANA ⬚ CENTRAL O'AHU

1972. Making a comeback are the native trees *koa* and *'iliahi*. *Koa* has sickle-shaped foliage and pale-yellow flower clusters. Early Hawaiians made surfboards and outrigger canoe hulls out of the beautiful red-brown wood. Today it is made into fine furniture.

*'Iliahi* or sandalwood has small dull-green leaves that appear wilted. The tree is partially parasitic, with outgrowths on its roots that steal nutrients from nearby plants. Early Hawaiians ground the fragrant heartwood into a powder to perfume their *kapa* (bark cloth). Beginning in the late 1700s, *'iliahi* was indiscriminately cut down and exported to China to make incense and furniture. The trade ended around 1840 when the forests were depleted of the tree.

Farther along the ridge is the native rain forest, dominated by *'ōhi'a* trees and *hāpu'u* tree ferns. *'Ōhi'a* has oval leaves and clusters of delicate red flowers. Early Hawaiians used the flowers in lei and the wood in outrigger canoes. The hard, durable wood was also carved into god images for *heiau* (religious sites). Beneath the *'ōhi'a* are *hāpu'u* tree ferns with delicate sweeping fronds. Their trunks consist of roots tightly woven around a small central stem. The brown fiber covering the young fronds of *hāpu'u* is called *pulu*.

At the helipad is a magnificent *lapalapa* tree. Its roundish leaves are arranged in groups of three and flutter in the slightest wind. Early Hawaiians used the bark, leaves, and purple fruit to make a blue-black dye to decorate their *kapa*. The leaves also make a distinctive lei.

Beyond the helipad, watch for *'apapane* and *'amakihi*, two colorful native birds. The *'apapane* has a red breast and head, black wings and tail, and a slightly curved black bill. In flight the bird makes a whirring sound as it darts among the *'ōhi'a* searching for insects and nectar. The *'amakihi* is yellowish green with a slightly curved gray bill and feeds on nectar, fruits, and insects. It is the most common native forest bird on O'ahu.

On the final climb, look for the native *loulu* palm, emerging out of the mist. It has rigid, fan-shaped fronds in a cluster at the top of a ringed trunk. Early Hawaiians used the fronds for thatch and plaited the blades of young fronds into fans and baskets.

As you near the top, listen for the Japanese bush warbler (*uguisu*), a bird often heard but rarely seen. Its distinctive cry starts with a long whistle and then winds down in a series of notes. There seems to be at least one bush warbler at the top of every Koʻolau ridge trail.

The view from the summit lookout is exceptional, weather permitting. Kaʻalaea (reddish earth) Valley lies 2,000 feet below. The windward coast stretches from Kualoa (long back) to Makapuʻu (bulging eye) Points. In Kāneʻohe (bamboo husband) Bay you can see three enclosed fishponds, Mōliʻi (small section), Kahaluʻu (diving place), and Heʻeia, from left to right. On the left are four windward valleys, Waiāhole, Waikāne, Hakipuʻu (hill broken), and Kaʻaʻawa (the wrasse fish). Dominating those valleys is the massive peak, Puʻu ʻŌhulehule (joining of waves hill). In the distance to the right is triple-peaked Olomana (forked hill).

For a shorter valley outing, take the Waimano Pool hike that starts from the same trailhead. Turn right at the junction by the hump and descend into the valley. The trail ends at a waterfall and two swimming holes. Total distance round-trip is 3.2 miles.

45

# Makapu'u Point

| | |
|---|---|
| LENGTH: | 3.0-mile loop |
| ELEVATION GAIN: | 600 feet |
| DANGER: | Low |
| SUITABLE FOR: | Novice, Intermediate |
| LOCATION: | O'ahu: Makapu'u Point State Wayside Park |
| TOPO MAP: | Koko Head |

## HIGHLIGHTS

This short, scenic loop climbs the windswept cliffs above the easternmost point on the island. Along the way are remnant fortifications, a lighthouse, and some rock scrambling. From ocean overlooks, you can often see humpback whales and colonies of seabirds.

## TRAILHEAD DIRECTIONS

**DISTANCE:**   (Downtown Honolulu to Makapu'u Point State Wayside Park) 16 miles

**DRIVING TIME:**   3/4 hour

At Ward Ave. get on Lunalilo Fwy (H-1) Koko Head bound (east).

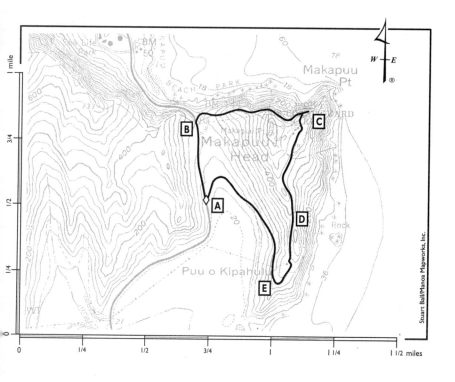

As the freeway ends, continue straight on Kalaniana'ole
Hwy (Rte 72).

The highway narrows to two lanes just past Koko Marina
Shopping Center.

Pass Hanauma Bay Nature Preserve and Sandy Beach Park
on the right and Hawai'i Kai Golf Course on the left.

The road swings left and begins the climb to Makapu'u
Lookout.

By the Kaiwi Shoreline sign, turn right into the main
parking lot for the Makapu'u Point hike and leave your car
there (elevation 40 feet) (map point A) (UTM 4Q 639332E,
2356466N) (Lat/Long N21.30472, W157.6567).

BUS: Route 22, 23, or 57 to Sea Life Park. Walk 0.5 miles along
Kalaniana'ole Hwy to Makapu'u Lookout. (This is the most
dangerous part of the hike because of the heavy traffic on the
narrow road.)

Walk back up the access road toward the highway.

As the road swings left, turn right onto a makeshift trail that leads through a grassy, rocky area to the Makapuʻu Lookout parking lot (map point B). If you miss the trail, walk along the highway to the lookout.

At the far end of the parking lot, climb two short flights of stairs to the upper viewing area.

Step between the railing and a rock wall and proceed along the edge of the cliff on a makeshift trail. Look for the low-lying native shrub *ʻilima papa* with its delicate yellow-orange flowers.

Pass three walled-up observation bunkers below and on the left.

Climb steadily along the cliff edge past a fourth bunker. As necessary, work right to avoid steep rock faces. Watch for *Schiedea globosa,* a prostrate native subshrub with narrow, somewhat fleshy leaves.

Pass a line of stunted ironwood trees on the left. The top of Makapuʻu Point Lighthouse appears dead ahead.

Reach a relatively flat, grassy area. In back is a rock face used by climbers.

Resume the steady ascent, roughly paralleling a water pipe and a utility line.

Pass a huge *pānini* cactus on the right.

Work left around the front of the cliff past some more ironwoods.

Pass a concrete water tank on the right. From there a short trail leads to the top of Makupuʻu Head (elevation 647 feet).

Descend briefly to a paved road and turn left on it.

Pass a memorial plaque honoring nine World War II airmen whose Catalina seaplane crashed nearby in 1942.

The road narrows to a path that climbs to a lookout (map point C) (UTM 4Q 639952E, 2356980N) (Lat/Long N21.30932, W157.65068). In season look for humpback whales below and frigate birds above.

From the lookout, retrace your steps back to the road.

In a level area, reach a junction. Turn left and down. (The road straight ahead soon ends and becomes a rough trail that ascends to the top of Makapuʻu Head.)

Descend along the crest of a ridge past night-blooming cereus and native *milo* trees.

Reach a junction with a gravel road. Continue straight on the main road. (The gravel road to the left leads past a red-roofed structure to the Makapuʻu Point Lighthouse, which is strictly off limits to the public.)

Just before a hump on the left, reach a junction marked by a whale sign (map point D). Continue straight on the paved road. (To the left an obscure trail marked with white paint descends steeply down the cliff to some tide pools and a double blowhole along the rocky shoreline.)

The road leaves the ridgeline at Puʻu o Kīpahulu and curves right through scrub *kiawe* trees.

Walk past an open black gate. Along the coast to the left is a prominent rock formation known as Pele's Chair.

Reach the main parking lot, which is lined with native *naupaka kahakai* shrubs (map point A).

## NOTES

Makapuʻu (bulging eye) Point is a very popular hike with tourists and locals alike. Most people walk up and back on the paved road from the main parking lot. If you are a novice hiker, that's exactly what you should do. More experienced hikers can try the loop route described above. It starts with a steep scramble along the edge of the Makapuʻu cliffs and ends with the pleasant stroll down the road.

Take this hike during winter (November–April) to see migrating humpback whales. The temperature is also cooler then, and the sun is less intense. Start early or late, or go on a weekday to avoid the crowds. Don't forget the two essentials for this hike: sunscreen and binoculars.

Near the start of the trail is the low-lying native shrub *'ilima papa.* It has oblong, serrated leaves about 1 inch long. The yellow-orange flowers strung together have been used to make regal lei, both in ancient and modern Hawai'i.

On the climb up, look out for the thorny *pānini* (prickly pear cactus). It has red or yellow flowers and a delicious, dark-red, pear-shaped fruit. Wear gloves when handling the fruit as the skin has small bristles. Don Marin, a Spaniard and advisor to King Kamehameha I, introduced *pānini* from Mexico in the early 1800s.

From the *makai* (seaward) lookout is a magnificent view along the windward coast to Mōkapu (taboo district) Point. Below are Makapu'u Beach and Sealife Park. Beyond is the broad sweep of lovely Waimānalo (potable water) Bay. The two islands offshore, Mānana and Kāohikaipu (Mokuhope), are state seabird sanctuaries. On a clear day, you can see the neighbor islands of Moloka'i and Maui across Kaiwi (the bone) Channel.

While at the lookout, scan the ocean for humpback whales. They migrate from the North Pacific to the Hawaiian Islands, arriving in October and leaving in May. The whales congregate off the leeward coast of Maui and occupy themselves calving, nursing, breeding, and generally horsing around.

From the lookout you can also see frigate birds and tropicbirds soaring overhead. Frigate birds are large, mostly black seabirds with slender wings and a forked tail. Early Hawaiians called them *'iwa* or "thief" because they often forced other seabirds to drop their food, which the *'iwa* would then catch in midair. The red-tailed tropicbird or *koa'e 'ula* is white with a black eye patch and two central tail feathers elongated into streamers. Tropicbirds feed by diving into the ocean for fish and squid. They nest in burrows or rock crevices on nearby Mānana Island.

The Makapu'u Lighthouse nestles on a shelf below the top of the cliffs. Completed in late 1908, the 35-foot tower houses the largest lighthouse lens in the United States. The kerosene lamp inside the lens was first lit on October 1, 1909. In November 1941, James Jones, author of the novel *From Here to Eter-*

*nity,* helped build five pillboxes on Makapuʻu Head. After the Pearl Harbor attack on December 7, he and fellow soldiers occupied those fortifications with machine guns and rifles to deter an anticipated Japanese invasion.

The short side trip to the top of Makapuʻu Head is well worthwhile. A makeshift trail starts from the water tank, parallels a water pipe, and then angles left to the summit (elevation 647 feet). From the bunker there, you can see the Koʻolau (windward) Range gradually rising to a flat-topped mountain, Puʻu o Kona (hill of leeward). On the leeward side are Koko Crater (Koheleplepe) and Hanauma Bay, and in the distance is Diamond Head (Lēʻahi).

On the way down, watch for native *milo* trees with glossy, heart-shaped leaves and yellow flowers. Hawaiian craftsmen carved the rich reddish-brown wood into bowls, dishes, and platters. The fruit is a flattened globe and produces a yellow-green dye.

As the road heads *mauka* (inland), look left along the coast for a prominent rock formation resembling a chair. According to legend, Pele, the goddess of fire, rested there before leaving Oʻahu for Maui and the Big Island. The Makapuʻu cliffs were also the site of Mālei, another ancient stone. It was a physical representation of the goddess Mālei, who watched over the *uhu* (parrot fishes) of Makapuʻu Point. Fishermen left offerings by the stone or sang to it to insure a good catch. The stone disappeared many years ago and has never been found.

# 46

# Olomana

| | |
|---|---|
| LENGTH: | 5.2-mile round-trip |
| ELEVATION GAIN: | 1,600 feet |
| DANGER: | High |
| SUITABLE FOR: | Intermediate, Expert |
| LOCATION: | Oʻahu: Olomana State Monument near Maunawili |
| TOPO MAP: | Mōkapu, Koko Head |

## HIGHLIGHTS

Olomana is the craggy, commanding mountain windward of Nuʻuanu Pali. The steep, narrow climb to its three peaks demands concentration, sure feet, and little fear of heights. From the summit is a panorama unsurpassed on Oʻahu.

## TRAILHEAD DIRECTIONS

| | |
|---|---|
| DISTANCE: | (Downtown Honolulu to Maunawili Loop) 11 miles |
| DRIVING TIME: | 1/2 hour |

At Punchbowl St. get on Pali Hwy (Rte 61 north) heading up Nuʻuanu Valley.

Go under the Pali through the twin tunnels.

Pali Hwy becomes Kalanianaʻole Hwy at the first traffic light (Castle Junction).

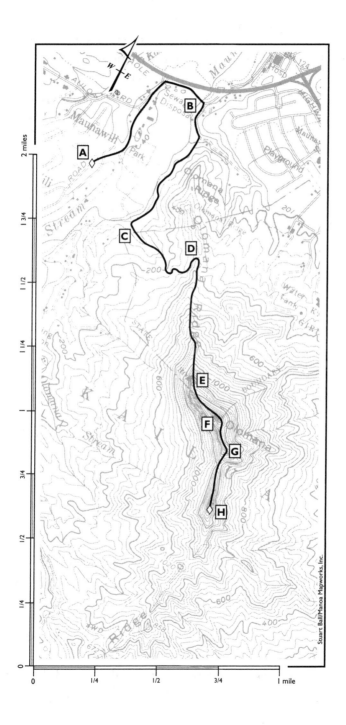

At the third traffic light, turn right on Aʻuloa Rd.

Shortly afterward the road forks; keep left on Maunawili Rd.

Pass Maunawili Valley Neighborhood Park on the left. The park has restrooms and drinking water.

As the road widens, enter Maunawili subdivision.

Park on the street just past the intersection with Maunawili Loop (elevation 80 feet) (map point A) (UTM 4Q 628078E, 2363711N) (Lat/Long N21.371, W157.76463).

BUS: Routes 56, 57, 57A, 70, or 77 to Kalanianaʻole Hwy and Aʻuloa Rd. Turn left on Luana Hills Rd. and pick up the description below. Route 77 runs only on weekdays.

## ROUTE DESCRIPTION

Walk back to Kalanianaʻole Hwy.

Just before reaching it, turn right on Luana Hills Rd., which parallels the highway.

After crossing Maunawili Stream on a bridge, turn right on the access road leading into Royal Hawaiian Golf Club (map point B).

As the road forks, keep right through a green gate and pass a security station on the left.

The golf club road ascends gradually past a white fence and then levels out.

As the road curves right and climbs, look for two thick yellow metal posts on the left.

Just past the second post, reach a signed junction (map point C). Turn left off the road, cross a narrow drainage ditch, and pick up the trail to Olomana. (Beyond the junction, the road is open only to club patrons.)

Ascend gradually along the right side of a gully.

Cross the gully near an abandoned pumping shack and keep left by a huge banyan tree.

Climb steadily up the side of Olomana Ridge through introduced forest. *Lauaʻe* ferns carpet the ground.

Gain the ridgeline at a small dip marked by a fencepost, a metal pipe, and a utility pole (map point D). Turn right, up the ridge.

Cross an eroded spot and enter an ironwood grove. Look for the native shrub 'ākia in the open sections.

Gradually ascend the flank of the mountain through a corridor of Christmas berry and laua'e. Watch out for a rusty barbed-wire fence on the right.

Begin climbing more steeply on a rocky trail (map point E).

Keep right up a long rock face partially covered by vegetation. A series of cables and ropes may provide some assistance.

Continue climbing very steeply. Underfoot are exposed rock dikes.

The angle of ascent decreases briefly through a hau grove (whew!).

Climb a short but nearly vertical rock face. A cable or rope may help in the ascent.

The ridgeline contracts to a thin rock dike.

Bear right off the ridge to avoid an especially narrow section.

Reach the summit of Olomana at a rocky outcrop (elevation 1,643 feet) (map point F) (UTM 4Q 629539E, 2362630N) (Lat/Long N21.36113, W157.75062). Admire the panoramic views of the windward coast and the Ko'olau cliffs.

Descend steeply to a saddle and then climb briefly to the second peak, known as Pāku'i (map point G). Among the grass and Christmas berry are the sprawling 'ūlei and the lanky koko'olau, both native shrubs.

Just past the summit of the second peak, turn sharp right and down to continue along the main ridge.

Descend precipitously to a saddle between the second and third peaks. A series of cables and ropes may aid in the descent over loose dirt and rock.

Begin climbing the very thin ridge of the third peak.

Inch left around a large dike section with a hole in it. A cable may provide some security.

Scramble up a long, steep rock face.

Keep right around a large free-standing boulder.

Bear right off the ridgeline and climb the final rock face.

Reach the flat summit of the third peak, known as Ahiki (map point H).

## NOTES

Olomana is Oʻahu's version of the Matterhorn. The main peak is a steep-sided pyramid that looks unclimbable from a distance. Closer inspection, however, reveals the classic route up the northwest ridge. Although thousands of hikers have taken that climb over the years, treat this alluring, dangerous mountain with respect.

Olomana (forked hill) has three distinct peaks. The elongated, razor-thin third peak is called Ahiki, and the second, central peak is Pākuʻi. Both are named after *konohiki* (overseers) of the ancient fishponds of Kaʻelepulu (the moist blackness), now called Enchanted Lake, and Kawainui (the big water). The first and highest peak is named after the legendary giant Olomana.

Olomana was a fearsome, evil warrior, 12 yards high, who dominated the windward side. None dared challenge him, not even the chief of Oʻahu. One day the chief commanded Palila, a brash young soldier, to rid the island of the giant. Palila journeyed to Kaʻelepulu, where he surprised Olomana by jumping up on his shoulder. The giant haughtily asked the boy soldier what he was doing up there and where he was from. Palila replied that he came from a temple on Kauaʻi noted for great warriors with supernatural powers. On hearing that, Olomana became afraid and begged for his life. Palila deftly struck the giant, cutting him in two. One part flew *makai* (seaward) and became Mahinui (great champion) mountain along the coast. The other part remained as the present peak of Olomana.

Much of the route up the mountain is a scramble over loose rock and dirt. The climb to the first and second peaks is an intermediate hike with medium danger. You must negotiate a narrow rock dike and a nearly vertical rock face just below the first peak. The descent from the second peak and the ascent to the third are for experienced, acrobatic hikers only. The rock is rotten, and the ridge plunges straight down on both sides. Test any ropes or cables that you find before using them. Take your time and be extraordinarily careful. There is no shame in turning back if you don't like what you see.

On the hike, look for the native dryland shrub *'ākia* in the open areas along Olomana Ridge. The shrub has dark branches jointed with white rings. Its leaves are bright green, oval, and pointed. Early Hawaiians pounded the leaves and bark and then dropped the mixture into tidal pools to poison the fish. The red-orange fruits were used in lei and as a poison for criminals.

From the top of the first peak is an awesome 360-degree view. *Makai* is the windward coast from Kualoa (long back) to Mōkapu (taboo district) to Makapu'u (bulging eye) Points. On a clear day, you can see the islands of Moloka'i and Maui across Kaiwi (the bone) Channel. *Mauka* (inland) is Maunawili (twisted mountain) Valley and the sheer, fluted cliffs of the Ko'olau (windward) Range. The massive peak to the left of Nu'uanu Pali (cool height cliff) is Kōnāhuanui (large fat testicles), the highest point in the Ko'olau Range. Try picking out the other major peaks on the summit ridge. From left to right are Pu'u o Kona (hill of leeward), Lanipō (dense), and Olympus (Awaawaloa). Beyond Kōnāhuanui are Lanihuli (turning royal chief) and Pu'u Keahi a Kahoe (hill of Kahoe's fire). In the distance is the steep pyramid of Pu'u 'Ōhulehule (joining of the waves hill).

Between the first and second peaks is the sprawling native shrub *'ulei*. It has small, oblong leaves arranged in pairs; clusters of white, roselike flowers; and white fruit. Early Hawaiians ate the berries and used the tough wood for making digging sticks, fish spears, and *'ūkēkē* (the musical bow).

From the second peak is a good view along the length of the mountain. Olomana is a remnant of the collapsed caldera of the old Ko'olau volcano. Filled with lava, the caldera stretched 8 miles from Waimānalo (potable water) to Kāne'ohe (bamboo husband). When the volcano became dormant, streams gradually eroded the softer lava, leaving intrusions of hard, dense rock known as dikes. Olomana remains because of its complex of narrow, vertical dikes over which you carefully scramble.

While resting on the third peak, look for small white nodules of opal in the dark lava. Over millions of years, volcanic gases altered the composition of the rocks in the caldera. In the process, excess silica collected in small cavities to form the white spheres, called amygdules.

# 47

# Maunawili

| LENGTH: | 7.4-mile round-trip |
|---|---|
| ELEVATION GAIN: | 600 feet |
| DANGER: | Low |
| SUITABLE FOR: | Novice, Intermediate |
| LOCATION: | O'ahu: Waimānalo Forest Reserve above Maunawili |
| TOPO MAP: | Honolulu, Koko Head |

## HIGHLIGHTS

This popular hike snakes along the base of the sheer, fluted Ko'olau cliffs. Along the way are lush gulches and ridge lookouts. An optional side trip leads to lovely Maunawili Falls, cascading into a deep swimming hole.

## TRAILHEAD DIRECTIONS

**DISTANCE:**   (Downtown Honolulu to Nu'uanu Pali State Park) 7 miles

**DRIVING TIME:**   1/4 hour

At Punchbowl St. get on Pali Hwy (Rte 61 north) heading up Nu'uanu Valley.

Just before the tunnels, turn right to the Pali Lookout.

Enter Nu'uanu Pali State Park.

Park in the lot (elevation 1,186 feet) (map point A)

(UTM 4Q 625041E, 2363157N) (Lat/Long N21.36621, W157.79396). Nonresidents must pay a parking fee.

BUS: Routes 56, 57, or 57A to Pali Hwy and Kamehameha Hwy (Castle junction). Walk 0.8 miles back up Pali Hwy to the viewpoint at the hairpin turn. Walk past the small parking lot and go through a gap in the guardrail on the left. Turn left on a connector trail to map point C and pick up the narrative there.

## ROUTE DESCRIPTION

Walk to the Pali Lookout.

Turn right down the ramp to Old Pali Rd.

Go through a gate by a Road Closed sign.

Descend gradually along the paved road, which is lined with yellow ginger. Encroaching vegetation and small landslides narrow the road to one lane or to a path in several spots.

After passing a rockfall on the right, reach a junction (map point B). Continue straight on the Maunawili Trail, which hugs the cliff on the right. (To the left a trail ducks under the Pali Highway to join the lower section of Old Pali Road.)

Keep to the right of a chain-link fence.

Descend gradually through three gulches. In the last one, cross intermittent Kahanaiki Stream.

Pass a viewpoint on the left.

Parallel a drainage ditch on your right.

By some plastic steps, reach a signed junction (map point C). Turn right, still on the Maunawili Trail. (To the left a connector trail descends to a small parking lot at the hairpin turn of the Pali Highway.)

Pass a small wood water tank on the right.

Contour into and out of three gulches through guava (*waiawī*) trees. *Kī* (ti) plants line the trail.

Cross over a prominent side ridge, known as Piliwale Ridge (map point D).

Break out into the open briefly through native *uluhe* ferns

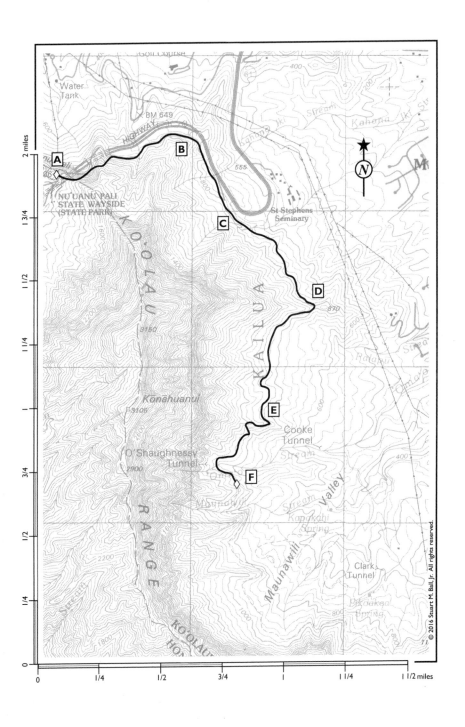

71

with scattered *ʻōhiʻa* trees above. *Mauka* (inland) are spectacular views of the Koʻolau cliffs.

Work into and out of a series of shallow gulches. Look for *kukui* trees in the gulches and Chinese ground orchids along the trail in winter.

Cross over a broad side ridge with a stand of ironwood trees above and on the right. Look *makai* (seaward) for triple-peaked Olomana.

Work into and out of another ravine and then cross over a narrow side ridge (map point E).

Descend into a deep ravine on two switchbacks and then contour through a series of shallow gullies. Before and after the switchbacks, watch for several native *māmaki* trees.

Enter a wide gulch with four waterfall chutes in back.

Cross a pair of rocky streambeds that join just below the trail. At the first one, a faint side trail on the right leads to the bottom of a waterfall chute and the OʻShaughnessy Tunnel.

In the next ravine, cross intermittent ʻŌmaʻo Stream by some struggling bamboo. Another faint side trail leads upstream to Smiling Falls, named for the shape of the rock dike at its base. After you leave the gulch, look behind for a fine view of the four waterfall chutes.

Reach a signed junction (elevation 880 feet) (map point F) (UTM 4Q 626263E, 2361286N) (Lat/Long N21.34922, W157.78231). Turn left and down to take the side trip to Maunawili Falls. Straight ahead, the Maunawili Trail continues to Waimānalo.

## NOTES

Maunawili is the showpiece of the Oʻahu trail system. Volunteer crews under the direction of the Sierra Club, Hawaiʻi Chapter, constructed 7 miles of trail during the summer and fall of 1991 through 1993. The remaining 2 miles were completed in 1993 by Boy Scouts, U.S. Marines, and prisoners from Oʻahu Correctional Facility. As described, the hike starts at the Nuʻuanu Pali Lookout and follows the first section of the trail to the Maunawili Falls junction.

With its well-groomed and graded treadway, the Maunawili Trail is popular with hikers, runners, and mountain bikers. To avoid the crowds, start early or go during the week. Better yet, try the hike right after a heavy rainstorm, when waterfalls suddenly appear out of every notch in the cliffs. Watch your footing in the slippery stream crossings, though.

The view at the Nuʻuanu Pali (cool height cliff) Lookout is world renowned. The windward coast stretches from Kāneʻohe (bamboo husband) to Kailua (two seas) Bays. In the distance to the right is triple-peaked Olomana (forked hill). From the old road, look back along the summit ridge to see the peak of Lanihuli (turning royal chief). Towering above you and frequently in the clouds is Kōnāhuanui (large fat testicles) (elevation 3,150 feet), the highest peak in the Koʻolau Range.

The Old Pali Road, which replaced earlier tracks over the Pali, was constructed in 1897 and opened to vehicle traffic a year later. It maintains a grade of 8 percent along its 1.7-mile length. The road switchbacks once through a tight bend known as the horseshoe curve or hairpin turn. Imagine what an adventure it was to drive a small car on this narrow, windy, winding road!

Lining the gulches along the Maunawili Trail are *kukui* trees. Their large, pale-green leaves resemble those of the maple, with several distinct lobes. Early Polynesian voyagers introduced *kukui* into Hawaiʻi. They used the wood to make gunwales and seats for their outrigger canoes. The flowers and sap became medicines to treat a variety of ailments. Early Hawaiians strung the nuts together to make *lei hua* (seed or nut garlands). The oily kernels became house candles and torches for night spearfishing.

While you are contouring below the cliffs, listen for the Japanese bush warbler (*uguisu*), a bird often heard but rarely seen. Its distinctive cry starts with a long whistle and then winds down in a series of notes. The bush warbler is olive brown on top with a white breast and a long tail.

Before and after the two switchbacks, look for *māmaki,* a small native tree. It has leathery, light-green leaves with toothed margins and prominent veins. Along the stems are the white, fleshy fruits. Early Hawaiians used the bark and sap in making *kapa* (bark cloth), and they also steeped the leaves to prepare a tea as a tonic. *Māmaki* leaves are a favorite food of the *pulelehua* (Kamehameha) butterfly, the state insect.

At the junction with the Maunawili Falls Connector Trail, take a break and admire the view. *Makai* (seaward) are Kailua and Waimānalo (potable water) Bays, with triple-peaked Olomana in front. *Mauka* (inland) loom the sheer, fluted Koʻolau (windward) cliffs from Makapuʻu (bulging eye) Point to Kōnāhuanui. Look back above the trail at the four waterfall chutes.

To get to Maunawili Falls, take the often-overgrown connector trail down a side ridge. At the signed junction by a bench, turn right and descend to Maunawili Stream. Cross the right fork and proceed up the right side of the left fork to the falls. At its base is a large, lower pool encircled by fern-covered cliffs. Up a slippery slope is a second smaller pool, where the waterfall splits in two. Enjoy a refreshing swim in the cool mountain water. If you plan to jump into the lower pool from the cliffs, be sure to check its depth first! The side trip to the falls and back adds about 2.5 miles to the hike length.

For a shorter, easier outing, use the alternate trailhead at the hairpin turn of the Pali Highway. Park in the small lot there, walk back up the access road, and go through a gap in the guardrail on the left. Turn left on the connector trail to map point C and pick up the narrative there. Starting from the hairpin turn reduces the hike length by about 3 miles and is a good option if you plan to visit the falls.

# 48

# Kahana Valley

| LENGTH: | 6.4-mile double loop |
|---|---|
| ELEVATION GAIN: | 400 feet |
| DANGER: | Low |
| SUITABLE FOR: | Novice, Intermediate |
| LOCATION: | O'ahu: Ahupua'a 'O Kahana State Park |
| TOPO MAP: | Kahana, Hau'ula |

## HIGHLIGHTS

This double-loop hike meanders around a vast, undeveloped windward valley. The intricate route has numerous junctions and stream crossings. Along the stream are deep, inviting pools and groves of mountain apple.

## TRAILHEAD DIRECTIONS

**DISTANCE:** (Downtown Honolulu to Ahupua'a 'O Kahana State Park) 25 miles

**DRIVING TIME:** 3/4 hour

At Punchbowl St. get on Lunalilo Fwy (H-1) heading 'ewa (west).

Take Likelike Hwy (exit 20A, Rte 63 north) up Kalihi Valley through the Wilson Tunnel.

As the highway forks, keep right for Kahekili Hwy (Rte 83 west).

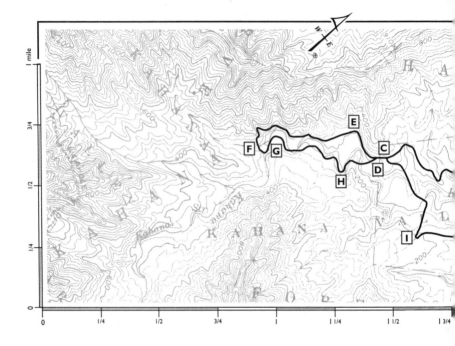

Kahekili becomes Kamehameha Hwy (still Rte 83), which continues up the windward coast.

Drive through the villages of Kahaluʻu and Waiāhole to Kaʻaʻawa.

Pass Crouching Lion Inn on the left.

The road curves left to go around Kahana Bay.

Cross Kahana Stream on two bridges.

By a large palm grove, turn left into Ahupuaʻa ʻO Kahana State Park.

Pass the front parking lot on the right and the visitor center on the left. A shelf by the front door contains park brochures and trail maps.

Just beyond the center are restrooms and drinking water in a green building on the right.

Drive another 0.5 miles into the valley on the paved road.

Park in the grassy area just before a locked gate with a stop sign (elevation 20 feet) (map point A) (UTM 4Q 615847E, 2383541N) (Lat/Long N21.55096, W157.88122).

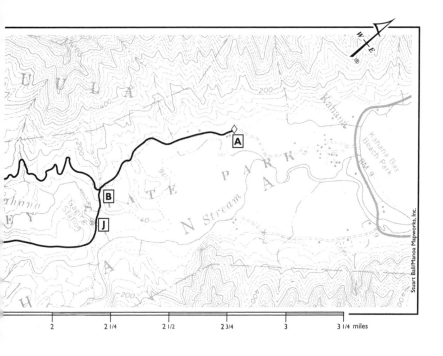

2       2 1/4      2 1/2      2 3/4      3      3 1/4 miles

**BUS:** Route 55 to the entrance of Ahupua'a 'O Kahana State Park. Walk 0.6 miles along the park access road to the locked gate.

## ROUTE DESCRIPTION

Continue along the paved access road on foot.

Pass houses on both sides of the road.

Go around a second locked gate. The road narrows to one lane.

Climb steadily through introduced forest.

On the left, pass two grass parking lots. The second one has a picnic table and a dirt road leading down to some *kalo* (taro) *lo'i* (terraces) by Kahana Stream.

Shortly afterward, reach a junction marked by hunting area and interpretive signs (map point B). After signing in at the hunter/hiker check-in mailbox, turn left and down on a dirt road. (The paved road curves right and up through a locked gate.)

Almost immediately, reach a signed junction. Turn right onto the Nakoa Trail. (The dirt road descends to Kahawainui Stream and is the return portion of the hike.)

Contour along the side of the valley through *hala* groves and *hau* tangles. Look for *hāpuʻu* tree ferns and mountain apple trees in this long section. In the openings, you can see Puʻu Manamana and Puʻu ʻŌhulehule on the ridge to the left.

Descend into a gully and turn right alongside it.

Bear left out of the gully and resume contouring through *hala* and *kī* (ti) plants.

Work into and out of a side gulch with a stream.

Go through a series of dense *hau* groves.

Descend briefly on a switchback and ford a small stream in a second gulch.

Descend into a third gulch on one switchback and cross another stream.

On the right, pass a rusted triangular tank trap left over from World War II army training.

Shortly afterward, reach a signed four-way junction in a clearing surrounded by *hala* trees (map point C) (UTM 4Q 614846E, 2381757N) (Lat/Long N21.53491, W157.89101). Continue straight across. (To the left the Nakoa Trail descends to Kahawainui Stream and is the return portion of the hike. To the right a trail leads to a water tank and the paved access road.)

Pass several observation bunkers partially hidden in the trees on the left.

Shortly afterward, reach a fork by a bamboo grove (map point D). Take the right fork. (The left fork leads down to Kahawainui Stream and is the return portion of the hike.)

Contour above Kahawainui Stream under magnificent Paraserianthes (albizia) and *kukui* trees.

Cross a side stream just after a grove of mountain apples.

Cross a second side stream by two mango trees.

Reach an obscure junction in a flat area surrounded by *hala* (map point E). Continue straight on the trail into the valley. (To the left a trail provides a shortcut to Kahawainui Stream.)

Cross several side streams in groves of mountain apple. The narrow trail hugs a cliff above the stream.

Swing left and down to reach another obscure junction by a large side stream (elevation 360 feet) (map point F) (UTM 4Q 614080E, 2381115N) (Lat/Long N21.52916, W157.89845). (To the right is the overgrown upper trail, which crosses the side stream and continues to the back of the valley.)

Parallel the side stream briefly, cross to its right bank, and then leave it behind.

Reach Kahawainui Stream and turn left downstream.

Cross the side stream again where it enters the main stream (map point G). Continue along the left bank of Kahawainui Stream.

Cross to the right bank of the main stream by two huge Paraserianthes trees with white-flecked trunks.

On the left, pass a sign marking nearby *lo'i*.

Ford the stream to the left bank at the tip of an island splitting the stream in two.

Cross the stream to the right bank by two large Paraserianthes trees.

On the right, pass a sign marking Pu'ulena (yellow hill), a swampy area where *kalo* was planted in mounds.

On the opposite bank of the stream are a large mango tree with exposed roots and a breadfruit tree.

Ford the stream to the left bank just before it turns sharp left (map point H). Nearby is a large mango tree and a deep, inviting pool with emerald-green water.

Continue downstream briefly and reach an obscure junction. Turn right and cross Kahawainui Stream to the right bank. (To the left a short trail leads back to map point E on the contour trail.)

The stream splits briefly. Traverse the island in between and then return to the right side.

Reach a large mango tree and a lovely pool.

Ford the stream there to the left bank and enter a bamboo grove.

Ascend through the grove, leaving the stream behind.

Work left and then straight up the slope on a narrow, rutted trail.

Reach the familiar junction with the contour trail (map point D) and turn right on it.

Reach the four-way junction again (map point C). This time, turn right downhill on the continuation of the Nakoa Trail.

Descend steadily through *hala* on an army road built of crushed coral.

Enter a *hau* grove.

Shortly afterward, ford Kahawainui Stream past two concrete bridge piers and turn right upstream.

Ascend steadily on a bench just below the ridgeline.

Reach a signed junction at the ridgeline (map point I). Turn sharp left down the ridge on another army road.

Descend gradually down the flat ridge through *hala*. Lining the trail are Chinese ground orchids, which bloom in winter.

Break out into the open briefly. The peak on the ridge to the left is Puʻu Piei.

Veer right, off the ridgeline onto a bench.

The trail curves left to reach Kahawainui Stream by a gaging station (map point J).

Ford the stream for the last time on a small dam. Watch your footing on the slippery concrete. At the dam is a large swimming hole popular with valley residents.

Climb gradually on an eroded gravel road.

A sign on the left marks an ʻauwai (ditch) for irrigating *loʻi*.

Reach the familiar junction by the hunting area sign (map point B). Turn right on the paved access road to reach your car.

## NOTES

This hike is an intriguing double loop in a largely undeveloped valley on the windward side. The initial stretch leaves something to be desired, but the stream loop is perhaps the most beautiful valley walk on the island. The water rushing by is cool and clear, and the pools are deep and inviting. There are few things better in life than spending a sunny afternoon by Kahawainui Stream.

Ahupua'a 'O Kahana (cutting) is a unique state park, established to foster and spread Native Hawaiian culture. About thirty families live in the lower section of the valley. They are helping to restore some of the ancient sites, such as Huilua (twice joined) Fishpond and *lo'i* (irrigated terraces for growing *kalo* [taro]). Years ago, the *ahupua'a* (land division) of Kahana supported a thriving community based on ocean fishing, taro farming, and fish raising.

During World War II, the U.S. Army established the Unit Jungle Training Center to better prepare its soldiers for combat in the Pacific Islands. The center had three layouts or courses of instruction: red and blue in Kahana Valley and green in nearby Punalu'u Valley. Soldiers learned to identify edible plants, build rope bridges across streams, and attack a mock-up Japanese village with pop-up targets. Look for remnant tank traps and bunkers near the four-way junction.

The trails in this wet valley are invariably muddy, sometimes overgrown, and occasionally obscure. Watch your footing while crossing the stream. If possible, change to tabis (Japanese reef walkers) or other water footwear for better traction on the slippery rocks. As always, do not ford the stream if the water is much above your knees.

Unfortunately, this magnificent valley harbors a large mosquito population. Local mosquitoes are usually laid back, but not so in Kahana. Bring insect repellent, cover up, or keep moving. For lunch, pick a sunny pool with a breeze, and you won't be constantly bothered.

On the first section of the Nakoa Trail are groves of tangled *hau* trees with large, heart-shaped leaves. Their flowers are bright yellow with a dark-red center and resemble those of a hibiscus. Early Hawaiians used the wood for kites and canoe outriggers, the bark for sandals, and the sap as a laxative.

Also common in the valley is the *hala* tree. It has distinctive prop roots that help support the heavy clusters of leaves and fruit on the ends of the branches. Early Hawaiians braided the long, pointed leaves, called *lau hala*, into baskets, fans, floor mats, and sails.

The wet side gulches are lined with *kukui* trees. Their large, pale-green leaves resemble those of the maple, with several distinct lobes. Early Polynesian voyagers introduced *kukui* into Hawai'i. They used the wood to make gunwales and seats for their outrigger canoes. The flowers and sap became medicines to treat a variety of ailments. Early Hawaiians strung the nuts together to make *lei hua* (seed or nut garlands). The oily kernels became house candles and torches for night spear fishing.

On the second loop, look for mountain apple trees (*'ōhi'a 'ai*) along the contour trail. They have dark, oblong, shiny leaves. In spring their purple flowers carpet the trail. The delicious pink or red fruit usually ripens in late July or early August. If none are in reach, shake the tree gently and try to catch the apples as they come down. The species is native to Malaysia and was brought over by early Hawaiians.

The walk along the stream is very pleasant, but the trail there may be obscure in spots. Follow the directions closely. Various colors of surveyor ribbon may mark the correct route, but don't count on it. If you do lose the trail, continue walking downstream until you pick it up again. Watch for the bamboo grove on the left bank where the trail leaves the stream for good.

On the return portion of the first loop, look for the Chinese ground or nun's orchid in winter. Its lovely flowers have tapered petals, which are white on the outside and reddish brown within. The lowest petal is a cream-colored tube with purple marking.

There are several variations to the route as described. You can, of course, do one or both loops in the opposite direction. However, the hike is complicated enough without having to read the narrative in reverse. For a short novice outing, walk only the first loop, on the Nakoa Trail. Be sure to visit the lovely pool near the bamboo by keeping left and down at the junction with the contour trail (map point D). Total distance for the first loop is about 5 miles. To shorten the second loop, turn left off the contour trail at map point E to reach the deep pool by the mango tree near map point H.

For a more difficult hike in the valley, explore the overgrown upper trail that leaves from the second loop and ends at the intake of Waiāhole Ditch. Across the intake is the start (end) of the Waiāhole Ditch Trail, which contours around the back of Kahana, Waikāne, and Waiāhole Valleys. Mountain man Richard H. (Dick) Davis of the Hawaiian Trail and Mountain Club reopened the upper trail in 1981–1982.

# 49

# Hau'ula-Papali

| | |
|---|---|
| LENGTH: | 7.4-mile double loop |
| ELEVATION GAIN: | 700 feet (Hau'ula), 800 feet (Papali) |
| DANGER: | Low |
| SUITABLE FOR: | Novice, Intermediate |
| LOCATION: | O'ahu: Hau'ula Forest Reserve above Hau'ula |
| TOPO MAP: | Hau'ula |

## HIGHLIGHTS

This intricate double loop traverses the foothills of the windward Ko'olau Range. From secluded viewpoints, you look down into deep, narrow gulches. Along the way are groves of stately Cook pines and some remnant native vegetation.

## TRAILHEAD DIRECTIONS

| | |
|---|---|
| DISTANCE: | (Downtown Honolulu to Hau'ula Beach Park) 30 miles |
| DRIVING TIME: | 1 hour |

At Punchbowl St. get on Lunalilo Fwy (H-1) heading 'ewa (west).

Take Likelike Hwy (exit 20A, Rte 63 north) up Kalihi Valley through the Wilson Tunnel.

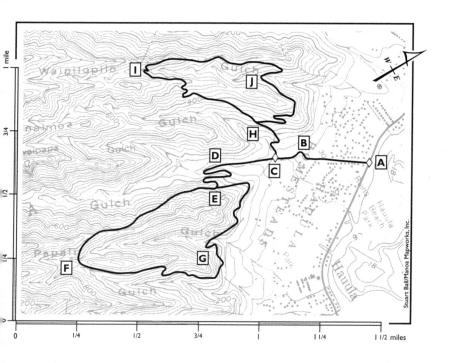

As the highway forks, keep right for Kahekili Hwy (Rte 83 west).

Kahekili becomes Kamehameha Hwy (still Rte 83), which continues up the windward coast.

Drive through the villages of Ka'a'awa and Punalu'u to Hau'ula.

Pass a fire station on the left and cross a bridge.

Look for Hau'ula Beach Park on the right. At the park are restrooms and drinking water.

Park on Kamehameha Hwy at the far end of the beach park near the intersection with Hau'ula Homestead Rd. Nearby are Hau'ula Congregational Church and the Hau'ula Base Yard (map point A) (UTM 4Q 612624E, 2390371N) (Lat/Long N21.61286, W157.91188).

**BUS:** Route 55 to Kamehameha Hwy and Hau'ula Homestead Rd.

Proceed *mauka* (inland) along Hauʻula Homestead Rd.

As the road curves left, continue straight on Maʻakua Rd.

Go around a yellow gate and pass a private driveway on the left.

The road forks by a utility pole (map point B). Take the left fork and go around another yellow gate.

Cross Hānaimoa Stream and swing right to reach a signed junction (map point C). Keep left on the paved road. (To the right is the Hauʻula Loop Trail, which is described later on.) Register at the nearby hunter/hiker check-in mailbox.

The road straightens out briefly by a concrete retaining wall.

Before the road curves right, reach a second signed junction (map point D). Bear left and down off the road onto the Maʻakua Ridge Trail. (To the right the road leads to the Maʻakua Gulch Trail, which is closed because of rockfall danger.)

Cross Maʻakua Stream presently and climb the embankment on the far side.

Work right and then left through a tangled *hau* grove.

Climb gradually up the side of Maʻakua Gulch on eight switchbacks. At the sixth one is a good view of Hauʻula town and the ocean. After the seventh, a short trail leads left to a covered picnic table.

At the eighth switchback by a bench, the trail splits to become a loop (map point E). Turn sharp right and start the Papali loop in a counterclockwise direction.

Switchback four more times and then steadily ascend *mauka* up the side of the ridge through mixed introduced forest. You can look deep into Maʻakua Gulch through breaks in the trees. Watch for *hala* trees with their prop roots.

Reach the ridgeline and stroll along it under shady Formosa *koa* trees.

By a large, yellow strawberry guava tree, reach a junction (elevation 800 feet). Bear left off the ridge and descend gradually into Papali Gulch. (A rough, makeshift route continues up the ridge.)

Cross the stream by a stand of *kī* (ti) shrubs and turn left downstream. Watch for native *pāpala kēpau* trees with their large, leathery leaves.

Climb gradually out of the gulch, which is lined with *kukui* trees.

Gain the narrow ridgeline briefly near a tall Cook pine and a mango tree (map point F) (UTM 0Q 612142E, 2388404N) (Lat/Long N21.59512, W157.91667).

Switch to the right side of the ridge and descend along the side of Punaiki Gulch on a series of twin switchbacks.

Break out into the open through *'ūlei*, a sprawling native shrub.

Contour around the front of the ridge under arching Christmas berry trees.

Descend once again into Papali Gulch to the stream and turn right.

Follow the rocky streambed briefly and then angle left onto the trail (map point G).

Climb out of the gulch on four switchbacks.

Contour along the front of the next ridge. A dark rock cliff overhangs the trail on the left.

Reach the end of the loop (map point E). Bear right and down.

Retrace your steps to the paved road and its junction with the Hau'ula Loop Trail (map point C).

Turn left off the road onto the trail to start the second loop.

Briefly parallel Hānaimoa Stream on your right and then cross it.

Ascend through ironwood trees on two long switchbacks. After the second switchback, look for *noni*, a small tree with large, shiny leaves and warty fruit.

The trail splits, becoming a loop (map point H). This time, keep left and start the loop in a clockwise direction.

Climb gradually up the side of Hānaimoa Gulch heading *mauka*. Switchback three times through an ironwood grove. At the first and third switchbacks are several sandalwood trees.

By a paperbark tree, reach the ridgeline and cross over it to the left.

Descend gradually into Waipilopilo Gulch.

Cross the stream between two small waterfalls and climb out of the gulch on two short switchbacks.

Reach the ridgeline (elevation 680 feet) (map point I) (UTM 4Q 611290E, 2389502N) (Lat/Long N21.60509, W157.92482) and turn right heading *makai* (seaward). Below on the left are the sheer walls of Kaipapaʻu Gulch. Look for a few native ʻōhiʻa trees and *pūkiawe* shrubs along the trail.

Descend steadily along the ridge. Steps are provided at steep, eroded sections.

Bear right off the ridgeline through a grove of ironwoods and then Cook pines. The ground near the trail is covered with *lauaʻe* ferns.

Switchback to the right and descend into Waipilopilo Gulch (map point J). Ignore a narrow trail continuing straight at the switchback.

Cross the stream again and climb out of the gulch.

Contour around the front of the ridge through Cook pines and ironwoods. Through gaps in the trees, you can see up the windward coast to Lāʻie Point and down the coast to Māhie Point on the far side of Kahana Bay.

Descend on two switchbacks through grass on rougher trail.

Reach the end of the loop (map point H) and turn left.

Retrace your steps back to the paved road (map point C).

Turn left on it to return to the highway (map point A).

## NOTES

Hauʻula-Papali is the perfect hike for beginners. The two loops are short, mostly shady, and surprisingly scenic. Along the trail are some easily identified native and introduced plants. Although in the same general area, each loop is different, so try them both. An inexpensive interpretive pamphlet, *Hauʻula Loop Trail: Field Site Guide* is available from Moanalua Gardens Foundation, whose address is listed in the appendix.

The route narrative describes the Papali (small cliff) loop first in a counterclockwise direction and then the Hauʻula (red *hau* tree) loop in a clockwise direction. You can, of course, do just one or both loops in either order or direction. The Hauʻula loop is somewhat easier and more popular than Papali. Neither loop is crowded, however, probably because of their distance from Honolulu.

Territorial Forestry built the two loops in the early 1930s to provide access to the Hauʻula Forest Reserve for tree planters, pig hunters, and fence builders. Trail crews finished the Papali loop first in December 1932 and the Hauʻula loop in April 1933. Civilian Conservation Corps workers regraded and cleared both loops in 1935. Even today the trails remain wide, well graded, and easy to follow for the most part. Watch your step, however, while crossing the rocky streambeds in the gulches. The Papali loop may be overgrown in spots with introduced shrubs.

On the trail, look and listen for the white-rumped shama. It is black on top with a chestnut-colored breast and a long black-and-white tail. The shama has a variety of beautiful songs and often mimics other birds. A native of Malaysia, the shama has become widespread in introduced forests such as this one.

Look for native *pāpala kēpau* trees in Papali Gulch. They have large, leathery, oval leaves and clusters of small, white flowers. Early Hawaiians smeared glue from the sticky, ripe fruit on poles to catch native birds for their feathers. Craftsmen then fashioned capes and religious objects from the bright red and yellow feathers.

On the return portion of the Papali loop, watch for the sprawling native shrub *ʻūlei* in the sunny sections. It has small, oblong leaves arranged in pairs; clusters of white, roselike flowers; and white fruit. Early Hawaiians ate the berries and used the tough wood for making digging sticks, fish spears, and *ʻūkēkē* (the musical bow).

Above Kaipapaʻu (shallow sea) Gulch on the Hauʻula loop are a few *pūkiawe* shrubs and *ʻōhiʻa* trees. *Pūkiawe* has tiny, rigid leaves and small white, pink, or red berries. *ʻŌhiʻa* has oval leaves and clusters of delicate red flowers. Early Hawaiians used the flowers in lei and the wood in outrigger canoes. The hard, durable wood was also carved into god images for *heiau* (religious sites).

On the return leg of the Hauʻula loop is a forest of tall Cook pines planted by Territorial Forestry in 1933. They have overlapping, scalelike leaves about 1/4-inch long, rather than true needles. Named after Captain James Cook, they are native to New Caledonia's Isle of Pines in the South Pacific between Fiji and Australia.

50

# Keālia

| LENGTH: | 6.6-mile round-trip |
|---|---|
| ELEVATION GAIN: | 2,000 feet |
| DANGER: | Low |
| SUITABLE FOR: | Intermediate |
| LOCATION: | Oʻahu: Kuaokalā and Mokulēʻia Forest Reserves above Mokulēʻia |
| TOPO MAP: | Kaʻena |

## HIGHLIGHTS

This hot, dry hike ascends a steep *pali* (cliff) en route to the summit of the Waiʻanae Range. While climbing, you may see fixed-wing gliders soaring above the north shore of Oʻahu. At the end is a scenic overlook of an undeveloped leeward valley.

## TRAILHEAD DIRECTIONS

**DISTANCE:** (Downtown Honolulu to Dillingham Airfield) 35 miles

**DRIVING TIME:** 1 hour

At Punchbowl St. get on Lunalilo Fwy (H-1) heading *ʻewa* (west).

Near Middle St., keep left on Moanalua Fwy (H-201) to 'Aiea.

By Aloha Stadium, bear right to rejoin H-1 to Pearl City.

Take H-2 freeway north (exit 8A) to Wahiawā.

As the freeway ends, continue on Rte 99 north (Wilikina Dr.), bypassing Wahiawā.

Pass Schofield Barracks on the left.

The road narrows to two lanes, dips, and then forks at a traffic light. Take the left fork toward Waialua (still Wilikina Dr., but now Rte 803).

Wilikina Dr. becomes Kaukonahua Rd. (still Rte 803).

At Thomson Corner with its flashing yellow light, continue straight on Farrington Hwy (Rte 930).

At the small traffic circle, bear left under the overpass to Mokulē'ia and Dillingham Airfield.

Pass Waialua Intermediate and High School on the left.

Drive through Mokulē'ia.

On the left, pass Dillingham Airfield and Glider Port, surrounded by a green fence.

At the far end of the airfield, turn left through the West Gate by a Low-Flying Aircraft warning sign. The gate is open from 7 a.m. to 6 p.m. daily.

Go around the end of the runway and head back along the other side.

Pass a low concrete building on the left.

Turn left into the paved lot in front of the airfield control tower and park there (elevation 20 feet) (map point A) (UTM 4Q 581997E, 238632N) (Lat/Long N21.57794, W158.20796).

BUS: None, within reasonable walking distance of the trailhead.

## ROUTE DESCRIPTION

From the lot, walk back across the access road and proceed along a wide, partially paved road heading *mauka* (inland).

By a trail sign, go around a chain across the road.

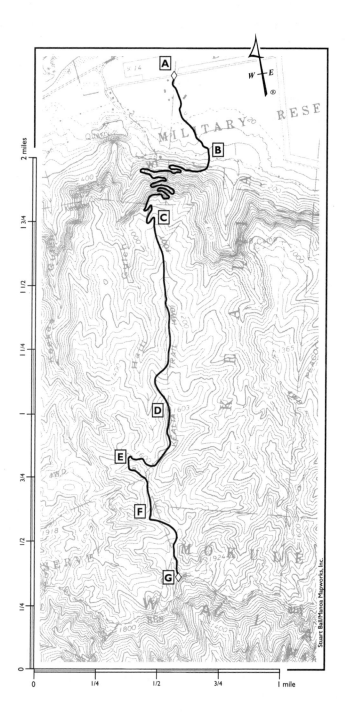

Bear left immediately, keeping a large concrete building on your right.

The road narrows to a gravel track through *koa haole* trees.

The track splits twice. Keep right at the first fork and left at the second one.

Go through an opening in a low green fence by a yellow warning sign (map point B) and immediately bear left on the Keālia Trail.

Work toward the base of the cliffs through grass and *koa haole*.

Pass a utility pole on the right.

Ascend the *pali* (cliff) gradually on nineteen switchbacks. Watch your footing on the loose rock.

After the second zigzag, look for native *lonomea* trees with dark green leaves.

At the third is a lone *noni* shrub.

After the fourth, views of the north shore begin to open up.

After the eighth, note the alternating layers of rough *ʻaʻā* and smooth *pāhoehoe* lava along the trail.

After the eleventh, watch for an inscription carved into the rock by a member of the CCC trail crew in 1934.

On the upper switchbacks are large native *alaheʻe* and *wiliwili* trees.

At the top of the cliff, reach a covered picnic table in an ironwood grove (map point C).

Pick up a dirt road at the far end of the grove.

Ascend gradually up the wide ridge through an introduced forest of silk oak, black wattle, and Christmas berry. Look for the native shrub *ʻaʻaliʻi* along the roadside.

Reach a junction by an old fence line. Turn right on the main road through two weathered wooden gateposts. (To the left a less-traveled dirt road heads downhill.)

Continue climbing through introduced ironwoods and pines.

Pass a rusted water tank on the left.

Enter Kuaokalā Public Hunting Area marked by a sign (map point D).

The road levels, dips briefly, and then resumes climbing around a hump in the ridge. Listen for the cackling cry of the Erckel's francolin.

As the road curves left in a eucalyptus grove, reach a junction (map point E). Continue left on the main road. (To the right another dirt road heads downhill.)

Ascend steeply up the side of the hump and then descend just as steeply to a saddle on the ridge.

Climb steadily until the road ends at a signed T junction (map point F). Turn left on Kuaokalā Access Rd. toward Mākua Valley. (To the right the access road leads to Ka'ena Point Satellite Tracking Station.)

Reach a signed junction. Bear slightly right and up on the Kuaokalā Trail, the less-traveled dirt road. (Kuaokalā Access Rd. veers left and leads to an abandoned Nike missile site and the Mākua Rim Trail.)

Reach the road end at a fence along the rim of Mākua Valley (elevation 1,960 feet) (map point G) (UTM 4Q 581528E, 2383274N) (Lat/Long N21.55044, W158.21264).

## NOTES

Keālia means "salt encrustation" in English. The name probably refers to sea salt along the coast, but it is also an apt description of your shirt after you finish the hike. Keālia is a hot, dry, unrelenting climb to the summit ridge of the Wai'anae Range. Switchbacks on the *pali* (cliff) and a dirt road to the top ease the gradient some. Magnificent views and a variety of native plants and introduced birds make the effort worthwhile.

The best time to take this hike is from February to April. The weather is cooler then, and you will miss the bird-hunting season. Whenever you go, drink plenty of water and use lots of sunscreen.

The switchback section is usually clear, wide, and well graded. However, don't sightsee and walk at the same time because of the nearby drop and the loose rock that sometimes litters the trail. On the road, watch out for the occasional four-wheel-drive vehicle. At the lookout, don't even think of descending into Mākua Valley, as it is a military range used for live-fire exercises.

On the initial zigzags, look for native *lonomea* trees. They have dark-green leaves with a prominent yellow midrib. Early Hawaiians strung the black seeds into *lei hua* (seed or nut garlands). The wood was used in house construction and to make spears.

Above the fourth switchback are superb views of the beautiful north shore of Oʻahu. Along the coast are the towns of Waialua and Haleʻiwa (house of the frigate bird). Beyond are Waimea (reddish water) Bay and Sunset Beach. In the distance is the Koʻolau (windward) Range. Directly below lies Dillingham Airfield. The large pond nearby was once a quarry used to mine rock for the airstrip and other construction projects. In the brackish water are farmed tilapia destined for Honolulu restaurants. Above the cliff and ocean, look for fixed-wing gliders and skydivers with their colorful parachutes.

After the eleventh zigzag, watch for some historical graffiti left by a member of the crew building the trail in 1934. He carved his initials, the date, and "C. C. C." for Civilian Conservation Corps. The Wahiawā Unit of the Corps began construction of the Keālia Trail in March and finally finished it in September. Whole sections of the route had to be blasted out of the lava rock. The holes near the inscription, however, are not left over from CCC blasting but were drilled more recently by geologists studying changes in the earth's magnetic field.

Along the upper switchbacks are native *wiliwili* and *alaheʻe* trees. *Alaheʻe* has small, oblong leaves that are shiny and dark green. Its fragrant white flowers grow in clusters at the branch tips. Early Hawaiians fashioned the hard wood into farming tools and hooks and spears for fishing.

*Wiliwili* has heart-shaped, leathery leaflets in groups of three. Flowers appear in the spring and are yellow-orange. Early Hawaiians used the soft, light wood for surfboards, canoe outriggers, and fishnet floats. The red seeds were strung together to form *lei hua* (seed or nut garlands).

Along the switchbacks and the road, look for a variety of introduced birds. Much in evidence is the white-rumped shama, a Malaysian songbird with a chestnut-colored breast. Watch for the red northern cardinal from the mainland and the red-crested cardinal from South America. Listen for the cackling cry of the Erckel's francolin, a brown game bird introduced from Africa. Look and listen for the iridescent peacock with its wailing call.

On the first road section, look for native ʻaʻaliʻi shrubs. They have shiny, narrow leaves and red seed capsules. Early Hawaiians used the leaves and capsules in making lei. When crushed or boiled, the capsules produced a red dye for decorating *kapa* (bark cloth).

After the uphill road walk, the summit lookout is a welcome sight. A thousand feet below lies the green expanse of Mākua (parents) Valley leading to the ocean. In back are the dark, sheer walls of ʻŌhikilolo (scooped-out brains) Ridge. To the left the Waiʻanae (mullet water) summit ridge gradually rises to flat-topped Kaʻala (the fragrance), the highest peak on the island.

For a longer hike, continue along the Kuaokalā (back of the sun) Trail to the right until turnaround time. The trail hugs the rim of Mākua Valley and then follows the coastal cliffs to Kaʻena (the heat) Point Satellite Tracking Station. For access through the tracking station to the Kuaokalā Trail, get a hiking permit and map from the Division of Forestry and Wildlife in Honolulu. See the appendix for the address.

# 51

# Wai'anae-Ka'ala

| | |
|---|---|
| LENGTH: | 8.6-mile round-trip |
| ELEVATION GAIN: | 3,500 feet |
| DANGER: | Medium |
| SUITABLE FOR: | Intermediate, Expert |
| LOCATION: | O'ahu: Wai'anae Kai Forest Reserve and Mt. Ka'ala Natural Area Reserve above Wai'anae town |
| TOPO MAP: | Wai'anae, Ka'ena, Hale'iwa |
| ACCESS: | Open, for groups of ten or less; for larger groups, obtain a special-use permit. See the appendix for more information. |

## HIGHLIGHTS

The highest mountain on O'ahu is flat-topped Ka'ala. This rugged hike climbs to its misty summit from the hot leeward side. En route and in the bog at the top is an amazing assemblage of native forest plants.

## TRAILHEAD DIRECTIONS

| | |
|---|---|
| **DISTANCE:** | (Downtown Honolulu to Wai'anae Kai Forest Reserve) 36 miles |
| **DRIVING TIME:** | 1 hour |

At Punchbowl St. get on Lunalilo Fwy (H-1) heading *ewa* (west).

Near Middle St., keep left on Moanalua Fwy (H-201) to 'Aiea.

By Aloha Stadium, bear right to rejoin H-1 to Pearl City and on toward Wai'anae.

As the freeway ends near Campbell Industrial Park, continue along the leeward coast on Farrington Hwy (Rte 93).

Pass Ko Olina resort on the left and Kahe Point power plant on the right.

Drive through Nānākuli and Mā'ili to Wai'anae town.

Pass Wai'anae Mall on the right.

Turn right on Wai'anae Valley Rd.

Turn left on a one-lane paved road (still Wai'anae Valley Rd.) by a bus turnaround marked with white curbs.

Pass several houses.

A locked gate blocks the road at the forest reserve boundary (elevation 580 feet) (map point A) (UTM 4Q 587829E, 2375049N) (Lat/Long N21.47584, W158.15222). Park in the dirt lot on the left across from a house.

BUS: Route 401 to the turnaround. Walk 1.1 miles along Wai'anae Valley Rd. to the forest reserve boundary.

## ROUTE DESCRIPTION

Register at the hunter/hiker check-in mailbox at the far end of the lot on the left.

Go around the locked gate and continue up the one-lane paved road on foot through scrub *koa haole* trees.

Pass a water tank on the left.

In a wooded area, the road levels off momentarily and passes Wai'anae Well I surrounded by a chain-link fence (map point B).

Ascend steeply through a mixed forest of *kukui*, silk oak, and coffee. Listen for the Japanese bush warbler.

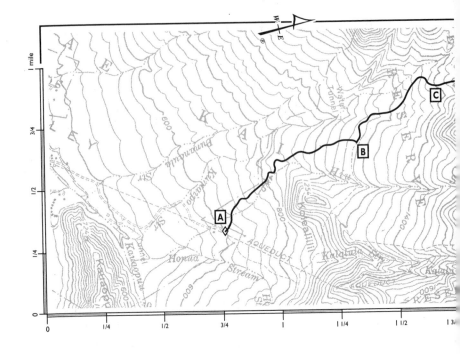

The pavement ends by Wai'anae Well II (map point C). Continue up a dirt road through Formosa *koa* trees.

Reach the end of the road by a covered picnic table. Take the trail on the right marked by several boulders. Nearby are some macadamia nut trees.

Ascend gradually along a broad ridge, keeping to its right edge. On the left are several *lo'i* (terraces) once used for growing *kalo* (taro).

Bear right around a large rock outcrop and pass a utility pole on the left.

After the ridge narrows, turn left down into a gully.

Cross the streambed and turn left downstream past some *kukui* trees.

Climb out of the gully and traverse a side ridge through strawberry guava and Christmas berry trees.

Work right, up a partially open ridge. Ignore obscure side trails on the left.

Bear left off the ridgeline into a broad gully.

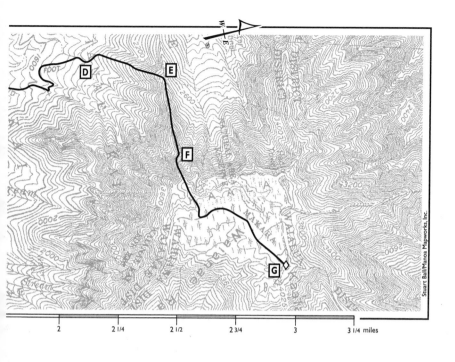

Stuart Ball/Manoa Mapworks, Inc.

| | | | | | |
|---|---|---|---|---|---|
| 2 | 2 1/4 | 2 1/2 | 2 3/4 | 3 | 3 1/4 miles |

Cross a very small streambed and reach an obscure junction (map point D). Take the right fork up the gully past some *kī* (ti) plants. (The trail to the left is the return leg of the Waiʻanae Kai loop.)

Work left out of the gully onto a side ridge and climb steeply up its left side.

The trail switchbacks once and then resumes going straight up.

Switch to the right edge of the ridge through native *koa* and *ʻōhiʻa* trees and *uluhe* ferns. Look for maile, a native twining shrub.

As the ridgeline nears, ascend very steeply, perhaps with the aid of a rope or cable.

Reach the top of Kamaileʻunu Ridge, a fence line, and a trail junction (map point E). Turn right up the ridge along the fence.

Almost immediately, reach an overlook of Waiʻanae Valley by some metal utility poles (elevation 2,720 feet). In front of the overlook are native *ʻaʻaliʻi* shrubs.

Climb steadily up the ridge through open native vegetation. Look for the native shrub *pilo*.

The ridge broadens and levels through a stand of *ʻōhiʻa ʻāhihi*.

Negotiate a series of large boulders on a steep and narrow section of the ridge. The last boulder is notorious. Scramble up to the right initially and then back to the left. A cable may provide some security.

Climb very steeply on the now-broad ridge through native forest. Between cables, look for *olomea* trees with their red-veined leaves.

Cut right, across the face of the ridge, and then resume steep scrambling. Several more cables may ease the climb.

Enter Mt. Kaʻala Natural Area Reserve marked by a sign.

The ridge narrows and the angle of ascent decreases as the top nears. Watch for *koliʻi*, a native lobelia.

Reach the Kaʻala plateau and bog (map point F).

Cross the bog on a narrow boardwalk through diverse native vegetation. Common are *lapalapa* trees and *kūkaemoa* (*alani*) and *pūʻahanui* (*kanawao*) shrubs.

Go through an unlocked gate, close it, and cross a helipad.

Reach paved Mt. Kaʻala Rd. and the summit near an FAA radar installation (elevation 4,025 feet) (map point G) (UTM 4Q 588804E, 2378582N) (Lat/Long N21.5077, W158.14262).

For the best views, turn right on the road. Just before reaching the main gate of the installation, turn left along the outside of the perimeter fence. Circle halfway around the fence to a grassy lookout. Do not enter the FAA installation, which is a secured area off-limits to the public, and do not go down the road.

## NOTES

The Waiʻanae-Kaʻala hike climbs to the summit of the highest mountain on Oʻahu from the leeward side. The route starts in a hot, dry valley and ends in a cool, wet bog. The misty walk through the native forest in the bog is one of the great hiking experiences on the island. After that, the summit, with its road, radar, and fleeting views is an anticlimax.

This rugged hike requires a number of cautions. The section through the boulders to the summit plateau is very steep and usually slippery. Watch your balance and footing constantly, especially on the descent. Test all cables before using them. If you feel uneasy about the exposure, turn around. On the final climb, blackberry bushes may overgrow the trail. Wear gloves and long pants for protection against the thorns. While crossing the bog, stay on the boardwalk to avoid damaging the vegetation. Finally, don't enter the FAA radar installation even though the main gate is sometimes open. The staff there does not welcome tourists!

On the ascent to the Wai'anae Valley overlook, watch for the native shrubs 'a'ali'i and maile. 'A'ali'i has shiny, narrow leaves and red seed capsules. Maile has glossy, pointed leaves, tangled branches, and fruit resembling a small olive. Its fragrant leaves and bark have been used to make distinctive open-ended lei, both in ancient and modern Hawai'i.

From the overlook, you can see Wai'anae (mullet water) and Lualualei Valleys to the right. On the left is Mākaha (fierce) Valley, backed by 'Ōhikilolo (scooped-out brains) Ridge. Ahead along Kamaile'unu (the stripped maile) Ridge are the imposing ramparts of Ka'ala (the fragrance).

On the final climb, take a break between cables and look for the small native trees, 'ōhi'a 'āhihi, pilo, and olomea. 'Ōhi'a 'āhihi have narrow, pointed leaves with red stems and midribs. Their delicate red flowers grow in clusters and are similar to those of the more common 'ōhi'a, which you saw on the way up. Pilo has reddish-orange berries and narrow leaves in a cluster at the branch tips. Olomea has shiny leaves with serrated edges and red veins and stems.

Olomea is a favorite habitat of endangered Hawaiian land snails. Look carefully for them on both sides of the leaves. One variety has a white, spiral shell and another has a brown, rounded shell. Do not disturb the snails or allow them to fall to the ground. Years ago, many valleys on Oʻahu had their own species of snail. Now most are gone because of shell collecting, habitat loss, and predation from introduced snails and rats.

On the flat top of the mountain is the Mt. Kaʻala Natural Area Reserve. Established in 1981, the reserve protects native plants and animals on 1,100 acres at the summit and along windward slopes of Kaʻala. For more information about the reserve, check the Division of Forestry and Wildlife website, whose address is listed in the appendix

After entering the reserve, keep your eye out for *koliʻi*, an unusual native *Trematolobelia*. It has a single woody stem with triangular leaf scars. Its long, slender leaves are arranged in a rosette resembling a dry mop head. A circle of horizontal stalks from the rosette bears the lovely scarlet tubular flowers. After flowering, the entire plant dies, leaving a ring of seed capsules.

The one-lane boardwalk makes for easy and reasonably dry walking through the misty bog. Take time to enjoy the incredible variety of native plants there. See if you can identify these three common ones: *lapalapa, pūʻahanui (kanawao),* and *kūkaemoa (alani). Lapalapa* trees have roundish leaves that are arranged in groups of three and flutter in the slightest wind. *Pūʻahanui,* a relative of hydrangea, has large, serrated, deeply creased leaves and clusters of delicate pink flowers. *Kūkaemoa* (chicken dung) shrubs have curled, dark-green leaves, which give off a slight anise odor. The fruits resemble miniature cauliflowers or chicken droppings.

From the lookouts along the perimeter fence at the summit, you can see the beautiful north shore, the Wahiawā (place of noise) plain, and, in back, the Koʻolau (windward) Range. In the distance are Pearl Harbor (Puʻuloa), Honolulu, and Diamond Head (Lēʻahi). Along the Waiʻanae summit ridge are the peaks of Kalena (the lazy one), Hāpapa (rock stratum), and Puʻu Kaua (war hill). If the view is obscured, wait a while, as the mist may lift suddenly.

The ridge and bog sections of the hike follow an old Hawaiian route across Kaʻala to Waialua. Natives used the Kūmaipō Trail to access the ridge route from either Mākaha or Waiʻanae Valley. To early Hawaiians, Kaʻala may have meant lofty and removed, even forbidding, an apt description of the mountain and this hike.

# 52

# Ka'ena Point

| LENGTH: | 5.8-mile round-trip |
|---|---|
| ELEVATION GAIN: | 100 feet |
| DANGER: | Low |
| SUITABLE FOR: | Novice, Intermediate |
| LOCATION: | O'ahu: Ka'ena Point Natural Area Reserve beyond Mākua |
| TOPO MAP: | Ka'ena |
| ACCESS: | Open, for groups of ten or less; for larger groups, obtain a special-use permit. See the appendix for more information |

## HIGHLIGHTS

Ka'ena is the westernmost point on O'ahu and a legendary entrance to the underworld. Along the hot, dry route are steep cliffs, pounding surf, and coastal native plants. You may also see humpback whales, nesting seabirds, and Hawaiian monk seals.

## TRAILHEAD DIRECTIONS

| DISTANCE: | (Downtown Honolulu to Ka'ena Point State Park) 42 miles |
|---|---|
| DRIVING TIME: | 1 hour |

At Punchbowl St. get on Lunalilo Fwy (H-1) heading *'ewa* (west).

Near Middle St., keep left on Moanalua Fwy (H-201) to 'Aiea.

By Aloha Stadium, bear right to rejoin H-1 to Pearl City and on toward Wai'anae.

As the freeway ends near Campbell Industrial Park, continue along the leeward coast on Farrington Hwy (Rte 93).

Pass Kahe Point power plant on the right.

Drive through Nānākuli, Mā'ili, and Wai'anae towns.

The road narrows to two lanes.

Drive through Mākaha and pass Kea'au Beach Park on the left.

On the right, pass 'Ōhikilolo Mākua Ranch and then Mākua Military Reservation with its observation post.

Enter Ka'ena Point State Park by Keawa'ula (Yokohama) Bay. In the first building on the right are restrooms and drinking water.

Park in the lot on the right at the end of the paved road (map point A) (UTM 4Q 577851E, 2383860N) (Lat/Long N21.5559, W158.24812). For safer parking, leave your car near the satellite tracking station guardhouse on the right or by the lifeguard stand on the left. Those options add 1 to 2 miles to the hike.

## ROUTE DESCRIPTION

Continue along the coast on a dirt road through scattered *kiawe* trees. The route roughly follows an old rail bed of the O'ahu Railway and Land Company. Watch for native *'iliahialo'e* shrubs (coast sandalwood) on the cliff side of the road.

Take the short, periodic trails on the left for a better view of the coves and tide pools along the shoreline and humpback whales in the ocean. Native *pā'ū o* Hi'iaka vines and low-lying *'ilima papa* shrubs carpet the ground.

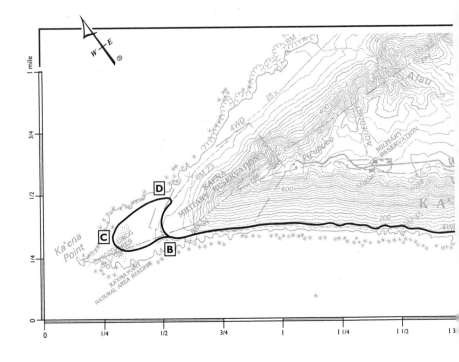

Just past a large boulder and before several railroad ties are two blowholes. One produces a jet of water, and the other sounds like a whale spouting.

Pass two sea arches.

Occasionally, walk on old wooden railroad ties. Note the alternating layers of rough *ʻaʻā* and smooth *pāhoehoe* lava in the road embankment. On the right, look for a lone *Kaʻena ʻakoko*, an endangered shrub found only in the Kaʻena area.

Pass an old utility pole on the right.

After passing a second pole, bear right and up on a make-shift trail to bypass a section where the road has washed out.

Go through a predator-proof fence and enter Kaʻena Point Natural Area Reserve (map point B).

Reach a junction. Keep left on the trail to the point. (To the right is the rail bed, which is the return portion of hike.)

Walk through sand dunes covered with coastal native plants, including *naupaka kahakai, naio, hinahina,* and *pōhinahina.* Look for nesting *mōlī* (Laysan albatross) in the winter and *ʻuaʻu kani*

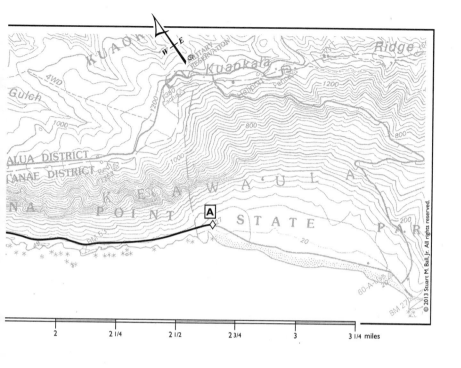

```
2        2 1/4        2 1/2        2 3/4        3        3 1/4 miles
```

(wedge-tailed shearwater) in the summer. Stay on the marked trail to avoid trampling the plants and disturbing the birds.

Reach a junction. Continue straight to a small beacon with an interpretive sign (map point C) (UTM 4Q 574603E, 2385885N) (Lat/Long N21.57433, W158.27939). Offshore is the legendary rock, Pōhaku o Kauaʻi. *Mauka* (inland) is Puʻu Pueo. Explore the inlets and tide pools along the shoreline. Watch for monk seals on the rocks or in the ocean, but do not approach or disturb them.

Return to the beacon and then turn left on the wide path heading along the other side of the point. Look for the native shrubs *ʻohai* and *naio*.

Reach a junction with the rail bed (map point D). For now, turn left.

Follow the rail bed to a large flat rock, marking Leina-a-ka-ʻUhane, a legendary entrance to the underworld.

To see more endangered *akoko*, walk through a nearby opening in the fence and meander along the upper road.

From the flat rock, backtrack to the junction with the trail from the beacon. This time, continue straight along the rail bed through a small cut in the rock.

Reach the familiar junction with the path to the beacon and retrace your steps back to the state park.

## NOTES

Ka'ena means "the heat," an apt description of the usually hot, dry, and windy western tip of O'ahu. Despite the heat, the hike along the coast to the point is richly rewarding. On view are wildlife, native plants, legendary sites, and the rugged beauty of an unspoiled shoreline. If the ocean is calm, go for a cooling swim at Keawa'ula Bay after the hike.

Take this hike during winter (November–April) to see migrating humpback whales and nesting *mōlī* (Laysan albatross). The temperature is also cooler then, and the sun is less intense. Don't forget the essentials for this walk: water, sunscreen, sunglasses, and binoculars. On the road, watch out for the occasional four-wheel drive vehicle and mountain bike. Along the shore, never turn your back to the ocean.

The route follows the abandoned rail line of the Oahu Railway and Land Company (OR&L), founded by businessman Benjamin F. Dillingham. In 1898, the company completed its main line from Honolulu to Hale'iwa and Kahuku, via the Wai'anae coast and Ka'ena Point. Pulled by steam locomotives, the narrow-gauge trains carried sugarcane, general freight, and passengers. The company shut down in 1947, a victim of upgraded roads, a sugar strike, and a maintenance backlog from World War II. Along the railroad right-of-way are remnant wooden ties and lava rock embankments.

Carpeting the ground and cliffs along the road are two low-lying native plants. *Pā'ū o Hi'iaka* is a vine with thick, elliptical leaves and pale-blue, bell-shaped flowers. The name means "skirt of Hi'iaka" and derives from a legend about the fire goddess Pele and her baby sister, Hi'iaka. One day, Pele went out to fish, leaving the baby asleep on the beach. When the goddess returned to shore, she found Hiʻiaka draped with a vine protecting her from the hot sun. ʻIlima papa is a prostrate shrub with oblong, serrated leaves about 1 inch long. The yellow-orange flowers strung together have been used to make regal lei, both in ancient and modern Hawaiʻi.

A predator-proof fence marks the boundary of the Kaʻena Point Natural Area Reserve. Established in 1983, the reserve protects the sand dune and boulder slope habitats of native coastal plants and provides a refuge for nesting seabirds. For more information about the reserve, check the Division of Forestry and Wildlife website, whose address is listed in the appendix. In the reserve, stay on the marked paths to avoid trampling vegetation and disturbing seabirds and their chicks. Leave your dogs at home, as they may attack and kill the chicks.

While walking in the reserve, look for three lovely native beach shrubs: hinahina and pōhinahina on the Waiʻanae side of the point and ʻōhai on the Mokuleʻia side. Hinahina has small white flowers and long, thick leaves arranged in rosettes. Shiny hairs on the leaf surface give it a silvery appearance and protect the plant from the strong sunlight. Pōhinahina has oval, gray-green leaves about 1 1/2 inches long and often forms extensive mats over the sand dunes. The lovely purplish-blue blossoms are clustered at the stem tips and are a favorite of lei makers. ʻŌhai has low-lying silver-green leaflets and scarlet winged and clawed flowers.

During winter, watch for a nesting colony of mōlī among the native shrubs on the dunes. Adult albatrosses are white with black upper wings and tail; chicks are fluffy brown. Courting pairs arrive in late fall and begin an elaborate mating ritual. The female lays a single egg in a makeshift nest scraped in the sand. By early summer, most mōlī have left Kaʻena to range widely over the North and Central Pacific Ocean.

From the beacon, look for monk seals lying on the rocks below or swimming in the ocean, but do not approach or disturb them. A sign near the beacon provides information about the seals' distribution, habits, and endangered status.

Ka'ena Point is the location of two significant Hawaiian legends. According to the first, the demigod and trickster Māui wanted to join all the islands together. From Ka'ena Point, he threw a great hook toward Kaua'i, hoping to snare the island. Initially the hook held fast, and Māui gave a mighty tug on the line. A huge boulder, known as Pōhaku o Kaua'i, dropped at his feet. The hook sailed over his head and fell in Pālolo Valley, forming Ka'au Crater, which is visible from the Lanipō hike.

Among old Hawaiians was a belief that when a person died, the soul left the body and traveled westward. Walk along the marked path on the Mokulē'ia side of the point to a large flat rock along the rail bed. The rock marks the area known as Leina-a-ka-'Uhane, the soul's leap. As spirits of the recently dead reached this westernmost point of the island, they were met by the souls of their ancestors, who guided them to Leina-a-ka-'Uhane for the final plunge into the sea on their way to eternity.

After visiting the entrance to the underworld, walk through a nearby opening in the perimeter fence, turn right, and stroll briefly along the upper road. Watch for the endangered Ka'ena 'akoko on the left. It is a low-lying shrub with rounded, gray-green leaves opposite each other and about 2 inches long. The slightly reddish branches have light-colored rings and a milky sap. This species of 'akoko is found only on the boulder-strewn slopes above the point.

You can also get to Ka'ena Point from the Mokulē'ia side. Follow the directions for the Keālia hike. Instead of turning into the airfield, continue along Farrington Hwy to the end of the paved road and park in the lot on the right.

## Hawai'i (the Big Island)

### Hawai'i Volcanoes National Park

P.O. Box 52
Hawai'i National Park, HI 96718
*Phone:* (808) 985-6000 (general), (808) 985-6178 (backcountry office)
*Website:* http://www.nps.gov/havo

*For:* park brochure, trail map, backcountry camping, rental cabins, and car camping at Nāmakani Paio

### State Parks

Division of State Parks
75 Aupuni St., Rm. 204
Hilo, HI 96721
*Phone:* (808) 961-9540
*Website:* http://www.hawaiistateparks.org

*For:* state parks brochures, backcountry camping, rental cabins, and car camping

### State Forest Reserves

Division of Forestry and Wildlife
19 E. Kawili St.
Hilo, HI 96720
*Phone:* (808) 974-4221
*Websites:* http://hawaii.gov/dlnr/dofaw, http://www.hawaiitrails.org

*For:* island recreation (trail) map and backcountry camping

# Kaua'i

## State Parks
Division of State Parks
3060 'Eīwa St., Rm. 306
Līhu'e, HI 96766
*Phone:* (808) 274-3444
*Website:* http://www.hawaiistateparks.org
*For:* state parks brochure, car and backcountry camping

## Kōke'e Museum
3600 Kōke'e Rd.
Kekaha, HI 96752
*Phone:* (808) 335-9975
*Website:* http://kokee.org
*For:* trail maps and pamphlets for the Kōke'e area

## State Forest Reserves
Division of Forestry and Wildlife
3060 'Eīwa St., Rm. 306
Līhu'e, HI 96766
*Phone:* (808) 274-3433
*Websites:* http://hawaii.gov/dlnr/dofaw, http://www.hawaiitrails.org
*For:* island recreation (trail) map, plant trail guides, and car and backcountry camping

# Maui

## Haleakalā National Park
P.O. Box 369
Makawao, HI 96768
*Phone:* (808) 572-4400
*Website:* http://www.nps.gov/hale

*For:* park brochure, trail map, backcountry camping, rental cabins, and car camping

## State Parks
Division of State Parks
54 S. High St., Rm. 101
Wailuku, HI 96793
*Phone:* (808) 984-8109
*Website:* http://www.hawaiistateparks.org
*For:* state parks brochure, cabin rentals, and car camping

**State Forest Reserves**
Division of Forestry and Wildlife
54 S. High St., Rm. 101
Wailuku, HI 96793
*Phone:* (808) 984-8100
*Websites:* http://hawaii.gov/dlnr/dofaw, http://www.hawaiitrails.org

*For:* island recreation (trail) map, plant and historical trail guides, and backcountry camping

## O'ahu

**Division of State Parks**
1151 Punchbowl St., Rm. 310
Honolulu, HI 96809
*Phone:* (808) 587-0300
*Website:* http://www.hawaiistateparks.org

*For:* state parks brochures and car camping

**Division of Forestry and Wildlife, Na Ala Hele**
  **(State Trail and Access Program)**
1151 Punchbowl St., Rm. 325
Honolulu, HI 96813
*Phone:* (808) 587-0166
*Websites:* http://hawaii.gov/dlnr/dofaw, http://www.hawaiitrails.org

*For:* hiking safely pamphlet, individual trail maps, backcountry camping, and special-use permits for and information about the Natural Area Reserves

**Moanalua Gardens Foundation**
1352 Pineapple Pl.
Honolulu, HI 96819
*Phone:* (808) 839-5334
*Website:* http://www.mgf-hawaii.org

*For:* pamphlets on Kamananui (Moanalua) Valley and Hau'ula Loop Trails

*Appendix*

# ⊞ FOR FURTHER REFERENCE ⊞

Ashley, Randy, and Jay Robinson. *Mauna Ulu Eruption Guide*. Hawai'i Volcanoes National Park, 2014.

Babb, Janet. *Kīlauea Iki Trail Guide*. Hawai'i Volcanoes National Park, 2014.

Baker, Nancy, and Kathy Valier. *Hiking in Haleakalā National Park*, 3rd ed. Hawaii Pacific Parks Association, 2014.

Ball, Stuart M., Jr. *The Backpackers Guide to Hawai'i*. Honolulu: University of Hawai'i Press, 1996.

———. *The Hikers Guide to O'ahu*, updated and expanded ed. Honolulu: University of Hawai'i Press, 2013.

———. *Native Paths to Volunteer Trails: Hiking and Trail Building on O'ahu*. Honolulu: University of Hawai'i Press, 2012.

Berger, Andrew J. *Hawaiian Birdlife*, 2nd ed. Honolulu: University of Hawai'i Press, 1988.

Bier, James A. *Reference Maps of the Islands of Hawai'i: Hawai'i*, 9th ed. Honolulu: University of Hawai'i Press, 2018.

———. *Reference Maps of the Islands of Hawai'i: Kaua'i*, 8th ed. Honolulu: University of Hawai'i Press, 2014.

———. *Reference Maps of the Islands of Hawai'i: Maui*, 9th ed. Honolulu: University of Hawai'i Press, 2017.

———. *Reference Maps of the Islands of Hawai'i: O'ahu*, 7th ed. Honolulu: University of Hawai'i Press, 2011.

*Bryan's Sectional Maps of O'ahu*, 2018 ed. Honolulu: EMIC Graphics, 2017.

Carlquist, Sherman. *Hawaii: A Natural History*, 2nd ed. Lāwai, HI: Pacific Tropical Botanical Garden, 1980.

Clark, John R. K. *The Beaches of the Big Island*. Honolulu: University of Hawai'i Press, 1985.

———. *The Beaches of Kaua'i and Ni'ihau*. Honolulu: University of Hawai'i Press, 1989.

———. *The Beaches of Maui County*. Honolulu: University of Hawai'i Press, 1989.

———. *The Beaches of O'ahu*. Honolulu: University of Hawai'i Press, 2004.

Dean, Love. *The Lighthouses of Hawai'i*. Honolulu: University of Hawai'i Press, 1991.

Emerson, Nathaniel B. *Pele and Hi'iaka*. Honolulu: 'Ai Pōhaku Press, 1997.

Gutmanis, June. *Pohaku: Hawaiian Stones*. Lā'ie, HI: Brigham Young University, 1986.

Hall, John B. *A Hiker's Guide to Trailside Plants in Hawai'i*. Honolulu: Mutual Publishing, 2004.

Hawaii Audubon Society. *Hawaii's Birds*, 6th ed. Honolulu: Island Heritage Publishing, 2005.

Hazlett, Richard W., and Hyndman, Donald W. *Roadside Geology of Hawai'i*. Missoula, MT: Mountain Press Publishing Company, 1996.

James, Van. *Ancient Sites of O'ahu*. Honolulu: Bishop Museum Press, 1991.

Juvik, Sonia P., and James O. Juvik. *Atlas of Hawaii,* 3rd ed. Honolulu: University of Hawai'i Press, 1998.

Kalākaua, David. *The Legends and Myths of Hawai'i*. Honolulu: Mutual Publishing, 1990.

Kane, Herb Kawainui. *Pele: Goddess of Hawaii's Volcanoes*. Captain Cook: Kawainui Press, 1987.

Kirch, Patrick Vinton. *Legacy of the Landscape*. Honolulu: University of Hawai'i Press, 1996.

Krauss, Beatrice H. *Plants in Hawaiian Culture*. Honolulu: University of Hawai'i Press, 1993.

Lamoureux, Charles H. *Trailside Plants of Hawaii's National Parks*. Hawaii Natural History Association and Hawaii Volcanoes National Parks, 1976.

Levin, Ruth. *Pu'u o Lokuana Trail Guide*. Hawai'i Volcanoes National Park, 2012.

MacDonald, Gordon A., Agatin T. Abbott, and Frank L. Peterson. *Volcanoes in the Sea,* 2nd ed. Honolulu: University of Hawai'i Press, 1990.

McMahon, Richard. *Camping Hawai'i*. Honolulu: University of Hawai'i Press, 1994.

Merlin, Mark. *Hawaiian Forest Plants*. Honolulu: Pacific Guide Books, 1995.

Miller, Carey D., Katherine Bazore, and Mary Bartow. *Fruits of Hawaii*. Honolulu: University of Hawai'i Press, 1991.

O'Connor, Maura. *A Walk into the Past*. Pamphlet. Honolulu: Moanalua Gardens Foundation, 1992.

Petersen, Lisa. *Mauna Loa Trail Guide,* 2nd ed. Hawaii Natural History Association, 1992.

Pukui, Mary Kawena, and Caroline Curtis. *Hawai'i Island Legends*. Honolulu: Kamehameha Schools Press, 1996.

Pukui, Mary Kawena, and Samuel H. Elbert. *Hawaiian Dictionary,* revised and enlarged ed. Honolulu: University of Hawai'i Press, 1986.

Pukui, Mary Kawena, Samuel H. Elbert, and Esther T. Mookini. *Place Names of Hawaii,* revised and enlarged ed. Honolulu: University of Hawai'i Press, 1981.

Roelofs, Faith. *Hau'ula Loop Trail: Field Site Guide*. Pamphlet. Honolulu: Moanalua Gardens Foundation, 1996.

Sohmer, S. H., and R. Gustafson. *Plants and Flowers of Hawai'i*. Honolulu: University of Hawai'i Press, 1987.

State of Hawai'i, Department of Health. *What Is Leptospirosis?* Pamphlet. Honolulu, 1992.

State of Hawai'i, Department of Land and Natural Resources. *'Awa'awapuhi Botanical Trail Guide*. Pamphlet. 1988.

———. *Ka'ena Point Natural Area Reserve*. Pamphlet. 2005.

———. *Mt. Ka'ala Natural Area Reserve*. Pamphlet. 1992.

———. *O'ahu Hiking Trails*. Individual trail maps, various dates.

———. *Pihea Trail Plant Guide*. Pamphlet. 1991.

———. *Recreation Map of Eastern and Western Kauai,* n.d.

———. *Recreation Map, Island of Maui,* n.d.

———. *Waihee Ridge Trail Native Plant Guide,* Pamphlet. 1993.

State of Hawai'i, Nā Ala Hele, Hawai'i Trail & Access System. *Maui History and Lore from the Lahaina Pali Trail*. Pamphlet.

Sterling, Elspeth P. *Sites of Maui*. Honolulu: Bishop Museum Press, 1998.

Sterling, Elspeth P., and Catherine C. Summers. *Sites of Oahu*. Honolulu: Bishop Museum Press, 1978.

United States Geological Survey. *Hawaii Volcanoes National Park and Vicinity*. Map. 1986.

Valier, Kathy. *On the Nā Pali Coast*. Honolulu: University of Hawai'i Press, 1989.

Wagner, Warren L., Derral R. Herbst, and S. H. Sohmer. *Manual of the Flowering Plants of Hawai'i*. Honolulu: University of Hawai'i Press and Bishop Museum Press, 1990.

Westervelt, William D. *Myths and Legends of Hawaii*. Honolulu: Mutual Publishing Company, 1987.

Wichman, Frederick B. *Kauai Tales*. Honolulu: Bamboo Ridge Press, 1989.

# ❊ INDEX ❊

'A'ali'i (shrub), 8, 28, 40, 133, 142, 148, 202, 215, 280, 285, 299, 365, 371
Āhinahina (shrub), 201, 208–209, 214
Ahupua'a o Kahana State Park, 349
'Aihualama, battle of, 305–306
'Ailā'au (god), legend of, 7
'Ākala (shrub), 71
'Ākia (shrub), 335
'Akoko (shrub), 380
Ala'ala wai nui (herb), 100
'Alae ke'oke'o (coot), 163, 168
'Alae'ula (moorhen), 168
Alahe'e (tree), 285, 364
Alani (tree), 372
'Alauahio (Maui creeper), 235, 241
Altitude sickness, xix
'Amakihi (bird), 22, 216, 234, 240, 300, 322
'Ama'u (fern), 40, 71, 208, 225, 273
'Anianiau (bird), 155, 163
'Apapane (bird), 16, 51, 70–71, 134, 147, 155, 216, 234–235, 240, 273, 300, 322

Ballpark Junction, 240
Banana poka (vine), xvii
Black Noddy. See Noio
Bus systems, xxvi
Byron, Captain George A., 93

Camp 10–Mōhihi Road, 164
Cardinal, red northern, 365
Civilian Conservation Corps, 23, 105, 213, 224, 248, 293, 357, 364
Clidemia hirta (shrub), xvii
Climate, of Hawai'i, xv
Clothing. See Hiking: clothing
Coffee, Arabian, 176
Cook, Captain James, 93
Cook Monument, 93

Cook pine, 293, 358
Coot, Hawaiian. See 'Alae Ke'oke'o
Creeper, Maui. See 'Alauahio

Damon, Samuel M., 313
Davis, Richard H. (Dick), 190, 351
Davis Falls. See Waimakemake Falls
Diamond Head, 301
Duck, Hawaiian. See Koloa

'Eke Crater, 274
'Elepaio (bird), 57–58, 71, 134, 147–148, 155, 163, 314
Emergencies. See Hiking: emergencies
Equipment. See Hiking: equipment

Flash floods, xx
Forestry and Wildlife, State Division of, 381–383
Francolin, Erckel's, 365

Goose, Hawaiian. See Nēnē
Guava, strawberry, 100, 168, 321

Hāhā lua (tree), 134
Hala (tree), 255, 261
Hala pepe (tree), 148–149
Halapē (area), 34
Haleakalā (volcano, crater), 201, 213–214
Haleakalā National Park, 382
Hame (tree), 57
Hanakāpī'ai Valley, 181
Hanakoa Falls, 182
Hāpu'u (tree fern), 7, 16, 23, 71, 115, 273, 322
Hau (tree), 261, 306, 314, 349
Hawai'i Volcanoes National Park, 381
Hawaiian Sugar Planters' Association, 306
Hawaiian Trail and Mountain Club, 299, 321

Hawaiian Volcano Observatory, 16–17
Hawk, Hawaiian. See 'Io
Hazards. See Hiking: hazards
Heat exhaustion, xix
Heat stroke, xix
Heiau (religious site), vvii, 120, 175, 190
Hi'ilawe Falls, 64
Hikes: danger rating of, xxiv; elevation
    gain of, xxii; highlights of, xxv;
    historical sights on, xxx–xxxi; length
    of, xxiii; location of, xxv; maps
    for, xxv; notes on, xxviii; route
    description of, xxvi–xxvii; suitable
    for, xxiv; swimming on, xxx–xxxi;
    trailhead directions of, xxv–xxvi;
    views on, xxx–xxxi; volcanic features
    on, xxx–xxxi
Hiking: clothing, xv–xvi; emergencies,
    xviii; equipment, xvi; hazards,
    xviii–xxii
Hilina Pali fault system, 28
Hinahina (shrub), 207, 225, 379
Hoapili (governor), 267
Honolulu mauka trail system, 307
Huluhulu, Pu'u. See Pu'u Huluhulu
Hunters, xxi
Hurricanes, xxii
Hypothermia, xix

'I'iwi (bird), 71, 155, 241
'Iliahi (tree), 14–15, 148, 186, 202, 216,
    300, 322
Iliahialo'e (shrub), 280
Iliau (shrub), 124–125, 142
'Ilima (shrub), 280, 299–300, 327–328
'Ilima papa (shrub), 33, 379
'Io (hawk), 8, 58
'Iwa (bird), 328

Jaggar, Thomas, 17, 79
Jaggar's Cave, 79
Jungle Training Center, 349
Junglefowl, red. See Moa

Ka'au Crater, 300–301
Ka'awaloa (village), 92–93
Ka'ena Point, legends of, 380

Ka'ena Point Natural Area Reserve, 379
Kahalaopuna (maiden), legend of, 305
Kaimuki Land Company, 299
Kalalau Trail, 175, 180
Kalani'ōpu'u (chief), 92–93
Kanawao (shrub). See Pū'ahanui
Karaka (tree), 134–135
Kaupō Trail, 208
Keāhua Arboretum, 106
Keanakāko'i (quarry), 16, 87
Keeling, Charles, 78
Kī (shrub), 100, 168, 306
Kīlauea Iki, eruption of, 8
King's Highway, 255, 267
Kīpuka, 71
Koa (tree), 71, 133, 142, 148, 168, 230,
    300, 322
Koa'e kea (tropicbird), 40–41, 101, 120,
    176, 182
Koa'e 'ula (tropicbird), 328
Koai'e Canyon Trail, 126
Kōke'e Museum, 382
Kōke'e Stream, 128
Kōlea (tree), 57
Koli'i (shrub), 372
Koloa (duck), 163
Kōnāhuanui (peak), 307
Kōnane (game), 33
Ko'olau Caldera, 335–336
Kōpiko (tree), 57, 273, 300
Kuamo'o-Nounou Trail, 101
Kuaokalā Trail, 365
Kuia Natural Area Reserve, 142
Kūkaemoa (shrub), 15, 372
Kūkaenēnē (shrub), 70
Kukui, Pu'u. See Pu'u Kukui
Kukui (tree), 105–106, 125, 341, 350
Kuli'ou'ou Valley Trail, 294
Kūpaoa (shrub), 202, 214–215

Lahaina Pali Trail, 279–280
Lama (tree), 46, 143, 181, 294
Lau hala (tree), 100
Lau'ulu Trail, 211
Lava: dikes, 336; trees, 22; tubes, 47;
    types of, xxi
Lehua makanoe (tree), 164

Index

Leiothrix, red-billed, 293
Leptospirosis, xix–xx
Lili'uokalani, Queen, 307, 315
Littering, xvii
Lonomea (tree), 364
Loulu (palm), 116, 322–323
Lyon Arboretum, 306

Maile (vine), 371
Makaleha Mountains, 106
Makapu'u Lighthouse, 328
Makauwahi Cave, 120
Māmaki (tree), 342
Māmane (tree), 202, 215, 235, 248
Marijuana, xxii
Māui (demigod), legends of, 208, 221, 301
Mauna Kea (volcano), eruption of, 86
Mauna Loa (volcano), eruption of, 41, 78
Mauna Loa Observatory, 78
Mauna Ulu (volcanic shield), eruption of, 23, 28
Maunawili Falls, 342
Mau'umae Ridge, 299
Melastoma candidum (shrub), xvii
Milo (tree), 94, 255, 267, 329
Moa (junglefowl), 125–126
Moalepe Trail, 105–106
Moanalua Gardens Foundation, 383
Moku'āweoweo Caldera, 79
Mōlī (albatross), 379
Monk seal, 379
Monterey pine, 235, 241
Mt. Ka'ala Natural Area Reserve, 372
Mountain apple, 350
Muliwai Trail, 62–64

Na Ala Hele (state trail program), 267, 293
Nā Pali Coast, 175, 180
Na'ena'e (shrub), 202, 214–215
Nāhuku lava tube. See Thurston lava tube
Naio (tree), 268
Nakamura, Charlie, 321
Nāulu Trail, 24
Naupaka kahakai (shrub), 47, 120, 175; legend of, 254–255

Nēnē (goose), 28, 143, 202–203, 208, 215
Noio (tern), 255
Nounou Mountain, legend of, 101
Nounou Mountain–East Side Trail, 101
Nounou Mountain–West Side Trail, 101
Nukupu'u (bird), 262

Oahu Railway and Land Company, 378
'Ōhā wai (shrub), 155, 162–163
'Ōhai (shrub), 285, 379
Ohala Heiau, 255
Ohe naupaka (shrub), 155–156, 162
'Ōhelo (shrub), 8, 70, 202, 208, 215–216, 248
'Ōhi'a, Pu'u. See Tantalus
'Ōhi'a (tree), 7–8, 16, 23, 51, 70, 106, 115, 133, 142, 148, 234, 273, 293–294, 300, 322, 357–358
'Ōhi'a 'āhihi (tree), 307, 315, 371
'Ōhi'a 'ai (tree). See Mountain apple
'Ōkolehao (liquor), 168–169
'Ōlapa (tree), 155
Old Pali Road, 341
Olomana, legend of, 334
Olomea (tree), 371
'Oma'o (bird), 8, 71
'Ō'ō, Pu'u. See Pu'u 'Ō'ō
'O'opu (fish), 262
Orchid, Chinese ground, 314–315, 350
Owl, Hawaiian. See Pueo

Pali Kapu o Keōua (cliff), 93
Pānini (cactus), 328
Pāpala kēpau (tree), 357
Parrotbill, Maui, 262
Pā'ū o Hi'iaka (vine), 285, 378–379
Peacock, 365
Pele (goddess), legends of, 7, 15–16, 87, 285, 329
Petrel, dark-rumped. See 'Ua'u
Pihea Trail, 155, 162
Pilo (shrub), 371
Plants, invasive, xvii
Pōhakukaluahine, legend of, 314
Pōhakupele (pillar), 155
Pōhinahina (shrub), 379

*Index*

*Pohuehue* (vine), 34
Poli'ahu (goddess), legend of, 87
*Pū'ahanui* (shrub), 372
*Pueo* (owl), 115, 163, 216
*Pūkiawe* (shrub), 8, 28, 40, 51, 70, 113,
    142, 148, 202, 208, 215–216, 230,
    235, 248, 357
*Pulu* (tree fern fiber), 7, 23, 322
Puna Coast Trail, 33–34
Pu'u Hinahina Trail, 135
Pu'u Huluhulu (cone), 22–23
Pu'u Kukui (peak), 274
Pu'u 'Ō'ō (cone), 23
Pu'u 'Ō'ō–Volcano Trail, 70

Redwood, 241
Rift zones, 22, 40, 248

Sandalwood. See *'Iliahi*
Shama, white-rumped, 105, 176, 306,
    313, 357, 365
Shipwreck Beach, 120
Sierra Club, Hawai'i Chapter, 306, 340
Silversword. See *Āhinahina*
Silversword Loop, 208
Sisal, 126, 186
Sleeping Giant, legend of, 101
Snail, Hawaiian land, 371–372
State Parks, Division of, 381–383
Strawberry guava. See Guava, strawberry

Tantalus (peak), 307
Tattler, wandering. See *'Ūlili*
Thurston lava tube, 7, 16
Ti (shrub). See *Kī*
Tropicbird. See *Koa'e kea; Koa'e 'ula*
Tsunami, xxii

*'Ua'u* (petrel), 249
*Uguisu.* See Warbler, Japanese bush
*'Uhaloa* (shrub), 28–29, 46–47, 92
*'Ūlei* (shrub), 63, 285, 335, 357
*'Ūlili* (tattler), 267
Upper Kahana Trail, 351

Waiāhole Ditch Trail, 350
Wai'ale'ale (mountain), 155
Wai'ānapanapa Cave, 256
Waiau Lake, 87
*Waiawī-'ula'ula.* See Guava, strawberry
Waimakemake Falls, 189–190
Waimano Pool, 323
Waimea Canyon, 125, 133; legend of, 134
Waimoku Falls, 262
Waipi'o Valley, legend of, 63
Waipo'o Falls, 133–134
Warbler, Japanese bush, 273, 294, 315,
    323, 341
Whale, humpback, 120, 280, 285, 328
Whitney Seismographic Vault, 17
*Wiliwili* (tree), 126, 364–365

# ❀ ABOUT THE AUTHOR ❀

STUART M. BALL, JR. has been hiking in Hawai'i for more than thirty years. He is a hike coordinator for the Hawaiian Trail and Mountain Club and is author of *Native Paths and Volunteer Trails: Hiking and Trail Building on O'ahu, The Backpackers Guide to Hawai'i,* and *The Hikers Guide to the Hawaiian Islands.* Retired from the Bank of Hawai'i, he holds a BA from Dartmouth College and an MBA from Stanford University.

ian route across Kaʻala to Waialua. Natives used the Kūmaipō Trail to access the ridge route from either Mākaha or Waiʻanae Valley. To early Hawaiians, Kaʻala may have meant lofty and removed, even forbidding, an apt description of the mountain and this hike.

At Punchbowl St. get on Lunalilo Fwy (H-1) heading 'ewa (west).

Near Middle St., keep left on Moanalua Fwy (H-201) to 'Aiea.

By Aloha Stadium, bear right to rejoin H-1 to Pearl City and on toward Wai'anae.

As the freeway ends near Campbell Industrial Park, continue along the leeward coast on Farrington Hwy (Rte 93).

Pass Kahe Point power plant on the right.

Drive through Nānākuli, Māʻili, and Waiʻanae towns.

The road narrows to two lanes.

Drive through Mākaha and pass Keaʻau Beach Park on the left.

On the right, pass ʻŌhikilolo Mākua Ranch and then Mākua Military Reservation with its observation post.

Enter Kaʻena Point State Park by Keawaʻula (Yokohama) Bay. In the first building on the right are restrooms and drinking water.

Park in the lot on the right at the end of the paved road (map point A) (UTM 4Q 577851E, 2383860N) (Lat/Long N21.5559, W158.24812). For safer parking, leave your car near the satellite tracking station guardhouse on the right or by the lifeguard stand on the left. Those options add 1 to 2 miles to the hike.

## ROUTE DESCRIPTION

Continue along the coast on a dirt road through scattered *kiawe* trees. The route roughly follows an old rail bed of the Oʻahu Railway and Land Company. Watch for native ʻiliahialoʻe shrubs (coast sandalwood) on the cliff side of the road.

Take the short, periodic trails on the left for a better view of the coves and tide pools along the shoreline and humpback whales in the ocean. Native *pāʻū o* Hiʻiaka vines and low-lying ʻilima papa shrubs carpet the ground.